Contents

Preface

Old Bailey Press textbooks are written specifically for students. Whatever their course they will find our books clear and concise, providing comprehensive and up-to-date coverage. Written by specialists in their field, our textbooks are reviewed and updated on a regular basis. A companion 150 Leading Cases, Revision WorkBook and Cracknell's Statutes are also published for this subject.

The traditional syllabus for English legal system has been expanded in recent times as a result of new modular courses being pioneered by higher education institutions. Such courses now include a heavy emphasis on European law and its influence on the English legal system. Consequently, to assist students on such courses this edition contains coverage of the European dimension.

The pace of change since the last edition has been considerable with major statutory change being provided for, but importantly at the time of writing, not fully implemented. The Criminal Justice Act 2003 impacts upon much of the criminal justice system and the Courts Act 2003 is also of major importance. Finally, the changes introduced by the Constitutional Reform Act 2005, particularly with regard to the role of Lord Chancellor, are noted.

Cases and materials up to March 2005 have been taken into account.

Table of Cases

Table of Statutes and Other Materials

Part I: Sources of Law

1

Introduction: Divisions and Sources of English Law

Divisions of English law

1.1 Historical background: origins and development of common law and equity

1.2 The division between civil and criminal law

1.3 Law of tort

1.4 Law of contract

1.5 Law of property

Sources of English law

1.6 Classification of sources

1.7 Custom

1.8 Legislation

1.9 Case law

1.10 Neutral case citation

1.11 European law

Divisions of English law

1.1 Historical background: origins and development of common law and equity

The Anglo-Saxon period prior to 1066

At this time the country was divided into various areas (or kingdoms) each with its own body of law based on the customs of the people who lived there. There was no uniform system of law because of the absence of any judicial machinery to require or produce it. Instead, the laws of Saxon and Danish kings were imposed on local traditions. These laws were known as 'dooms'.

These laws were conservative and harsh in character, reflecting a society in which violence, robbery and death dominated everyday life.

The effect of the Norman Conquest 1066

Social conditions did not change significantly after the Conquest because William I did not try to impose Norman law on local conditions or customs, at least not immediately. The process of change was gradual but nevertheless dramatic because of the introduction of the feudal system. Under this system all land was owned by the King, so that at a stroke the country became a united kingdom, replacing the local kingdoms that had existed prior to 1066.

In return for various services the King granted land to his barons and other followers. They in turn granted land to tenants in return for services. This process was known as 'subinfeudation'. The result was a single kingdom but one in which different laws continued to exist in different areas, eventually collected together in the Domesday Book 1086.

William I introduced a central government based at Westminster. His closest advisers were known as the King's Council or 'Curia Regis' (arguably an early precedent for the modern Cabinet system of government).

At first, the Council performed judicial functions as well as legislative and administrative ones, but gradually the judicial functions were delegated to committees of the Council, which became the royal courts of justice. The first court to emerge was the Court of Exchequer which dealt with the collection of taxation. The next was the Court of Common Pleas, which dealt with disputes between individuals such as contract and tort. The final court to appear was the Court of King's Bench, dealing with criminal law and also any civil matter of public importance affecting the King.

At first the royal courts sat only at Westminster Hall but, in order to maintain law and order throughout the kingdom, the practice arose of sending judges into the provinces on 'assize' or 'circuit'. These judges acted under the authority of various 'royal commissions' granted to them by the Norman kings in order to try criminals.

The reforms of Henry II (1154–1189)

Henry II, a lawyer by character, laid the foundations for a system of common law, through the following reforms:

1. *the Assize of Windsor (1179)*: this placed the circuit system on a regular and permanent basis;
2. *the Assizes of Clarendon (1166) and Northampton (1176)*: these established the system of criminal justice which brought about the development of trial by jury

and the investigation by the royal judges of the charges made against offenders presented by the local courts – the origin of the committal system;

3. *the Grand Assize (1179)*: introduced a new method of trying cases of disputed ownership of land, leading to the modern system of determining title to land. The civilised nature of this system helped put a stop to the use of force by those claiming wrongful dispossession of their lands.

The circuit system of royal justice administered a system of national law which was not qualified in any way by local custom. The reforms of Henry II helped to develop a national legal system based on 'common law', a law common to all persons and parts of England and Wales. At regular periods the travelling judges, who were known as 'justices in eyre', held a 'General Eyre' in each locality dealing with all the legal and fiscal matters of that area in one sitting. The General Eyre gradually died out by the mid-fourteenth century but the regular circuit system survived into modern times.

Early common law and the forms of action

Early common law was characterised by an obsession with procedural law. A system developed whereby a civil dispute had to be brought before the appropriate royal court by a writ. Each writ was drawn up to fit the precise facts of that dispute and all writs were collected on a register of writs so as to provide precedents of procedure, known as 'forms of action'.

However, the system quickly became rigid because judges, fearing a flood of actions as a result of the popularity of royal justice, stopped the issue of new forms of action, so that a litigant only had a right of action if he could find a form to fit exactly the facts of his case. Later, the strictness of this approach was relaxed to allow the issue of writs which were reasonably similar to those already on the register of writs. Nevertheless, the obsession with preserving existing forms of action was a major obstacle to the development of new rules and principles, particularly in the fields of contract law and tort.

The early system was also extremely technical and if not followed precisely could lead to failure to obtain any remedy for the wrong suffered. Frustrated litigants sometimes petitioned the King for a remedy, because the King was the 'fountain of justice'. Some of these petitions were granted and the popularity of this led to an increase in the number of petitions. The King referred them to the Lord Chancellor, one of his closest advisers, who was not only a lawyer but also regarded as keeper of the King's conscience. It was not surprising therefore that the various Lord Chancellors decided cases as much on principles of morality as on strict law.

The origins and development of equity

The body of rules and principles developed by the Lord Chancellors became known as 'equity' because they were based on concepts of fairness and justice (from the

Latin, 'aequitas'). They were applied in a special court of the Lord Chancellor known as the Court of Chancery which began to recognise and enforce new rights and duties, thus providing an alternative system of justice to that of the common law courts. New remedies were also developed by the Chancery Court. Among the new rights and remedies invented by Equity in early times were those listed below.

1. *The trust* (or 'use' in early times): Party A is given the legal title to property to hold it for the benefit of Party B.
2. *The equity of redemption*: the mortgagor has the right to regain his property from the mortgagee.
3. *The doctrine of part performance*: in certain situations the law requires written contracts. If there is no writing and yet one party performs his part of the contract, equity in the past would compel the other party to perform his part of the contract.
4. *The equitable lease*: the law requires leases over three years long to be in a deed. Equity will enforce leases that do not meet this requirement.
5. *The doctrine of equitable estoppel*: a party to a contract informs the other party that he does not intend to rely on his strict legal rights. In certain circumstances he will not be able to go back on this undertaking (for the full story of how this important doctrine was developed in the twentieth century see Lord Denning's accounts in the *Discipline of Law* (1979), pp197–223, and *The Closing Chapter* (1983), pp254–257).
6. *Restrictive covenants*: equity will enforce restrictive covenants against parties who were not parties to the original agreement, hence circumventing the common law rule of privity of contract.
7. *Contractual licences*: these now give some right to remain in property.
8. *The remedy of injunction*: a mandatory injunction is an order to perform an act; a prohibitory injunction is an order not to perform an act; a 'quia timet' injunction is an order not to do an act that a party is planning to do in the future, ie it is based on speculative evidence and requires more proof than for an ordinary prohibitory injunction; and an 'interlocutory' injunction may be granted before the full trial to preserve the situation until the trial can be held.
9. *The remedy of specific performance*: an order to perform a contract; it is granted only where the common law remedy of damages would not be adequate compensation for the breach, eg a contract for the transfer of land or of a rare or personal chattel.
10. *The remedy of rectification*: a written document that does not reflect the true intention of the parties will be corrected in certain circumstances.
11. *The remedy of rescission*: a contract will be rescinded (ie set aside as if it had not been made) where one of the parties is the victim of some unfairness or wrongdoing.
12. *The remedy of account*: to return money fraudulently obtained.
13. *Delivery-up and cancellation of documents*: a document may be returned to court to be cancelled, eg a void lease, conveyance, negotiable instrument.

14. *The process of discovery of documents*: in civil litigation to require each side to disclose to the other all relevant documents in their possession, custody or control. This has become 'automatic' in modern litigation and is based on the 'cards on the table' philosophy, discouraging trials by ambush and encouraging sensible evaluation of the strength of an opponent's case, sometimes resulting in an out-of-court settlement.
15. *The subpoena*: an order to compel the attendance of a witness at court.
16. *The appointment of a receiver*: after one side has obtained a judgment against the other side, a financial manager may be appointed to recover debts and administer affairs. This is known as 'equitable execution', but tends to be more expensive than other methods of enforcing judgment.

During modern times equity has demonstrated its potential to continue developing new rights and remedies. From the interlocutory injunction has developed the 'Anton Piller order' (now known as a search order) and the 'Mareva injunction' (now referred to as a freezing injunction). The Anton Piller order allows inspection of and prevents disposal of goods, documents, etc that may be needed in evidence at the trial: *Anton Piller KG* v *Manufacturing Processes Ltd* [1976] Ch 55. The Mareva injunction prevents disposal of assets abroad, ie it has the dramatic effect of 'freezing assets' and preventing the normal conduct of the party's financial affairs; accordingly it may only be granted if it is established that there is a real danger of the party trying to avoid probable judgment at trial by getting rid of assets in the meantime: *Mareva Compania Naviera SA* v *International Bulk Carriers SA* [1975] 2 Lloyd's Rep 509.

The story of the Anton Piller order is told by Lord Denning in the *Due Process of Law* (1980) pp123–130 and in *The Closing Chapter* (1983) pp235–239. The story of the Mareva injunction is told in the *Due Process of Law* at pp133–151 and in *The Closing Chapter* at pp225–239.

All equitable remedies are discretionary, so that even if a litigant wins a case on the merits the remedy might be withheld if, for example, the winning litigant had himself been guilty of unconscionable conduct during the dispute. This became the maxim that 'He who comes to equity must come with clean hands' and was applied in the case of *Webster* v *Cecil* (1861) 30 Beav 62, where Cecil had offered to sell certain property and stated that the price would be £1,100. He meant to write £2,100. Webster was well aware that Cecil had made a slip of the pen but he snapped up the offer and sued for specific performance. The court refused the remedy owing to his inequitable conduct.

Equity developed other maxims to emphasise its flexible character and its concern for fair dealing. Examples are given below.

Equity is equality
This can be illustrated by reference to tenancies. At common law, if property were given to A, B and C, they took a joint tenancy therein which meant that if A died

his share passed to B and C, not to A's relatives. When B died, C became entitled to the whole interest. However, if the gift had been made to 'A, B and C as tenants in common' A's interest on his death would pass under his will or intestacy; the same would happen to B's interest when B died and C's when C died. Equity preferred the tenancy in common and accordingly wherever possible would interpret words as creating such a tenancy even if common law would have interpreted them as creating a joint tenancy. Similarly, equity would construe a tenancy in common whenever two or more persons purchased property with money found in unequal shares or where two or more lend money upon a mortgage in equal or unequal shares, even though in each case the conveyance or mortgage was expressed as jointly, or as joint tenants.

Equity looks on as done that which ought to be done
This is well illustrated by the case of *Walsh* v *Lonsdale* (1882) 21 Ch D 9. Lonsdale had agreed to lease a mill to Walsh for a period of seven years, such agreement being in writing. The rent was to be paid quarterly in arrears but Lonsdale was entitled to demand one year's rent in advance if he so desired. No lease was ever actually executed but Walsh entered into possession and paid his rent as stipulated. Lonsdale then demanded a year's rent in advance. Walsh refused to pay. Lonsdale sued for specific performance and won because the court treated the agreement for the lease as being as good as the lease itself, as if it had been formally executed.

Equity looks to the intention rather than the form
Similar to the preceding maxim, it enables equity to disregard formal procedural requirements in order to ascertain and implement the real intention of the parties.

Equity acts in personam
This maxim emphasised that equity could act against the physical person of the defendant by imprisoning him for contempt of court if he failed to obey an injunction, or order for specific performance, etc. A consequence of the maxim is that equity will not entertain a suit unless the defendant is within the jurisdiction of the court and amenable to such orders.

Equity will not suffer a wrong to be without a remedy
This maxim was used to justify the invention of new rights and duties which would not otherwise be developed because of the rigidity of the common law system of forms of action. The trust is a shining example of the exercise of the maxim.

Equity does nothing in vain
Equity's jurisdiction was based on its integrity and therefore equity would not make an order likely to prove useless or unenforceable, eg an order for specific performance of a contract for personal services. Alternative remedies that might have

the desired persuasive effect would be granted instead, eg an injunction preventing the party performing those services elsewhere, or imprisonment for contempt.

Hence, whereas common law remedies were granted as of right on the merits, equity was and is a discretionary system sometimes criticised for arbitrary decision-making. In early times it was said that 'equity varies with the length of the Chancellor's foot' (John Selden). In early times equity provoked a jealous reaction from the common law judges because, despite its potential for arbitrariness, equity proved popular with litigants and consequently the common law courts lost revenue to the Court of Chancery (in those early times courts were private enterprise institutions which charged fees for the dispensation of justice). The tension between the courts of common law and equity became serious when the Court of Chancery claimed exclusive jurisdiction over cases in which the defence was of an equitable nature, and the Court would issue a 'common injunction' against the plaintiff in such a case to prevent him from continuing the action at common law or, if he had already obtained a judgment in damages, from enforcing that judgment. Disobedience of the common injunction was punished by imprisonment for contempt of Chancery. The common law judges objected to the practice and eventually the dispute was referred to James I (1603–1625) in the *Earl of Oxford's Case* (1615) 1 Rep Ch 1. The King ruled that in all future cases of conflict between rules of common law and equity, equity should prevail, but that as far as possible equity should follow the rules of common law and only intervene where common law provided inadequate remedies. The compromise was accepted and it no longer became necessary to issue common injunctions.

Equity became a body of legal principles which were described by Maitland as a 'gloss on the common law' and by Hammond as 'supplemental and superior in quality to the common law'. During the nineteenth century a number of statutes were passed which were designed to harmonise the administration of the two systems of law. For example, the Common Law Procedure Acts 1852–1860 allowed common law courts to grant equitable remedies and the Chancery Amendment Act (Lord Cairns' Act) 1858 allowed the Court of Chancery to grant the common law remedy of damages in lieu of an injunction where appropriate. A more modern illustration can be found in *Page One Records* v *Britton* [1967] 3 All ER 822 (pop group 'The Troggs' took on another manager in breach of a restrictive covenant with existing manager, who sought injunction. Held: damages in lieu because Troggs could not survive without a manager). The relevant rule is now contained in the Supreme Court Act 1981, s50.

The harmonisation process culminated in the Judicature Acts 1873 and 1875 which restructured the court system and fused the administration of common law and equity. The courts of common law and the Court of Chancery became divisions of a single High Court with one set of procedures, under which common law and equitable principles and remedies could be applied in all divisions of the High Court. The rule that equity must prevail in the event of conflict was put into statutory form and is today contained in s49(1) Supreme Court Act 1981:

'Every court exercising jurisdiction in England and Wales in any civil cause or matter shall continue to administer law and equity on the basis that, whenever there is conflict or variance between the rules of equity and the rules of the common law, with reference to the same matter, the rules of equity shall prevail.'

The Judicature Acts did not fuse common law and equity, which remain distinct systems, as illustrated by the first case decided after those Acts which involved a conflict between the two systems: *Walsh* v *Lonsdale*, above. Consequently, equity has survived as a system capable of inventing new rights and remedies in areas where common law is deficient.

1.2 The division between civil and criminal law

A major division in English law is between criminal and civil law.

There is a fundamental distinction between crimes and civil wrongs which are dealt with by different courts and by very different procedures. Some of the main differences between criminal and civil cases are set out below.

While it is important to be able to tell whether an act is criminal or not it is not easy to define exactly what a crime is. There are certain tests which may be applied to distinguish criminal acts.

Criminal cases	*Civil cases*
1. In general any citizen can bring a criminal prosecution.	Generally only the person wronged may sue.
2. Brought in the name of the Crown in trials on indictment and usually prosecuted by public authorities.	Brought by private individuals.
3. An individual cannot discontinue a prosecution at will as it is brought in the public interest.	The plaintiff may discontinue at any time.
4. The Crown may put an end to the prosecution by the entry of a nolle prosequi by the Attorney-General or by decision of the Crown Prosecution Service.	The Crown cannot interfere to prevent the maintenance of a civil case.
5. The Crown may pardon a crime.	The Crown cannot pardon a civil wrong.
6. The consent of the victim is usually irrelevant to a criminal charge, eg assault.	The consent of the 'victim' will in most cases prevent him from suing.

Criminal cases	*Civil cases*
7. Sanctions primarily intended to protect the community and punish the offender (although in some cases the court can compensate the victim as well).	Remedies primarily intended to compensate the victim (although in some cases extra damages are awarded as a punishment).
8. Criminal law attempts to regulate the behaviour of the whole community.	Civil law attempts to regulate relationships and behaviour between individuals.

1.3 Law of tort

In general terms a tort is a civil wrong arising from a breach of duty created not by agreement but by operation of law.

Such a breach gives rise to a cause of action for unliquidated (ie unspecified in amount) damages. The law of tort enables compensation to be made to a person for damage caused to him by another, but not all damage is actionable. The law of tort specifies when a person who has suffered damage can sue for compensation.

While some torts are also crimes a tort has no general moral character. Not all anti-social conduct constitutes a tort (eg perjury which harms another), while some conduct is tortious even though it causes no harm (eg trespass).

In general when an act is both a crime and a tort both criminal and civil proceedings may be taken in respect of the same act. However, if the victim of a minor assault brings a summary prosecution against the offender no civil proceedings may subsequently be taken in respect of that assault whether or not the offender is convicted. This forces the victim to decide whether he wishes to institute civil or criminal proceedings and avoids unnecessary proceedings for a fairly minor wrong. The police do not usually take proceedings in such cases to allow the victim to make this choice.

1.4 Law of contract

While the modern law of contract developed from the same root as the law of tort, the old action of trespass, they are now significantly different. The important difference is that in contract the obligations are primarily fixed by the parties themselves whereas the duties enforced by the law of tort are imposed by the law, although they may be varied contractually.

Some conduct is both a breach of contract and a tort. Thus if a taxi driver causes an accident in which his passenger is injured he is both in breach of his contractual obligation to convey his passenger safely and in breach of his duty to take care imposed by the tort of negligence. It is not usually important to consider whether certain conduct is both a tort and a breach of contract. The plaintiff may pick which is the most advantageous to him or he may plead both in the alternative (but of course, he cannot have two lots of damages). In general it is more advantageous to sue in tort as the measure of damages is wider, aggravated damages might be recoverable, the limitation period operates from a later date and damages which may be too remote in contract may be recoverable in tort.

1.5 Law of property

The law of property in land is complex and has developed over many centuries, and there are now many legal and equitable interests which can exist in land. A freeholder, a lessee, a mortgagee and a neighbour whose drains run under the land in question all have different interests in the land. The law of property in goods is less complicated.

Goods

Ownership or title to goods is described as 'property'. Thus where the Sale of Goods Act 1979 refers to the transfer of ownership the words used are 'the transfer of the property in the goods'.

This is general property, and a legal interest in goods which is less than ownership is called special property. Examples are hirers and bailees, and these forms of special property are based on possession.

Distinguish between ownership, possession and custody as follows.

1. If I buy a book I have ownership of the book.
2. If I agree to lend you the book for a week you have possession of the book. This means that you have a legal right to have that book for the week.
3. If you take the book without asking my permission, you have custody of the book but you have no right to retain it.

Land

Land cannot be owned absolutely because in theory the Crown is the ultimate landowner. Individuals hold land from the Crown, and the form of holding is known as 'tenure'.

In the Middle Ages there were several forms of tenure but they are no longer of practical importance. While tenure relates to the relationship between the lord and his tenant, the interest which the latter has in his land is termed an 'estate'. There were many types of estate at common law, but since 1 January 1926 there are only two legal estates in land: (1) a fee simple absolute in possession (freehold); and (2) a term of years absolute in possession (leasehold). 'In possession' means that the estate owner is entitled now and does not have to wait for a future event, and it includes the right to rent and profits. Thus where land is leased the landlord freeholder has a legal fee simple and the tenant has a legal term of years. It is this possibility of several estates and interests co-existing in the same piece of land which makes the law of land more complicated than the law relating to property in goods.

Apart from the two legal estates there are many other legal and equitable interests in land.

Real and personal property

This is a classification of property which derives from an early legal procedure. At first the Royal courts were mainly interested in acquiring jurisdiction over pleas of the Crown (crimes) and disputes over land. The earliest forms of action were those directed to recovering land and were known as real actions, as the thing (in Latin, res) in dispute could actually be recovered. Interests protected by these actions were called real property, or realty.

Actions for dispute over chattels were known as personal actions because at first the plaintiff could not insist on the return of the thing itself, and the subject matter of such actions were known as personal property, or personalty. Until the fifteenth century leases were treated as purely contractual matters and were classed as personal property. This classification persists despite the fact that a lease can now be a legal estate in land.

The difference between real and personal property is of little importance since the property legislation of 1925.

Personal property can be divided into two classes.

1. Choses in possession, which are something capable of physical possession, such as goods.
2. Choses in action, which are rights in intangible property that can only be enforced by action (eg debts, copyrights, stocks and shares). Choses in action can only be transferred by some document or formality.

Sources of English law

1.6 Classification of sources

An important aspect of any legal system is its source of law, and the English legal system has many sources – their significance varying from area of law to area, and from one period of history to another. For example, in the Anglo-Saxon period prior to the Norman Conquest of England in 1066, law was largely customary and there was little interference in law by the Crown. A few hundred years later, there had been a momentous change and the common law, derived from the authority of case law, was becoming the dominant source. In the twentieth century, case law is still of great importance, but legislation has become very much more significant over the last century or so – a trend which has been increased by the United Kingdom's membership of the European Union.

There are numerous ways of classifying sources, not always distinct.

Formal sources

These are the sources from which a legal system ultimately derives its validity and effect: for example John Austin (1790–1859) saw laws as the commands of a sovereign, to whom a habit of obedience is owed, which are enforced by sanctions.

Historical sources

These are the historical origins and development of different rules of law, deriving from separate sources (eg the common law, equity, the Law Merchant, Roman Law, Canon Law, European Law, legislation and custom).

Legal sources

These are the authorities for existing rules of law (eg case law, legislation and custom). The comparative importance of these matters has varied greatly over the last thousand years – custom now having a very minor role to play in the law, though it was of prime importance before the development of the common law.

Literary sources

The written records of legal rules, such as statutes, European legislation, law reports, statutory instruments, and, to a lesser extent, legal textbooks.

1.7 Custom

In a wide sense of the word, custom is of great historical significance. Before the developing common law extinguished the local variations of law, English law was 'custom' in the sense that, with the exception of limited royal intervention, law varied from area to area, shire to shire, town to town.

These local customary laws were not written down and were administered by the local courts. However, with the rapid development of the royal courts and royal justice which provided a law 'common' to the entire realm (that is, it was of even application and did not vary with the locality), the local customary law went into a decline and disappeared. However, though not much is known about communal, customary justice, it is clear that parts of it did exert an influence on the developing common law.

In the modern law, custom has a very limited role to play and a narrower meaning: that is, a particular rule which has existed since 'time immemorial' and must have obtained legal status within a particular location. Custom should be distinguished from mere trade usage which is simply a factual question of usual practice within a given trade and which is not subject to the stringent tests for establishing custom providing the usage is legal and reasonable. One use for trade usage is to imply terms into contracts.

Basic definition

In the *Tanistry Case* (1608) Dav Ir 28 custom was defined as 'such usage as has obtained the force of law' and is binding as regards the particular places, persons and things with which it is concerned.

The main characteristics of custom are as follows.

1. It must have existed in fact, or by presumption, since time immemorial, namely, 1189.
2. The custom must be local, that is, confined to a particular locality. A custom cannot exist in one place which purports to confer a right to something in a different locality: *Re Ecclesfield Inhabitants* (1818) 1 B & Ald 348 (Lord Ellenborough CJ). Contrast this with the common law which is not (within England and Wales) confined to any particular locality.
3. Custom is an exception to the normal operation of the common law – though many customs have been abolished by legislation.

Essential elements of custom

Time immemorial
The custom must be shown to have existed since 1189, the time fixed by the Statute of Westminster I, 1275 as 'time immemorial' (viz the first year of the reign of Richard I). In some cases, it is sufficient to raise a presumption of antiquity, for example by showing that a continuous customary user has existed for as long as living memory can go: *Angus v Dalton* (1877) 3 QBD 85 at 103–104. Of course, such a presumption is open to rebuttal, such as by evidence indicating that the custom began after 1189.

Must be reasonable
This requirement means that if the alleged custom is without a legal reason, it will not be upheld. 'Unreasonableness' in this context can mean that the custom arose from accident or by the permission of another, for example from a royal grant and not from a right arising in ancient times. The reasonableness of a custom is to be

adjudged at the time it began, and a custom is not unreasonable merely because it is not consistent with the common law: *Tanistry Case*, above.

Further, if the custom is repugnant to the principles of the common law it will not be upheld, for example if it entails placing a disproportionate burden on some for the benefit of others: *Wolstanton Ltd* v *Newcastle-under-Lyme Corporation* [1940] 3 All ER 101 (HL).

Must be certain

The custom alleged must be clear and certain not only in respect of the nature of the right claimed but as to the custom itself. A custom must be certain:

1. as to its general nature;
2. as to the persons alleged to be affected; and
3. as to the locality in which it is alleged to be affected (eg a town, manor, parish or county).

Must be obligatory

Unless the custom carries with it obligatory force it will not be upheld, since in that case it does not have the characteristic of a rule of law.

Must not have been interrupted

To be valid a custom must have existed without interruption since time immemorial. A mere lack of use for a period does not necessarily mean that the custom has been extinguished, though it makes it more difficult to establish.

Creation and enjoyment

Provided that the requirements stated above have been fulfilled, it is unnecessary to prove how the custom originated. However, the right claimed by virtue of custom must be enjoyed as of right (viz by virtue of the custom) and without violence, secrecy or the permission of another (nec vi nec clam nec precario): *Alfred F Beckett Ltd* v *Lyons* [1967] 1 All ER 833 (CA).

As noted in the section above, non-user will not of itself extinguish the custom though it may raise an inference that no such custom existed particularly if non-user was not accidental or due to natural causes.

Customary rights may even exist over the land of another (eg rights of entry for recreation or taking water, rights of way), and are in the nature of easements ('quasi-easements').

1.8 Legislation

Introduction

The modern importance attached to legislation and the overriding effect of Parliament's will manifested through statute has not always existed, though statutes (in one form or another) have existed for many centuries. Ancient statutes did not follow the modern form nor did they always enjoy the respect and obedience given to modern legislation by the judiciary.

Parliament initially played a minor role in law-making though it gradually developed functions of ratification of royal decrees and initiator of royal legislation (by presenting grievances to the Crown). In the modern law, statute law fulfils a number of important functions, since it not only expresses the will of the democratically elected Parliament (insofar as their will is clearly expressed in statute) but carries out social, legal and administrative reforms. With the generally conservative approach of the judiciary and the constraints of the doctrine of precedent, major legal reform is usually left to Parliament: see, for example, *Lim Poh Choo* v *Camden & Islington Area Health Authority* [1980] AC 174 (HL) where the House declined to initiate major reforms of the law governing damages for personal injury:

> '... so radical a reform can be made neither by judge nor by modification of rules of court. It raises issues of social, economic and financial policy not amenable to judicial reform, which will almost certainly prove to be controversial and can only be resolved by the legislature after full consideration of factors which cannot be brought into clear focus, or be weighed and assessed, in the course of the forensic process ... it is this limitation, inherent in the forensic process, which sets bounds to the scope of judicial law reform ...' (Lord Scarman)

The 'limitation' referred to is that the court is always confined to the issues raised and argued by the litigants and is very rarely in a position to consider the full implications of a major change in the law. Parliament is, however, in such a position and is further able to make use of reports of the Law Commission (a permanent body set up to consider issues of law reform) or a Royal Commission specially set up to consider a particular area of the law.

Modern legislation

Since 1973 there have been two major sources of legislation binding within the English legal system: the traditional parliamentary legislation was joined by that of the European Communities on the coming into force of the European Communities Act 1972. European law is dealt with in detail in Chapters 16 and 17.

The modern authority of statute law is clear and is quite able to alter and abolish sections of the common law: subject to the restraints of the democratic system, laws may also be enacted contrary to morality or religion. Further, international law is only made part of English law by statutory incorporation: *Attorney-General for Canada* v *Attorney-General for Ontario* [1937] AC 326 at 347–348.

With the exception of private member's bills most legislation is initiated by the government. The initial impetus may be that of the government seeking to implement its own party policy, or from the Law Commission (or Royal Commission) pointing out defects in the existing law and making recommendations for reform. Government bills are usually dealt with by the government ministry or department most concerned and their proposals form the basis of instructions sent to parliamentary counsel who draft the bills. The drafting of a bill involves consultation between counsel (who is a qualified barrister) and the relevant ministry (or even the Cabinet if it is sufficiently important).

Prior to its introduction into Parliament, the final draft of the relevant bill is approved by the department whose concern it is. It is also attended by counsel who drafted it, and who will draft any subsequent amendments made during its passage. The basic stages in the passage of a bill are as follows.

1. Introduction of the Bill.
2. First reading.
3. Second reading.
4. Committee stage.
5. Report stage.
6. Third reading.
7. Royal Assent.

Form and functions of modern legislation

Form

In brief, there are a number of forms of legislation. The most important form is, of course, an Act of Parliament which is enacted in accordance with the unlimited legislative power of Parliament subject to compliance with European Community law. It is now well established that no court may impugn an Act or go behind it in order to see if there were irregularities of procedure: *British Railways Board* v *Pickin* [1974] AC 765.

The most commonly used version of an Act is the Queen's Printer's Copy though various editions are published (not least by Old Bailey Press), with or without commentaries, and as appendices to practitioners' works.

Functions

Reform and revision of law. This function of legislation (viz reform of 'lawyers' law') is not a function in which Parliament generally initiates, except where it has other implications. The initiative for legal reform usually comes from the Law Commission or specially appointed Royal Commissions, usually on ministerial recommendation. A separate Criminal Law Revision Committee deals with reform of the criminal law.

Social legislation. This form of legislation deals with wider and often more fundamental issues than simple revision of the substantive law. It often involves a wholesale abolition of existing principles and the creation of a new system or structure of rules: for example, major reforms of taxation, such as the creation of capital transfer tax to replace estate duty in the Finance Act 1975 (consolidated in the Capital Transfer Tax Act 1984). Capital Transfer Tax is now called inheritance tax and the 1984 Act has been renamed accordingly. While some minor revisions of the law (and some major, such as the new approach to tax planning – *Furniss* v *Dawson* [1984] 2 WLR 226 (HL)) are carried out by the courts, particularly the House of Lords, social reform is almost wholly outside the scope of the activities of the judiciary. Indeed, it is not normally in a position to take such steps and the judges are not democratically acceptable as instigators of social reform.

Consolidation. It often happens that when Parliament enacts a statute on a particular topic (eg the parts of the Finance Act 1975 dealing with capital transfer tax), the new law requires amendment which is dealt with by subsequent statutes – and additions and deletions are made as the effects and problems of the new law become apparent with time. A consolidating statute is one which brings together all the statutory provisions on a given topic and, together with any consequential amendments, puts them into one statute. An example is the Taxation of Chargeable Gains Act 1992 which consolidated the many statutory provisions relating to the taxation of chargeable gains.

Codification. In areas of the law which are well developed and the principles of which are well worked out in a body of case law and statute, statutes are sometimes enacted which bring together all the rules (both common law and statutory) and present them in a single statutory code. From thenceforth, the new statute is the starting point in that area of the law and case law will, in time, build up around the codified provisions. Examples are the Criminal Law Act 1977 (conspiracy), the Criminal Attempts Act 1981 and the Police and Criminal Evidence Act 1984.

The operation of statutes

Geographical operation

There is a presumption that an Act of Parliament is operative throughout the United Kingdom but nowhere else unless a contrary intention appears in the Act. In practice statutes normally have a section which deals with the issue of where it will be applicable.

Temporal operation

A statute comes into force on the day it receives the Royal Assent unless some other date is specified in the Act itself: Interpretation Act 1978. Very often Acts now provide that they are to come into force on 'a day to be appointed' usually by a Minister or by Order in Council (ie by Statutory Instrument).

Often sections of an Act are brought into operation at different times: for example the Children Act 1989, various sections of which were brought into force on different dates and which was not fully in force until 14 October 1991.

There is a presumption against retrospective operation except for certain financial and revenue statutes: *R* v *Fisher* [1969] 1 All ER 100 and *Wilson* v *Dagnall* [1972] 1 QB 509.

Obsolescence

A statute never becomes ineffective due to the passage of time and, if it is desired that it should no longer be in force, it must be repealed, unless it was stated to be for a fixed period, or for a particular purpose, long since gone. Repeal must be by statute, and can be either express or implied, implied repeal of an earlier statute being the result of an enactment of a later inconsistent statute. Since 1965 the Law Commission has been systematically reviewing the statute book and repealing obsolete statutes in regular Statute Law Repeal Acts.

Subordinate legislation

Despite the ever increasing volume of primary legislation, the complexities of governing modern society necessitates the delegation of legislative functions to inferior bodies, such as Ministers and local authorities. Clearly Parliament simply does not have the time or resources to enact in the form of primary legislation, which can be fully debated and scrutinised by both Houses, every single piece of legislation that is needed. The result is subordinate (or delegated) legislation: that is, legislation produced by an inferior body which nevertheless has the force of law.

Subordinate legislation may be classified: according to purpose; or according to procedure.

Classification according to purpose

Regulations for the purpose of bringing a statute into operation. Some statutory instruments are designed to bring into force the whole or part of an Act of Parliament which for some reason it is not desired to put into effect immediately upon Royal Assent. There may be more than one of these Commencement Orders per Act and there is in general no requirement as to the time after Royal Assent in which such an order must be brought in.

Regulations for the purpose of amending statutory provisions. For example the European Communities Act 1972, s2(2), delegates power to give effect to Community obligations. Orders in Council and Ministerial regulations made under these delegated powers have the effect of Acts of Parliament and may be made even where they conflict with Acts of Parliament.

Regulations which add to, explain, or give effect to general statutory provisions.

Regulations for the purpose of clothing a statute. The general principles of a piece of legislation may be expounded in the 'framework' statute, but it is left to the subordinate authority to clothe that statute, by means of delegated legislation, with the detail necessary to give it effect.

Classification according to procedure

This is the way of implementing the law-making power. The main kinds of delegated legislation are as follows.

Orders in Council. These are the oldest and most dignified form of delegated legislation, and are made by the Queen 'by and with the advice of Her Majesty's Privy Council'. Only those Orders in Council made under statutory authority may be classified as delegated legislation, and they must be distinguished from those Orders in Council made under the Royal Prerogative.

Ministerial regulations. Ministers of the Crown may be empowered to make regulations and issue directions, rules and orders relating to matters within their departmental jurisdiction.

Local authority and other bye-laws. These comprise rules made by local authorities and other statutory undertakers, for the regulation, administration or management of the district or service administered by the authority or undertaking concerned.

Miscellaneous categories. These include local authority orders (for example compulsory purchase orders), and measures taken by the General Synod of the Church of England.

1.9 Case law

Law reporting, in one form or another, has been an integral feature of the English legal system since the thirteenth century. The earliest reports may simply have been notes of cases collected on scraps of parchment, passed around by members of the profession for their own use. At some stage, reporting became popular enough to be performed on a wider (though unofficial) basis and the Year Books, the great series of medieval reports, began late in the reign of Edward I.

The Year Books ceased in 1535, and were ultimately superseded by the so-called innominate reports, which initially did not differ in style from the Year Books. With the appearance of reporters and commentators such as Plowden and Coke later in the sixteenth century, reporting underwent a revolution and a new thoroughness and attention to detail became apparent, in addition to the provision of learned comment.

The late seventeenth and eighteenth centuries saw a decline in the standard of reporting which was not overcome until the appearance of Burrow's Reports in the late eighteenth century. Gradually, there was an increase in professional and judicial supervision of reporting, and haphazard methods of reporting were replaced by periodical series of reports. Eventually, in 1865 the Incorporated Council of Law reporting was set up and the official Law Reports began, which continue to be produced now in the following series:

AC	Appeal Cases
QB	Queen's Bench Division
Ch	Chancery Division
Fam	Family Division

Until the new Family Division was set up, there was a series of Probate Reports (P), dealing with the reports of cases in the Probate, Admiralty and Divorce Division.

In addition to the official series (which contain the summarised arguments of counsel, and are checked by the judges responsible for the judgments), the Incorporated Council also produces the Weekly Law Reports (WLR) which appeared in 1953 to replace Weekly Notes (WN). Volumes 2 and 3 WLR reproduce all the cases to be printed in the official series and Volume 1 contains cases not reported in the official series which are considered of interest.

Various other series of reports also exist, the main commercial series of general reports being the All England Law Reports (All ER). Other major series include:

Cr App R	Criminal Appeal Reports
CMLR	Common Market Law Reports
ECR	European Court Reports (the official reports of the European Court of Justice)
RTR	Road Traffic Reports
STC	Simon's Tax Cases
Lloyd's Rep	Lloyd's List Reports (commercial law)

Current Law contains a brief summary of most cases on a monthly basis (as well as noting recent articles), whether reported or not. *The Times* and other newspapers also publish abbreviated reports which are sometimes cited in court.

Unreported cases may be cited to the court, transcripts being obtainable (depending on the court) from the official shorthand writers. In the case of Court of Appeal decisions, transcripts are available in the Supreme Court library. The computerised system LEXIS makes available, inter alia, a comprehensive collection of English and other cases. However, the House of Lords has warned against the use of unreported Court of Appeal authority: see *Roberts Petroleum Ltd* v *Bernard Kenny Ltd* [1983] 2 AC 192 discussed in Chapter 3, section 3.1.

Case law is of great importance as a source of law because of the potential for judicial law reform: see, for example, *Woolwich Building Society* v *Inland Revenue Commissioners* [1992] 3 WLR 366 (HL). The issue of judicial law reform is explored in detail in Chapter 3.

1.10 Neutral case citation

At the beginning of 2001, the courts introduced a new method of case citation as well as a new system using paragraph numbers. These changes are primarily intended to assist in the researching and use of cases from the internet and they conform with emerging international practice. The system of citation is referred to as neutral citation, as it does not refer to any particular law report. The format is as follows:

1. House of Lords: [2003] EWHL (followed by allocated case number);
2. Court of Appeal (Civil Division): [2003] EWCA Civ (followed by allocated case number);
3. Court of Appeal (Criminal Division): [2003] EWCA Crim (followed by allocated case number);
4. High Court (Administrative Court): [2003] EWHC Admin (followed by allocated case number).

1.11 European law

The European Community and European Union

The United Kingdom acceded to the European Economic Community (as it then was) on 1 January 1973 and from that date European Community law has been an important source of English law. If a national law of a member state conflicts with Community law, the latter prevails: see *Costa* v *ENEL* [1964] CMLR 425. The framework of the European Union and the implications of Community law are explored in detail in Chapters 16 and 17.

The European Convention on Human Rights

English law has also been affected by the United Kingdom's incorporation of the European Convention on Human Rights. The influence of human rights jurisprudence as a source of law increased dramatically since the Human Rights Act 1998 came into force. The Act incorporates the bulk of the Convention into English law, enabling judges to apply its provisions directly to English cases instead of indirectly. The historical influence of the European Convention and the impact of the Human Rights Act 1998 are explored in detail in Chapter 18.

2

Interpretation of Legislation and Law Reform

Interpretation of legislation

2.1 Introduction

2.2 The canons of interpretation

2.3 Other principles of construction

2.4 Aids to interpretation and construction

2.5 The influence of the European Convention on Human Rights and the impact of the Human Rights Act 1998

2.6 Judges as law reformers

Law reform

2.7 Law reform bodies

2.8 Examples of reform

Interpretation of legislation

2.1 Introduction

There is nothing unusual in the process of interpretation: it is the ordinary function of the courts to interpret statutory provisions (viz give meaning to the provisions) and apply them. Problems occur when statutory words are unclear, or at least are not instantly susceptible of a clear interpretation, and the court must resolve uncertainties and, occasionally, resolve ambiguities in the language used. This latter process can be distinguished from the everyday interpretation of statutes and is sometimes called statutory construction so as to distinguish it from the more ordinary function. In the great majority of cases, litigation does not involve problems of construction: usually the argument turns on the application of clear provisions to the disputed facts of the case.

The problem of uncertainty arises generally because it is unclear whether the particular statutory provisions are meant to cover the factual situation before the court. This can be a particular problem when a situation arises which the draftsman clearly did not envisage, not necessarily because the drafting was badly done, but perhaps because the situation could not have been foreseen (especially if the statute is quite an old one) and is quite novel. After all, draftsmen cannot be expected to foresee and be able to cope with every possible eventuality: what they must do is draft provisions within their terms of reference and try to ensure that the principles are sufficiently clear to enable the courts to deal with new situations as they arise.

Ambiguity is a problem which tends to occur less frequently than uncertainty and is the problem of a particular word or phrase, used in a statute, which gives rise to two or more meanings. Since many statutes create new 'legal situations' (ie venture into areas not previously covered by statute), all of these competing meanings may be quite plausible – the problem is rarely dealt with simply by stating that one possible construction is so 'absurd' that it can be discarded. An example of ambiguity is provided by *Fisher* v *Bell* [1961] 1 QB 394, where the question arose whether a display of 'flick-knives' was included in the phrase 'offer for sale' in the Restriction of Offensive Weapons Act 1957. A strict contractual analysis of the display indicated that it was merely an invitation to treat and not an 'offer for sale', and so the court held, finding the shopkeeper not guilty of an offence under the Act.

Sometimes a provision is so badly drafted that it is almost impossible to construe sensibly – such as the ill-fated s16(2)(a) of the Theft Act 1968 (*R* v *Royle* [1971] 3 All ER 1359 – 'a judicial nightmare', per Edmund Davies LJ at p1363) which was ultimately replaced by an entire Act, the Theft Act 1978. Fortunately, such occurrences are rare, but where it is 'abundantly clear' that the court should declare an error and correct a statute it will do so: *Inco Europe Ltd and Others* v *First Choice Distribution and Others* [2000] 2 All ER 109 (HL).

As should already be quite clear, the function of the courts in interpreting and construing statutes is a vital one, since it is the courts which must 'give life' to the provisions by considering and applying them. To a certain extent (much greater in cases of uncertainty and ambiguity) the court is responsible for the development of the law created by a particular statute. In cases of clear and easily applicable provisions, the possibility of judicial discretion is much less, but in cases of construction, a court may have the 'last word' in the meaning and scope of a statute – at least, until Parliament intervenes. The judicial function was put quite strongly by Lord Reid in *Black-Clawson International Ltd* v *Papierwerke Waldhof-Aschaffenburg AG* [1975] AC 591:

> 'We are seeking the meaning of the words which Parliament used. We are seeking not what Parliament meant but the true meaning of what they said.'

This appears to focus on the fact that the courts are not concerned with the abstract notion of parliamentary intention but with the words by which Parliament seeks to make its intention manifest. Lord Wilberforce in the same case contrasted the different functions of Parliament and the courts:

> 'Legislation in England is passed by Parliament and put in the form of written words. This legislation is given legal effect ... by virtue of judicial decision, and it is the function of the courts to say what the application of the words used to particular cases or individuals is to be.'

He noted that the frequently repeated statement 'that it is the function of the courts to ascertain the intention of Parliament' can, if too 'unreflectingly' repeated, lead to 'neglect of the important element of judicial construction' which is not confined to a 'mechanical analysis' of words, but should be related to matters such as:

> 'Intelligibility to the citizen, constitutional propriety, considerations of history, comity of nations, reasonable and non-retroactive effect and, no doubt, in some contexts, to social needs.'

See also the purposive approach to statutory construction explained in *Pepper* v *Hart* [1993] 1 All ER 42 (HL): see section 2.2 below.

It is traditionally said that the approach of the judiciary can be classified by reference to the three canons (or rules) of statutory interpretation, the literal, golden and mischief rules. In addition to these three main rules, there are a number of other rules of construction, as well as presumptions of construction. However, as will be seen, none of these so-called rules are truly rules because much depends on the approach of the particular judge.

2.2 The canons of interpretation

The literal rule

The literal rule of interpretation is that the intention of Parliament is to be found by giving the words their ordinary and literal meaning. The general rule was stated by Lord Esher MR in *R* v *Judge of the City of London Court* [1892] 1 QB 273:

> 'If the words of an Act are clear, you must follow them even though they lead to a manifest absurdity. The court has nothing to do with the question whether the legislative has committed an absurdity.'

Thus, on this approach, the court does not consider the result of the application of the rule, which may or may not be sensible. Examples of applications of this rule where the results are at least questionable include *Inland Revenue Commissioners* v *Hinchy* [1960] AC 748 where the House of Lords held that a penal provision that a person delivering an incorrect tax return should forfeit 'treble the tax which he ought to be charged under this Act' (ie the Income Tax Act 1952, s25(3)(a)) meant that the penalty was three times the whole amount payable for the relevant year. Parliament showed that it had intended only three times the amount unpaid by changing the law shortly afterwards. See also *Fisher* v *Bell*, above, where 'offer for sale' was construed strictly in accordance with standard contract law. Was this, in fact, the 'plain meaning', or was that simply a non-technical meaning of 'display to encourage sale' – which is what the Act of 1957 appears to have been attempting to prevent?

The literal rule was the product of the nineteenth century and reached its most extreme expressions during that time. The extreme nineteenth-century view was typified by a dictum of Lord Halsbury in *Hilder* v *Dexter* [1902] AC 474:

'In construing a statute I believe the worst person to construe it is the person who is responsible for its drafting. He is very much disposed to confuse what he intended to do with the effect of the language which in fact has been employed.'

Compare the dictum of Lord Reid in *Black-Clawson*, quoted above.

The inflexibility of the literal approach when applied with full rigour can be seen in relation to the judicial attitude to 'omissions': that is, the willingness to give sense to a statute by reading in additional words in order to further the intention of Parliament. In *Seaford Court Estates Ltd* v *Asher* [1949] 2 KB 481 Lord Denning said:

'... if the makers of the Act had themselves come across this ruck in the texture of it, how would they have straightened it out? He [the judge] must then do as they would have done. A judge must not alter the material of which it is woven, but he can and should iron out the creases.'

Another classic example is *Magor and St Mellons* v *Newport Corporation* [1952] AC 189; [1951] 2 All ER 839. Under the Local Government Act 1933, compensation was payable to two district councils which had their boundaries reduced by the expansion in the boundaries of Newport Corporation. However, the two councils were ultimately amalgamated into one and Newport Corporation argued that no compensation was payable since it was only payable to surviving councils and, in fact, they were not surviving, having been abolished to form one new one. The Corporation succeeded. However, in the Court of Appeal, Denning LJ dissented on the basis that the obvious intention was to provide compensation and said he had:

'... no patience with an ultra-legalistic interpretation which would deprive them of their rights altogether ... we sit here to find out the intention of Parliament ... and carry it out, and we do this better by filling in the gaps and making sense of the enactment than by opening it up to destructive analysis.'

In the House of Lords, Lord Simonds was very critical of this approach:

'The duty of the court is to interpret the words that the legislature has used. Those words may be ambiguous, but, even if they are, the power and duty of the court to travel outside them on a voyage of discovery are strictly limited ... [and of Denning LJ's dictum said] it appears to me to be a naked usurpation of the legislative function under the thin disguise of interpretation and it is less justifiable when it is guesswork with what material the legislature would, if it had discovered the gap, have filled it in. If a gap is disclosed, the remedy lies in an amending Act.'

However, it is not always the case that the courts will take such a strict approach: in many constructions there is an element of filling gaps, since the words must be interpreted and a gloss put on them in order that they might be made to operate in practice. For example, in *Nothman* v *Barnet London Borough Council* [1979] 1 All ER 142 (HL); [1978] 1 WLR 220 (CA) the court had to construe para 10 of Sch 1 of the Trade Union and Labour Relations Act 1974 which limited the right not to be unfairly dismissed and excluded it in cases, inter alia, where an employee at the date of dismissal had reached 'the normal retiring age ... or, if a man, attained the age of 65, or, if a woman, attained the age of 60'.

In the Court of Appeal Lord Denning dealt with the problem in his usual robust manner:

'... Whenever the strict interpretation of a statute gives rise to an absurd or unjust situation, the judges can and should use their good sense to remedy it (by reading words in, if necessary) so as to do what Parliament would have done had they had the situation in mind.'

The House of Lords split three to two over the construction of those words, the majority holding that para 10 specified two limits, one for when there was a 'normal retiring age' and one when there was not. The minority held that the limits were cumulative and that the plain meaning was that the earlier should apply. The objection of the majority to this approach was that it involved: 'tacking on to the end of it the words "whichever is the earlier" ' (Lord Salmon at p146).

Equally, it could be said of the majority that their approach required the insertion of the words 'where there is no normal retiring age'. Curiously enough, with the exception of Lord Russell, both majority and minority considered they were applying the 'literal meaning': 'I think that the words are clear and free from ambiguity' (Lord Diplock, dissenting).

All the Law Lords expressed strong disapproval of Lord Denning's comments in the Court of Appeal, on the ground that Lord Denning was crossing the line between interpretation and judicial legislation. The constitutional objections to judicial creativity in this field surfaced again in *Duport Steels Ltd* v *Sirs* [1980] 1 WLR 142 (HL). Lord Denning's approach to statutory construction in this case drew strong condemnation from the Law Lords on the ground that he was trying to advance a policy in conflict with the plain words of an Act of Parliament simply because he found the parliamentary policy 'unjust'. Lord Diplock emphasised the constitutional doctrine of the separation of powers as justification for confining the judiciary to the interpretation and application of statute law:

'Where the meaning of the statutory words is plain and unambiguous it is not for judges to invent fancied ambiguities as an excuse for failing to give effect to its plain meaning because they themselves consider that the consequences of doing so would be inexpedient, or even unjust or immoral.'

Lord Scarman agreed, saying:

'... in the field of statute law the judge must be obedient to the will of Parliament as expressed in its enactments ... Unpalatable statute law may not be disregarded or rejected merely because it is unpalatable.'

Hence the literal rule is a constitutional virtue in safeguarding the sovereignty of Parliament, the separation of powers, the rule of law and, indeed, the independence and impartiality of the judges themselves. However, as will be seen, it is difficult to maintain such constitutional purity in the face of judicial determination to apply the law as humanely and fairly so far as it is possible to do so.

The golden rule

This so-called golden rule is said to apply in cases where the plain meaning of the words produce a 'manifest absurdity'. In *Grey* v *Pearson* (1857) 6 HL Cas 61, Parke B (later Lord Wensleydale) said:

'... the grammatical and ordinary sense of the words is to be adhered to, unless that would lead to some absurdity, or some repugnance or inconsistency with the rest of the instrument, in which case the grammatical and ordinary sense of the words may be modified, so as to avoid the absurdity and inconsistency but no farther.'

In *River Wear Commissioners* v *Adamson* (1877) 2 App Cas 743, Lord Blackburn said:

'I believe it is not disputed that what Lord Wensleydale used to call the golden rule is right, viz that we are to take the whole statute together and construe it all together, giving the words their ordinary significance, unless when so applied they produce an inconsistency, or an absurdity or inconvenience so great as to convince the court that the intention could not have been to use them in their ordinary signification, and to justify the court in putting on them some other significance, which, though less proper, is one which the court thinks the words will bear.'

An example of the application of this rule (and they are comparatively rare) is *R* v *Allen* (1872) LR 1 CCR 367: the word 'marry' in s57 of the Offences Against the Person Act 1861 (bigamy) was construed so as to give effect to the least absurd result, namely, 'go through a ceremony of marriage' – the alternative 'contract a valid marriage' would be impossible, since it is not possible to contract a valid marriage when one is already validly married. However, the rule is not entirely clear in its extent (quite apart from problems of application, see below), for on one reading it closely resembles the literal rule:

'The golden rule is that the words of a statute must prima facie be given their ordinary meaning.' (Viscount Simon in *Nokes* v *Doncaster Amalgamated Collieries* [1940] AC 1014.)

The usual meaning is that of Parke B, quoted above. Even in that case, there must be a manifest absurdity before the court will depart from an otherwise plain meaning – and cases such as *IRC* v *Hinchy, Fisher* v *Bell* and *Magor and St Mellons* v *Newport* indicate that odd 'literal' constructions do not automatically lead to use of the golden rule.

The mischief rule and modern purposive construction

The 'mischief' rule is a departure from the other two rules in that it concentrates, not solely on the words of the statute, but on the purpose for which Parliament enacted the statute. It is derived from *Heydon's Case* (1584) 3 Co Rep 74 (Court of Exchequer), where the court 'resolved' that four matters are to be had regard to:

'1st What was the common law before the making of the Act.
2nd What was the mischief and defect for which the common law did not provide.
3rd What remedy the Parliament hath resolved and appointed to cure the disease of the Commonwealth.
And,
4th The true reason of the remedy; and then the office of all the Judges is always to make such construction as shall suppress the mischief, and advance the remedy.'

The narrow application of this rule occurs where the literal rule cannot be applied due to ambiguities. An example of this occurred in the case of *Kruhlak* v *Kruhlak* [1958] 2 QB 32, where it was decided that a 'single woman' for the purpose of affiliation proceedings was a woman with no husband to support her and that did not necessarily mean an unmarried woman (ie the mischief was a woman with an illegitimate baby and no means of support).

In *Universal Corporation* v *Five Ways Properties* [1979] 1 All ER 552 (CA) Buckley LJ said that:

'... that doctrine [viz the mischief rule] ... does not entitle the court to disregard the plain and natural meaning of wide general terms in a statute. If the language is equivocal and requires construction, then the doctrine is a proper one to refer to; but if the language is quite plain then the duty of the court is to give effect to what Parliament has said.'

See also the dictum of Viscount Simons in the *Hanover* case, below, for a potentially wider approach.

In the *Black-Clawson* case, Lord Diplock noted that the original meaning of this canon of construction was that only the statute itself could be looked at to ascertain the mischief. Now, however, certain documents extraneous to the statute can be used 'with caution'. In that case, the HL held that use could be made of the report of the Law Commission (or equivalent) to discover what the mischief was (and for no other use) for which the statute was enacted. As Lord Reid pointed out:

'... the mischief which this Act [Foreign Judgments (Reciprocal Enforcement) Act 1933, s8] was intended to remedy may have been common knowledge 40 years ago. I do not think that it is today. But it so happens that a committee ... made a full investigation of the matter and reported some months before the Act was passed.'

The advantage of this approach is that, at least, it requires the court to consider the purpose of the statute and to construe the words in that context: see *NWL Ltd* v *Woods* [1979] 1 WLR 1294 (HL).

In *Attorney-General* v *Jones* [1990] 1 WLR 859 the Court of Appeal was called upon to consider the meaning of s42 of the Supreme Court Act 1981. Lord Donaldson MR concluded that the section is ambiguous and that it followed 'that it is both permissible and necessary to have regard to its purpose, to the mischief at which it is directed'. Again, in *Southern Water Authority* v *Nature Conservancy Council* [1992] 3 All ER 481 the question arose as to whether, for the purposes of s28 of the Wildlife and Countryside Act 1981, a water authority was an 'occupier' of land by reason of carrying out ditching operations on it. After noting that the Act itself demonstrated that 'occupier' had no fixed meaning, Lord Mustill said: 'We must therefore consider what kinds of occupier must have been intended to fall within the prohibition with which we are here concerned'. His conclusion ('that the section was never intended to apply to persons such as the ... water authority') was reinforced by consideration of other provisions of the Act and their effect.

There is a growing tendency, perhaps encouraged by Europe, towards a purposive construction of statutes which do not deal with penal or revenue matters and this principle is not limited to statutes passed after the principle had been authoritatively declared by the courts: *R* v *Registrar-General, ex parte Smith* [1991] 2 WLR 782. Indeed, in *Pepper* v *Hart* [1993] 1 All ER 42 Lord Griffiths felt able to say:

'The days have long passed when the courts adopted a strict constructionist view of interpretation which required them to adopt the literal meaning of the language. The courts now adopt a purposive approach which seeks to give effect to the true purpose of legislation and are prepared to look at much extraneous material that bears on the background against which the legislation was enacted.'

See further section 2.4, below.

2.3 Other principles of construction

In common with most rules and principles governing the interpretation of statutes, the following principles are not of mandatory application and much depends on the particular problem before the court, as well as the preferences of that court.

The statute should be read as a whole

This is obviously an important principle since words often take on a particular, more precise, meaning when they are placed in the context of other words. Since the courts profess to be giving effect to the intention of Parliament, to read statutory words out of context could scarcely be justified. As Cross writes, 'it is difficult to believe that the notion of construction in complete isolation was ever taken wholly seriously' though there are isolated examples of attempts to do such, even in the twentieth century: see Lord Greene's criticism of the trial judge in *Re Bidie* [1948] 2 All ER 995.

In *Attorney-General* v *Prince Ernest Augustus of Hanover* [1957] AC 436 (HL) it was held that:

> '... the Act (enacted in Queen Anne's reign) must be construed as it would have been construed immediately after it became law.' (Lord Normand)

Viscount Simonds made what were then somewhat 'revolutionary' remarks concerning 'context':

> '... words, and particularly general words, cannot be read in isolation, their colour and context are derived from their context ... I use "context" in its widest sense, which I have already indicated as including not only other enacting provisions of the same statute but its preamble, the existing state of the law, other statutes in pari materia, and the mischief which I can, by those and other legitimate means, discern the statute was intended to remedy.'

This passage was cited by Lord Upjohn in *DPP* v *Schildkamp* [1971] AC 1, 23. Its importance lies in the fact that it recognises that a reasonable result often cannot be achieved by a 'purely semantic process' (Cross), by simply trying to construe the actual words and only looking to the object of a statute when the words lead to doubt.

Ejusdem generis

This simply means that when a series of words is used, a series of particular words followed or preceded by general words, such as 'and other such' or 'including', the general words must be construed with reference to the particular words. The particular words (there must be at least two to make a 'series': *Allen* v *Emmerson* [1944] KB 362) are said to make a genus, that is, a category or 'family' of objects. To include a particular matter or situation within the general words, they must be shown to be ejusdem generis ('of the same type') with the particular words.

In *Powell* v *Kempton Park Racecourse Co* [1899] AC 143 (HL) the court had to decide whether a racecourse was comprised in the definition of 'house, office, room ... or other place' within the Betting Act 1853. It was held not to be ejusdem generis with those places, ie 'other place' was confined to indoor places.

Presumptions

Presumptions, when they are used, merely presume that a given approach is to be taken (eg penal statutes are strictly construed), but such a presumption always gives way to contrary intention (express or implied). Common presumptions include the following.

1. Penal statutes are construed strictly in favour of the accused. For example, in *R v Highbury Corner Magistrates' Court, ex parte Di Matteo* [1991] 1 WLR 1374, Watkins LJ said:

   '... the words used in s43 [of the Powers of Criminal Courts Act 1973] should be given their natural and ordinary meaning, unless on a reading of the section there are two possible interpretations, in which case, this being a penal provision, the interpretation most favourable to the defendant should be adopted.'

   In *Wychavon District Council* v *National Rivers Authority* [1993] 2 All ER 440 Watkins LJ said that it was a well-known truism that:

   '... where ... a word appears ... in a penal section and ... it is capable of bearing more than one meaning, the meaning most favourable to the subject must be adopted.'

2. Criminal offences usually require fault (that is, mens rea: *Sweet* v *Parsley* [1970] AC 132).
3. Statutes are not intended to derogate from common law rights.
4. Statutes are not intended to have retrospective effect.
5. Parliament, when enacting statutory duties in apparently absolute terms, is to be presumed not to have intended that those terms should apply so as to reward serious crime committed in the past; likewise, Parliament must be presumed not to have intended to promote serious crime in the future: *R* v *Registrar-General, ex parte Smith* [1991] 2 WLR 782.
6. United Kingdom legislation does not apply to foreign persons outside the United Kingdom where acts are performed outside the United Kingdom: *Arab Bank plc* v *Mercantile Holdings Ltd* [1994] 2 All ER 74.

The principle that an ambiguity in a statute should not be construed in a manner which derogates from common law rights does not constrain the courts to invent an ambiguity or to construe an ambiguity in a way which does not make good sense: per Lord Templeman in *Waltham Forest London Borough Council* v *Thomas* [1992] 3 WLR 131.

In *Pepper* v *Hart* [1993] 1 All ER 42 Lord Mackay of Clashfern LC suggested that any ambiguity in a taxing statute should be resolved in favour of the taxpayer. However, the majority approach, which favours a purposive approach to the interpretation of statutes, and the use of external aids such as Hansard to discover Parliament's 'true' intention, may mean that the use of presumptions will become less common in future years.

Conflicting provisions

It was sometimes suggested that where there is a conflict between two sections in the same Act, the last of them must prevail. This is not the case. In such circumstances, if the provisions cannot be reconciled, the court must determine which is the leading provision and which the subordinate and which must give way to the other: *R* v *Moore* [1995] 4 All ER 843 (court gave 'rectifying construction' to conflicting provisions of the Powers of Criminal Courts Act 1973).

Subordinate legislation

Where this is doubt, subordinate legislation is to be construed so as not to be ultra vires the enabling Act: *Raymond* v *Honey* [1983] 1 AC 1.

Reconciliation with European Community law

Primary or subordinate legislation enacted to give effect to the United Kingdom's obligations under Community law must be interpreted as far as possible so as to achieve the intended results, even though this may involve a departure from a literal application of the words which the legislature has chosen to use: per Lord Diplock in *Garland* v *British Rail Engineering Ltd* [1983] 2 AC 751. See also per Lord Dillon LJ in *Morris Angel and Son Ltd* v *Hollande* [1993] 3 All ER 569 (CA). See further Chapter 17.

When United Kingdom judges are required to interpret European Community law itself they must follow the same principles of interpretation as the European Court of Justice, ie because EC law is expressed in generalised terms of principle, and is full of gaps and lacunae, judges must fill in those gaps according to the spirit of Community law. This is known as the European 'teleological' approach: per Lord Denning MR in *Bulmer (HP) Ltd* v *J Bollinger SA* [1974] 3 WLR 202 (CA). It will be seen that United Kingdom judges have adopted a more purposive approach to the construction of purely domestic law (section 2.4 below), but it should be noted that this approach falls well short of the kind of judicial creativity employed for the interpretation of European Community law.

2.4 Aids to interpretation and construction

Internal aids

These are matters appearing within the Queen's Printer's Copy of the Act, and can, with a few exceptions, be used to construe the individual provisions of that Act: that is, the court may read the statute as a whole, in order to understand the provisions from their context. Indeed, it is often the case that a statute will contain a specific section defining certain key words used throughout all, or part, of the statute.

The matters to which the court may have regard in construing statutory provisions are as follows.

1. *The long title* – the formal description of the Act, placed at its beginning (in *R* v *Secretary of State for Foreign and Commonwealth Affairs, ex parte Rees-Mogg*

[1994] 1 All ER 457 Lloyd LJ said 'the days are long since past when courts declined to regard the long title as an aid to construction').

2. *The short title* – the shorter title used for reference.

3. *Schedules* – these are fully part of the statutory provisions, in any case, and have the same legal force as the individual sections themselves.

4. *Preambles* – in older legislation preambles were often included, being (sometimes) lengthy expositions of the purpose of the enactment. They are rarely used in modern legislation, but may be used to construe the statute: see *Prince Ernest Augustus of Hanover*'s case, above.

Marginal notes may not be used to interpret an Act since these are simply summaries of particular sections and are not part of the statute: *Re Woking Urban District Council* [1914] 1 Ch 300, 322. However, regard may be had to them for an indication of the mischief with which the Act is dealing: *R* v *Kelt* [1977] 1 WLR 1365. Further, the traditional view was that punctuation should be disregarded, but it seems that this is no longer the position unless to take account of it would so alter the sense as to be contrary to the plain intention of the statute: *Hanlon* v *The Law Society* [1981] AC 124.

Statutory history

In some cases the historical development of particular statutory provisions may be used to construe the modern version, particularly if there is a change in the words used. In *Stoke-on-Trent City Council* v *B & Q (Retail) Ltd* [1984] 2 All ER 332, the House of Lords made use of the statutory predecessors of the Local Government Act 1972, s222, in order to decide whether the council had authority (usually vested in the Attorney-General) to use an injunction (a civil law remedy) to prevent a breach of the criminal law – in this case, the legislation prohibiting Sunday trading. The addition to the current Act of words not in the predecessor section were held to grant that authority to local councils. See also *Armah* v *Government of Ghana* [1968] AC 192.

External aids

These are matters lying outside the actual statute itself, some of which may be used as an aid to construction. Examples include the Interpretation Act 1978, dictionaries, reports from law reform bodies and reports of parliamentary debates in Hansard. Each will be considered in turn.

The Interpretation Act 1978

This contains some basic rules, eg that male includes female, singular includes plural unless otherwise stated in the statute, and that an Act comes into force as soon as it receives Royal Assent unless the date for its operation is expressly postponed by the Act in question.

Dictionaries

These would seem to be useful, especially if the court is seeking to discover the ordinary, 'literal' meaning of a word. However, much depends on the individual tribunal, and there are instances of dictionaries being used and others where their use is rejected. In *R* v *Callender* [1992] 3 All ER 51 the Court of Appeal sought assistance from the Shorter Oxford English Dictionary in establishing the meaning of 'employment' in the context of s16 of the Theft Act 1968: see also *R* v *McFarlane* [1994] 2 WLR 494 (reference was made to Oxford dictionaries when deciding that 'clipper' was a prostitute for purposes of s30(1) of the Sexual Offences Act 1956).

Law Commission (or Royal Commission) reports

Reports of committees, such as the Law Commission, are not generally admissible, but they are admissible in order to discover the 'mischief' which a particular statute was enacted to remedy, though it had once been thought that such reports were even inadmissible on this point: *Assam Railways and Trading Co Ltd* v *IRC* [1935] AC 445. However, in the *Black-Clawson* case (above) the House of Lords held that such reports could be used to ascertain the mischief – but no further. The reason is quite clear, and was noted as early as 1898 by Lord Halsbury in *Eastman Photographic Materials Co Ltd* v *Comptroller General of Patents* [1898] AC 571 at 575:

'I think no more accurate source of information as to what the evil or defect which the Act ... now under consideration was intended to remedy could be imagined than the Report of that Commission which had led to the particular enactment.'

See also dicta of Lord Denning MR in *Letang* v *Cooper* [1965] 1 QB 197, to similar effect.

Reports of Parliamentary debates – Hansard

For many years it could be said that the use of these was absolutely prohibited: see Lord Wilberforce in *Black-Clawson*. His Lordship gave two reasons why this was so. The first is a practical objection: 'the courts would merely have to interpret ... two documents instead of one'. The second is a constitutional objection, concerning the division in function between Parliament and the courts: 'it would be a degradation of that process if the courts were to be merely a reflecting mirror of what some other interpretation agency might say'.

However, in *Pepper* v *Hart* [1993] 1 All ER 42 the House of Lords (Lord Mackay of Clashfern LC dissenting) concluded that the time had come to relax, in certain circumstances, the rule prohibiting courts from referring to parliamentary material as an aid to statutory construction. The relaxation applies (in the words of Lord Browne-Wilkinson):

'... where: (a) legislation is ambiguous or obscure, or leads to an absurdity; (b) the material relied on consists of one or more statements by a minister or other promoter of the Bill together if necessary with such other parliamentary material as is necessary to understand such statements and their effect; (c) the statements relied on are clear.'

The case which gave rise to this decision concerned the interpretation of s63 of the Finance Act 1976. There was no doubt that the section was ambiguous and that statements made by the responsible minister during the Bill's passage through Parliament were clear. Accordingly, their Lordships were able to take account of the minister's statements, as recorded in Hansard in deciding upon the section's meaning.

An example of a court (the House of Lords) exercising its new but restricted ability to refer to statements made by a minister in Parliament and recorded in Hansard is *Scher* v *Policyholders Protection Board (No 2)* [1993] 4 All ER 840 where the House of Lords was called upon to construe certain provisions of the Policyholders Protection Act 1975. The House consented to receive, in accordance with *Pepper* v *Hart*, extracts from the parliamentary records of debates during the committee and report stages of the passage of the Policyholders Protection Bill through the House of Lords (see also *Chief Adjudication Officer* v *Foster* [1993] 2 WLR 292). However, in *R* v *Secretary of State for Foreign and Commonwealth Affairs, ex parte Rees-Mogg* [1994] 1 All ER 457 the court refused to look at Hansard because, inter alia, the statutory provision in question was not ambiguous.

Lord Browne-Wilkinson's three conditions for the use of Hansard do not apply to the interpretation of United Kingdom primary or delegated legislation which implements international or European Union law, where a broader, purposive approach and a more generous use of Hansard is permitted: *Three Rivers District Council* v *Bank of England (No 2)* [1996] 2 All ER 363 (QBD, Commercial Court).

Whilst many commentators welcomed *Pepper* v *Hart* as a sensible step for ascertaining legislative intentions, some have criticised it:

> 'Reference to Hansard necessarily sets an interpretation within the immediate contemporary understanding of the government of the day … It risks imposing a literalism in interpretation … on the basis of an interchange, possibly in a nearly empty chamber late at night, indicative only of what [the government] would like the law to be.' (David Robertson, *Judicial Discretion in the House of Lords* (1998), pp171–172, 183, Clarendon Press, Oxford.)

Lord Bingham makes clear, in *R* v *Secretary of State for the Environment, Transport and the Regions, ex parte Spath Holme Ltd* [2001] 2 WLR 15, that the ability to use Hansard as a guide to statutory intention is a device that is to be used only sparingly. He stated:

> 'I think it important that the conditions laid down by the House in *Pepper* v *Hart* should be strictly insisted upon. Otherwise, the cost and inconvenience feared by Lord Mackay, whose objections to relaxation of the exclusionary rule were based on considerations of practice not principle (see p615G), will be realised. The worst of all worlds would be achieved if parties routinely combed through Hansard, and the courts dredged through conflicting statements of parliamentary intention (see p631F), only to conclude that the statutory provision called for no further elucidation or that no clear and unequivocal statement by a responsible minister could be derived from Hansard.' (p211)

A similar restrictive approach was adopted again by the House of Lords in the later decision in *Wilson* v *Secretary of State for Trade and Industry* [2003] 3 WLR 568.

2.5 The influence of the European Convention on Human Rights and the impact of the Human Rights Act 1998

The Human Rights Act 1998 has brought about fundamental changes in statutory interpretation. Section 3 of the 1998 Act provides that 'So far as it is possible to do so, primary legislation and subordinate legislation must be read and given effect in a way which is compatible with the Convention rights' (ie the European Convention on Human Rights). This applies to existing or future legislation. It is unlikely that s3 will be interpreted as overturning all the existing principles of statutory construction, but there is little doubt that it will encourage judges to take a much more purposive approach based on the morality of legislation and the spirit of the Convention.

For details of the Act see Chapter 18, and see further Marshall 'Interpretating Interpretation in the Human Rights Act' [1998] PL 167 and Klug 'The Human Rights Act 1998, *Pepper* v *Hart* and All That' [1999] PL 246.

2.6 Judges as law reformers

It has been seen that the process of statutory interpretation offers opportunities (albeit limited ones) for judges to develop legal principles and reform aspects of law. In Chapter 3 judicial law reform will be considered in the context of the doctrine of precedent – but again the conclusion will be that the scope for such reform is inevitably limited for constitutional reasons, not least the sovereignty of Parliament. The main engine for law reform is the legislature and in practice this means the governing party, influenced by its political ideology, public opinion, pressure groups and the like. It is also influenced by the work of non-political law reform bodies, on which judges, lawyers and academics play important roles. The rest of this chapter is concerned with the work of these law reform bodies.

Law reform

2.7 Law reform bodies

Standing committees

In 1959 the Home Secretary set up the Criminal Law Revision Committee to examine such aspects of criminal law as the Home Secretary may from time to time refer to it. The first important reference was the law of larceny and similar offences which resulted in the Theft Act 1968. Subsequently, the Lord Chancellor established the Statute Law Commission, the Law Reform Committee and the Commission on Private International Law.

The Law Commission was set up by the Law Commission Act 1965 for the purpose of promoting the reform of the law. The Commission consists of a chairman (a High Court judge) and four others, all of whom must be persons appearing to the Lord Chancellor to be suitably qualified by the holding of judicial office, by experience as a person having a general qualification (within the meaning of s71(3) of the Courts and Legal Services Act 1990), or as a teacher of law in a university.

In their twenty-fifth annual report (1990) the Commission observed that the ultimate proof of the value of their work comes only when Parliament decides to give legislative effect to their recommendations. In practice this means that they must find favour with the government, and that either a Bill must be included in the government's legislative programme, or that a Private Member who is successful in the ballot for Private Members' Bills decides to introduce a Bill giving effect to the recommendations in one of the Commission's reports.

In its twenty-eighth annual report, published in April 1994, the Commission complained that only four of its reports had been implemented since 1990 and that more than thirty, many of them uncontroversial, were awaiting legislative attention. This was despite efforts by the Law Commission to improve its communications with MPs and raise its profile with the general public. Indeed, its efforts appeared to backfire when the tabloid press and some MPs criticised its 1992 Report (No 207) on reform of family property law for 'subverting family values'. It seems likely that the role of the Law Commission will be confined by political pressures to making only technical improvements in branches of the law. See further Cretney 'The Law Commission: True Dawns and False Dawns' (1996) 59 MLR 631.

Ad hoc committees

Over the last 100 years many changes in law have been based on the reports of Royal Commissions or official committees. They are made up of a cross-section of people who are often experts or are concerned in the matters in question. However, the members are not sitting full time and so they are slow and not suitable for matters requiring long-term continuing examination. The committee makes recommendations which must be considered by the Minister concerned and if he is satisfied proposals are put before Parliament.

2.8 Examples of reform

Law Commission

Examples of reports implemented, in whole or in part, include *Family Law: Review of Child Law: Guardianship and Custody* (Law Com No 172) – Children Act 1989; *Law of Contract: Minors' Contracts* (Law Com No 134) – Minors' Contracts Act 1987; *Deeds and Escrows* (Law Com No 163), *Transfer of Land: Formalities for Contracts for Sale etc of Land* (Law Com No 164); and *Transfer of Land: The Rule in Bain v Fothergill* (Law Com No 166) – Law of Property (Miscellaneous Provisions) Act 1989; *Corroboration of Evidence in Criminal Trials* (Law Com No 202) – ss32 and 33 Criminal Justice and Public Order Act 1994; *Rape within Marriage* (Law Com No 205) – s142 Criminal Justice and Public Order Act 1994; and *Statute Law Revision: 13th Report* (Law Com No 179) – Statute Law (Repeals) Act 1989 (which continues the long tradition of repealing specified enactments which are no longer of practical utility).

Some recent reports include: *Double Jeopardy and Prosecution Appeals* ((2001) Law Com No 267), *Bail and the Human Rights Act 1998* ((2001) Law Com No 269), *Limitation of Actions* ((2001) Law Com No 270), *Land Registration for the Twenty-First Century: A Conveyancing Revolution* ((2001) Law Com No 271), *Third Parties – Rights against Insurers* ((2001) Law Com No 272) and *Evidence of Bad Character in Criminal Proceedings* ((2001) Law Com No 273).

The Law Commission's Annual Report 2004 provides details of both the work of the Law Commission in recent years and its plans and targets for the future. In the year covered by this Annual Report they published the first part of their report on renting homes: a project which impacts upon a third of the population. Also completed was a joint project with the Scottish Law Commission on the law of partnership. There are over 500,000 partnerships in the United Kingdom, producing an annual turnover of £136 billion. Partnerships represent an important part of the economy, but they operate under legislation which is over 100 years old and in need of updating. A research project, which aims to produce a code of compensation for those whose land is compulsory purchased or affected by development schemes, was also completed. The present rules are thought to be needlessly complex and uncertain. The Criminal Justice Act 2003 was a clear indication of the importance of the work of the Law Commission. The 2003 Act enacted wholly, or in part, four of their reports: Evidence in Criminal Proceedings: Hearsay and Related Topics; Double Jeopardy and Prosecution Appeals; Bail and the Human Rights Act 1998; and Evidence of Bad Character in Criminal Proceedings. During the year they also started a new high profile law reform project on Partial Defences to Murder.

Royal Commissions

An example of extensive reform can be seen in the changes in the law resulting from the Royal Commission on Criminal Procedure (1981) Cmnd 8092 and recommendations on several aspects of the criminal process. Its recommendations have largely been implemented in two Acts.

1. The Police and Criminal Evidence Act 1984 dealing with police powers in the investigation of offences.
2. The Prosecution of Offences Act 1985 dealing with the prosecution of offences.

Another notable example is the work of the Royal Commission on Criminal Justice (1993) Cmnd 2263. The Commission investigated the causes of miscarriages of justice in the criminal justice system and its eventual findings and proposals have led to many reforms of the law of evidence, criminal procedure and the appeal system, notably the setting up of the Criminal Cases Review Commission.

3

The Doctrine of Precedent

3.1   Introduction

3.2   Stare decisis: meaning

3.3   Principal elements of stare decisis

3.4   The operation of precedent within the hierarchy of the courts

3.5   The European Court of Justice (ECJ)

3.6   The European Court of Human Rights (ECHR)

3.7   The House of Lords

3.8   The Court of Appeal

3.9   The High Court

3.10 Other courts

3.11 Reform proposals

3.1 Introduction

It is an important aspect of the English legal system that most of the major rules and principles of the common law have been developed (often by accident) and further elaborated in the daily work of the courts in resolving the disputes brought to them. Unlike most major continental jurisdictions (including Scotland), which are based upon the 'civil law' system of the Romans, statute and codified law have not played such an important part in the development of English law although the vast growth of legislation over the last century or so has altered this balance very significantly.

Traditionally it is said that judges do not make law, but only declare what the law is, by considering and applying rules laid down in previous cases, which themselves were based on the rules of earlier cases and so on. However, this 'declaratory' theory of law is simplistic in the following aspects.

1. It overlooks the fact that the judges must of necessity extend and modify existing

rules insofar as the established rules must be applied to new cases, to new situations. In the words of Lord Radcliffe:

> 'Judicial law is always a reinterpretation of principles in the light of new combinations of facts ... true, judges do not reverse principles, once well established, but they do modify them, extend them, restrict them or even deny their applicability to the combination in hand.' (*Not in Feather Beds*, 1968.)

2. It overlooks the creative function of the more 'dynamic' lawmakers amongst the judiciary (more apparent at certain periods of history than others) who develop existing rules into a new form which it is possible to categorise as 'new law'. For example, the 'distillation' of the principle in *Hughes* v *Metropolitan Railway* (1877) 2 App Cas 439 by Denning J in *Central London Property Trust Ltd* v *High Trees House Ltd* [1947] KB 130 to 'create' a new form of equitable forbearance (promissory estoppel). The classic statement of the heart of the modern tort of negligence, the duty of care, by Lord Atkin in *Donoghue* v *Stevenson* [1932] AC 562 was a departure from precedent and a generalisation of more limited rules.

Nevertheless, it remains true that the judicial process of applying and developing the law is largely a conservative one and radical change is left to Parliament.

Precedent, in the sense of treating like cases alike and following established rules of law and practice, has been present in the English legal system for many centuries, as is clear from the continued interest in law reporting from the thirteenth century onwards. However, the medieval view of decided cases was not that of the twentieth century, which sees the decision in the case itself as binding. The medieval attitude was that decisions were examples of the application of rules of law, several examples demonstrating an established custom which would be very persuasive in a medieval court.

The modern doctrine only emerged in the nineteenth century with the establishing of an official system of reliable law reporting which, of course, is indispensible to the operation of the doctrine. Formerly, any report of a case made by a barrister was regarded as reliable, as this was usually a precondition to the citation of a report in court. Now, however, a report by a solicitor or a person having a Supreme Court qualification (within the meaning of s71 of the Courts and Legal Services Act 1990) has the same authority as if it had been made by a barrister: s115 of the 1990 Act.

Although there is no rule that an unreported decision may not be put before the court in a subsequent case, almost invariably precedents will be contained in law reports. Indeed, in *Roberts Petroleum Ltd* v *Bernard Kenny Ltd* [1983] 2 WLR 305, Lord Diplock opined that the House of Lords should not allow the citing before it of transcripts of unreported judgments of the Court of Appeal unless they contained a statement of some principle of law the substance of which could not be found in any law report. The *Practice Statement (Judgments)* [1998] 2 All ER 667 confirms the procedural practice followed by the Court of Appeal (Civil Division) and High

Court in this area, namely that leave to cite unreported cases will not usually be granted unless counsel are able to assure the court that the transcript in question contains a relevant statement of legal principle not found in reported authority and that the authority is not cited because of the phraseology used or as an illustration of the application of an established legal principle. For a critique, see Bennion 'Citation of Unreported Cases: A Challenge' [1998] NLJ 1520.

It is surprising to note that there is no official control over which cases are and are not reported. It is arguable that this is an unhappy state of affairs given the obvious importance of law reports to the doctrine of precedent in the English legal system.

In addition to the generally conservative views of judges, the doctrine is upheld for a number of reasons.

Fairness

It is based on a principle of 'fairness', that is treating like cases alike. This is also convenient in that it is obviously wasteful of effort to reconsider every like case and consider what the applicable principles should be. Precedent allows a judge to have a ready-made solution to hand, with the possibility of distinguishing previous decisions if they are significantly different. Most cases do not involve disputes as to the principles to be applied at all, since these are usually clear, but rather disputes as to the facts and the application of the rules to those facts.

Certainty

In theory, with the large number of points of law which have already been decided, it should be a relatively simple matter to discover the relevant principles applying in the particular case. Of course, the many variations in facts and circumstances mean that in some cases, the relevant principles are unclear (or their application is uncertain). However, the great majority of cases do not involve disputes as to the law, only as to the facts and the application of those rules.

Flexibility

The fact that the decisions are decisions of judges, and not statutory provisions, means that they can be subsequently overruled or distinguished (see below) where they are incorrect, cease to be applicable or are simply not applicable to the instant case.

Predictability

Predictability relates to the certainty argument. With the large number of reported decisions it should, in theory at least, be relatively easy to predict on the basis of those decisions the relevant rules applicable and the result of the present case. This enables legal advisers to give to their clients more precise and accurate advice as to what are their chances of success in bringing or defending a particular claim. Consequently, the settlement of claims and disputes, saving time and money for all concerned, becomes more likely.

A fairly typical example of the judicial attitude is shown by Russell LJ's speech in *Gallie* v *Lee* [1969] 2 Ch 17 (CA):

> 'I am a firm believer in a system by which citizens and their advisers can have as much certainty as possible in the ordering of their affairs ... an abandonment of the principle that this court follows its own decisions on the law would I think lead to greater uncertainty and tend to produce more litigation ...'

3.2 Stare decisis: meaning

The doctrine of binding precedent or 'stare decisis', stated briefly, is that any previous decision of a court, depending upon its position in the hierarchy of courts, is binding on a subsequent judge who is dealing with a case which is not reasonably distinguishable from that previous decision.

The doctrine arises out of the rule that it is not the function of a judge to make new law but only to decide cases in accordance with the law as it exists. Thus in effect it is part of the doctrine of the separation of powers.

It is the statement of law made by the judge in his judgment which may (or may not) be binding. Such statements may be either 'ratio decidendi' or 'obiter dicta'.

3.3 Principal elements of stare decisis

Ratio decidendi

It is ironic that the ratio, the heart of the doctrine, is so difficult to define since it is the ratio alone which is binding on future courts (within the court hierarchy). The status of the ratio is well illustrated by a dictum of Lord Reid's in *Nash (Inspector of Taxes)* v *Tamplin & Sons Brewery (Brighton) Ltd* [1952] AC 231:

> 'It matters not how difficult it is to find the ratio decidendi of a previous case, that ratio must be found. It matters not how difficult it is to reconcile that ratio when found with statutory provisions or general principles, that ratio must be applied to any later case which is not reasonably distinguishable.'

Two points can be made about the ratio decidendi.

1. Only pronouncements of law can be ratio.
2. Only those reasons (or reason) which are necessary to reach the decision in the particular case can be ratio.

The combination of the findings of fact and the items in these two points are responsible for the judgment in the case. As the American jurist Wambaugh put it:

'When a case turns on only one point the proposition or doctrine of the case, the reason for the decision, the ratio, must be the general rule without which the case must have been decided otherwise ...'

A L Goodhart regards the ratio as the legal principle to be derived from the judge's decision on the basis of the facts regarded by the judge as material. However, Goodhart's test does not really help decide which facts are regarded by a court as material.

One major difficulty which occasionally arises is the inability of later courts, or lawyers, to discover the ratio of a particular case. In these circumstances, the various attempts at defining 'ratio' may be of some help, but often it is in the difficult cases that these attempts break down – particularly if, as sometimes happens, in a multiple-judge court, each judge gives a different reason for his decision (or one judge gives separate reasons for his decision).

A further problem is when it is impossible to discover the legal basis for the decision of the court on the facts: for example, the case of *Elder, Dempster & Co Ltd v Paterson, Zochonis & Co Ltd* [1924] AC 522 (HL). In *Scruttons Ltd v Midland Silicones Ltd* [1962] 2 WLR 186 (HL) Lord Reid said of the *Elder, Dempster* case:

'It can hardly be denied that the ratio decidendi of the *Elder, Dempster* decision is very obscure ... when I look for such a principle I cannot find it, and the extensive and able arguments of counsel ... have failed to discover it.'

In such a case, the only binding element of the judgment is the decision itself and it only binds in cases which are not reasonably distinguishable. However, in the *Midland Silicones* case Lord Reid held that the *Elder, Dempster* case was distinguishable in several respects. Further it will only be principles of law which are binding. Therefore words which are construed in a certain way in one contract need not have the same effect in future contracts: see *Ashville Investments* v *Elmer Contractors* [1988] 3 WLR 867.

Obiter dicta

These are legal reasons or pronouncements which are not necessary for the decision in the case, and hence are not ratio and not binding. They are therefore said to be obiter – 'by the way'. In *Behrens* v *Bertram Mills* [1957] 1 All ER 58, Devlin J said:

'If a judge gives two reasons, both are equally binding. But he may make an obiter observation – it is equally possible for it to be an additional reason, but he may not wish to make it part of the ratio, for example, because he is not sufficiently convinced of its cogency to give it the full authority of precedent.'

Although an obiter dictum (plural – 'dicta') is not binding on subsequent courts, some may be influential or 'persuasive' in later cases in helping make up a judge's mind on a novel or difficult point (see 'persuasive authority', below). If such dicta are used in a later case they may become binding if they are made part of a later ratio decidendi. Well-known examples of influential obiter dicta are the 'neighbour principle' of Lord Atkin in *Donoghue* v *Stevenson* [1932] AC 562 (HL) and the extension of this to negligent misstatements in *Hedley Byrne* v *Heller & Partners Ltd* [1963] 3 WLR 101 (HL).

Persuasive authority

These are decisions and dicta which are not binding but may strongly influence future decisions which use them as support – this is particularly so if such dicta are part of the judgments of respected judges. Such authority includes the following.

1. Obiter dicta – see above.
2. Recommendations of the Privy Council – these are paticularly influential, since the Judicial Committee is usually made up of Law Lords.
3. Decisions of courts of Commonwealth jurisdictions.
4. Decisions of Scottish or Irish courts, even though they are not part of the English legal system.
5. Decisions of courts inferior to that hearing the case.

Distinguishing

It is inherent in the doctrine of 'treat like cases alike' that where a case is sufficiently dissimilar then the previous rule need not be followed – the two cases may be distinguished. It is often said that a previous case can only be distinguished if it is 'reasonable' to do so, eg if the material facts are dissimilar. Of course, what is reasonably distinguishable depends on the particular cases and the particular court – some judges being more inclined to 'distinguish' disliked authorities than others. If the notion is carried to extreme lengths then judges would be able to avoid the unpleasant consequences of applying disliked rationes by distinguishing them on inadequate grounds. While distinguishing is an important factor in maintaining fairness and flexibility in stare decisis, if carried to such lengths it would undermine the system.

Overruling and reversing

Overruling

A court of competent jurisdiction within the hierarchy of the courts may declare that the decision in a previous case is no longer good law: for example because that previous court did not correctly interpret the law or because the later court considers that the rule of law contained in the previous ratio is no longer supportable or desirable. An example of the former is the overruling of *Horsler* v

Zorro [1975] Ch 302 by the House of Lords in *Johnson* v *Agnew* [1979] 2 WLR 487, and an example of the latter is the House of Lords' decision in *Miliangos* v *George Frank (Textiles) Ltd* [1975] 3 WLR 758 which overruled previous authority that judgments could not be given in foreign currency. Cases may also be overruled by statute.

It should be remembered that only courts of competent jurisdiction may overrule previous precedents. For example, the House of Lords may overrule the decisions of any court in the legal system, including its own: see, for example, *Murphy* v *Brentwood District Council* [1990] 3 WLR 414 where the House of Lords overruled its own decision in *Anns* v *Merton London Borough* [1977] 2 All ER 492. The Court of Appeal (Civil Division) may neither overrule a decision of the House of Lords nor its own previous decisions. This is so even if the reason for the earlier decision is now questionable or clearly wrong. In the *Miliangos* case (above), the Court of Appeal had sought to alter the foreign currency rule itself by following its own earlier decision in *Schorsch Meier GmbH* v *Hennin* [1975] QB 416, which had refused to follow earlier House of Lords' authority (*Re United Railways of Havana and Regla Warehouses* [1961] AC 1007) affirming the currency rule. The House of Lords agreed that the rule should be changed, but that it was not the function of the Court of Appeal to disregard House of Lords' authority:

'Courts which are bound by the rule of precedent are not free to disregard an otherwise binding precedent on the ground that the reason which led to the formulation of the rule embodied in such precedent seems to the court to have lost cogency ...' (Lord Simon)

However, whilst the Court of Appeal cannot overrule a decision of the House of Lords, or one of its own previous decisions, it is permitted to 'depart' from (ie not follow) such a decision in limited circumstances: see further section 3.8 below.

The effect of overruling a previous authority is that authority is treated as 'bad law' and is no longer binding either on subsequent courts, or the court itself which is overruling it. In effect, this gives overruling 'retrospective' effect since it affects not only future cases, but the present one also – even though that case arose before the precedent was overruled. Indeed, this can seem unfair to parties who may have relied on that precedent only to find it overruled on appeal. This is one reason why courts are reluctant to overrule well-established precedent and accounts, in part, for the fact that the House of Lords rarely overrules its previous decisions.

Reversing

This is simply an overturning, on appeal, of the decision of the court below that hearing the appeal. The appeal court will then substitute its own decision.

Per incuriam statements

A decision which is reached per incuriam is one reached through 'want of care'. A Court of Appeal decision reached per incuriam is not binding on subsequent Courts of Appeal: *Young* v *Bristol Aeroplane Co Ltd* [1944] KB 718 (CA). Similarly, the High Court is not bound by one of its own previous decisions reached per incuriam: *Younghusband* v *Luftig* [1949] 2 All ER 72.

Per incuriam does not signify mere carelessness on the part of the court, or the fact the case was badly argued or judgment badly reasoned. It is confined to the narrow grounds of failure to consider binding authority or statute. In *Morelle Ltd* v *Wakeling* [1955] 2 QB 379 (CA) Lord Evershed MR stated that:

> '... the only cases in which decisions should be held to have been given per incuriam are those of decisions given in ignorance or forgetfulness of some inconsistent statutory provision or of some authority binding on the court concerned: so that in such cases some part of the decision or some step in the reasoning on which it is based is found, on that account, to be demonstrably wrong.'

In *Secretary of State for Trade and Industry* v *Desai* (1991) The Times 5 December Scott LJ said that to come within the category of per incuriam it must be shown not only that the decision involved some manifest slip or error but also that to leave the decision standing would be likely, inter alia, to produce serious inconvenience in the administration of justice or significant injustice to citizens.

However, this rule does not appear to permit the Court of Appeal to ignore decisions of the House of Lords. In *Cassell* v *Broome* [1972] AC 1027 Lord Denning MR held the House of Lords' decision in *Rookes* v *Barnard* [1964] AC 1129 to be per incuriam on the basis that it ignored previous House of Lords' decisions. He was rebuked sternly by the House of Lords who considered that the Court of Appeal 'really only meant' that it 'did not agree' with the earlier decision:

> 'Even if this is not so, it is not open to the Court of Appeal to give gratuitous advice to judges of first instance to ignore decisions of the House of Lords.' (Lord Hailsham)

Similarly, it had been assumed that the High Court could not use the per incuriam principle in order to depart from a decision of the House of Lords or Court of Appeal, but, rather surprisingly, the principle was invoked by the High Court in order to depart from a decision of the Court of Appeal: *Hughes* v *Kingston-upon-Hull City Council* (1998) The Times 9 December, which is considered in Chapter 8, section 8.6.

3.4 The operation of precedent within the hierarchy of the courts

It is a fundamental to the doctrine of precedent that it operates within the system of the courts and the authority of a decision and a court's ability to overrule a previous decision depends on its position within that hierarchy. Each court will be considered in turn.

3.5 The European Court of Justice (ECJ)

Except as to questions of the interpretation of European law (referred under art 234 of the EC Treaty) the ECJ has no authority within the English legal system. Where it has authority its decisions are binding on the courts of member states, but not binding on itself.

3.6 The European Court of Human Rights (ECHR)

The importance of the decisions of the ECHR has been increased now that the Human Rights Act 1998 has been implemented. Section 2 of the 1998 Act requires a court determining a question relating to a Convention right to 'take account' of the opinions and decisions of the ECHR. Whilst these decisions will not be strictly binding, they will become highly persuasive whenever provisions of the 1998 Act are being applied.

3.7 The House of Lords

As the final court of appeal in the English legal system, the decisions of the HL are binding on all courts beneath it in the hierarchy. The HL for the greater part of the twentieth century also regarded itself as bound by its own decisions, following *London Street Tramways Co* v *London County Council* [1898] AC 375:

> 'I do not deny that cases of individual hardship may arise ... but what is that occasional interference with what is perhaps abstract justice, as compared with the inconvenience ... of having each question subject to being re-argued.' (Lord Halsbury)

However, in 1966 the HL changed its opinion and issued a *Practice Statement* [1966] 1 WLR 1234:

> 'Their Lordships regard the use of precedent as an indispensable foundation upon which to decide what is the law and its application to individual cases. It provides at least some degree of certainty upon which individuals can rely in the conduct of the affairs, as well as a basis for orderly development of legal rules.
>
> Their Lordships nevertheless recognise that too rigid adherence to precedent may lead to injustice in a particular case and also unduly restrict the proper development of the law. They propose, therefore, to modify their present practice and, while treating former decisions of this House as normally binding, to depart from a previous decision when it appears right to do so.
>
> In this connection they will bear in mind the danger of disturbing retrospectively the basis on which contracts, settlements of property and fiscal arrangements have been entered into and also the special need for certainty as to the criminal law.
>
> This announcement is not intended to affect the use of precedent elsewhere than in this House.'

The 1966 *Practice Statement* was considered by Lord Bridge of Harwich when the House of Lords overruled in *R* v *Shivpuri* [1986] 2 WLR 988 their own decision in *Anderton* v *Ryan* [1985] 2 All ER 335. He felt that the *Statement* was 'an effective abandonment of [the House's] pretension to infallibility' and, where there was an error, it was better that it should be speedily corrected. Lord Hailsham was prepared to distinguish *R* v *Shivpuri* from *Anderton* v *Ryan* but the clear statement that the earlier case has been overruled is a welcome sign of a seeking to achieve as much clarity in the law as possible rather than relying upon fine and perhaps misleading distinctions.

The *Practice Statement* did not alter the fundamental attitude of the House of Lords to precedent, but allowed the House more flexibility in changing its mind. However, as can be seen, the House of Lords also emphasised the need for certainty, and the power which the *Practice Statement* acknowledged has been used very sparingly. In *Miliangos* v *George Frank (Textiles) Ltd* [1975] 3 WLR 758 the Law Lords said that the 1966 *Statement* could be utilised in civil law if a better rule can be stated, provided that no procedural difficulties arise from the change in the law.

It is perhaps the undesirability of causing uncertainty which has often led the House to decline to overrule established authority and to say that such matters are best left to Parliament. A good example of this is *Jones* v *Secretary of State* [1972] 2 WLR 210 where seven Law Lords considered the earlier decision of *Re Dowling* [1967] AC 725, and though four considered it to have been wrongly decided they refused to overrule it. Little guidance was forthcoming as to when the House would overrule previous precedents. Lord Reid said that a change would be considered in old authority 'where some broad issue is involved', but that 'it should only be in rare cases that we should reconsider questions of construction of statutes and other documents'.

Lord Wilberforce stated his fears concerning too willing an approach to reconsider statutory construction on the basis that litigants would take a chance and appeal in the hope of persuading the House to reconsider. Lord Simon suggested that inconvenience in the construction of statutes caused by judicial interpretation should more appropriately be left to the consideration of Parliament. Lord Pearson was concerned that the advantage of finality should not be lightly thrown away 'by too ready use of the recently declared liberty to depart from previous decisions'.

Nevertheless, where a court is faced with conflicting decisions of the House of Lords as to the construction of a statute, the later decision should be followed, certainly where the court believes that the earlier House of Lords' decision would have been reversed if the House in the earlier case had been aware of the principle enunciated in the later House of Lords' decision: *Moodie* v *Inland Revenue Commissioners* [1993] 1 WLR 266, itself a decision of the House of Lords.

The House of Lords is also prepared to adopt an 'activist' approach so as to modernise the common law where there is an overpowering need to do so, even if it means overruling precedents which have stood for many years, in both civil law

(*British Rail* v *Herrington* [1972] 1 All ER 749 on occupiers' liability to child trespassers) and the criminal law.

In *R* v *R (Rape: Marital Exemption)* [1991] 4 All ER 481 (HL) the House held that the common law rule that a husband could not be guilty of raping his wife because marriage implied the wife's consent to sexual intercourse was obsolete. Such a retrospective change to the criminal law does not infringe the European Convention on Human Rights because it is a progressive and foreseeable evolution of the common law through judicial law-making: *CR* v *UK* (1995) The Times 5 December (ECHR).

The Law Lords have shown greater hesitation in effecting change in other areas, where the need for change may still be highly contentious. In these areas the 'leave it to Parliament' argument has prevailed: examples are the reduction of what would otherwise be murder to manslaughter in a particular class of case: *R* v *Clegg* [1995] 1 All ER 334 (HL); and the abolition of the presumption of doli incapax in the area of children's liability for crimes: *C* v *DPP* [1995] 2 All ER 43 (HL). In the latter case the 'leave it to Parliament' approach led quite swiftly to statutory abolition of the presumption of doli incapax: s34 Crime and Disorder Act 1998. In *C* v *DPP*, above, Lord Lowry gave the following guidance on the propriety of judicial law-making:

> '... (i) if the solution is doubtful, the judges should beware of imposing their own remedy;
> (ii) caution should prevail if Parliament has rejected opportunities of clearing up a known difficulty or has legislated while leaving the difficulty untouched;
> (iii) disputed matters of social policy are less suitable areas for judicial intervention than purely legal problems;
> (iv) fundamental legal doctrines should not be lightly set aside;
> (v) judges should not make a change unless they can achieve finality and certainty.'

The issue of judicial law-making has continued to trouble the Law Lords in several cases. In *Westdeutsche Landesbank Girozentrale* v *Islington London Borough Council* [1996] 2 All ER 961 (HL) the Law Lords were divided three to two on the question whether the rules of equity should be judicially developed so as to permit an award of compound interest on a judgment for repayment of money had and received. The majority were against such development, taking the view that Parliament had twice legislated on the matter and that therefore it must be left to Parliament to amend that legislation in order to provide the remedy in question. The two dissenting Law Lords (Lords Goff and Woolf) were prepared to develop the law of restitution to provide the remedy in order to meet the 'moral justice' of the case. Lord Goff made the following observations on the creative role of judges:

> '... it is the great advantage of a supreme court that, not only does it have the great benefit of assistance from the judgments of the courts below, but also it has a greater freedom to mould, and remould, the authorities to ensure that practical justice is done within a framework of principle. The present case provides an excellent example of a case in which this House should take full advantage of that freedom ...
> ... It would be strange indeed if the courts lacked jurisdiction in such a case to ensure that justice could be fully achieved by means of an award of compound interest, where it

is appropriate to make such an award, despite the fact that the jurisdiction to award such interest is itself said to rest upon the demands of justice. I am glad not to be forced to hold that English law is so inadequate as to be incapable of achieving such a result. In my opinion the jurisdiction should now be made available, as justice requires, in cases of restitution, to ensure that full justice can be done. The seed is there, but the growth has hitherto been confined within a small area. That growth should now be permitted to spread naturally elsewhere within this newly recognised branch of the law. No genetic engineering is required, only that the warm sun of judicial creativity should exercise its benign influence rather than remain hidden behind the dark clouds of legal history.'

In another case the Law Lords were again divided three to two on the issue of judicial law reform, but this time Lord Goff found himself in the majority favouring such reform. In *Kleinwort Benson Ltd* v *Lincoln City Council and Other Appeals* [1998] 4 All ER 513 (HL) the Law Lords held (Lords Browne-Wilkinson and Lloyd dissenting) that the common law rule precluding recovery of money paid under a mistake of law should no longer be maintained. Since such judicial development is retrospective in effect the decision enables those who entered transactions in reliance on the overruled decisions to re-open them, ie the decision effectively allows the six-year limitation period to run afresh – a bold piece of judicial law reform! The majority were convinced, however, that the need to meet the 'moral justice' of the case must prevail over any problems the change of law might cause in the commercial world. The minority, whilst agreeing on the need for the change, preferred to leave the whole issue of reform of restitution law and limitation periods to Parliament. For a critique: see Bennion 'A Naked Usurpation?' [1999] NLJ 421. In *R* v *Kansal (Yash Pal) (Change of Law)* [2002] 2 AC 69 the House of Lords (in the interests of consistency) refused to depart from its decision in *R* v *Lambert* [2001] 3 WLR 206 even though the later court thought that the earlier decision was incorrect.

3.8 The Court of Appeal

For the purposes of the doctrine of precedent a 'full court' (of five or more judges) has the same authority as that of a three-judge court or even a two-judge court since they are all sittings of equal status: *Langley* v *North West Water Authority* [1991] 3 All ER 610.

In general, both divisions of the Court of Appeal are bound by the decisions of the House of Lords and by their own previous decisions. To this general rule there are some exceptions.

The Civil Division

Four exceptions are established, the first three of which have been taken from *Young* v *Bristol Aeroplane Co Ltd* [1944] KB 718.

1. Where there are conflicting Court of Appeal decisions, the Court of Appeal may choose which one to follow.

2. The Court of Appeal may disregard one of its own previous decisions if it cannot be reconciled with a decision of the House of Lords. If such a decision was later in time than the House of Lords' decision and had overlooked the House of Lords' decision it would be covered by the per incuriam exception, below. If it had not overlooked the House of Lords' decision but had chosen not to follow it (eg because it thought the House of Lords' decision was reasonably distinguishable) it is for the Court of Appeal to decide at its discretion whether the apparently conflicting Court of Appeal precedent should be followed – clearly if the House of Lords' precedent was not reasonably distinguishable the Court of Appeal must disregard the conflicting Court of Appeal precedent.

   If the House of Lords' decision was later in time than the conflicting Court of Appeal decision then the Court of Appeal may choose to follow the prior Court of Appeal decision if it believes that the House of Lords' decision involved only a general consideration of the issues raised by the earlier Court of Appeal decision and has not substantially undermined its authority. If, however, this is not the case it would appear that the Court of Appeal must treat the conflicting Court of Appeal precedent as impliedly overruled by the later House of Lords' decision: *R* v *Secretary of State for the Home Department, ex parte Al-Mehdawi* [1989] 1 All ER 777 (CA).

3. It may disregard a decision of the Court of Appeal reached per incuriam, ie without due care, for example as a result of overlooking a relevant binding authority: *Rakhit* v *Carty* [1990] 2 All ER 202, *Rickards* v *Rickards* [1989] 3 WLR 748 and see further *Per incuriam statements* at section 3.3 above.

4. As a result of *R* v *Brent London Borough Council Housing Benefit Review Board, ex parte Khadim* [2001] NPC 7 the Court of Appeal will not be bound where a proposition of law was assumed rather than established.

Note that the 1966 *Practice Statement* gives no power to the Court of Appeal: *Davis* v *Johnson* [1978] 2 WLR 553 (HL). In this case, in the Court of Appeal, Lord Denning MR had suggested that the 1966 *Practice Statement* could be adopted by the Court of Appeal (Civil Division) so as to enable the judges to reform the law in a sensible and humane manner. However, when the case went to the House of Lords the Law Lords were strongly critical of Lord Denning's attempts to confer on the Court of Appeal a wider discretion than that given by *Young* v *Bristol Aeroplane Co Ltd*. Lord Diplock observed that it is the House of Lords, as the appellate court of last resort, which is best placed to reform the law judicially. Further, to extend the 1966 *Practice Statement* to the Court of Appeal would greatly undermine certainty and predictability of law-making.

Criminal Division

The rules laid down in *Young* v *Bristol Aeroplane Co Ltd*, above, have been used as guidelines by the Criminal Division, which also applies the doctrine of stare decisis less strictly than the Civil Division in cases where the liberty of the subject may be affected by previous decisions in which the law has either been misapplied or misunderstood: *R* v *Taylor* [1950] 2 KB 368, *R* v *Gould* [1968] 2 WLR 643 and *R* v *Newsome; R* v *Browne* [1970] 2 QB 711.

Both divisions – a summary of the rules of precedent

In *Limb* v *Union Jack Removals Ltd* [1998] 2 All ER 513 at 522–523 Brooke LJ summarised some of the aspects of the doctrine of precedent in so far as it relates to both divisions of the Court of Appeal. He suggested that the following five principles can be derived from the authorities.

1. Where the court has considered a statute or a rule having the force of a statute its decision stands on the same footing as any other decision on a point of law.
2. A decision of a two-judge Court of Appeal on a substantive appeal (as opposed to an application for leave) has the same authority as a decision of a three-judge or a five-judge Court of Appeal.
3. The doctrine of per incuriam applies only where another division of the court has reached a decision in ignorance or forgetfulness of a decision binding upon it or of an inconsistent statutory provision, and in either case it must be shown that if the court had had this material in mind it must have reached a contrary decision.
4. The doctrine does not extend to a case where, if different arguments had been placed before the court or if different material had been placed before it, it might have reached a different conclusion.
5. Any departure from a previous decision of the court is in principle undesirable and should only be considered if the previous decision is manifestly wrong. Even then it will be necessary to take account of whether the decision purports to be one of general application and whether there is any other way of remedying the error, for example by encouraging an appeal to the House of Lords.

3.9 The High Court

As a court of first instance

The divisions of the High Court sitting as trial courts are bound by decisions of the courts superior to them, but are not binding on themselves. An example of a refusal by a High Court judge to follow a decision of another High Court judge, both sitting at first instance is the case of *Re Jeffrey S Levitt Ltd* [1992] 2 All ER 509. Although Ferris J had made his decision after full argument, Vinelott J felt compelled to reach a different conclusion, not least because a House of Lords' speech and certain statutory provisions had not been drawn to Ferris J's attention, and subsequent decisions, one of the Court of Appeal, supported his (Vinelott J's) view of the matter. However, judges still tend to follow the decisions of their fellow puisne judges on the basis of judicial comity (mutual co-operation) and certainty. In *Colchester Estates* v *Carlton Industries* [1984] 2 All ER 601 Nourse J in the Chancery Division was faced with two conflicting first instance decisions (*Swallow Securities* v *Brand* (1983) 45 P & CR 328 and *Hamilton* v *Martell Securities* [1984] 1 All ER 665). He said that, since the second decision was not given in ignorance of the first, the general rule was that a first instance judge should follow the second judgment of the two conflicting cases, in the interests of certainty.

Where a judge of first instance is confronted by conflicting decisions of the Court of Appeal, in the later of which the earlier had been fully considered, he is bound to follow the later decision: *Miliangos* v *George Frank (Textiles) Ltd* [1975] 3 All ER 801.

It had been thought that the High Court could not invoke the per incuriam rule as justification for departing from a House of Lords or Court of Appeal decision, but the rule was used for this purpose in *Hughes* v *Kingston-upon-Hull City Council* (1998) The Times 9 December: see further Chapter 8, section 8.6.

As an appeal or review court: Divisional Courts

Usually Divisional Courts of the High Court have treated the rules of *Young* v *Bristol Aeroplane Co Ltd*, above, as equally applicable to them, and for this purpose a full court of five judges has the same authority as one composed of three or even two judges: *Younghusband* v *Luftig* [1949] 2 All ER 72.

In *R* v *Governor of Brockhill Prison, ex parte Evans* [1997] 1 All ER 439 the Divisional Court departed from several of its own previous decisions concerning judicial review of prison governors. Lord Bingham CJ emphasised that the Divisional Court should not depart from its own decisions unless satisfied that they are clearly wrong, especially where public officials such as prison governors have founded their practice on those decisions. See also *R* v *Greater Manchester Coroner, ex parte Tal* [1984] 3 WLR 643.

3.10 Other courts

The inferior courts are bound by the decisions of those above (ie the superior courts). The position of the Crown Court, as a superior court, is unclear – though it may be that a High Court judge sitting in the Crown Court is in the same position as a puisne judge sitting in the High Court at first instance.

3.11 Reform proposals

Though the doctrine of precedent exists for a number of reasons, including certainty and predictability, it is not entirely clear that it does not go too far and lead to rigidity and inflexibility, particularly given the reluctance of the House of Lords and the general inability of the Court of Appeal (Civil Division) to overrule their own decisions. The 'leave it to Parliament' view in the House of Lords does not necessarily mean that Parliament will deal with the matter immediately, quickly, or even at all.

The following matters could be said to mitigate the harshness of the doctrine.

1. Appeals.
2. Parliamentary reform.
3. Distinguishing – must generally be 'reasonable', though see Lord Reid in *Jones* v *Secretary of State* (above).
4. *Young* v *Bristol Aeroplane* exceptions – of limited application.

Should the Court of Appeal be permitted to depart from its own previous decisions (see above)? Would this necessarily mitigate some of the rigours of the doctrine – or would there be similar reluctance to overrule as the House of Lords has shown?

It has been suggested that the courts could adopt the practice of 'prospective overruling', under which the effect of a change in the law would take place only from a future date and would not affect those who have reasonably relied on the overruled decision, such as the parties in the case which is resulting in the decision to overrule. This practice is followed in the superior courts of the United States of America. In Europe the European Court of Justice adopts a modified version of prospective overruling by giving the benefit of the change in the law to the party in the case who persuaded the court to make the change. Both kinds of prospective overruling offend the principle that like cases should be treated alike and have been opposed on this ground by some senior judges, including Lord Mackay, the former Lord Chancellor. However, other senior judges have expressed support for the concept of prospective overruling: for example Lord Browne-Wilkinson in *Prudential Assurance Co* v *London Residuary Body* [1992] 3 All ER 504 at 512b.

It has also been suggested that a codification of the law would solve, or at least alleviate, some of the problems which are created by the operation of the doctrine of precedent (eg too much case law and other sources of authority; inflexibility, etc). However, this would depend on what type of codification was selected. Broadly speaking, there are two main types of codification.

1. The type predominant in English legislation such as the Theft Act 1968 and the Sale of Goods Act 1979 (this Act really consolidates the original Act of 1893, which had codified the then existing case law, with case and statute law which occured in the interim), that is, an amalgamation and reform of all the law relating to a given topic and putting it in the form of a single statute. This does not affect the basic operation of stare decisis, but merely creates a new starting point from which new case law will build up (in interpreting the statute) – with some reference, perhaps, to the pre-codification of the law.

2. The type predominant in civil law jurisdictions on the Continent (such as France or West Germany) where the code is absolute and there is no doctrine of stare decisis at all. Cases are not binding authority and the practice of the courts does not become a source of law until the point is established by the agreement of many different judgments.

It will be noted that the two main types of codification are quite different in their operation. The effect of the first type on the present system would not be fundamental, since the doctrine of precedent would still remain, with all its attendant problems (and advantages). The only positive advantage would be that the source of law on a given topic would now be concentrated in one place and that some of the previous problems would be ironed out – it would prevent the accretion of too much case law. However, case law on the interpretation of the new codified statute would soon appear. The effect of the second type, on the other hand, would be radical since it would involve an abolition of the doctrine of stare decisis and the development of new techniques for the interpretation of the new code. It is true that some of the problems with the present system would be dealt with (eg the existence of too much authority) but new problems would be created. It would have to be decided, for example, how the code would be constructed: should it be detailed, dealing with every conceivable situation or should it merely lay down more general guidelines and directions for the courts to follow? The sort of problems that this type of codification might engender are as follows.

1. If the code is a detailed code (of the 'absolute' second type), then this will entail the need for a better system of law reform and revision, since it will be no longer be possible for judges to develop the law on a case-by-case basis. Certainty would be achieved, but at the cost of rigidity and slowing down of the development of legal principles.
2. If the code is more general, laying down fairly broad guidelines and rules but leaving a certain amount to judicial discretion, this would permit more flexibility to cover novel situations, but perhaps only in return for too much discretion and consequential uncertainty (of course, much depends on the issue of the desirability of certainty in the law).
3. Uncertainty as to the interpretation of the new code and its relation to the old law.
4. The need to develop new techniques for the interpretation of the code.
5. The time and cost needed to codify the law.

Part II: The Personnel of the Legal System

4

The Judiciary and the Magistracy

The judiciary

4.1 Independence, impartiality and immunity of the judiciary

4.2 Functions of a judge

4.3 Appointment to judicial offices

4.4 Selection of judges

4.5 Training of judges

4.6 Alternative methods of selection for a judiciary

4.7 Removal and retirement

The magistracy

4.8 Lay magistrates (Justices of the Peace)

4.9 District judges (formerly stipendiary magistrates)

4.1 Independence, impartiality and immunity of the judiciary

Judicial independence

In his Hamlyn lectures delivered in 1994 the then Lord Chancellor, Lord Mackay, explained judicial independence in the following terms:

> 'What do I mean by the independence of the judiciary? I mean that every judge in deciding a case does so according to his own judgment, in the words of the judicial oath, "according to the laws and usages of this realm, without fear or favour, affection or ill-will". This means, among other things, that a judge deciding a case should do so without any influence being brought to bear upon him to decide it one way or another by any agency outside himself.'

The prime agency would be considered to be the executive, ie the government, both in the form of the House of Commons and all its departments and other branches. That is not to say that the government does not have a vital role to play in the passing of law but it is not to interfere directly with the judicial process. There is a separation of powers that amounts to a delicate balancing act. The executive, the legislature and the judiciary are three separate organs of state and central power is separated between them to prevent abuses in the exercise of power. Therefore, the legal system exists as an autonomous system, free from direct interference from the state, and the judicial function is exercised independently, free from direct control by the legislature or the executive. This judicial independence, however, exists alongside the sovereignty of Parliament. It is equally as important to the separation of powers that Parliament is the supreme law-making authority. Thus, whilst the judiciary enjoy a certain autonomy of decision-making and judicial immunity, they remain at the same time bound by the laws written by the legislature. To preserve the balance of power between themselves and the executive and legislature, convention dictates that they are not to take part in politics and cannot be a Member of Parliament at the same time as holding judicial office. Again by convention, since we do not have a written constitution, when the Law Lords sit in their legislative capacity in the House of Lords their role is to debate the legal aspects of the proposals presented in a Bill. They are to shun any temptation to take part in political controversy surrounding the Bill and they must remain neutral as to politics, ie 'apolitical' in that they are not to voice opinion expressly based on party politics.

This conceptually difficult constitutional role of the judiciary emerged from the pre-nineteenth-century development of our legal system and the new role of the judiciary within it. Right up to the end of the 1600s the monarch enjoyed a power that was barely limited by the constitution. Judges held office at 'the pleasure' of the ruling monarch and could be removed at his/her pleasure. By 1701 the long revolutionary struggle of Tudor and Stuart times brought about the limited constitutional monarchy that we now have. Parliament had secured a limited sovereignty and the independence of the judiciary within that scheme of things was secured by the Act of Settlement 1701. Since then it has evolved into an actual separation of the powers that is hard to define, because what happens in reality is a complex constitutional balance of power found in:

1. the relationship between the executive and the legislative body;
2. the relationship between the legislature and the judiciary;
3. judicial review of the actions of the executive;
4. a measure of judicial interpretation of legislation carried out in accordance with interpretation rules that are, for the most part, created by the judiciary themselves;
5. a limited judicial law-making role carried out within the confines of the operation of the doctrine of judicial precedent that, again, was largely created and continues to be developed by the judiciary themselves.

The complexity of this balance of power came to be highlighted in 1995 when the Home Secretary announced the government's intention to introduce mandatory sentences for certain crimes. Here we had political pressure on the government to respond to public disquiet over sentencing, which was seen by many as being far too lenient, sitting in direct conflict with the independent right of the judiciary to determine sentences within the confines of the rules laid down. The Lord Chief Justice, Lord Taylor of Gosforth, broke with tradition and delivered a scathing attack both on the government's proposals and on their lack of constitutional integrity in attempting to introduce them in this way. His attack was a direct challenge to the Home Secretary's attempted use of his penal powers and there is little doubt that he spoke with the support of most of the judiciary and of the legal profession in general. The Home Secretary was interfering with the sentencing powers of the judiciary: the sacred right to judicial independence was being undermined and the rule of law was being threatened. Lord Donaldson of Lymington, a former Master of the Rolls, who described the proposals as 'an attack by politicians on the Judiciary as a whole', summed up Lord Taylor's view in 'An Unwise Path' published in *The Guardian* newspaper in 1996:

'As Lord Taylor, the Lord Chief Justice, has pointed out, the rule of law, to which all the political parties subscribe, requires that the criminal law shall be governed by established principles, for it is this law which defines what is regarded as unacceptable and punishable by society. It should not be subject to arbitrary change according to the vagaries of fashion. Whilst change there must be, it should be evolutionary. It should be based upon the result of extensive research and consultation with all those involved in the sharp end of the system, ie the judiciary including the magistracy, the Parole Board, the probation service, prison visitors, the prison service, the police and many others. This has not happened, and it is far from clear to what extent it will now happen ...

The criminal law is a basic part of the fabric of society, and any proposal for change needs to be carefully researched and take full account of the professional views of all concerned. This has certainly not happened on this occasion. Indeed, the core proposals for mandatory minimum life sentences are contrary to most professional advice.'

In the body of his article Lord Donaldson gave detailed discussion of the import of the proposals and roundly dismissed the idea that these were, as the government claimed, introducing 'honesty in sentencing'. He argued out the reasons why certain of the proposals would result in a judge passing sentence which that judge believed to be unjust. In respect of the proposed minimum sentences he said:

'It is one thing to be required to be lenient. It is quite another to be required to be unjust ...

If, which is by no means clear, the general level of sentences for these offences is too low, the remedy lies in the Lord Chief Justice and the Court of Appeal giving guidance.'

In respect of the proposed mandatory life sentence he said:

'This proposal is intended to meet a real problem – the fear that such offenders may be released only to strike again. But it is not the right solution. Instead Parliament should empower judges to pass a new sentence of "x years to life". The offender would remain in prison for at least x years and would only be released if and when an appropriate court, rather than the Parole Board, was satisfied that he was no longer a risk to the public, and once so released he should be a free man.

Such a sentence would be honest. It would mean what the judge said. It would also leave the future freedom of the judiciary where it belongs, and where the European Convention on Human Rights expects it to be. This is not to disparage the Parole Board, for which I have great respect, but it is not a judicial body. Furthermore it would still have a role to play in giving advice to the courts.'

It can be seen from these few extracts that Lord Donaldson was sending a clear message to the government that sentencing powers were not their prerogative and were mainly a matter for the judiciary sitting in the courts. Attacks such as these on the decision-making authority of the executive have come increasingly to the fore. A great deal of what has gone on over the last 20 years has been seen as interference with the important independent role to be played by the judiciary. The astonishing departure from tradition of Lord Taylor's speech in the House of Lords can in large measure be explained by the growing antagonism between the judiciary and the government of the day. From when he took office in 1987 to the time he relinquished the post to Lord Irvine in 1997, Lord Chancellor Mackay pushed through reforms that fundamentally altered the framework of the legal system. As a Scotsman and, therefore, an outsider to the English legal system, Lord Mackay was described as being able 'to view the fulminations of the English legal establishment with a certain detachment': Nigel Lawson, former Cabinet minister, in *The View from No 11 – Memoirs of a Tory Radical* (1992) Bantam Press. Under his Lord Chancellorship the fulminations of the English legal establishment certainly did meet up against a strong character intent on bringing the English legal system into the twentieth century, whether screaming and kicking or not, and examples of Lord Mackay's at times near head-on conflict with the judiciary are legion.

Lord Mackay expressed his staunch belief in the independence of the judiciary and there should be no doubt that he did see the preservation of that independence as being crucial to maintaining the balance of power. The point at which he ran a thin line between his separate responsibilities to the executive and to the judiciary was in the interpretation of what this 'independence' meant in the modern state. There was a fundamental change in attitude going on in the Lord Chancellor's Department. Judicial independence was no longer being treated as a right of the judiciary to be free from interference in all legal matters, but was rapidly being restricted to the notion that a judge had a right to try an individual case without interference from the executive or the legislature. Not unnaturally, this sea-change in thinking was met by considerable opposition, but it went to the root of matters to such an extent that it provoked rhetoric to the point of open criticism in the House of Lords, a lot of which was conducted along the lines of comparison with the encroachment on judicial independence by the German Ministry of Justice during the 1920s and 1930s. The warning notes were that change was being brought in not openly through proper use of all the arms of state, but 'by stealth' and 'via the backdoor'. The theme was probably started by Lord Elwyn-Jones, a Law Lord, when he warned that oppression does not necessarily stand on the doorstep wearing 'a toothbrush moustache' and 'a swastika armband' and it was taken up by Lord Lane (Lord Taylor's predecessor) speaking as Lord Chief Justice in the House of Lords during the debate 'The Legal Profession: Reform Proposals' (7 April 1989) when he quoted from Lord Elwyn-Jones and warned that 'loss of freedom seldom happens overnight ... It creeps up insidiously: it creeps up step by step and all of sudden the unfortunate citizen realises that it has gone'. Some five years later the theme lived on. Lord Oliver of Aylmerton speaking in the House of Lords debate 'The Judiciary: Independence' (27 April 1994) used it to condemn the change in attitude in the Lord Chancellor's Department:

> 'Recent pronouncements in this House have seemed to indicate that the noble and learned Lord, the Lord Chancellor and his department interpret the principle of judicial independence in a very much more restricted sense [than the previously accepted view] and as meaning simply this: that judicial independence is infringed only if an attempt is made to dictate or influence the decision in a particular case ... On that analysis, a direction in the 1930s by the German Ministry of Justice that judges were not to decide disputes in favour of members of the Jewish faith or against party members would have been no infringement of their judicial independence – and that, of course, is palpably absurd.'

Rhetoric of this nature spoken by a judiciary that diligently sought to shun all political comment is the surest indication that the proposed reforms, and the method by which they were being pushed through, had well and truly upset the judiciary's view of the balance of powers. Inextricably entwined with all of this was concern over attempts by the government to curtail judicial review of executive decisions, and the growing conviction that a great deal of legislative change had more to do with economic advantage to the Treasury than with preserving the integrity of the judicial system. Time and again over the 1990s the Law Lords used the second chamber to strenuously oppose measures introduced by the executive. The Constitutional Reform Act 2005 had two major impacts on this issue. Firstly, the Law Lords would no longer be based in the second chamber as a Supreme Court was provided for. Secondly, the statute contains a guarantee of judicial independence.

Impartiality

Whilst the independence of the judiciary is of fundamental constitutional importance, it cannot be allowed to vindicate bias on the part of a judge in reaching a decision in any particular case. The impartiality of a judge is essential to the fair administration of justice and the judicial oath taken by a judge on appointment to the bench includes the pledge to act 'without fear or favour, affection or ill-will'. This embraces a number of concepts but in respect of impartiality it carries the ideology that a judge will act without any form of bias. Thus, in addition to political, racial and sexual bias, it includes bias founded on some particular association with persons involved with the case.

Actual impartiality is relatively easy to deal with. A judge is automatically disqualified from sitting as a judge if she/he has a direct financial interest in the outcome of the case or is so closely connected to one of the parties in the case as to share their interest in the outcome. This amounts to actual bias and rarely occurs because it is obvious to the judge in question, and probably others as well, that an interest needs to be declared. It is more usual for complaints to be made of apparent bias in the form of some kind of non-financial interest in the case. This is a considerably more difficult issue. Appearance of impartiality is as important as actual impartiality but it can be difficult for an individual to know where the line is to be drawn. In *R* v *Gough* [1993] 2 WLR 883 the House of Lords laid down a test for apparent bias based on the question 'is there in the view of the court a real danger that the judge was biased?'. In essence, this brings 'real danger of bias' forward as the determining factor and precludes a complainant from being able to rely on mere reasonable suspicion of bias alone. There have been problems with this test. Courts in Canada, Australia and New Zealand have either refused to apply it or have modified it so as to make the relevant test the question: 'whether the events in question give rise to a reasonable apprehension or suspicion on the part of a fair-minded and informed member of the public that the judge was not impartial': *Webb* v *R* (1994) 181 CLR 41 (High Court of Australia).

In the UK two cases have been significant for the clarification of how the *Gough* test is to be applied. The first of these is the *Pinochet Ugarte* case. General Pinochet was the head of the government junta in Chile from 1973–74 and head of state of the Chilean Republic from 1974 to 1980. In 1988 the Central Court of Criminal Proceedings in Madrid issued an international warrant for his arrest, alleging that the General had engaged in acts of genocide and torture of Chilean and Spanish nationals in Chile between 1973 and 1979. General Pinochet was at the time staying at a London hospital and warrants for his arrest were issued under s8(1) of the Extradition Act 1989 by stipendiary magistrates sitting at Bow Street Magistrates' Court. The Divisional Court quashed these warrants on the basis that the applicant enjoyed state immunity in respect of the alleged acts. The Commissioner of Police of the Metropolis and the Spanish government appealed to the House of Lords. This appeal was heard in November 1998 by five Law Lords, one of whom was Lord Hoffmann who, it turned out, had previously acted as Chairman and Director of Amnesty International Charity Ltd, a company that carried out the charity aspects of the work of Amnesty International. The latter had been joined as a party to the proceedings before the House of Lords and was arguing for extradition. Lawyers for Amnesty International argued that there could be no sovereign immunity from extradition in cases where the allegations involved such grave crimes as authorising murder, torture and similar violations of fundamental human rights. By a majority of three to two the Law Lords accepted this argument and allowed the appeal. Lord Hoffmann, who did not declare his association with the related company, was one of the majority.

Shortly thereafter Lord Hoffmann's association with Amnesty became known and lawyers for General Pinochet then lodged a petition asking the House of Lords to set aside the ruling on the ground of appearance of bias. The matter was viewed with the gravest concern. The senior Law Lord, Lord Browne-Wilkinson, and four other Law Lords who had not been involved with the appeal were convened to hear the application. They held that the automatic disqualification rule was not confined to cases of pecuniary interest alone. It had equal application to cases where an adjudicator was a supporter of, or was connected with, a cause or interest group involved in the case before him. Accordingly, by unanimous agreement, their Lordships found that Lord Hoffmann was automatically disqualified as a matter of law by reason of his association with a charity linked to and sharing the same aims as Amnesty International, one party to the case. The earlier ruling was therefore set aside and a rehearing ordered: *R* v *Bow Street Metropolitan Stipendiary Magistrate, ex parte Pinochet Ugarte (No 2)* [1999] 2 WLR 272; [1999] 1 All ER 577 (HL).

The decision therefore clarified that 'promotion of a cause' was to be treated as actual bias and so was not subject to the *Gough* test for apparent bias. This rather upset the apple cart since it had always been generally assumed that non-pecuniary advantage did fall within the general notion of apparent bias. A pecuniary advantage is easily identifiable and is the issue that arises in most civil cases since they are more usually concerned with issues of economic advantage. The decision about automatic disqualification can then turn on the much simpler evidence that a judge will stand to make some financial gain or loss out of the decision reached and the issue can be determined on the basis of the de minimus rule and remoteness. The decision of the House clarifies that it does not follow from this that all other forms of civil case fall outside the automatic disqualification rule. Lord Browne-Wilkinson described the rationale of the automatic disqualification rule as being that 'a man cannot be a judge in his own cause'. On the basis of this rationale it follows that a judge cannot adjudicate on anything which involves a cause which is in some way his own, including cases where the decision reached will favour a judge's non-pecuniary interest in the promotion of the cause in question. Assessing the effect of such allegiances on impartiality involves a qualitative assessment and leaves a considerable degree of uncertainty as to what will constitute actual bias as opposed to apparent bias. Indeed, it rather leads to the idea that there is no distinction to be drawn and this is given some weight by the fact that Lord Chancellor Irvine wrote to Lord Browne-Wilkinson proposing that in future a judge must disclose any matter giving rise to the appearance of a conflict of interest concerning a case in which she/he is about to adjudicate or hear an appeal.

The decision in the case, and the proposal of the Lord Chancellor, came in for a good deal of criticism. A number of people saw the decision of the House as being a reaction to the considerable adverse publicity that surrounded the matter and an attempt to 'whitewash' the severe blow it had dealt to the prestige of the most senior judges in the English legal system. The whole affair had done considerable damage to the perception of an independent and impartial judiciary and there were calls that a much closer scrutiny system be introduced. It was suggested by some that this should be on the lines of the American system, where challenges to judges' interests and public 'vetting' of applicants to the bench are routine. It is accepted that judges cannot be required to avoid outside interests since that would be contrary to their freedom to be associated with lawful activities, but the case highlights the fact that some form of recognisable system needs to be in place both to protect the judiciary and to enable parties to decide whether to object to a particular judge hearing their case.

The passing of the Human Rights Act 1998 brought a new dimension to the problem. Article 6 of the European Convention on Human Rights guarantees the citizen an 'independent and impartial tribunal'. In the wake of the decision in *Pinochet Ugarte (No 2)* there was a growing awareness of the extent to which the ruling opened up the opportunity to challenge judges on the ground of bias. In 2000 a special sitting of the Court of Appeal was convened as part of the actions brought under *Locabail (UK) Ltd* v *Bayfield Properties Ltd; Locabail (UK) Ltd* v *Waldorf Investment Corporation; Timmins* v *Gormley; Williams* v *Inspector of Taxes; R* v *Bristol Betting and Gaming Licensing Committee, ex parte O'Callaghan* [2000] 1 All ER 65. The appeals concerned four test cases in which litigants claimed that the judge or tribunal chairman should have stood down because of links with the case. Each case alleged a different form of bias:

1. that the Deputy Judge was also a solicitor with the firm that acted for the applicant (*Locabail (UK) Ltd* v *Bayfield Properties Ltd* and *Locabail (UK) Ltd* v *Waldorf Investment Corporation*);
2. that the chair of an employment tribunal hearing an unfair dismissal against the Inland Revenue had been employed by the Inland Revenue some 30 years previously (*Williams* v *Inspector of Taxes*);
3. that the presiding county court recorder hearing a claim arising out of a road traffic case was a member of an organisation which campaigned for reforms to the law to help accident victims and had published trenchant views on the issue of personal injury litigation in an article (*Timmins* v *Gormley*);
4. that the judge's refusal to allow the applicant's application of judicial review be set aside on the ground that the judge's family owned property that had been let to the defendant (*R* v *Bristol Betting and Gaming Licensing Committee, ex parte O'Callaghan*).

One could say that everything was beginning to come out of the woodwork, including the intimation that pecuniary advantage to one's relatives gave rise to bias. This extension arose from the consideration given not only to Lord Hoffmann's interests in Amnesty International but also to those of his wife who was a keen supporter of the charity and had done work for them. Lawyers had been quick to see the considerable potential to claim bias afforded by the ruling in *Pinochet Ugarte (No 2)* and now had the force of the Human Rights Act 1998 on their side as well. The unprecedented convening of a Court comprising the Lord Chief Justice, the Master of the Rolls and the Vice-Chancellor illustrates the importance with which the matter was viewed. The object of the sitting was to establish new guidelines on the circumstances in which a judge could be challenged and disqualified on the ground of bias. This was the Court's opportunity to clear up some of the problems caused by the automatic disqualification of Lord Hoffmann and they utilised the opportunity to the full. It held:

1. that proof of actual bias was required for automatic disqualification of an adjudicator;
2. that automatic disqualification on the grounds of pecuniary interest is subject to the de minimus rule;
3. that the pecuniary interest of an adjudicator's partner or relative results in automatic disqualification only where it could be said that the interest of that other person was so close to that of the adjudicator's as to be indistinguishable from cases where the pecuniary interest was the adjudicator's interest;
4. that the automatic disqualification rule extends to cases involving non-pecuniary interest only where it could be shown that the adjudicator has a close connection with one of the parties to the litigation;
5. that beyond cases of automatic disqualification, the test to be applied was that laid down by the House of Lords in *R* v *Gough* (above) ie 'real danger of bias'.

The Court clarified that a real danger of bias might arise where:

1. there was a friendship or personal animosity between the adjudicator and a member of the public involved in the case; or
2. if an adjudicator had doubted the credibility of a party in previous proceedings in outspoken terms suggesting that he was unable to approach a party's evidence with an open mind; or
3. if for any other reason there were real grounds for doubting the judge's ability to ignore extraneous considerations and bring an objective judgment to bear on the issues before him.

The Court expressed the view that factors such as religious persuasion, ethnic or natural origin, gender, age, class, means or sexual orientation would not amount to a sensible objection to the adjudicator hearing the case. The Court also doubted whether a challenge could ever succeed on the basis that the adjudicator or his close family had a particular social or educational background, employment history, political associations, was a member of any social, sporting or charitable bodies, or had Masonic associations (for this latter see further below). Also regarded as unimportant were previous judicial decisions, extracurricular utterances and membership of the same Inn, circuit or Local Law Society.

This is a very clear set of guidelines which puts the issue of when a judge should declare an interest onto a very much clearer footing than it has ever been on before. There can be little doubt that it will curb the growing tendency to challenge judges' decisions on the grounds of bias and thereby restore to the system the stability that is needed if justice is to work effectively. The Court also clarified the position under the Human Rights Act 1998 in that it confirmed that an adjudicator who allows his judicial decision to be influenced by partiality or prejudice deprives a litigant of the right to a fair trial by an impartial tribunal and violates a most fundamental principle on which the administration of justice rests. However, every case of alleged bias must turn on its particular facts, with real doubt being resolved in favour of disqualification.

The Court also took the opportunity to address the problems raised by the Lord Chancellor's proposal that every judge be under a duty to declare all possible conflicts of interest. It decided that it would be wrong for a judge to disqualify him/herself on the basis of a tenuous objection and that, instead, if a judge had a connection with a person who was a party to the case or an organisation which was a party or which promoted a cause which was central to the outcome of the case, that judge ought to disclose that connection in advance of the hearing so that the parties had the opportunity to object to it. The 'automatic disqualification' principle of *Pinochet Ugarte (No 2)*, above, was to be applied only in rare cases of actual bias where the judge's interest (whether pecuniary or non-pecuniary) was of such a nature that justice could not be seen to be done if she/he presided in the case. In cases of apparent bias, a pre-trial objection to the judge, or post-trial disqualification of the judge, would be valid and appropriate only where there had been a real danger or possibility of bias.

As a result of the guidelines laid down by the Court, only one of the four appeals was granted. It was the personal injuries claim in *Timmins* v *Gormley* where the Court felt that the involvement of the recorder in campaigns to reform the law to help accident victims was sufficient to establish a real danger or possibility that the compensation award had been tainted by bias or prejudice. A retrial was ordered.

In *Lawal* v *Northern Spirit Ltd* [2004] 1 All ER 187 the House of Lords felt it was improper for a part-time judge in Employment Appeal Tribunals to appear as an advocate before such tribunals.

As mentioned above, the Court of Appeal viewed association with the Freemasons Society to be a matter that did not give grounds for a challenge. It is likely that a good number of serving judges are members of this ancient and exclusively all-male organisation. The reason that this has given concern is that it is a secret society dedicated to protecting the interests of its members who individually pledge to help one another in every way. There is no means of knowing whether the judge or any other person involved in the proceedings is a member so bias could be occurring without any means of identifying it. In 1998 there were calls for judges to be prohibited from remaining as a member of the society, but the Lord Chancellor rejected these on the ground that he was not empowered to prevent any member of the judiciary from belonging to a lawful association. In an attempt to give greater openness and dispel any public fears about potential bias, Jack Straw, the Home Secretary, encouraged the establishment of a voluntary register so that judges (and magistrates) could declare their membership of the society. He cannot compel disclosure since the society is lawfully a secret one, and compulsory disclosure was in any case strongly resisted by the judiciary on the ground that it would be a step towards politicisation of judges. The Lord Chancellor's Department put out a preliminary questionnaire and out of approximately 5,000 judges, 247 judges declared themselves to be Freemasons and 64 refused to make any declaration.

Immunity

Immunity is an extension of the principle of an independent judiciary. In order for a judge to be able to act as an independent and effective arbiter of the law she/he must be able to express opinion on the law and on the situation to which it is to be applied without fear of law suits from the parties. Accordingly, the judiciary cannot be sued in a civil action for anything done or said while acting in their judicial capacity. In *Sirros* v *Moore* [1975] QB 118, the Court of Appeal held that a judge who had wrongly ordered a detention was immune from action since he had acted in good faith in his judicial capacity.

The notion of immunity goes beyond that of good faith within the exercise of judicial function. In strict terms a judge is immune from suit even if she/he has acted in bad faith. This position is reached by reasoning out the doctrine of judicial independence to its ultimate conclusion: freedom from interference by any agency embraces freedom from suit. However, acting in bad faith is acting contrary to the judicial oath, ie 'without fear or favour, affection or ill-will', and it can be argued that a judge therefore has no authority to act in a corrupt or malicious way, ie such behaviour is outside their jurisdiction and ultra vires. This is not the view that is taken but it may be a view that is tested in the future since it is anomalous for the judiciary to have immunity against an abuse of their position of authority when such immunity is not available to any other public servant.

The Courts and Legal Services Act 1990 removed the old system under which immunity varied according to the status of the judge. It used to be that judges in the inferior courts were liable for damages for actions done in excess of their actual authority, but they now enjoy the same immunity as judges in the superior courts. This extension includes magistrates. Likewise, neither the Lord Chancellor nor any of the designated judges is liable in damages for anything done or omitted in the discharge or purported discharge of any of their functions: Part II of the Courts and Legal Services Act 1990, s69(1).

4.2 Functions of a judge

These may be summarised as follows.

1. Supervisory – conduct of the trial.
2. Sole arbiter of any legal issue.
3. In civil cases the judge alone decides fact and law, but certain actions (eg libel

and slander) may be tried with a jury: s69 of the Supreme Court Act 1981. In jury cases the judge must leave fact-finding to the jury.

4. In civil cases the judge decides quantum of damages unless this decision falls to be made by the jury, eg in defamation cases. However, even in these cases judicial guidance can be given to the jury in the matter of assessing damages.
5. To interpret, clarify and give effect to the law.
6. In criminal cases, the role of summing up to a jury.
7. In criminal cases, passing sentence.
8. In exceptional cases, to reform the law. Whilst in theory judges cannot create new rules of law, in practice this must inevitably happen either through the development of judicial precedents or through the process of statutory interpretation. In rare cases where there is no authority to guide them, judges may feel compelled to create new principles of law: see, for example, in civil law, *R v Human Fertilisation and Embryology Authority, ex parte Blood* [1997] 2 All ER 687 (CA); and, in criminal law, *Shaw v Director of Public Prosecutions* [1962] AC 220 (HL).

In addition to the purely judicial functions outlined above a judge may be called upon to exercise quasi-judicial functions involving a mixture of fact-finding, administration and policy formulation, eg when chairing a Royal Commission or a tribunal of inquiry.

4.3 Appointment to judicial offices

The arrangements for the senior judiciary are in a state of flux. The Constitutional Reform Act 2005 retains the office of the Lord Chancellor and makes changes to the way in which the functions vested in that office are handled. In practice a system in which the Minister for Constitutional Affairs takes over the role of the Lord Chancellor is already operative and the Act makes provision for this (some matters will become the responsibility of the Lord Chief Justice). Lord Falconer, the present Minister for Constitutional Affairs, does not sit as a judge, and separating judicial from other functions is one of the aims of these reforms. Under the terms of the 2005 Act the Lord Chancellor, or the person who performs the role, need not be a member of the House of Lords (as a second chamber within Parliament) and need not be a lawyer. The Constitutional Reform Act 2005 also provides for a President of the Courts of England and Wales, a post which will be assumed by the Lord Chief Justice. The Act sets out the responsibilities of the President of the Courts of England and Wales and the courts to which the presidency applies. In his role as President of the Courts of England and Wales, the Lord Chief Justice is to be responsible for representing the views of the judiciary of England and Wales to Parliament, the Minister (that is, the Secretary of State for Constitutional Affairs) and Ministers of the Crown generally. He is also to be responsible, within the resources made available by the Minister, for maintaining appropriate arrangements for the welfare, training and guidance of the judiciary of England and Wales, and for maintaining appropriate arrangements for the deployment of the judiciary of England and Wales and allocating work within courts. The Act also provides for a new statutory post of Head of Criminal Justice, which will be held ex officio by the Lord Chief Justice of England and Wales or, after consultation with the Minister, by his nominee. Provision is also made for the Lord Chief Justice to appoint a Deputy Head of Criminal Justice. The creation of these new posts mirrors the existing statutory posts of Head and Deputy Head of Civil Justice, established by s62 of the Courts Act 2003. Additionally, provision is made for a new statutory post of Head of Family Justice, which will be held ex officio by the President of the Family Division. The Lord Chief Justice may also appoint a Deputy Head of Family Justice. A further change introduced by the 2005 Act is that an independent commission to appoint judges is to be established.

The major judicial offices at present are the Lord Chief Justice, the Master of the Rolls, the President of the Family Division of the High Court, the Vice-Chancellor and the Senior Presiding Judge for England and Wales. In addition to these offices, judges are appointed to sit in courts at the various levels within its hierarchy and these judges are referred to as: the Lords of Appeal in Ordinary, the Lords Justices of Appeal, the puisne judges of the High Court, deputy judges of the High Court, circuit judges, recorders, and district judges.

The traditional constitutional view is that judges are 'servants of the Crown'. This remains true to the extent that most of the judiciary is appointed and, in certain circumstances, removable by the Crown, but the modern judiciary certainly does not hold office at the 'pleasure' of the monarch in the sense that it was thought of in former times. The independence of the judiciary confirmed by the Act of Settlement in 1701 effectively removed all direct control over the judiciary in the exercise of their office by the ruling monarch or by his/her ministers. The Queen acts on the advice of the Prime Minister for the appointment of the Minister for Constitutional Affairs, the Lord Chief Justice, the Master of the Rolls, the President of the Family Division of the High Court, the Vice-Chancellor, the Lords of Appeal in Ordinary and the Lords Justices of Appeal. For the appointment of the 'puisne' judges of the High Court, circuit judges and recorders, the Queen acts on the advice of the Minister for Constitutional Affairs. It is only Justices of the Peace and district judges (including those formerly known as stipendiary magistrates) who are appointed directly by the Minister for Constitutional Affairs.

Lord Chief Justice

This appointment is made by the Crown on the recommendation of the Prime Minister after consultation with the Lord Chancellor (a role taken over by the Minister for Constitutional Affairs). The Lord Chief Justice is the senior judge and can sit as President of the High Court. He is President of the Criminal Division of the Court of Appeal and formally the senior judge in the Queen's Bench Division. In practice, however, the Lord Chief Justice will normally sit in the appellate courts, and usually the Court of Appeal or the Queen's Bench Divisional Court.

The appointment of the Lord Chief Justice can give rise to considerable constitutional debate. In 1995 the then serving Master of the Rolls, Sir Thomas Bingham, was appointed Lord Chief Justice to replace Lord Taylor who sadly had to retire early due to ill health. Shortly before his retirement Lord Taylor delivered an attack in the House of Lords on the Home Secretary's plan to introduce mandatory prison sentences for certain crimes, saying that justice is better served if sentencing is left to individual judges deciding individual cases than by politicians motivated by electoral success and political fashion: see further section 4.1. The fact that he did this raised considerable debate about the apolitical role that the Lord Chief Justice is traditionally supposed to play in the administration of justice. It also gave rise to debate about whether his successor should return to the neutrality of the traditional view or dispense with judicial quietism in the manner of Lord Taylor. Lord Bingham thus took office at a time of constitutional sensitivity. That he carried out the role successfully is shown by his promotion to senior Law Lord in which office, amongst other things, he took responsibility for deciding which Law Lords hear which cases. His appointment was unusual as the position usually goes to the next senior serving Law Lord according to the date of appointment. It was, therefore, a promotion that amounts to a shake-up of the House of Lords and perhaps symbolises a notable stage in its evolution. Part of the background to this may be the mess that the House found itself in after appointing Lord Hoffmann to the *Pinochet Ugarte* case: see further section 4.1. Most of the 100 or so cases currently heard each year by the House of Lords are concerned with commercial and taxation matters. It is now likely that an increasing number of cases will be on the fundamental freedoms laid down by the European Convention on Human Rights and, in particular, the rights of the individual against the state.

Master of the Rolls

This appointment is made by the Crown on the recommendation of the Prime Minister, usually after consultation with the Lord Chancellor (a role taken over by the Minister for Constitutional Affairs). The Master of the Rolls is President of the Civil Division of the Court of Appeal. This is a key position. Although the House of Lords is the final appellate court, the number of civil appeals heard by the House in an average year is about 50 while it is over 1,500 in the Civil Division of the Court of Appeal.

President of the Family Division

The holder of this position is responsible for the management and organisation of the Family Division of the High Court and presides as a judge in that Division. As the President of a division of the High Court, the holder is also an ex officio member of the Court of Appeal. The appointment is made by the Crown on the advice of the Prime Minister.

Vice-Chancellor

The Vice-Chancellor carries out the function of organising the business of the Chancery Division and sits as a judge in that Division. As a senior appointment of the High Court, the holder is also an ex officio member of the Court of Appeal. The appointment is made by the Crown on the advice of the Prime Minister.

Senior Presiding Judge for England and Wales

This office was created by the Courts and Legal Services Act 1990. A Senior Presiding Judge is appointed from the Lords Justices of Appeal and two Presiding Judges are appointed from the High Court to administer the operation of the six Crown Court circuits.

Lords of Appeal in Ordinary

Normally referred to as the Law Lords, these are the judges that sit in the House of Lords. They are ennobled on appointment to their position by the Queen and hold office 'during good behaviour' which means that a Law Lord may be stripped of his ennoblement and removed from office on the address of both Houses of Parliament.

The maximum number of servicing Law Lords is set at 12. This can be altered by Order in Council. Although full members of the House of Lords, there is a constitutional presumption based on the separation of powers that they will not take part in political debate. Their role within the constitution is that of judiciary, as the Law Lords sitting in the highest appellate court in the land, and as members of the legislature for consideration of proposed legislation in the second chamber of the House. The Law Lords are, however, on occasion prompted to participate in what can be seen as political debate and this is especially true where the proposed legislation affects the administration of the system of justice. Examples of such involvement have been seen in recent times with the passing of the Access to Justice Act 1999, the Human Rights Act 1998, and the Courts and Legal Services Act 1990. Appointment rests on certain criteria. The Constitutional Reform Act 2005 provides for the removal of these members of the judiciary from the second chamber and the establishment of a Supreme Court. They must have held 'high judicial office', as defined by s25 of the Appellate Jurisdiction Act 1876 (eg a judge of the High Court or the Court of Appeal), for not less than two years, or for not less than 15 years have been:

'(a) person who has a Supreme Court qualification, within the meaning of s71 of the Courts and Legal Services Act 1990;

(b) an advocate in Scotland, or a solicitor entitled to appear in the Court of Session and the High Court of judiciary; or

(c) a practising member of the Bar of Northern Ireland.'

(Section 71(2), Sch 10, para 1, Courts and Legal Services Act 1990.)

Lords Justices of Appeal

These are the Lords who constitute the majority of the Court of Appeal. The Supreme Court Act 1981 failed to consider the appointment of a female Lord Justice and for some time all their Lordships, whether male or female, had to be referred to as Lord Justice. This rule has now been changed and the title Lady Justice may be used.

Appointment is by the Crown on the advice of the Prime Minister and is for judges who hold a ten-year High Court qualification within the meaning of s71 of the Courts and Legal Services Act 1990 or who are a judge of the High Court. The maximum number of Lord Justices is set at 38 and there are currently that number in post (or 39 if the Master of the Rolls is included in the count). They sit in the Court of Appeal, either Division, but usually the court is organised so that at least one appeal judge has experience of the branch of law involved in the case before the court.

High Court judges

Properly known as the 'Justices of the High Court' but often called by their old name of 'puisne' judges which is pronounced like 'puny' (ie 'pewnee') and used as a reference to their junior or subordinate status within the judiciary. They must have a ten-year High Court qualification, within the meaning of s71 of the Courts and Legal Services Act 1990, or be a circuit judge who has held that office for at least two years, and are appointed by the Crown on the advice of the Lord Chancellor.

Until the passage of the 1990 Act appointments were restricted to practising barristers (usually Queen's Counsel) of at least ten years' experience of advocacy or barristers who had become circuit judges. The 1990 Act permitted solicitor circuit judges to be considered for appointment and also provided for the extension of rights of advocacy in the High Court to solicitors. Eventually this should lead to more solicitor judges being appointed to the High Court bench. In 1994 Lord Mackay, the then Lord Chancellor, also used his delegated powers under the 1990 Act to lift the ban on employed government lawyers working for the government legal service and Crown Prosecution Service from becoming judges after retirement.

On appointment High Court judges receive a knighthood. In 2000 the Lord Chancellor proposed that the statutory ceiling on the number of High Court judges be raised to from 96 to 106. The increase was designed to cope with the anticipated volume of work generated by the Human Rights Act 1998 which came into force in October 2000.

In addition to serving as a judge in one of the three divisions of the High Court (Queen's Bench Division, Chancery Division and Family Division), a High Court judge hears the more serious offences tried on indictment in the Crown Courts, eg murder cases.

Circuit judges

The position of circuit judge was introduced by the Courts Act 1971. All county court judges, who until then were exclusively concerned with civil work, became circuit judges and, additionally, were assigned to the Crown Court. Circuit judges now, therefore, undertake a mixture of civil and criminal work as do their High Court counterparts. They are appointed by the Crown on the advice of the Lord Chancellor and are addressed as Your Honour (His Honour, etc).

By virtue of the Courts and Legal Services Act 1990, Sch 10, para 31, no person is qualified to be appointed a circuit judge unless she/he has a ten-year Crown Court or ten-year county court qualification within the meaning of s71 of the 1990 Act; or she/he is a recorder; or she/he has held a full-time appointment for at least three years in one of the offices listed in Pt IA of Sch 2 to the 1971 Act, which include coroners, taxing masters of the Supreme Court, stipendiary magistrates and district judges.

Section 52 of the Criminal Justice and Public Order Act 1994 provides that, in certain circumstances (eg an appeal against conviction otherwise than before a High Court judge), circuit judges are able to act as judges of the Court of Appeal (Criminal Division).

Recorders

They are appointed by the Crown on the advice of the Lord Chancellor (the role has now been taken over by the Minister for Constitutional Affairs). They serve as part-time judges of the Crown Court. They must have a ten-year Crown Court or county court qualification under s71 of the Courts and Legal Services Act 1990. The appointment is often regarded as an 'apprenticeship' since a recorder who demonstrates judicial ability may be appointed as a circuit judge or High Court judge.

District judges

The original district judges were created by s74(1) and (2) of the Courts and Legal Services Act 1990 which provided that the offices of registrar, assistant registrar and deputy registrar for each county court district and district registrar, assistant district registrar and deputy district registrar for each district registry of the High Court, became the offices of district judge, assistant judge and deputy district judge respectively. The office of registrar of the principal registry of the Family Division of the High Court became the office of district judge of the principal registry of the Family Division. They also include what were stipendary magistrates who operate in the magistrates' courts.

District judges hear the less serious cases and are appointed by the Lord Chancellor (a role that has been taken over by the Minister for Constitutional Affairs). They must meet the seven-year general qualification under the Courts and Legal Services Act 1990.

The composition of the judiciary

In November 2004 the composition of the judiciary was as follows.

Lords of Appeal in Ordinary	12
Heads of Divisions	5
Lords Justices of Appeal	37
High Court Judges	107
Chancery Division	17
Queen's Bench Division	72
Family Division	18
Circuit Judges	636
Recorders	1,339
Recorders in Training	49
District Judges	415
Deputy District Judges	739
District Judges (Magistrates' Court)	126
Deputy District Judges (Magistrates' Court)	147

4.4 Selection of judges

An account is offered of the development of the system for the appointment of judges to the present time. For the future, as a result of the Constitutional Reform Act 2005, an independent commission will undertake the role.

The development of the independence of the judiciary from the Crown, the executive and the legislature allowed the choice of appointment for judicial posts to take on a mystery of its own and the selecting of the judiciary to become shrouded in secrecy. There was no promotion structure as such since it was thought that judges might allow the prospect of promotion to a higher court to influence the way that they reached their decisions. Instead, appointment for senior judicial posts was 'by invitation of the Lord Chancellor' and was exclusively from the ranks of Queen's Counsel (ie QCs simply hoped to be invited to take a post). Such invitations were decided on the basis of 'soundings' taken in confidence from serving judges and senior practising lawyers which were then compiled into files on potential candidates. The subject of a file had no opportunity to check the accuracy of the information in it nor to challenge recommendations that may have been made by those consulted by the Department. Indeed, the sources of recommendations were kept strictly confidential. There were no formal interviews and no reasons were given for particular decisions. The final decision about appointment was in the hands of the Lord Chancellor.

Whatever the merits of this 'soundings' system might have been, it had the unfortunate result of favouring Queen's Counsel who belonged to the 'right social group' and the 'elite' chambers. For centuries our judiciary has comprised mainly white, middle-aged and establishment-minded men who share the same background of a public school education followed by Oxford or Cambridge ('Oxbridge') and belong to the same social clubs. A study in 1970 found that of 359 judges 81 per cent had been to public schools and 76 per cent to 'Oxbridge', and a survey in 1991 of 123 senior judges showed that over two-thirds had passed through public schools and 'Oxbridge'. They were overwhelmingly middle aged or elderly, only two being under 50 and more than half over 60; there were then no members of racial minorities and only three women in the upper echelons of the judiciary. Solicitors, who outnumbered barristers as practising lawyers by about seven or eight to one, were dismissed as being entirely unsuitable for judicial office because of their different training and experience, ignoring the fact that the great bulk of justice in England and Wales is dispensed by lay magistrates who at the time had virtually no legal training.

Appointment was on the basis of a candidate's 'standing' and 'temperament', the specifics of which remained undisclosed but appeared to be based on very subjective criteria that had a lot to do with maintaining the 'establishment status quo' and very little to do with ensuring equal representation of women, ethnic minorities and other minority groups within society. Indeed, it was argued that the judiciary was becoming increasingly unrepresentative of the diverse needs of modern society as a whole. The entire process was decried as having 'built-in head winds' which ensured the perpetuation of a class-ridden and discriminatory 'old boy network'. Its secretive and discriminatory practices were no longer acceptable to the modern world which values equality for all and its related concepts of openess, impartiality, and the securing of a class-less society.

Some inroad into the problem was made by the widening of the pool from which the judiciary can be selected enacted as part of the Courts and Legal Services Act 1990. It introduced changes in rights of audience for the profession and this allowed appointment to the High Court and to the Court of Appeal to include qualification based on ten years' exercise of such right of audience in the High Court. Similarly, a ten-year right of audience in the Crown Court or county courts acts as qualification for appointment to the posts of circuit judge, recorder and assistant recorder. The requirement that solicitors serve three years as a recorder before appointment as a circuit judge has been abolished. In addition, three years service as a district judge is qualification for appointment as a circuit judge. In the year 2000 the potential pool from which judges can be appointed was further widened by s37 of the Access to Justice Act 1999 which provides that employed lawyers, including those employed by the Crown Prosecution Service, have rights of audience in courts to the same extent as their counterparts in private practice. The Act also permits all barristers and solicitors full rights of audience on call to the Bar or admission to the Roll.

The changes introduced by the Courts and Legal Services Act 1990 were to be welcomed in that they gave a greater number and variety of persons the opportunity to hold judicial office but they did not in themselves address the underlying disquiet with the actual method of appointment. It took another four years before the calls for open competition for judicial posts with selection based on stated criteria were conceded to, and then only in the face of mounting evidence that public confidence in the judiciary was waning. In 1994 the Lord Chancellor announced that advertisements would be placed for the junior judicial posts of circuit judge, district judge and recorder in the Crown Courts and county courts. In the case of circuit judge, this replaced the system of application on the basis of recommendation that previously pertained. This was followed in 1998 by the first advertisement ever for a vacancy on the High Court bench, a momentous event in the history of the judiciary in that it displaced a centuries old tradition of appointment by invitation only.

Advertisement necessitated the publication of criteria for appointment to replace the old criteria of 'standing' and 'sound temperament'. For the first time the Lord Chancellor's Department revealed the kind of qualities looked for in candidates for judicial office. In addition to the legal and administrative skills demanded by the post, the list includes such as: fairness, humanity, courtesy, integrity, honesty, communication skills, community experience and contacts. This awesome list of attributes no doubt has as much to do with restoring public confidence in the judiciary as it does with setting criteria for appointment. All advertisements contain a pledge that applications will be considered 'regardless of ethnic origin, gender, marital status, sexual orientation, political affiliation, religion or (subject to the physical requirements of the office) disability'.

The interviews for both types of posts are conducted by 'panels'. Applicants short-listed for junior judicial posts are interviewed by a panel which includes a serving judge, a lay person and an official of the Lord Chancellor's Department (now the Department for Constitutional Affairs). Applicants for vacancies on the High Court bench are interviewed by a panel consisting of a judge, a civil servant from the Lord Chancellor's Department (now the Department for Constitutional Affairs) and a lay person. The panel does not make the appointment but instead makes recommendations to the Lord Chancellor (the role now having been taken over by the Minister for Constitutional Affairs) who still uses a form of 'sounding' in that he makes his final decision not solely on the advice received from the interview panels but also on the results of confidential consultations with judges and practitioners who have direct knowledge of the candidate's talents, experience, and professional merits. In a response to continuing hostility from the profession about the lack of disclosure of information obtained by these consultations, Lord Irvine instructed that any adverse allegations made about a candidate, and the source of them, are to be disclosed to that candidate, who will then be given an opportunity to rebut them. This, however, has not been enough to assuage the criticism of the new system and its fiercest critic has been the legal profession itself. The Law Society even threatened to boycott the entire appointment process and have repeatedly called for an independent Judicial Appointments Commission to be established. This idea was first put forwad by Lord Williams of Mostyn, fomer Chairman of the Bar Council and a Labour peer, who described Lord Mackay's changes to the system as being no more than 'cosmetic tinkering to no lasting or sensible purpose' and called for the Judicial Studies Board to be given independent status from the Lord Chancellor's Department with full responsibility for the appointment and training of the judiciary. The idea was rejected by Lord Mackay and his successor Lord Irvine. Both pledge their faith in the consultations system as a means of preserving the integrity of appointments to the bench. Criticism is rebutted with the claim that the information gathered is used impartially for a systematic and objective evaluation of an individual's merits, taking thorough account of all the relevant qualities of a candidate, including his/her humanity, courtesy and understanding of people and society.

The debate took on a new surge of ferocity when the statistics produced for 1998 recorded a very low percentage of representation of women and ethnic minorities amongst the junior judicial posts and none at all for the High Court bench and higher posts. In a series of speeches during 1998, in which he reiterated his intention to modernise the appointments system so as to promote fairness and equality of opportunity, Lord Irvine rejected the use of what he called 'quick fix solutions' to tackle the low representation of women and ethnic minorities among the judiciary on the grounds that would undermine the fundamental principle that the best qualified candidates must be appointed regardless of gender or race. The use of positive discrimination, fast-track methods of promotion and quotas were, therefore, firmly rejected and the Lord Chancellor's Department instead set about trying to find schemes to make the judicial system more sympathetic and responsive to the needs of women and minorities. Ideas for improvements came in thick and fast and included the following.

1. Appointing candidates as district judges for three to four weeks as a period of probation which, if successfully completed, would be followed by promotion to assistant recorders.
2. The introduction of a 'shadowing' system to enable prospective applicants to spend time with a judge so as to obtain knowledge of, and confidence in, the discharge of judicial functions.
3. Creating a system of permanent part-time judges in the High Court and on circuit (which might prove attractive for women in combining a judicial career with the responsibility of bringing up a family).
4. Introducing psychological tests for candidates to assess character and detect undesirable prejudices.

5. Widening the pool of candidates to include pure academic lawyers and those working in quasi-legal environments such as legal advice centres, the probation service, local authorities legal services, government advisory groups and so on. There is a good proportion of women and ethnic minorities in these occupations. The widening of the pool to bring in all the legal profession brought in by the Courts and Legal Services Act 1990 helped to break down the notion that Queen's Counsel, or even practising barristers, are the best persons for judicial appointment and paved the way to a realisation that judges can be drawn from any quarter, ie that being a player in the game is not necessarily a prerequisite for being a good referee! The passing of the Human Rights Act 1998 has done much to assist this view. The thrust of the European Convention on Human Rights is to secure to everyone within their jurisdiction the rights and freedoms defined in art 1 of the Convention, and these include amongst many others the right to liberty and security, to a fair and public hearing, and to an effective remedy. These are matters of justice and fairness, rather than strict legality. Strict adherence to precedent and ability with the other judicial formalities of the English system do not create the prerequisite for the appointment of a judge in such a system. It is however an absolute prerequisite that the judiciary are chosen in an open and fair manner, are properly trained to do the job, and then proceed to act in all ways in a fair and justifiable manner. In many European jurisdictions there is some semblance of this objective in the career-structured judicial systems used; this is discussed below at section 4.6.

6. The establishment of a Judicial Appointments Board composed of lay persons with some experience of the justice system to advise the Lord Chancellor on senior judicial appointments and be under a duty to provide reasons for its advice. This is essentially a modification of the Law Society's recommendation for a Judicial Appointments Commission. A Commission would act independently of the Lord Chancellor's Department and this was seen by many as being the major stumbling block to the success of the recommendation. The idea of an advisory board was more favourably received and following the disappointing results of the 1998 statistics for judicial appointments it started to gather strength. Such a system was introduced by the Constitutional Reform Act 2005.

By the end of 1998 it was clear that detailed consideration needed to be given to the whole question of how judicial appointments were to be conducted and in response to this Lord Irvine appointed Sir Leonard Peach, the Commissioner for Public Appointments, to undertake a review of the system, to include evaluation of the appointment of Queen's Counsel. The Peach Report was published in December 1999. It recommended that the system of confidential soundings be retained but suggested that anxieties about its operation in regard to ensuring equality of opportunity could be allayed through the appointment of an ombudsman to ensure independent monitoring of the procedures for choosing judges and Queen's Counsel.

The Lord Chancellor immediately recommended that this proposal be implemented and the post of Commissioner for Judicial Appointments has been created. It is a part-time post and does not replace the current appointments system. Instead the Commissioner is able to hear complaints about the appointment system from individuals, as well as audit the system. The Lord Chancellor also recommended implementation of two other proposals in the Report, namely, that the advocacy requirement no longer be relied on as the criterion for judicial appointment, thereby encouraging the appointment of more solicitor-judges, and that performance appraisal be introduced for newly appointed judges.

The Lord Chancellor's response to the Peach Report did not receive a warm welcome and in 2000 the Law Society published a report in which it roundly criticised the reforms undertaken as being a wasted opportunity for radical change to the appointments system. It highlighted the continuing lack of representation of women and ethnic minorities and called again for the establishment of an independent appointments Commission. The report emphasised the increasing importance and impact of judicial decisions and the increased need to respond to this following the implementation of the Human Rights Act 1998.

During 1999 the Lord Chancellor's Department carried out a survey of members of the legal profession. The results were published in a report entitled *Factors Affecting the Decision to Apply for Silk and Judicial Office*. The results revealed that although there is general support for the improvements already made to date, such as advertising of posts and giving feedback to applicants, there is still a large degree of dissatisfaction. High among the most popular of the recommendations put forward by those questioned were reform of the consultation process and the establishment of a Judicial Appointments Commission. The end of this process of reform may now be in sight as the Constitutional Reform Bill 2004 provides for a Judicial Appointments Commission to be responsible for recruiting and selecting judges. The Commission is to report to the Minister on who has been selected, for the Minister to make the appointment or the recommendation to The Queen. It also makes provision for a Judicial Appointments and Conduct Ombudsman, who will investigate any complaints, and for disciplinary procedures in relation to the judiciary.

Data is collected in relation to the ethnic background of the judges and the material in a government report states the position as at 1 November 2004 (Ethnic Minority Appointments (2004) London: Department for Constitutional Affairs). The same report also provides information as to the gender of the judiciary. It appears that we are not quite an equal opportunity society, though there has been a change from the even worse situation that existed in the past. The difficulty is that in order to be appointed as a judge, you need the necessary experience. Thus it is the lack of opportunity to start and develop legal careers that is the initial problem. Some further steps are being taken in terms of widening access – by, for example, allowing people to be appointed at a lower age than that which was usual in the past. Nevertheless, all of the members of the House of Lords, all of the Judges of the

Court of Appeal and all of the Heads of Division are white. Women do slightly better as they make up ten of the 107 High Court judges, two of the 37 members of the Court of Appeal and the Head of the Family Division is female. Progress is most notably seen in the one female member of the House of Lords and the one member of the High Court who is from an ethnic minority. Data for the other courts is presented in tabular form.

Gender and ethnic background of the lower judiciary

	Men	Women	Total	% Ethnic minority
House of Lords	11	1	12	0
Heads of Division	4	1	5	0
Court of Appeal	35	2	37	0
High Court	97	10	107	1
Circuit Judges	569	67	636	2
Recorders	1,164	175	1,339	5
Recorders in Training	35	14	49	12
District Judges	350	83	433	4
Deputy District Judges	616	189	805	3
District Judges (Magistrates' Courts)	101	25	126	4
Deputy District Judges (Magistrates' Courts)	114	33	147	8

The government wants to attract more women, minority group, ethnic and disabled judges. A Department for Constitutional Affairs consultation paper seeks to increase diversity in the profession: the problems identified in the judicial statistics, just noted above, are thus being addressed (Increasing Diversity in the Judiciary (2004), London: Department for Constitutional Affairs). Formal career breaks, more flexible sitting arrangements and a drive to urge women, minority group, ethnic and disabled lawyers to apply to become judges, are among measures being considered. At the same time it is emphasised that merit must remain the criterion on which judicial appointments are made. The problem is easily stated as at present only 15.8 per cent of court judges are women and just 3.4 per cent come from minority ethnic groups. Work-shadowing schemes for would-be applicants, changes to age limits, the involvement of independent lay members in sifting and interviewing for office, part-time sitting for judges below High Court level and the publication of an annual judicial appointments report are amongst the other possibilities being reviewed. A more diverse judiciary is essential if the public's confidence in its judges is to be achieved.

4.5 Training of judges

Prior to 1979 there was no system in place for any form of training prior to appointment to the bench or for continuing professional development after appointment. This was in great measure due to the notion of the independence of the judiciary. Freedom from interference carries with it the idea that a judge is to be 'free in thought and independent in judgment'. Implicit faith in judicial decision-making has, however, diminished over recent decades. This is in part associated with the method by which judges were appointed in that the traditional view was that practise at the Bar, and more particularly experience as Queen's Counsel, was sufficient experience to take on the functions of a judge. This rather ignored the view that on appointment to the bench an individual had to transform themselves overnight from ferocious fighting counsel to contemplative and fair-minded adjudicators. There was also the problem that society was beginning to perceive of the judiciary as having become unrepresentative of modern views and beliefs. There were a number of highly publicised comments made by judges sitting in court which revealed complete lack of knowledge of famous sports people, pop groups and media celebrities as well as total unfamiliarity with popular pastimes and other general affairs of society. John Mortimer, an English lawyer and well known writer, commented that the 'pronouncements of some judges, before and since retirement, have gone beyond endearing eccentricity to give some cause for alarm'. The judiciary did seek to redress some of the allegations made and it would be wrong to tar the whole of the judiciary with the same brush. As Lord Edmund-Davies, a former Law Lord commented: 'Judges are human beings, have families of their own, families have troubles ... they are not set apart, they have to lead pretty normal lives off the bench'.

Judicial independence acts both for and against the argument for judicial training. On the one hand the imposition of training, even though carried out by the Department for Constitutional Affairs, carries with it the potential for executive interference in judicial decision-making. An executive driven more by managerial concerns and cost savings can put pressure on the Department for Constitutional Affairs to incorporate all manner of restrictions on the freedom of judicial decision-making in the guise of 'training'. It lies open, therefore, to be condemned as yet another example of 'stealth by the back door' in the diminishing of the constitutional right to judicial independence. On the other hand judicial independence leaves the judiciary formally unaccountable for its decisions. The task of remedying 'wrong' decisions is left to the process of appeal. Disapprobation may be expressed within the confines of the profession and the judge may even be reprimanded, but these affairs are rarely conducted in public and there is no formal machinery by which society is involved in complaints. Whatever the effects of internal discipline might be, as far as the public is concerned there is little to no outward display of disciplinary action and judges whose conduct has been the subject of public criticism usually remain on the bench. There is good argument for protection of security of tenure as an essential prerequisite to judicial independence in that without it judges would have to be mindful of keeping their office if they were to reach a more controversial decision. In such an environment the system would quickly degenerate into one of decisions made to maintain the status quo, a situation that is not necessarily always in the best interests of the public.

In short, the whole question of training represents a delicate balancing act but, notwithstanding the force of any counter-argument to judicial training, there was sufficient disquiet over the attitude and competency of certain of the judiciary to prompt change. The findings of Lord Bridge in his *Report on Legal Education and Training* (1978) led directly to the establishment of the Judicial Studies Board in 1979 'to determine the principles on which judicial studies should be planned, to approve the proposed forms of the study programmes and to observe them in operation': Lord Chancellor's Department, 1998. It was a compromise solution that addressed both the need for some form of training and the need to maintain judicial independence. It was not constituted as an independent body but operated as part of the Lord Chancellor's Department and on a part-time basis with very limited resources. Originally it was responsible only for the full and part-time training of the Crown Court judiciary and arranged courses and seminars for trainee assistant recorders and new circuit judges. As the value of its work came to be appreciated more government funds were provided and it underwent considerable expansion in the mid-1980s. Most especially, in 1985 its role was expanded to include the training of full and part-time judiciary of the county courts, lay and stipendiary magistrates, judicial chairmen and members of tribunals.

During the 1990s there were renewed calls to improve judicial awareness of the needs of minority groups and the Board were the obvious body to carry out such a role. In 1991 an advisory committee on cases concerning members of ethnic minorities was established and from its work there arose a training programme aimed first at educating judges (and magistrates) on basic cultural differences of the main ethnic minority communities and then at identifying the areas that most commonly cause offence. The programme also involves sessions in racial awareness as part of the compulsory training and refresher courses for judges and magistrates. In 1996 the Board announced more spending for 'equal treatment' training designed to cover gender awareness, and sensitivity to unrepresented parties, witnesses, jurors, victims and their families, children and persons under physical and mental disability. Confidence in the work of the Board was confirmed in 1996 when it was given an independent budget and separated from the Lord Chancellor's Department; a major step given the fears prevalent at the time over the general erosion of judicial independence and the safeguarding of the rule of law following certain of Lord Chancellor Mackay's reforms. In the same year the Board was also granted a special budget of £1,050,000 by the Lord Chancellor's Department to spend on case management training in preparation for the civil procedure reforms stemming from the implementation of Lord Woolf's Report *Access to Justice* (1996) – the implementation date being 26 April 1999. Lord Chancellor Irvine, who took office in

1997, also appointed 30 civil judges to oversee this training. Whilst preparation for the Access to Justice Act 1999 may have been a major boost to the work of the Board, it has paled into near insignificance against the role that the Board has had to undertake to prepare the judiciary for their obligations under the Human Rights Act 1998 which came into force in October 2000. This has required a comprehensive training programme for judges, magistrates and tribunal members at a cost of some £4.5 million. The Lord Chancellor's Department has also provided judges with access (either through textbooks or information technology) to the judgments of the European Court of Human Rights.

In its general work, the Board now provides longer and more detailed courses of training and arranges seminars for judges of all levels on specific matters. Refresher seminars are organised for circuit judges and recorders to which newly appointed Queen's Bench Division judges are invited to attend. There remains, however, a reluctance to introduce too much 'education' and 'monitoring' in the fear that it might undermine the independence of the judiciary, and that it may lead to a professional career judiciary of the sort found in continental legal systems.

4.6 Alternative methods of selection for a judiciary

A 'career judiciary'

Reference has been made in sections above to the career-structured judiciary found in some of the civil law systems of mainland European countries. The basic idea of these is that certain lawyers are chosen at an early stage in their career to be trained for the job of being a judge. Unlike our judges, therefore, their training is specific to the work of a judge and they do not go through years of practice as general lawyers (eg advocates) before being appointed to the bench. All English judges, from the ranks of Lords of Appeal in Ordinary to county court judges, are at present usually chosen from the ranks of practising lawyers, mainly barristers but with a steadily increasing number of solicitors. Appointment will usually be to one of the lower courts with promotion to the higher courts/appellate courts.

The French have one of the most straightforward systems. Their judges do not practise as advocates at all but are immediately trained at a national Judges' College (the École Nationale de la Magistrature). Entrance is for postgraduate law students through competitive exams and interviews. Training at the college lasts for two years, during which the trainee judge receives a salary (in other countries training can last for up to six years!). Training involves courses on criminology, penology, procedural law, evidence, how to handle witnesses, psychology, ethnic awareness and so on. Exams are held in each subject. On graduating from the College the typical young French judge will start as an examining judge (a juge d'instruction) in criminal law in a small town, deciding whether there is sufficient evidence to prosecute and supervising the collection of evidence by the police. She/he will then preside over trials, possibly starting as a juvenile court judge. During tenure she/he must undergo compulsory continuous education involving refresher courses, often lasting at least a week for each course. Promotion is determined by relevant central government civil servants and is decided, according to vacancies, on the basis of experience, interests and wishes.

In the English legal system there have been such substantial improvements in the training of judges that some have argued we are moving closer to the establishment of a judicial training college and a career-structured judiciary. However, in 1996 Henry LJ, the head of the Judicial Studies Board, said that such developments did not represent the first steps towards the creation of such a college but rather were part of a gradualist approach designed to satisfy an independent-minded and critical clientele. Civil code legal systems like the French one do not sit in the same constitutional framework as our legal system. Our unwritten constitution relies on its own unique method of ensuring a separation of powers and a central part of the safeguarding of the rule of law is the independence of the judiciary both from the executive and from the legislature. Career-structured judiciary are effectively a part of the civil service and, as such, are not wholly independent from the executive. Nor are they wholly independent from the legislature and the way in which they carry out their judicial decision-making function is a reflection of this. Civil code law is written in very much more general terms than our Acts of Parliament. In their interpretation of these codes the judges enjoy a much higher level of discretion than our judges despite the introduction of a more purposive style of interpretation loosely based on European methods.

An elected judiciary

The United States uses appointment and election as two separate methods for selecting its judges. All federal judges are appointed by the President on the approval of the Senate which carries out any necessary investigation into a candidate's character and standing for the post. It has been suggested that our holders of high judicial office should be subjected to similar confirmation hearings conducted by, for example, a select committee of the House of Commons. Lord Chancellor Mackay expressed dislike for the notion of prior examination which he described as being a process conducted:

> '... to discover and analyse the previous opinions of the individual in detail. I question whether the standing of the judiciary in our country, or the public's confidence in it would be enhanced by such an enquiry, or whether any wider public interest would be served by it.'

All other US judges (eg state and local) are usually elected to office, either as a straight 'first time appointment' election or as an election to confirm their continuation in a post to which they were appointed for a given trial period. In the main it is the American Bar Association that carries out the most extensive investigation into a candidate's suitability for the post and this includes questioning the candidate as well as taking the opinions of judges, lawyers, academics and a wide range of other persons or bodies that may have something to say on the opinions held by the candidate or activities they have been involved in during their lives. Public examination of the candidate is also conducted by pressure groups and minority groups who have a vested interest in ensuring that any nominee holds the views that they prefer. All in all, a great deal of time, money and effort goes into producing evidence in favour, or against, any nominee and the entire process is politically charged in a way that does not pertain to the selection of the English judiciary. Lord Mackay took the view that 'The British people would not feel that this was a very satisfactory method of appointing the professional judiciary', and this does seem to be the majority view both of society in general and the legal profession in particular.

4.7 Removal and retirement

Judges of the High Court and above hold office during good behaviour subject to a power of removal by the Monarch on an address presented by both Houses of Parliament. This provision derives from the Act of Settlement 1701, and is now contained in the Supreme Court Act 1981.

Judges below High Court level (eg circuit judges and recorders) may be removed from office on the grounds of incapacity or misbehaviour by the Lord Chancellor, a role now performed by the Minister for Constitutional Affairs. Discipline is administered by the Minister usually through private letters of reprimand.

Resignation from the bench is unusual; in February 1998 Harman J resigned from the High Court bench following severe criticism from the Court of Appeal concerning his dilatory and negligent conduct in delivering judgment in a civil case.

It has sometimes been suggested that an independent 'judicial conduct tribunal' should be set up to supervise judicial standards and to advise the Minister on questions of discipline and removal.

The general retirement age for all judges is 70: s26 Judicial Pensions and Retirement Act 1993. The Minister has power under the 1993 Act to extend the service of circuit judges and recorders, a year at a time, up to the age of 75 if he considers it desirable in the public interest.

4.8 Lay magistrates (Justices of the Peace)

The relevant statute is the Justices of the Peace Act 1997, which consolidates earlier legislation.

Appointment of lay magistrates

Lay magistrates are appointed by the Minister for Constitutional Affairs on behalf of the Crown from people who have been put forward by local party political organisations, or by leading members of the community or by voluntary organisations, and those put forward are in general people of standing, generally with a record of good service to the community. Indeed, individuals may put themselves forward for consideration. The Minister is assisted by local advisory committees (about 94) and he attempts to maintain as far as possible a balance between the sexes, political parties, social classes and races.

The greatest difficulty in attempting to obtain magistrates representative of the community as a whole is that their services are unpaid, although they may receive allowances to cover travelling expenses, subsistence and financial loss occasioned by the performance of their duties.

There are few formal qualifications. On appointment a magistrate must be over 21 and (unless there are exceptional circumstances) below 65 (50 in the case of a juvenile bench) and must normally reside within 15 miles of the boundary of the Commission of the Peace to which he or she is appointed. There are no formal 'character' qualifications, although the following, among others, will not be accepted.

1. A person convicted of certain offences, or subject to certain court orders.
2. An undischarged bankrupt.
3. A serving member of the monarch's forces.
4. A member of the police service or the spouse of such a member.
5. A close relative of a person who is already a magistrate on the same bench.

In January 2004 there was a total of 29,705 Justices of the Peace in England and Wales. Of the total, 14,555 were men and 15,150 were women. During 2004, 1,002 men and 805 women were appointed Justices of the Peace.

During the summer of 1998 Lord Irvine revised the procedures for appointing lay magistrates. The reforms include the introduction of a clear job description for magistrates, and the six key qualities defining the personal suitability of candidates are declared to be: good character; understanding and communication; social awareness; maturity and sound temperament; sound judgment; and commitment and reliability. Lord Irvine urged the local advisory committees which recommend appointments to put forward suitable candidates who reflect the communities they serve in terms of gender, ethnic origin, occupation, geographical location and political persuasion.

Training of lay magistrates

A frequent criticism is that lay magistrates do not need to be legally qualified. However, all newly appointed magistrates undergo training under the supervision of the Judicial Studies Board. The objects of the training are to enable justices to understand their duties, to obtain sufficient knowledge of the law to follow normal cases, to acquire a working knowledge of the rules of evidence and to appreciate the nature and purpose of sentences. The first stage of training consists mainly in attending court as an observer, and instruction on the duties of a justice of the peace, on the practice and procedure in courts, and on the methods of punishment and of treatment. The second stage must be completed within 12 months of appointment and consists of further instruction and visits to certain penal institutions. Magistrates also undergo refresher training. Special training is given to those magistrates who deal with juvenile or family matters.

A new training programme was launched by Lord Irvine in the autumn of 1998. The new training involves 'hands on' practical experience (eg sitting in courts) and sessions in equality awareness. Experienced magistrates act as monitors on the new courses.

Removal and retirement

Magistrates are removable by the Minister for Constitutional Affairs for good cause (eg conviction of a serious offence). Lay magistrates retire at 70.

Immunity

Under s108 of the Courts and Legal Services Act 1990 no action lies against a Justice of the Peace (or a justice's clerk) in respect of any act or omission when acting in the execution of his duty and with respect to any matter within his jurisdiction, but an action will lie if the matter was not within his jurisdiction and it is proved that he acted in bad faith.

Functions of lay magistrates

These may be summarised as follows.

1. Issuing of warrants and summonses.
2. Granting and withholding bail.
3. Exercising summary jurisdiction.
4. Presiding over committal proceedings.
5. Matrimonial and guardianship jurisdiction (in the family proceedings court) and other limited civil jurisdiction.
6. Administrative functions (eg granting licence applications).
7. Juvenile jurisdiction. The youth court is not an independent court but is the magistrates' court sitting in a special capacity.
8. Administering oaths or taking affidavits for the purposes of an application for a grant of probate or letter of administration.

The magistrates' clerk

Lay magistrates can only sit if they have a qualified clerk. The clerk must advise the magistrates as to the law and practice, but he/she must not interfere with their decision and the decision is liable to be quashed by an order of certiorari if this is seen to happen: *R* v *Eccles Justices, ex parte Farrelly* (1992) The Times 17 June. The clerk, who must have a five-year magistrates' court qualification within the meaning of s71 of the Courts and Legal Services Act 1990 or then be or previously have been a justices' clerk, is a salaried official. He/she is a key figure in the magistrates' courts. It is important that the magistrates themselves must make the decisions, yet lay magistrates often need to call on the help of the clerk who brings points to their attention. The responsibilities of the magistrates' clerk also include the consideration of applications for legal aid in criminal cases.

4.9 District judges (formerly stipendiary magistrates)

In November 1999 the Lord Chancellor anounced that the title of 'stipendiary magistrate' was to be changed to 'district judge'. The term 'stipendiary' denoted that these were magistrates who were salaried and the title differentiated them from lay magistrates who are not. They must have a seven-year general qualification within s71 of the Courts and Legal Services Act 1990 and they are appointed by the Minister for Constitutional Affairs. Their salary is determined by the Home Secretary. Retirement is at 70, although the Minister may grant extensions up to 75 if he believes it to be in the public interest.

The system of full-time salaried magistrates was set up at the end of the eighteenth century to deal with defects in the administration of justice in London. The system was retained when it became apparent that they were needed in order for the system to cope with the ever-increasing workload of the magistrates' courts. Unlike the lay magistracy, they sit alone and do not require the assistance of a magistrates' clerk. Most large conurbations now have both types of magistrate and in 2004 there were 126 district judges. The magistrates' courts now undertake a vast quantity of work and at the same time as he announced the forthcoming change in their title the Lord Chancellor indicated his intention to appoint more district judges so as to cut the backlog of cases that have built up in criminal prosecutions. District judges are generally thought to be more efficient than lay magistrates in disposing of cases and also more independently minded when it comes to assessing evidence (it is often said that lay magistrates rely too much on the advice of their clerk and are too willing to believe police evidence). However, the cost of replacing all lay magistrates with district judges would be prohibitive and is not a realistic option.

5

The Jury System

5.1 Representation by society

5.2 Selection, empanelment and discharge of the jury

5.3 The use of the jury in civil cases

5.4 The majority verdict of the jury in criminal cases

5.5 The right to trial by jury in criminal cases

5.6 Jury deliberations

5.7 Alternatives to the jury system

5.8 Summary of the arguments for and against the jury system

5.1 Representation by society

The jury represents a microcosm of society and offers trial by one's equals. It is probably the most closely guarded tradition of our legal system. Moves for its reform are met with strong opposition but there is mounting reason for some form of change in the face of the growing body of evidence that juries are not only unpredictable and fallible but also wholly unsuitable for a some of the complex cases that they are called to hear. The notion of the jury as 'a little parliament' that represents a cross-section of society's views is falling to be dismissed as romantic myth. The discussions in this chapter will explore some of the reasons for this sea-change in thinking. It does, however, have to be emphasised at this early stage that there remains considerable support for the jury system and many believe that the decline in its use has gone far enough. Up until only about 150 years ago the vast majority of cases were tried by a jury. Today the jury operates in a minority of cases. Less than 1 per cent of civil cases are tried by jury. Of the 3 per cent of criminal cases for which jury trial is at present available, only about 1 per cent actually have their outcome determined by a jury because in the majority of cases the defendant pleads guilty on all or most counts.

The jury as the bulwark of our freedom

The right to be tried 'by one's peers' (ie equals) is an ancient tradition. For several centuries it has been cherished as an institution of utmost constitutional importance to be fiercely guarded as an inviolable right. The rhetoric sung in its praise has been almost unquestioning of the value of a lay element randomly introduced into the trial procedure to act as the sole judges of the facts. In the mid–eighteenth century Blackstone, a legal writer, described it as 'this sacred bulwark of our nation' and that basic sentiment has lodged itself at the heart of the British legal system with such tenacity that it seems almost unshakeable. Lord Denning, sitting as Master of the Rolls in *Ward* v *James* [1966] 1 QB 273, said:

> 'It has been the bulwark of our liberties too long for any of us to seek to alter it. Whenever a man is on trial for serious crime, or when in a civil case a man's honour or integrity is at stake, or when one or other party must be deliberately lying, then trial by jury has no equal.'

The notion of the jury as the bulwark of freedom in a democratic state runs through most of the views expressed in favour of the system. Blackstone viewed the jury as the barrier between the liberties of the people and the prerogative of the Crown and, in a more modern context, this translates as the jury being a 'little parliament' made up of ordinary citizens which acts as the ultimate counter-balance to the power of 'the establishment' and, therefore, 'the lamp that shows that freedom lives': per Lord Devlin.

The time-honoured notion is that the jury finds on its conscience. When this idea is combined with that of their role as preservers of freedom, the results can be quite startling. In *R* v *Kronlid and Others* (1996) The Times 31 July three women charged with criminal damage to a Hawk fighter plane that had been sold by the British government to the Indonesian government were found not guilty by the jury despite their admission that they had caused the damage. Their defence rested on the claim that by s3 of the Criminal Law Act 1967 it is lawful to commit a crime to prevent the commission of another crime by the use of 'such force as is reasonable in all the circumstances'. The crime they sought to prevent was the anticipated use of the plane by the Indonesian government as a weapon of genocide against the population of East Timor, which country they had annexed by force with much killing. The prosecution brought evidence that the British government had agreed the export licence only after receiving assurances that the plane would not be used in this way. The jury's unexpected acquittal of all three women has to be regarded as a statement of disapproval of the actions of the British government. Rather than vote on the evidence, they voted on their consciences which, it would appear, had told them that agreements motivated by commercial advantage made between governments are not necessarily to be trusted.

There are many other examples of this 'exercise of society's conscience' by juries. One that raised considerable controversy about the right of the jury to find in favour of the defendant in open defiance of the law was the acquittal of Clive Ponting, a civil servant who leaked official secrets to a journalist which exposed the fact that the British government had lied to Parliament over the circumstances surrounding the sinking of the Argentinian vessel, the *General Belgrano*, during the Falklands war. The jury would seem to have ignored, or completely misunderstood, the careful explanation given by McGowan J on what is meant by 'in the interests of the state', the defence raised by Ponting under the Official Secrets Act: *R v Ponting* [1985] Crim LR 318. A justifiable criticism of such unchecked freedom of the jury is that it is inconsistent. The year after the *Ponting* case a jury convicted a defendant whose moral outrage led her to leak official secrets to reveal the wrongdoings of a government department, even though the leak presented no threat to national security: *R v Tisdall* (1984) 6 Cr App R 155. Supporters of the jury's role as guardian against unfair laws and oppressive prosecutions tolerate, or perhaps turn a blind eye to, such inconsistency on the grounds that it is preferable to the imposition of laws that society (as represented by the jury) want re-written. In her article 'The Lamp that Shows that Freedom Lives – Is it Worth the Candle' [1991] Crim LR 740 Penny Darbyshire raises two objections to such a preference: 'First, in the absence of a reasoned decision, how do we know whether juries acquit out of sympathy of for some extraneous reason? Secondly, the argument ignores the potential for wrongful convictions in allowing the jury to re-write the law.'

Since judges are criticised for irrational decisions as to the law and inconsistencies in sentencing, it seems anomalous to sanction a body that can reach decisions on the facts on irrational grounds and rewrite the law at will. There is, nonetheless, strong support for the jury system voiced by people from all walks of society and it must be assumed that the jury's role as a conveyor of discontent in the subject matter of laws or rules of evidence forms a part of this endorsement.

Competency of the jury

The idea that 'Trial by jury is indeed the foundation of our free constitution; take that away, and the whole fabric will soon moulder into dust', as expressed by Lord Camden in the eighteenth century, is seen by many as being an over-sentimental view of the value of a group of lay persons selected at random and asked to hear matters on which they have no expertise. The winds of change have led society away from unfailing confidence in lay representation. Modern society believes in, and strives toward, things like equality, minority representation and a class-less society. The selection process for juries leaves doubt as to their representative character and inextricably entwined in this debate is the doubt about the competency of lay people to deal with some of the complex cases that now come before the courts.

It can be argued that the affairs of man are always complicated and that, relatively speaking, there is no difference in complexity as between our lives and those of former generations. The argument thus runs that if lay representation was a satisfactory process in the past, it is equally as satisfactory now. Those that disagree with this train of thought see things like our advances in forensic and medical knowledge and the complexity of events leading to serious frauds as resulting in evidence too complex to be comprehensible to anyone other than an expert in the field. Some support for this view can be found in cases indicating difficulties juries appear to have had in determining innocence or guilt. Notes sent by juries to the trial judge have indicated difficulties with determining the fine distinction between murder and manslaughter on the basis of abstruse psychological evidence, and difficulties with determining liability on the basis of complex technical evidence presented in defamation, personal injury and serious fraud cases.

The jury is seen as valuable counter-weight to the formal procedures of a trial and the technicalities of the rules of evidence. Supporters of the system claim that if it was not for the presence of a jury, evidence might not be so thoroughly examined and important information might get pushed aside by lawyers who have become case-hardened. It is certainly true that the need to present facts to the jury demands rigorous investigation on the part of the lawyers and the quantity of conflicting facts produced may be the deciding factor in casting doubt. On the other hand, of course, it is that quantity of conflicting information that serves to make jury trials all the more complex on their facts, and when the subject matter of the trial is already complex, as with defamation and serious fraud trials, the jury can get lost in all the evidence produced on their behalf.

Concern over the adequacy of a jury to hear complex cases mainly centres on their competence to understand evidence presented in serious fraud trials. In 1995 there was considerable controversy when a fraud trial heard at Newport Crown Court collapsed after six months at an estimated cost of £2 million when the trial judge, Crowther J, ruled that the evidence had become too unmanageable and too difficult for the jury to understand. The following year the unexpected acquittal of Ian and Kevin Maxwell in 1996 after a lengthy serious fraud trial at the Old Bailey provoked a similar outcry. They may, of course, have been correct verdicts but the public surprise with which they were received cannot be entirely ignored. There was open debate about whether the unmanageable quantity of complex and technical evidence presented during the trial was comprehensible only to experts in the field. It was felt by some that the jury had become so confused by the evidence that they felt bound to give the benefit of the doubt to the accused and acquit them. Hundreds of weighty documents crammed with complex financial data were presented to the jury in the Brent Walker trial in 1994 which ran for months and cost £5 million. The same was true for the seven-month long Guinness trials and Henry LJ, who presided over them, was prompted to state that 'Serious fraud is near the limit of criminal jurisprudence. There is a risk that a system designed for very different trials may be tested to destruction.'

So is this a good reason to abolish juries for complex trials, or indeed for any trial? Whilst there does appear to be strong evidence of the difficulties experienced by a group of 12 lay people to get at the truth of a complex issue presented to them on an adversarial basis, there is also evidence that this is mainly confined to cases of exceptional complexity. The majority of criminal cases turn upon the credibility of simpler evidence and the general view is that a typical jury probably is capable of reaching a fair result in such cases. Given that juries are now used only in a small part of the administration of criminal justice, there will have to be very good cause for them to be abolished altogether and what is known about their operation would not yet seem to have provided such cause.

Research conducted within the confines of the parameters allowed does reveal evidence of wrong or questionable verdicts, but the conclusions that may be drawn from them are conflicting. Statistics compiled by Baldwin and McConville (*Jury Trials* (1979)) found that some 25 per cent of acquittals and 5 per cent of convictions on a sample of 500 cases were questionable. McCabe and Purves (*The Jury at Work* (1972)) who worked with 'shadow juries' and sampled 173 jury acquittals, found that the majority of these could be attributed to a weak prosecution case, but that 9 per cent (15 cases) were reached in doubtful circumstances in that they denied the evidence on which they should have been based. Their conclusion, however, was that juries were diligent in following the evidence and putting aside their prejudices. This sits in sharp contrast with the view of Baldwin and McConville who concluded that there should be concern about the 'arbitrary and unpredictable business' of trial by jury for serious crimes. Notwithstanding results such as these, it has to be borne in mind that questionable acquittals may not be the result of confusion, sympathy for the defendant or antipathy for the victim, but based on the juries' perception of the high burden of proof in criminal cases and their desire to carry out their duty with fairness and justice.

At the end of the day, it is perhaps the fact that each juror swears an oath to give a true verdict according to the evidence that provides the best argument to any justification of irrational decision-making, perverse verdicts, wrongful convictions or acquittals, and verdicts based on some notion of society's conscience. They are instructed to find on the evidence and not on other sources that they choose to include at will.

The future of the jury system

Despite evidence that criticisms of the jury are founded, calls for the total abolition of the jury system meets with opposition bordering on the emotional. This was noted by the Faulks Committee on Defamation (1975), which recommended the retention of juries for defamation cases, and it attributed such emotional support as deriving 'from the undoubted value of juries in serious criminal cases where they stand between the prosecuting authority and the citizen': para 496 of the Report. The criminal case for which blind support starts to be called in question is serious fraud and the Roskill Committee on Fraud Trials (1986) presented a slightly less charitable view in their observation at para 8.21 that 'Society appears to have an attachment to jury trial which is emotional or sentimental rather than logical'. Logic is struggling to the fore and there is increased endeavour to replace the jury in certain cases with an alternative that continues to meet the demand of being representative of the public voice, for example, panels made up of lay experts either to sit instead of the jury or to advise the traditional jury.

It would seem that the 'overwhelming evidence' in favour of retention of the jury system found by the Report of the Royal Commission on Criminal Justice in 1993, which advised against the abolition of the traditional jury, is not going to disappear lightly and that the jury still has a place in the scheme of things. Its survival, however, is likely to depend on how well the system can be adapted to meet new criteria. Jury trials are costly and add to the length of time taken to hear the case, which in turn contributes to the unacceptable delays in the system of justice that the government is striving to combat. Whilst it may be generally accepted that the jury system is a fundamental and deeply entrenched constitutional right that should be reformed or replaced only for very good cause, the winds of change are blowing in and, for criminal cases, the cost to the taxpayer may yet be that 'very good cause'.

5.2 Selection, empanelment and discharge of the jury

Qualification for service

Random selection is carried out by computer and relies on drawing names from local electoral registers. Any person between the ages of 18 and 70, who is on the electoral register and has been ordinarily resident within the United Kingdom for at least five years since the age of 13, is qualified for jury service.

Panels of potential jurors for the various cases are drawn up by an officer of the court and summoned to attend. These lists may contain as many as 150 names. The first erosion of the random selection principle occurs with the reduction of these numbers through disqualification, ineligibility, excusals and deferment.

1. Schedule 1, Pt 1 of the Juries 1974 Act, as amended by the Juries (Disqualifications) Act 1984, classed four categories of people as ineligible for jury service: the judiciary, members of the legal profession and other persons connected with the administration of justice (eg in prisons, the probation service, the Crown Prosecution Service), members of the clergy or religious orders and the mentally ill. The Criminal Justice Act 2003 has drastically reduced the classes of ineligible jurors to just the mentally ill.
2. Schedule 1, Pt II of the 1974 Act, as amended, disqualifies any person who has been sentenced to a term of imprisonment or custody, including youth custody, of five years or more. Also disqualified are persons who, within the last ten years, have served a sentence, or had a suspended sentence imposed on them, have been placed on probation or had a community service order made against them. To this has been added persons on bail in criminal proceedings: s40 Criminal Justice and Public Order Act 1994. Crimes punishable by fines do not affect eligibility to serve as a juror. The period of disqualification depends on the

type of sentence, its length and how recently it was made. However, imprisonment for a term of over five years results in disqualification for life.

3. Under ss8 and 9 and Sch 1, Pt III of the 1974 Act, eligible persons may claim to be excused as of right if they have more pressing duties than jury service. This category includes members of the medical professions, members of armed forces and Members of Parliament. In addition, jurors between 65 and 70 are excused if they do not wish to sit upon the jury and, under s42 Criminal Justice and Public Order Act 1994, a practising member of a religious society or order whose beliefs are incompatible with jury service may be excused.

4. Section 9B, as inserted by s41 of the Criminal Justice and Public Order Act 1994, and s10 provide for circumstances in which there may be doubt as to the capacity of a juror to serve on account of physical disability or insufficient understanding of English. Such a person is brought before the judge who must then determine whether or not the person should act as a juror. The presumption is that a person should serve and the judge must affirm the jury summons unless she/he is satisfied that the person will not be able to act effectively as a juror. There have been a number of instances where profoundly deaf persons have been discharged on the grounds that the signer they rely on to follow the proceedings is not permitted to retire with the jury to the jury room. By law only 12 persons are allowed in the jury room: see *Re Osman* [1995] 1 WLR 1327.

5. Under s120 Criminal Justice Act 1988 the court has a discretion to defer jury service if the person summoned shows good reason, eg personal involvement with the case, childcare problems, a previously booked holiday, etc. Deferral means that their duty to sit on a jury is put off to a later time. In some cases they may be released from jury service, for example, in *R* v *Guildford Crown Court, ex parte Siderfin* [1989] 3 All ER 73 a juror was excused from service on the basis of a conscientious objection to serving on a jury.

Jury service is a public duty and it is compulsory for all those not disqualified, ineligible or excused to attend. Failure to attend on the specified date and unfitness for service through drink or drugs are contempt of court and punishable by a fine.

The initial process of exceptions, excusals and disqualification is left with the individual who is required to truthfully declare their disqualification or ineligibility. Thereafter primary responsibility to ensure that jurors are eligible and competent to serve is with the appropriate court officer and, ultimately, the judge. Any party to the proceedings is entitled to inspect the list of potential panel members that is first drawn up. Such inspection provides only the names and addresses of the listed panel. In practical terms, therefore, it is the prosecution, with its state resources, that is able to make any real use of the list and this advantage to the prosecution is addressed by the tight restrictions placed on investigations into a juror's background that can be undertaken by the Crown (see *Jury vetting*, below). There is a fairly wide permission to check on previous convictions of a juror and it is expected that such checks will become automatic when there are centrally held computer records of criminal convictions.

Once selected, a juror will receive a set of notes explaining the functions of a juror and the procedure of the jury service. Since April 1996, everyone called for jury service is shown a 17-minute video about the functions of a juror which includes information about eligibility requirements and courtroom procedures.

Jury vetting

Vetting is a process undertaken by the police on behalf of the Crown in which the background of potential jurors is checked to ensure that they are 'sound' (ie suitable in terms of political beliefs, etc) to decide a particular case. The practice of vetting first became public in an official secrets trial in 1978 when it was discovered that a little known set of guidelines laid down by the Attorney-General which, it turned out, had been in use since 1974, had been used by the prosecution to check the 'soundness' of the jurors on the panel list in terms of their loyalty to the state, ie that they did not hold strong anti-establishment political beliefs. A new trial was ordered and there was considerable hue and cry over the whole affair as a result of which new guidelines were issued. These have been subsequently revised and the current guidelines are published as *Practice Note (Attorney-General's Guidelines on Jury Checks)* [1988] 3 All ER 1086.

Vetting can be viewed as the most invidious of the methods used to shape the constitution of a particular jury and the guidelines make it clear that in all ordinary cases jurors should be selected at random from the panel and that disqualification should be on the grounds set out in the 1974 Act or by challenge for cause in open court. It is only in the two special cases identified in the guidelines that the prosecution has a right to check on a juror's background, namely:

1. cases where national security is involved and evidence might be heard in camera (ie heard privately with public and press excluded), and there is a danger that the juror, either voluntarily because of political beliefs or involuntarily under pressure, might disclose sensitive information given in camera; and
2. cases where a terrorist offence is alleged and the juror holds extreme political views likely to prevent him/her from being impartial or lead to him/her putting undue pressure on other jurors.

The guidelines lay down the procedure for the vetting. Clause 6 envisages that in most cases there will only be a need for a 'limited investigation of the panel' by checking police criminal records and that further checks should only need to resort to the records of police Special Branch. These investigations are carried out by the police. It is only in cases of national security that investigation may additionally involve the security services and checks into records held by them. The checking of police Special Branch records and security service records have to be 'authorised checks', ie they require the personal authority of the Attorney-General on the application of the Director of Public Prosecutions. It is the Director of Public Prosecutions who decides what information ought to be brought to the attention of the prosecuting counsel. The Crown's right of stand by (see below) of a juror subject to an authorised check can be exercised only with the authority of the Attorney-General and the defence is not informed of the reasons for stand by. Other than this, the defence will be given an indication of why a juror may be inimical to the interests of the prosecution case.

The trial judge also has a discretion to order a security check on a jury during a trial but he must do so only after informing both prosecution and defence of such intention: *R v Obellim* [1997] 1 Cr App R 355.

There has been much discussion about the propriety of jury vetting. In *R v Sheffield Crown Court, ex parte Brownlow* [1980] QB 530 Denning and Shaw LJJ sitting in the Court of Appeal expressed opinion, obiter dicta, that jury vetting in all its forms was constitutionally wrong since it was not provided for by legislation, eg the Juries Act 1974, and was contrary to the principle of random selection. However, the Court of Appeal subsequently declared that vetting by means of checking criminal records was lawful on the ground that it was necessary in the public interest to ensure, inter alia, that disqualified persons did not sit on juries: *R v Mason* [1981] QB 881. Recommendations of the Association of Chief Police Officers are annexed to the Attorney-General's 1988 guidelines which make recommendations in the light of the decision in *R v Mason*, and these include checks where it is believed that in a previous related abortive trial an attempt was made to interfere with a juror or jurors.

Empanelment of the jury: challenge for cause

Those that are left from the panel of potential jurors as eligible for service after disqualification and excusals have been determined are allocated to an actual jury by means of a ballot conducted in open court which comprises shuffling cards with their names on and selecting the first 12 names called out. These 12 people will be sworn in unless there are any challenges.

Challenging represents another modification of the principle of random selection, though it is now less of problem in this respect since the abolition in 1988 of the defence right to 'peremptory' challenges (ie challenges without giving reasons). Hitherto, defence counsel did have a limited opportunity to 'pack' the jury in their favour in that they could object to up to three potential jury members without showing cause. Despite considerable opposition from civil liberties groups, the right was abolished by s118(1) of the Criminal Justice Act 1988 on the recommendation of the Roskill Committee on Fraud Trials which condemned it as interfering with the random selection process. In practice it was only really a problem in cases involving several defendants who could combine their rights to peremptory challenge.

Consequently, both the prosecution and the defence may only 'challenge for cause' (ie state good reasons for a challenge), and such a challenge is heard by the trial judge either 'in camera' (ie the courtroom is cleared of jurors, members of the public and the press) or in chambers: s118(2) of the 1988 Act.

A challenge for cause can be made either to the whole panel, though this is rare, or to an individual juror and it must be made on one (or more) of the three grounds under s12(4) of the 1974 Act:

1. that the juror is not qualified to serve;
2. that the juror is biased and proof of actual bias is available;
3. that the juror may be reasonably suspected of bias, ie there is apparent bias.

The first ground may be established as a result of jury vetting (see above). Since jurors cannot be questioned prior to a challenge, the opportunity to establish much of a cause for grounds (2) or (3) is seriously lessened. Ground (2) will be established if the juror has had actual dealings with the defendant, or has lost money or property as a result of the defendants actions, or has been involved in matters to do with the case in some other way. Establishing cause for the third ground is obviously the most difficult of all the challenges for cause. The test is one of 'real danger of bias' and this was laid down by the House of Lords in *R* v *Gough* [1993] 2 WLR 883 which was an appeal to have a conviction set aside on the grounds of injustice by reason of bias. One of the jurors on a conspiracy to commit robbery case discovered after conviction and sentence that he lived next door to the brother of the accused with whom the accused had conspired. The Court of Appeal decided that there was no danger that the accused might not have had a fair trial and this was upheld by the House of Lords, which stated that the correct test to adopt in deciding whether a decision should be set aside on the grounds of alleged bias is whether there was a real danger of injustice having occurred as a result of the alleged bias.

Empanelment of the jury: stand by

The prosecution, on behalf of the Crown, has a special right to 'stand by' a member of the jury panel, ie exclude that juror who is then held in reserve and used only if no other members of the jury panel remain available for jury service at the end of the challenges (which is most unlikely to happen since the abolition of peremptory challenges brought by the defence).

Stand by is not based on cause in that no reason need be given, and can be exercised by the prosecution in addition to their right to challenge for cause. This imbalance of rights was recognised by the Roskill Committee which recommended that if the defence rights to peremptory challenge were abolished then the prosecution's right to stand by should also be abolished. This was not done and the 1988 Act made no reference to the stand by procedure. The wholly unreasonable advantage that this gave to the prosecution was eventually addressed by *Practice Note* [1988] 3 All ER 1086 issued by the Attorney-General which states two grounds on which it is proper for the Crown to exercise its power to stand by a juror.

1. If a vetting approved by the Attorney-General reveals information justifying the concern that a juror may be a security risk, the Attorney-General may authorise the use of the stand by procedure (see further under *Jury vetting*, above).
2. The prosecution may exercise the right to stand by where a person who is about to be sworn in is manifestly unsuitable to act as a juror in the case and the defence agrees that the exercise of the right to stand by would be appropriate.

Discharge of the jury or a juror

The jury will be discharged when it has given its verdict but there are certain circumstances when the trial judge may discharge the whole jury or any individual juror during the course of the trial.

For criminal trials the rule is that the jury must not fall below nine persons. Accordingly, the trial judge has discretion to allow the trial to continue if up to three members are discharged, eg on compassionate grounds because of the death of a close relative, because they fall ill, 'or for any other reason': s16(1) of the Juries Act 1974.

If it is accidentally disclosed that the accused has a criminal record, the whole jury will be discharged since this would be prejudicial to the defence case. In such a case trial will proceed again and usually with a new jury.

It is not necessary that the jury be prevented from separating (eg going home at night), either before or after the judge has given his summing-up: s13 of the Juries Act 1974, as amended by s43 of the Criminal Justice and Public Order Act 1994. If the jury is instructed not to separate after the summing-up has been given by the judge and one juror does separate, it may not be necessary to discharge the whole jury: see *R* v *Chandler* (1992) The Times 16 April, where one juror separated himself from the rest for about 15 minutes. In *R* v *Knott* (1992) The Times 6 February the jury was discharged when one member caused criminal damage at the hotel the jury were staying at overnight.

Where in the course of a trial the judge becomes aware of friction or dissension amongst the jury as whole, the whole jury should be questioned in open court through their foreman to ascertain whether, as a body, it anticipates bringing in a true verdict according to the evidence. It is a matter for the judge's exercise of discretion as to whether he discharges the whole jury, or whether he discharges individual jurors up to three in number: *R* v *Orgles* [1993] 4 All ER 533.

Since the passing of the Human Rights Act 1998 there has been some challenging of this judicial discretion in respect of allegation of racial bias of jurors. In *Gregory* v *United Kingdom* (1998) 25 EHRR 577 the European Court of Human Rights decided that the issuing of a strong, clear and carefully worded warning to the jury that they must decide the case on the evidence alone and ignore all personal prejudice was sufficient, in the circumstances, to deal with the situation of a request that one juror be discharged for racial bias.

An example of circumstances that do require the discharge of a juror or the jury as a whole can be found in *Sander* v *United Kingdom* Application No 34129/96 (2000) The Times 12 May. One juror informed the court that other jurors were making racist jokes and passing racist remarks. The trial judge asked the whole jury to consider whether each of them was able to try the case according to the evidence and not their prejudices. He decided not to discharge the jury on the basis of the receipt of a written confirmation of their assurance signed by the whole jury, including the juror who had raised the matter in the first place. The claimant was found guilty of conspiracy to defraud but his co-accused, who was also Asian, was acquitted. The claimant sought to argue that he had been denied the right to a fair trial within the meaning of art 6 of the European Convention on Human Rights on the grounds that the trial judge should not have disclosed to the whole jury the details of the information received from the juror, and that the whole jury should have been dismissed. The Court of Appeal dismissed the appeal on the grounds that in the circumstances there was no real risk of bias and that it was satisfied that the conviction was safe.

The European Court of Human Rights, in recognition that it was the policy of the European Convention on Human Rights to robustly combat racism throughout all Member States, held that there had been a violation of art 6 of the Convention. The relevant test was that any court must be impartial from both a subjective and an objective point of view. Thus, although on balance there was insufficient evidence to conclude that any juror was in fact racist (the subjective test), from the objective point of view there were legitimate doubts that the trial was heard by an impartial jury. The jury should have been dismissed and the claimant had been denied a fair trial. The Court stated that the case was decided on its facts and in reaching this conclusion they took a number of factors into consideration. These included the fact that racist jokes had been made in the context of court proceedings, the fact that an open admission of racism could not easily be expected in court, and the fact that there was an inconsistency in the actions of the juror who raised the concern and subsequently signed a joint statement refuting it. In the opinion of the Court these all led to a reasonable impression that racism on the part of the jury could not be dispelled. The decision is an important precedent for the application of s2 of the Human Rights Act 1998 in the UK, and it has been reported (The Times 10 October 2000) that following the *Sander* decision, a whole jury was dismissed and a retrial ordered at a cost of £45,000 on evidence that a juror had passed a racist remark.

The principle of random selection

The concept that the accused is to be tried by his/her equals finds expression in the idea that a jury must be representative of ordinary society. This does not lead to the conclusion that the jury must be representative of the individual. There is strong opposition to what is known as 'packing' juries with jurors of the same ethnic origin, social class or political persuasion as the accused. The process of 'random selection' of juries is intended to prevent this but it does not guarantee that the jury will constitute a valuable cross-section of society, nor even that it will produce a jury suitable to act as arbiters of fact in the particular case.

The first question that has to be asked is whether 'random' selection can produce a 'representative' jury. If something is random it is, by definition, going to produce any sort of result. There is no reason why it should not eventually produce a potential panel comprised entirely of white male Conservative voters, or any other such unrepresentative list. The fact that the system has to allow challenge for cause and stand by is proof in itself that random selection does not always create the type of representative jury that society desires.

The second question is whether a general cross-section of the public is in any case what is needed to hear some of the actions brought before the courts. Serious fraud trials stand out in this category but they are not alone. All the serious crimes and a good quantity of civil actions brought in the High Court have a tendency to evidence that is inter-laced with complex issues, the presentation of which lasts for weeks rather than days and would be capable of mentally exhausting a panel of experts in the field, let alone a lay person with little experience of day-long intensive deliberation.

When it comes to complex trials that may last six months or more, requests from individuals who wish to be excused from service by reason of employment, booked holidays and so on, are more favourably looked on and the outcome is a jury chosen because they are available rather than from a general cross-section of society. Lord Donaldson, a former Master of the Rolls, commented in a letter to *The Times* in 1996, on the inevitably of a jury selected to hear a serious fraud case by this process being made up of those 'who would not otherwise be more gainfully occupied' and as such 'wholly unrepresentative'. It has been suggested that a compensation scheme be introduced whereby employers and employees who suffer disruption as a result of long jury service and others who have to suffer inconvenience, for example, the cancellation of a booked holiday, would be paid some compensation by the state. Attention could then be switched to giving a traditional jury considerable guidance in the complex aspects of evidence without undue concern over the extent to which this lengthened the trial. Since trials already cost amounts running into hundreds of thousands of pounds, this is not a desirable solution as regards the litigants. Given the present pressure on funding that already exists in the provision of the whole system of justice, it is unlikely that such a scheme, or at least one of any effectiveness in terms of compensation paid, will be introduced.

Implicit in Lord Donaldson's criticism is the view that a jury selected from those who are left may lack sufficient intellect to understand the evidence, as well as possibly lack responsibility to deliver an objective and carefully considered verdict. Another former Master of the Rolls, Lord Denning, in his book *What Next in the Law* (1982) at pp70–78, similarly argued that random selection can produce 'irresponsible' jurors and that prospective jurors ought to be interviewed to assess their suitability and even required to produce character references. So far, the

English legal system has resisted all attempts to introduce such selection measures. The American system, by contrast, allows potential jurors to be cross-examined by each side for weeks prior to the trial, but the English legal system has so far resisted all calls to employ formal interviews, tests or questions to determine the suitability of juries.

The trial judge does have some discretion to allow some questioning of jurors during empanelment but this is usually reserved for cases of political sensitivity. In ordinary cases judges are reluctant to permit questioning of jurors to elicit bias. For example, in *R* v *Andrews* (1998) The Times 15 October the defence requested that a questionnaire be put to the potential jurors to establish whether they had been affected by substantial adverse publicity concerning the accused prior to the trial. The Court of Appeal upheld the trial judge's decision to refuse this request on the ground that such questioning was of doubtful efficacy and might be counter-productive in bringing the attention of the juror to prejudicial matters. It was said that questioning of potential jurors, whether orally or by use of a questionnaire, was to be avoided save in the most exceptional circumstances, such as where it was alleged that potential jurors might have a direct interest in the case (eg by having lost money in transactions which formed the basis of the trial). The Court maintained the view that juries have to be trusted to be faithful to their oaths to return true verdicts in accordance with the evidence.

Others have expressed concern about the under-representation of ethnic minorities on juries even in areas where there are sizeable numbers of minority households. It has been argued that it is unfair if a black defendant is faced with an all-white jury: see further Herbert 'Racism, Impartiality and Juries' [1995] NLJ 1138. Following the decision in *R* v *Ford* [1989] 3 WLR 762, it would appear that the trial judge is not required as a matter of fairness to ensure a racially balanced jury even in cases with sensitive racial overtones. The Royal Commission on Criminal Justice (1993) Cmnd 2263 (the Runciman Report) recommended that in exceptional circumstances cases either side should be able to apply to the trial judge to ensure the selection of a jury containing up to three people from ethnic minority communities, with one or more of this group of three coming from the same ethnic minority as the accused or the victim of the crime if either side should so request. However, any move towards race quotas on juries has so far been resisted by the senior judiciary on the ground that they would seriously undermine the principle of random selection which ensures a trial by one's equals, regardless of race, rather than by one's racial group.

It may be that the answer to these problem lies not in 'packing' a jury with members as desired by the prosecution and/or the defence but rather in ensuring that random selection is carried out in such a way as to reflect accurately the local population. Electoral registers do not always provide a true record of all persons who would be eligible for jury service. People who move around a lot, for their work or because they are students, for example, may not appear on the electoral register of the place they are currently living in, and a number of people for various reasons, deliberately avoid being on the registers by failing to return their electoral forms. Alternative methods lie in other data systems such as social security numbers or driving numbers which could be used to supplement the electoral register. These have not been seriously considered and the Runciman Report in 1993 merely suggested that every endeavour be made to ensure the accuracy of the local electoral registers. The Criminal Justice Act 2003 provides for the wider involvement of the community as a whole in jury service.

5.3 The use of the jury in civil cases

The erosion of the use of juries in civil cases started in the mid-nineteenth century. Prior to that most civil cases were tried by juries. Statutory limitation of cases that could be tried by jury was first introduced in 1933 and by the mid-twentieth century it was more common for an action to be heard by a judge alone than by jury. Much of this decline has been due to the complexity of issues involved in High Court civil actions and the quantity of highly complex technical data that is presented. In these circumstances, trial by jury becomes very lengthy and they are in any case not suitable actions to be heard before a jury comprising lay people selected at random.

The right to a jury in civil cases

The right to a jury trial in the Queen's Bench Division is now provided for by s69 of the Supreme Court Act 1981. Under s69(1) the right is limited to four types of cases: fraud, defamation, malicious prosecution and false imprisonment. The Defamation Act 1996 has since abolished trial by jury for defamation claims of £10,000 or less. The right under s69(1) is not 'absolute'. It is qualified by the discretion of the court to deny the claim for jury trial if it is of the opinion that the trial requires 'prolonged examination of documents or accounts or any scientific or local investigation which cannot conveniently be made with a jury'.

For all other cases s69(3) gives the trial judge a discretion to order a jury trial if he thinks fit, eg because of public interest considerations. There is, however, a presumption against jury trial, though the similarity of any other tort for which a jury trial is requested to any of the torts listed in s69(1) is not a factor to be taken into account in the exercise of judicial discretion: *Racz* v *Home Office* [1994] 2 WLR 23 (HL). In *Ward* v *James* [1966] 1 QB 273; [1965] 1 All ER 563 the Court of Appeal held that the exercise of judicial discretion in these cases is for 'special cases' and to be exercised only in 'exceptional circumstances'.

The majority of civil actions brought in the Queen's Bench Division are for damages for personal injury, which fall under s69(3). The nature of the scientific and technical evidence produced in these claims usually serves to give the judge good reason for refusing to order trial by jury. In *H* v *Ministry of Defence* [1991] 2

WLR 1192 it was held that the issues of law and evidence involved were too complex for a jury to assess damages on a rational basis. Similarly, in *Singh* v *London Underground* (1990) The Independent 25 April, a case involving a claim for personal injuries sustained in the fire at Kings Cross underground station, the court found that the technical issues in combination with the wide issues involved in the case were unsuitable for trial by a jury.

There was much criticism of the inclusion of defamation in the s69(1) category of cases. They are notorious not only for the length of time that it takes to hear the action before a jury but also for the level of award that juries make in them: see further below. In 1975 the arguments for the complete abolition of juries in defamation cases was rejected by the Faulks Committee on Defamation but the Committee did recommend that they should be subject to the same judicial discretion as all other civil cases.

A jury of eight persons may sit in county court trials and a jury of 12 persons in High Court trials. For both types of trial it is comparatively rare for there to be a request for trial by jury, even when the right is available, since costs must be paid by the losing party and litigants are, not unnaturally, reluctant to take on the risk of the escalating costs of a lengthy jury trial. The combined effect of this and the statutory limitations is that less than 1 per cent of civil cases are now tried by jury.

Assessment of compensation in civil cases

When a civil jury sits in a case it has the function of determining liability and, if finding in favour of the claimant, the task of assessing compensation. In recent years concern has been expressed over an apparent tendency by juries to award very large sums of compensation, particularly against newspapers in defamation cases and against police in false imprisonment and malicious prosecution trials. Sums used to be in thousands and there was concern when they went to being tens of thousands: they can now be in millions. A right of appeal against such awards has been provided by statute. Section 8 of the Courts and Legal Services Act 1990 provides that the Court of Appeal may set aside an award of damages by a jury which the Court regards as excessive (or inadequate) and may substitute such sum as appears to the court to be proper. This power has been interpreted so as to be exercised consistently with art 10 of the European Convention on Human Rights, which declares the need to safeguard freedom of expression. In *Rantzen* v *Mirror Group Newspapers* [1993] 3 WLR 953 the Court of Appeal reduced a jury's award of libel damages from £250,000 to £110,000 on the ground that the former sum was excessive and inhibited press freedom. Similarly, in *Sutcliffe* v *Pressdram Ltd* [1990] 1 All ER 269 the Court of Appeal stated that it would reassess the damages of £600,000 awarded to the wife of Peter Sutcliffe, the serial killer convicted for the murder of a number of prostitutes, but this became unnecessary when she separately settled for £60,000.

In *Ward* v *James* [1966] 1 QB 273; [1965] 1 All ER 563 the Court of Appeal held that trial judges should not give any specific guidance to juries on appropriate sums in particular cases. As a result trial judges were deterred from offering any guidance to juries on how to assess adequate and reasonable compensation. A change of practice occurred in *John* v *Mirror Group Newspapers Ltd* [1996] 2 All ER 35. In this case the Court of Appeal, in reducing a compensation award for defamation, said that trial judges would be able in future to provide guidance to defamation juries in the way that they assessed damages. Sir Thomas Bingham MR (as he then was) said that, without such guidance, the jury 'were in the position of sheep loosed on an unfenced common, with no shepherd'. He added that giving guidance to a jury would not undermine its constitutional position but rather buttress its constitutional role by rendering jury proceedings more rational and so more acceptable to public opinion. The principle laid down in *John* v *Mirror Group Newspapers Ltd* has since been extended to trials involving the assessment of compensatory and exemplary damages for false imprisonment, malicious prosecution and consequential torts: see *Thompson* v *Commissioner of Police of the Metropolis* [1977] 2 All ER 762. However, the Faulks Committee on Defamation 1975 shared the concern expressed by the Court of Appeal in *Ward* v *James*, above, as to the suitability of juries to determine the level of damages awarded and recommended that for defamation cases the function of the jury should be limited to deciding issues of liability, leaving the assessment of damages to the judge. The call for a reform of this type is likely to be strengthened if juries continue to award damages that are considerably higher than that expected by the court. It is interesting that the Court of Appeal took the step of overturning the very high award for libel given by a jury to Bruce Grobbelaar, the former professional footballer, on the grounds that the jury's decision was 'perverse' and inconsistent with the evidence: *Grobbelaar* v *News Group Newspapers Ltd* [2001] 2 All ER 437. Whilst many will welcome this as being a sensible decision there are those that will not and will view it as a serious erosion of the jury system.

5.4 The majority verdict of the jury in criminal cases

The jury in criminal cases comprises 12 persons. They hear trials on indictment brought in the Crown Court and their function is to determine the guilt or innocence of the accused on the basis of the factual evidence presented in court. The trial judge will instruct the jury to try to reach a unanimous verdict, but if the jury cannot agree after a reasonable period of deliberation the judge may then direct them on a majority verdict: s17 Juries Act 1974.

It can be that jurors are discharged: see further section 5.2 above. Where the jury comprises 11 members the judge may accept a majority verdict of ten members. If there are ten jurors, nine must agree and if the jury comprises only nine people, it must reach a unanimous verdict.

By s17(3) of the 1974 Act, the court may only accept a majority verdict of guilty if the foreman of the jury states in open court the numbers who agreed on and dissented from the verdict. This requirement is mandatory but the discharge of a jury is not a bar to the rectification of a verdict so as to comply with s17(3): *R* v *Maloney (Peter James)* (1996) The Times 25 March (CA).

The majority verdict is intended to overcome the problem of one juror with an intractable view holding out against the rest and lessens the need for an expensive retrial. It can be argued that justice must be done to protect the innocent even if that means extra cost and that if one juror has doubt then there must be a need for the others to reassess the evidence. Financial considerations, however, can equally be argued to be in the public interest and in any event the majority verdict is justifiable on the grounds that it thwarts a juror with extremist views and helps to prevent 'jury nobbling', ie undue pressure being put on a juror(s) to vote in a particular way. Intimidation of jurors and witnesses is an offence under s54 of the Criminal Procedure and Investigations Act 1996 and the High Court has the power to set aside an acquittal and to order a retrial if it is in the interests of justice to do so. Intimidation can be by threat of physical or financial harm: s51.

5.5 The right to trial by jury in criminal cases

The overwhelming majority of criminal cases are dealt with under the summary jurisdiction of the magistrates' courts for which there is no jury. For those that are heard on indictment in the Crown Court, the majority need no jury because the defendant pleads guilty on all counts. There are then the cases in which the trial judge directs the jury to acquit, so the final proportion of cases in which a jury actually decides the outcome of the case is about 1 per cent.

There is little argument that this 1 per cent should be tried by jury, save for the concerns for the use of the jury in serious fraud cases, but there is an argument that they are not required for the other cases, most of which are those 'triable either way'. The Criminal Justice Act 2003 provides for a defendant's right to trial by jury to be restricted where there is a large risk of interference with the jury.

Serious fraud cases

As mentioned above (section 5.1), concern over the adequacy of a jury to hear complex cases mainly centres on their competence to understand evidence presented in serious fraud trials. The acquittal of Ian and Kevin Maxwell in 1996 after a lengthy serious fraud trial at the Old Bailey highlighted a number of the reasons for this concern. They may, of course, have been correct verdicts but the public surprise with which they were received cannot be entirely ignored. There was open debate about whether the unmanageable quantity of complex and technical evidence presented during the trial was comprehensible only to experts in the field.

In 1998 the government invited discussion of four proposals to reform the use of the jury in serious fraud cases.

1. Abolition of the jury and its replacement with a special tribunal composed of a trained judge and two specialist members who would have expertise in commercial affairs.
2. Abolition of the jury and its replacement with a trained single judge or panel of trained judges, sitting with or without commercial advisors.
3. Retaining jury trial but restricting the role of the jury to issues of dishonesty, with a single trial judge making all other decisions.
4. Replacing the traditional jury with a special jury selected by qualifications or tests or who could demonstrate specialist knowledge (eg City of London accountants and auditors).

No action has yet been taken but the proposals represent a major step forward in thinking. It is felt by many that expert assessors, rather than lay people selected at random, are the proper panel to assess complicated evidence, ask relevant and searching questions and generally perform the inquisitorial function that is required for an adversarial trial. The proposals reflect recommendations made in the Roskill Report on Fraud Trials in 1986 which recommended that the jury should be replaced by a panel of judges and professional assessors. Under this recommendation, serious fraud cases would be decided by the trial judge with the help of a panel of expert assessors such as accountants and auditors.

5.6 Jury deliberations

The trial judge's directions

It is not necessary that the jury be prevented from separating (eg going home at night) after the judge has given his summing-up: s13 of the Juries Act 1974, as amended by s43 of the Criminal Justice and Public Order Act 1994. Clearly, if the jury does separate there is a danger that a jury might be influenced by outside events or pressures and hence the trial judge must give appropriate warnings to a jury who are to separate prior to reaching their verdict. In *R* v *Oliver* (1995) The Times 6 December, the court said that the trial judges' directions to a jury who were about to separate should include the following points:

1. that the jury must decide the case on the evidence and the arguments that they had seen or heard in court and not on anything they might have seen or heard or that they might see or hear outside the court room;
2. that the evidence had been completed and that it would be wrong for any juror to seek for or to receive further evidence or information of any sort about the case;
3. that the jury must not talk to anyone about the case save to other members of the jury and then only when they were debating in the jury room;

4. that when they left court they should try to set the case they were trying on one
   side until they returned to court and retired to their jury room to continue the
   process of deliberating about their verdict or verdicts.

The secrecy of the jury room

When the jury retire to the jury room to consider their verdict, they conduct their
deliberations in secret. When they return their verdict they are not required to give
reasons for how their decision has been reached or to disclose any other form of
information on how they reached the conclusion they did. In other words, the
verdict of the jury is sovereign.

The prohibition on disclosure of deliberations is imposed by s8(1) of the
Contempt of Court Act 1981 which makes it a contempt of court, and therefore an
offence, for any person to obtain, disclose or solicit any particulars of statements
made, opinions expressed, arguments advanced or votes cast by members of a jury in
the course of their deliberations. In *Attorney-General* v *Associated Newspapers Limited*
[1994] 2 AC 238; [1994] 1 All ER 556 it was held that this total prohibition included
indirectly obtained disclosures obtained not from the jurors themselves, but from an
outside party conducting research into juries who had placed an advert offering
payment to jurors if they took part in this research. The newspaper had used the
results of some of this research in an article on a fraud trial. On a proper
construction of s8, the word 'disclose' covers disclosure from A (ie the juror) to B
(ie the researcher) and from B to C (ie the newspaper) and thence from C to the
public at large.

Once they retire to the jury room the jury is not allowed to communicate with
anyone other than the judge and an assigned court officer. The court's primary
concern during the period of their deliberations is to ensure that they are kept
inviolate and free from outside influence or eavesdropping: *R* v *Bean* [1991] Crim
LR 843. If the jury send a note to the judge during their deliberations, the judge
must disclose the terms of the note to counsel for both sides and reconvene the
court without the jury to invite submissions on the matter. It is wrong for the judge
to give these directions to the jury through the medium of the court clerk. The jury
must be recalled to be given directions on the matter by the judge: *R* v *Green* [1992]
Crim LR 292.

Part of the sovereignty of the jury verdict is that it is unchallangeable on appeal
and the Court of Appeal will not receive evidence of discussions which take place in
the jury room. This rule was reaffirmed by the Court of Appeal in *R* v *Miah; R* v
Akhbar (1996) The Times 18 December. The Court of Appeal has also shown great
reluctance to investigate allegations of impropriety in jury proceedings, including
information later received that a jury has considered matters obtained from sources
other than that presented in evidence. In *R* v *Thompson* [1962] 1 All ER 65 the
court even refused to make enquiries where it was later contended that the majority
wanted to acquit until a juror produced a list of previous convictions. However, in *R*

v *Young (Stephen)* [1995] 2 WLR 430 the Court of Appeal did take the unusual step of investigating the deliberations of a jury who had been sent to an hotel overnight and decided to contact the deceased by means of an ouija board to find out whether her husband had killed her! It thought there to be a real danger that that some jurors may have been influenced by 'messages' so a retrial was ordered. In any case the jury should not have continued their deliberations overnight: *R v Tharakan* (1994) The Times 10 November.

There is strong opposition to any erosion of the jury's right to secret deliberations and there are a number of good reasons for this:

1. the verdict is final so there can be no 'follow on' actions on the basis of it alone, which in some cases might become a stream of actions that do more to damage the course of justice than promote it;
2. no disclosure of reasons prevents the occurrence of an unreliable account of their deliberations that would lead to misunderstanding of how they did reach their verdict, which relates both to the above and to misuse of such information into research on how juries should be used;
3. it goes a long way to protecting jurors from outside influence and harassment;
4. they have freedom of discussion without fear of disclosure of either that information or their individual identities in expressing it, which promotes full and frank discussion without concerns for later criticism being levelled, or indeed, possible retribution for their views;
5. it enables jurors to move from one view to the opposite of it without having to provide a carefully reasoned explanation of the factors that tipped the balance for them;
6. it encourages them to bring in a verdict based on their conscience rather than on what they perceive will be thought of, after later inquiry, as the correct verdict to have reached.

The counter-arguments are:

1. that it would make juries more accountable and that this in turn might make them consider some of their reasoning more carefully;
2. that it would reveal areas of the law that might need reform on the basis of society's expectations if juries were consistently voicing opinion that an area of the law ran against what they thought to be acceptable;
3. that it would reveal the extent to which individual jurors were reluctant to bring in the verdict that they did and identify the factors that tipped the balance for them;
4. that it would reveal irrational reasoning, inferences that were incorrectly drawn from the evidence, decisions reached on the basis of information that should not have been relied on, and indications of undue influence to conform being exerted within the jury itself, all of which would allow 'perverse' verdicts or other injustices to be rectified.

In *R* v *Mirza* [2004] 1 AC 1118 the primacy of the secrecy of jury trial was upheld by the House of Lords. The case concerned a Pakistani man who had lived in England since 1988. He was convicted, by a majority jury verdict (ten to two), of six counts of indecent assault on his step-daughter. English was not his first language and he had had the assistance of an interpreter at is trial. The jury found this suspicious and on two occasions sent notes to the judge about the matter. They were told not to take the use of the interpreter into account. Six days after the verdict a juror wrote a letter to counsel for the appellant. It suggested that the jury reached their verdict on perverse grounds which included a racial element, that some of the jury thought that the use of an interpreter was a devious ploy and that they had no insight into the defendant's culture. It also stated that the direction by the judge that the use of the interpreter was not a matter that should count adversely against the defendant seemed to have been ignored. The Court of Appeal had felt itself to be bound by the decision of a differently constituted Court of Appeal in *R* v *Qureshi* [2002] 1 WLR 518, which had stated in absolute terms the rule concerning the secrecy of the deliberations of the jury after verdict. The House of Lords similarly felt that they should not interfere.

Whilst accepting the ability of the House of Lords to state the law, it is still possible to wonder if the arguments of the majority in the case are compelling. Perhaps Lord Slynn, who dissented, is on safer grounds when, in short, he argues that the outrageous cannot be tolerated. It is certainly no answer to say that a concerned juror should speak up before the verdict, because as this case shows sometimes they do not do so. One partial solution would be to require each individual juror to declare that they did not have concerns as to the jury deliberations or lack of them. The plan now is for research to be carried out in relation to the jury system: it is probable that Lord Slynn's concerns will be vindicated.

Prohibition on research

One of the difficulties in making a rational assessment of the competency of juries is the dearth of knowledge about how they reach their verdict. The prohibition under s8 of the Contempt of Court Act 1981 includes disclosure for the purposes of academic research into the operation of juries. The Royal Commission on Criminal Justice (1993) recommended that s8 should be amended to permit genuine academic research but this was not implemented. There is strong opposition to any erosion of the jury's right to secret deliberations. Some senior judges feared that exposing the jury to open scrutiny would focus attention onto their weaknesses at the expense of reinforcing their strengths, so that instead of restoring public confidence in its role there would be calls for its abolition and the consequent loss of a constitutional safeguard for the citizen.

Until some form of research into their operation is permitted, it remains impossible to assess with certainty the ability of a passive group of 12 lay people to get at the truth of a complex issue presented to them on an adversarial basis. Conclusions may only be inferred from the decisions they reach, the length of time it takes them to reach a decision, notes they send to the judge during their deliberations and other surrounding information such as the composition of the jury. All of these are unsatisfactory determinants of the adequacy of the jury to deal with complex and technical evidence which is the information that is needed to make a rational decision as to what types of trial they should be used for.

In the United States of America jurors are frequently interviewed by the media as to their reasons for reaching particular decisions but there is considerable reluctance to introduce such an open inquiry here, based on the fear that media interest in any case may have an undesirable influence on the future deliberations of a another jury in a similar case.

Most cases turn upon the credibility of evidence and the typical jury probably is capable of reaching a fair result. It is cases of exceptional complexity that give rise to doubts, but in the absence of empirical research there can only be speculation about the difficulty that a typical jury may have in deciding guilt or innocence. One result of the *Mirza* case, noted above, is that some form of research on the jury is likely to take place.

5.7 Alternatives to the jury system

The independence of the jury from the judiciary and executive provides a constitutional safeguard for the citizen so unique and strong in character that no satisfactory alternative has yet been found. It is unlikely to be abolished completely in the near future at least. Successful reform will lie with improvements to the existing system that will enable juries to be retained whilst making them more effective.

The Report of the Royal Commission on Criminal Justice (1993) recommended that instead of outright abolition or the implementation of full alternatives, steps be taken to encourage proactive participation from jurors. In particular, it recommended simplification of the presentation of complex evidence, a minimal use of jargon and technicality to simplify the issues, dispensing with lengthy speeches from counsel and increased use of audio-visual aids to assist communication. Jurors are then to be encouraged to ask questions on points on which they are confused and for clarification of facts.

It has since been suggested that the computerisation of evidence should be introduced with provision of laptop computers for jurors for use during the trial, but the obvious need to select for computer literacy again raises issues about the need to preserve a randomly selected jury.

The fact that pro-active participation would do little in a case where the evidence has admittedly become too complex for the jury to understand goes a long way toward rebutting the claim that this is a solution to the problem for cases like serious fraud crimes. The Royal Commission on Criminal Justice, in recognition of the particular complexity of evidence in serious fraud trials, recommended a change of approach away from criminal penalties and over to a system of regulatory penalties similar to that used in some states in USA where the Securities and Exchange Commission administers the process of discipline as an alternative to the adversary system of trial.

This recommendaton has not been taken up and the solution for ensuring a fair and objective trial for complex cases would be more likely to sit in a reform of the adversarial system of law that permits more proactive involvement of the jury. Jury participation would reveal the point at which a case takes on such exceptional complexity as to be beyond the comprehension of the lay person and alternatives could be considered to deal with these isolated cases without the clutter of the other issues involved in retaining the jury system as a whole. There could, for example, be a process by which evidence that the jury indicate they cannot understand, despite attempts to simplify and explain it, are referred to a panel of experts appointed independently for the purpose (for example, by the Department for Constitutional Affairs) and whose advice is taken into account by the jury in their deliberations.

It is felt by many that expert assessors rather than lay people selected at random are the proper panel to assess complicated evidence, ask relevant and searching questions, and generally perform the inquisitorial function that is required for an adversarial trial. In 1986 the Roskill Report recommended that the jury should be replaced by a panel of judges and professional assessors. Serious fraud cases, for example, would be decided by the trial judge with the help of a panel of expert assessors such as accountants and auditors. The proposal was not implemented because of the strong opposition at the time to any form of abolition of the jury and the Government chose instead to reform the nature of fraud trials: Criminal Justice Act 1987.

Other alternatives are trial by a judge sitting alone who would assess questions of law and fact, and trial by a bench of three to five judges and no jury. Judges are less likely to be distracted from main issues but there is a danger that they will become case-hardened and perhaps pro-prosecution minded in criminal trials. The jury acts as a counter-balance to 'the establishment' and, if randomly selected, brings a diversity of knowledge of everyday occurrences and social norms and expectations that a judge sitting alone cannot replicate and a bench of judges is unlikely to represent. The Roskill Report proposal for trial by a composite tribunal of lawyers and lay people goes considerably further toward meeting this goal so can be viewed as being a better alternative to total judicial control.

5.8 Summary of the arguments for and against the jury system

The lists presented below summarise the arguments for the retention and the abolition of juries into ten points each. They are intended to draw together the threads of the various matters discussed within this chapter and do not represent definitive lists.

Arguments raised in favour of juries

1. The jury, since it is random selected from a wide range of the population, is best able to reflect the views of society. When a person's liberty is at stake it is a matter of principle that she/he should be tried by his/her peers.
2. The jury is regarded by the public as the 'bulwark of individual liberties'. Justice must be seen to be done: per Lord Denning MR in *Ward* v *James* [1966] 1 QB 273.
3. Fact-finding is a matter of common sense and does not require specialised legal training.
4. The opinion of 12 jurors is better than the single opinion of the judge since it is more likely to prevent individual biases governing the course of the fact-finding.
5. The jury is less 'prosecution minded' than many judges and magistrates, being an 'organ of dis-establishment'. It can be totally independent because it is unaccountable.
6. Juries are barometers of public feeling on the state of law, eg by deliberately acquitting against the weight of the evidence to express disapproval of a 'bad' or 'unpopular' law.
7. There is no satisfactory alternative to a lay jury. Its presence demands that evidence is properly aired and fully explained. All suggestions for alternatives fall to be criticised on the grounds that court proceedings and the fact-finding process will become institutionalised, or establishment minded, and that persons who continually act as arbiters of fact in an area are likely to become case hardened.
8. The presence of a lay jury goes some way to ensuring that proceedings are kept simple. Rather than abolish their use for complex trials, the trials should be reformed to simplify procedures and rules of evidence.
9. The jury is particularly suited to judge questions of defamation (civil jury) since the test which is applied is that of 'right thinking people generally': *Sim* v *Stretch* [1936] 2 All ER 1237.
10. It is incorrect to dismiss all juries as incompetent, biased, and lacking in public duty. There is good evidence that juries do perform their task faithfully, with due diligence and in full recognition of the public duty they are performing.

Arguments raised against the use of juries

1. The argument that random selection produces a jury that is representative of society is fallacious. Juries can comprise those that were left as available at the end of the selection process.

2. The jury is uneducated in the law and is often unable to weigh evidence correctly and appreciate the significance of certain matters.
3. Complex fraud cases are particularly likely to cause problems for the lay jury. The Roskill Report (1986) recommended the replacement of the jury in such cases by a judge sitting with expert assessors.
4. There is evidence that juries are unable properly to understand some of the more complex distinctions in the law that have a bearing on their fact finding, eg the distinction between murder and manslaughter.
5. The present law of evidence in criminal cases is much distorted by the need to accommodate the biases and inexperience of the jury and to keep from them matters which would unduly prejudice them against the accused, but which are not actually relevant to the weighing of evidence in the case (eg informing them of the accused's criminal record which may be totally irrelevant to the present case).
6. The jury may be too easily swayed by good oratory from counsel. Conversely, they may reach a verdict on the basis that counsel was weak, disorganised, or seemed to be lacking in confidence in what she/he said in support of the accused. The same factors may apply to evidence given by witnesses, the police, or even the accused. Sympathy (or the opposite) for the accused or the victim cannot form the basis of a rational decision reached on a logical consideration of the facts.
7. Jurors may be dominated by two or three strong-minded individuals on the jury.
8. It is not possible to guarantee that there has been absolutely no tampering with the jury.
9. Juries may bring in perverse verdicts (ie against the weight of the evidence) as the result of irresponsible decision-making. A perverse verdict is contrary to the juror's oath.
10. Their unaccountability by virtue of the secrecy of the jury room gives the jury an unacceptable freedom of decision-making which runs contrary to democratic principles in that it is not for the jury to re-write the law; society has established an accountable executive and a legislature for that purpose.

6

The Legal Profession

6.1 Introduction: the divided legal profession

6.2 Solicitors

6.3 Barristers

6.4 The Crown Prosecution Service

6.5 The future of the legal profession

6.1 Introduction: the divided legal profession

Unlike the position in most systems of law, the English legal profession is not a single profession exercising various functions, but a divided profession comprising barristers and solicitors. This division is a historical one stretching back into the twelfth and thirteenth centuries when, as a result of the growing complexities of the developing system of justice, claimants began to employ agents and experienced representatives to plead their cases before the courts. In modern times the divided profession has been justified on the ground that there is a continuing need for specialisation of function.

Practising barristers have been regarded as specialists in advocacy; it has been argued that the specialised nature of court proceedings requires a practical knowledge of the adversary system and an intimate awareness of the rules of evidence and procedure. Comparisons were often drawn with the medical profession; solicitors were regarded as 'general practitioners' dealing with routine problems, but referring a client to a specialist (a barrister) if his or her claim needed to be conducted in a court ('the operating theatre'). Lord Donaldson, a former Master of the Rolls, once expressed the view that it would be as impractical to merge solicitors and barristers as it would be to merge the professions of doctor, dentist and veterinary surgeon: 'No-one suggests that those professions should be fused because the divisions between them represent natural demarcation lines in terms of the public's needs. The same is true of the law': letter to *The Times*, 30 July 1996.

However, this contention can be disputed on the ground that there is no evidence of specialist training in the legal profession comparable to that found in the medical profession. Until 1969 barristers received no training at all in the art of advocacy, and until 1989 the practical training element of the Bar examinations consisted of a very short period of elementary exercises in pleading and drafting for which there were no formal examinations. Since 1989 the Bar examinations have laid more emphasis on formal appraisals of practising skills but they have still been criticised for giving inadequate tuition. The Royal Commission on Criminal Justice (1993) Cmnd 2263 recommended that practising barristers needed compulsory continuing education in areas such as forensic science and psychology. The 'apprenticeship' which a young barrister must serve as a 'pupil' to a senior barrister before being allowed to practise has also been criticised for being an inadequate training period.

Hence, it is not surprising that the basis for the divided profession has been attacked as fallacious, particularly when it was used to justify a monopoly of advocacy rights enjoyed by barristers in the higher courts. Steps were taken to break this monopoly under the Courts and Legal Services Act 1990 but, as discussed in section 6.2 below, they did not lead to the changes in the traditional discharge of lawyers' functions that were intended. The Access to Justice Act 1999 represents a further attempt to break this monopoly and open legal services to the public. If solicitors in the coming years respond to the Act then it will, no doubt, encourage more calls from some quarters for a single fused legal profession. If this happened this would mean common legal training with graduates joining firms of lawyers, with each firm developing a specialist department of advocates if it so wishes, as, for example, in Canada, where the specialist advocates have retained the title of 'barristers'. Alternatively, there might be common legal training but a continuing division of practitioners so as to allow a distinct corps of higher court advocates, as happens in New Zealand and some Australian states.

Fusion, or significant moves towards it, would, it has been argued, provide a more rational and cost-effective basis for a modern legal profession. In theory a client would be paying one lawyer instead of two (or more) for all the work on his or her case, including advocacy in court if required. However, opponents of fusion and of moves towards it have argued that large city firms would employ the best advocates, thereby reducing client choice and the geographical spread of legal advice (at present any solicitor in England and Wales has right of access to any barrister in independent practice). It has also been argued that an independent Bar is a valuable safeguard of the constitution: a barrister is expected to put his or her duty to the court above any loyalty he or she may feel to his or her client. An employed lawyer who appears as an advocate for his or her employer might be faced with a conflict of interest; if the employed lawyer is a Crown prosecutor, his or her employer is the state, and the potential conflict of interest could have serious implications for citizens' rights.

Hence, opponents of fusion and of extended rights of advocacy (which they see as inevitably leading to fusion) have fought a long campaign in defence of the traditional system. These opponents mainly comprise the Bar and the senior judiciary; during the 1980s the campaign against the proposed reforms eventually contained in the Courts and Legal Services Act 1990 was known as 'Bar Wars'. The changes brought about by the Access to Justice Act 1999 were not fought so robustly, and this was probably explained by a degree of resignation to change.

6.2 Solicitors

There are approximately 70,000 solicitors in independent practice working for firms ranging from big city partnerships of 300 or more to small rural partnerships of six or less, including some one-man/one-woman practices. In addition, a number of solicitors work as employed legal advisers in various fields, such as local government, commerce, the government legal service and the Crown Prosecution Service.

Qualification

The road to becoming a solicitor depends upon whether one is a law graduate, a non-law graduate or a mature student for whom work experience may be a substitute for a degree.

A 'qualifying' law degree is one which has covered the seven 'foundations of legal knowledge' (contract law, law of tort, criminal law, constitutional and administrative law, land law, trusts and European Union law) and a course on the English legal system. The holder of a qualifying law degree is eligible to attend the one-year full-time Legal Practice Course (LPC) at the Law Society's College of Law (or other approved institution). This is followed by a two-year 'training contract' with a law firm during which time a 'professional skills course' must be taken. This is finally followed by admission to the roll.

Non-law graduates must take a conversion course in the seven 'foundations of legal knowledge' and the English legal system. This course is known as the Common Professional Examination (CPE) and may be taken in one year by full-time students. Successful completion of the CPE enables the graduate to proceed to the LPC and then along the same route as law graduates.

Functions

A solicitor in independent practice working for a law firm operates like a businessman with an office to run and substantial correspondence. He or she deals with the preparatory stages of litigation (interviewing witnesses, collating evidence and following procedural requirements of the court) and has direct contact with his or her clients. However, the bulk of a solicitor's work is non-litigious and includes conveyancing, drafting wills, the supervision of settlements, administration of estates, matrimonial problems and matters arising from employment, immigration and company law. Many solicitors handle a cross-section of work but there is a trend towards specialisation, especially in London and the cities.

Rights of advocacy (rights of audience)

Solicitors in independent practice

Traditionally, such solicitors had very restricted opportunities to appear as advocates in the courts. They have long had rights of audience in the magistrates' courts, county courts and before certain tribunals. They have also been allowed to appear in certain types of non-jury cases in the Crown Courts, eg in proceedings on appeal from the magistrates' court or in committals for sentence from the magistrates' court. The opportunity to obtain greater rights of advocacy came with the passage of the Courts and Legal Services Act 1990. Under ss27–33 of the 1990 Act rights of audience were extended to those persons who could satisfy criteria established by their professional governing bodies, provided that those criteria have been approved by a panel comprising the Lord Chancellor (the role has now been taken over by the Minister for Constitutional Affairs) and senior judges.

The solicitors' governing body, the Law Society, eventually made rules which were approved by the judges' panel enabling solicitors in independent practice of at least three years' experience to apply for a higher courts' qualification upon successful completion of training courses and tests in advocacy, evidence and procedure (courses and tests being run by and set by the Law Society). Applicants also need to show experience of advocacy – at least two years' experience in the magistrates' courts and county courts. On successful completion of the course the solicitor becomes a 'solicitor advocate'.

A holder of the higher courts' (criminal proceedings) qualification has rights of audience in the Crown Court and in other courts in all criminal proceedings. A holder of the higher courts' (civil proceedings) qualification may appear in the High Court and in other courts in all civil proceedings. The holder of the higher courts' (all proceedings) qualification may appear in all courts in all proceedings.

According to Law Society figures, by 2003 there were 1,787 solicitors with extended rights of audience. So after a slow start the number of Solicitor Advocates has started to increase significantly.

The Lord Chancellor expressed his disappointment in the small number of Solicitor Advocates in the 1998 White Paper, *Modernising Justice*, and stated his intention to address the issue. The result is s36 of the Access to Justice Act 1999. This section permits the Law Society to grant full rights of audience to its members. In other words it allows the Law Society to give all solicitors the right to appear as advocates in all courts at all levels. Interestingly, the Law Society has not decided to grant this right automatically, but instead will extend rights of audience for individual solicitors who undertake a period of post-LPC training and assessment. This position, namely that all solicitors have rights of audience in the lower courts, and can extend this by a period of further training and assessment, appears little different from the regime that operated following the Courts and Legal Services Act 1990. However the Law Society has made the period of training and assessment less onerous. Further, now under Law Society rules, a solicitor can qualify for extended rights of audience within 12 months of qualifying.

Employed solicitors

Traditionally rights of audience for employed solicitors, such as those employed by corporations, local government or the Crown Prosecution Service, have been very limited. Over the years they, with the general support of the Law Society, have sought to have rights of audience equal to their counterparts in private practice. In June 1995 the Lord Chancellor's Advisory Committee on Legal Education and Conduct (now replaced by the Legal Services Consultative Panel) recommended (by a majority of nine to eight) that employed lawyers should continue to be denied the right to apply for advocacy certificates under the system established by the Courts and Legal Services Act 1990.

In 1997 new rules were approved which amounted to a very limited relaxation of the restrictions applying to employed solicitors wishing to exercise advocacy rights in the higher courts. These rules however maintained significant restrictions and employed solicitors were unable to appear as advocates on their own in the following situations:

1. for the prosecution in criminal proceedings committed for trial to the Crown Court;
2. in civil proceedings in the higher courts in any hearing intended to dispose in whole, or in part of, the merits of the case; and
3. for local authorities in care proceedings.

Though the Bar welcomed the restriction on criminal proceedings as being necessary to prevent the establishment of a state prosecution service, the new rules were seen as a blow to employed solicitors, particularly those employed by the Crown Prosecution Service. The government was unhappy with the situation and overruled these restrictive rules with s37 of the Access to Justice Act 1999. The section gives employed solicitors, including those employed by the Crown Prosecution Service, the same rights of audience as those in private practice. The only restriction now permitted under the section is that the Law Society can require that the rights be exercised only on behalf of the employer.

Regulation and discipline

Solicitors are officers of the Supreme Court and were originally regulated and disciplined by the judges. However, this function is now exercised partly by the Law Society and partly by the courts.

The Law Society was constituted by Royal Charter in 1845 and has always been a voluntary organisation: about 85 per cent of solicitors are members. Under the Solicitors Act 1974 it makes training regulations, provides club facilities and maintains the roll of solicitors (under the formal supervision of the Master of the

Rolls). A solicitor found in serious breach of professional rules may be 'struck off' the roll, ie suspended from the ability to practise. Solicitors are accountable to the Law Society for such matters as the handling of clients' money and insurance cover for claims arising from their work. Discipline is administered in serious cases by the Solicitors' Disciplinary Tribunal, comprising solicitors and lay members. Appeal lies to the High Court or, in certain cases, to the Master of the Rolls. The Tribunal makes an annual report to the Lord Chancellor (whose role has now been taken over by the Minister for Constitutional Affairs).

Complaints by clients against solicitors can be made to the Office for the Supervision of Solicitors (Ofsol), established in 1996 to replace the much criticised Solicitors' Complaints Bureau. Although Ofsol is a Law Society institution it operates on procedures designed to speed up the handling of complaints and to improve communications between all those involved in a complaint.

The solicitors' profession is also supervised by the Legal Services Ombudsman, an institution set up by ss21–26 of the Courts and Legal Services Act 1990. The Ombudsman's general function is to investigate the way in which a complaint has been dealt with by, inter alia, the Law Society (and the Bar Council: see section 6.3 below). A person who is unhappy about the way the professional body has dealt with his complaint can bring the matter to the attention of the Ombudsman. Section 49 of the Access to Justice Act 1999 permits the Ombudsman to make a binding order for payment of compensation following an investigation into a complaint against the Law Society or an individual solicitor. However, the Ombudsman may not investigate, inter alia, any issue which is being or has been determined by, inter alia, the Solicitors' Disciplinary Tribunal.

The Office of the Legal Services Ombudsman completed 1,731 cases in 2003/2004. A total of 1,485 new cases were accepted for investigation. The Ombudsman was satisfied with the way in which the Law Society's Office for the Supervision of Solicitors (Ofsol) handled complaints in only 53 per cent of the cases investigated. In January 2002 the Ombudsman used her powers under s24(1) of the Courts and Legal Services Act 1990 to make a number of recommendations to the Law Society in relation to their new Consumer Redress Scheme. The Ombudsman was concerned that the Scheme was disappointingly unambitious and unlikely to deliver the necessary improvement in public confidence. Nor was she persuaded that the appointment of a Lay Commissioner would add anything other than symbolic value to the Law Society's complaint-handling arrangements.

A review of the regulatory process in relation to legal services is being carried out by Sir David Clementi. Zahida Mansoor, the Legal Services Ombudsman, suggests that the professional bodies should continue to play a part in regulation but that this would be within and subject to a framework of an independent regulatory system.

Relationship with clients

As far as a solicitor's relationship with his client is concerned, a solicitor owes both contractual and tortious duties of care, arising from his retainer by his client – which also (depending upon its scope) gives him his authority to act for that client. Until recently there was limited immunity from a suit for damages for breach of that duty of care, but only so far as the solicitor was carrying out litigation work which would have been carried on by a barrister had one been engaged.

However in *Arthur J S Hall* v *Simons* [2000] 3 WLR 543 the House of Lords removed this remaining immunity from suit. Now solicitors are in the same position as any other type of professional and can be sued in negligence for any aspect of their work.

The confidential relationship of solicitor and client which arises out of the solicitor's fiduciary duty has important consequences, notably the fact that all communications between them are 'privileged' and cannot be required to be disclosed in evidence without the client's consent: *Wheeler* v *Le Marchant* (1881) 17 Ch D 675. The reason for this privilege is to allow the client to be free to obtain legal advice without fear of disclosure.

Liability to third parties

A solicitor can be sued in contract or tort by third parties. In the former his liability is usually governed by the law of agency. He can therefore be indemnified by his client for acts within the scope of his authority. Where he acts without his client's authority he can be sued for breach of warranty of authority: *Yonge* v *Toynbee* [1910] 1 KB 215. A solicitor's liability in tort is governed by the usual principles applicable under the law of torts. Under the rapidly developing tort of negligence, particularly in respect of negligence causing economic loss (purely financial loss), a solicitor may be liable to beneficiaries for loss caused by faulty drafting of a client's will, even though the beneficiary is not in a contractual relationship with that solicitor: *Ross* v *Caunters* [1979] 2 All ER 580.

6.3 Barristers

There are over 10,000 barristers in independent practice, ie self-employed, working from sets of chambers (on average 20 members to a set in London and 15 to a set in the provinces). A set of chambers shares secretarial facilities and the services of a 'practice manager' (formerly known as a barristers' clerk), who negotiates fees with solicitors and distributes work among the barristers. Each barrister must pay rent for his 'tenancy' in chambers, plus contributions to overheads such as the salary of the practice manager (who may alternatively be paid commission on fees earned by the barristers).

A number of barristers work as employed legal advisers in various fields, such as local government, commerce, the government legal service and the Crown Prosecution Service. An increasing number of barristers are employed by firms of solicitors.

Qualification

A barrister can only practise if he has been 'called to the Bar' of one of the four Inns of Court (Inner Temple, Middle Temple, Gray's Inn and Lincoln's Inn). These are very old institutions dating back to the fourteenth century.

In order to be called to the Bar and to practise in England and Wales, a prospective applicant must complete the following three stages.

The academic stage

This involves either passing a qualifying law degree course or passing the CPE conversion course. For the definition of a qualifying law degree and CPE: see section 6.2, above.

The vocational stage

After joining one of the Inns the student must take the one-year full-time Bar Vocational Course (BVC). The course is practical; it teaches and assesses the skills needed by a barrister. In particular it teaches advocacy and legal writing skills. On successful completion the student is eligible to be 'called to the Bar' with his Inn. At this stage the student is a non-practising barrister.

The practical stage

After being called to the Bar, the pupil barrister embarks on a one-year period of apprenticeship known as 'pupillage' which is supervised by a pupil master. The first six months are spent in chambers as a non-practising pupil and, on satisfactory completion of this period, the pupil is issued with a provisional practising certificate. He/she may then accept work ('briefs') and appear in court and, at the end of another six months (possibly spent in a different set of chambers), a final certificate is issued.

The latest edition of the Bar's Code of Conduct permits, for the first time, pupillage to be taken outside chambers. Such external training may only be taken with organisations that have been authorised.

In the past, the average pupil received no income during pupillage, but things are now very different. Apart from scholarships and low interest loans, many chambers give 'awards', that is payment, during pupillage. However, with the increasing cost of the BVC, and competition from solicitors for the best law students, the Bar Council has recognised the need to secure a minimum award for all pupil barristers. All pupillages must now be funded to a minimum level of £5,000 in the first six months and £5,000 (by way of guaranteed receipts or award) during the second six months. This is important as, following the Court of Appeal decision in *Edmonds* v *Lawson* (2000) The Times 16 March, pupil barristers are not entitled to the national minimum wage.

Continuing education

Newly qualified barristers are required to undergo further training. For example those involved in jury trial work are required to undergo compulsory training in advocacy. The introduction of continuing education is to help improve standards, and reflects public concern at inconsistent standards of advocacy, particularly in criminal trials. The advocacy programme requires completion of 42 hours of training, including refresher courses on changes in the law.

Queen's Counsel

Queen's Counsel (QCs) or 'silks' (because of their silk gowns) are the senior practitioners of the Bar and they constitute about 10 per cent of its practising membership. After ten to 15 years' practice as a junior (all barristers who are not silks are known as 'juniors') a barrister may apply to the Lord Chancellor, a role now being performed by the Minister for Constitutional Affairs, to 'take silk' (ie to be appointed QC) and on doing so changes his/her practice considerably: the heavy load of a junior in drafting pleadings and paperwork is lost and greater fees may be charged. There is also an increase in status, and judges will (naturally enough) tend to respect the arguments of silks to a greater extent than juniors. Indeed, almost all puisne judges are appointed from the ranks of the silks.

The rule that a QC could not appear in court without a junior was abolished in 1977, though it is still the usual practice – the junior bearing the greater part of the preliminary work (particularly the paperwork). In consequence of this, the client whose case is difficult enough to merit engaging a QC to argue it in court often will have to pay both the QC's fees and those of his/her junior. Solicitor advocates are also eligible to apply for silk.

Appointment to the office of Queen's Counsel is approved by the Queen on the recommendation of the Lord Chancellor (whose role has now been taken over by the Minister for Constitutional Affairs). There has been much criticism of the appointments system, not least because of its secrecy and, allegedly, its dependence on patronage. A working party (chairman Michael Kalisher QC) appointed by the Bar Council to consider the appointment of Queen's Counsel submitted its report in June 1994. It did not recommend any structural change in the selection system, but it suggested ways in which it could be improved. For example, there should be formal published criteria for the grant of silk: appointments should be based solely on merit with no positive discrimination in favour of women or ethnic minorities. In 1999 the Peach Report on the appointments processes for judges and QCs recommended that the existing process for the appointment of QCs be retained but with some changes. These included giving more weight to the information supplied by the candidates themselves, and separation of appointment for QC from any consideration of suitability for the judiciary. The Lord Chancellor implemented the recommendations. The role of Queen's Counsel is still under review and a further consultation document was issued by the Department for Constitutional Affairs in 2003.

The Queen also appoints Queen's Counsel honoris causa, an honour for lawyers – including solicitors – who have made a distinguished contribution in the legal field otherwise than as practising advocates, for example as academics.

Functions

The basic work of a practising barrister (or 'counsel' as he or she is also known) is advocacy and litigation, though there is a certain amount of paperwork to do in even the most litigious practices – typically settling pleadings and giving written opinions on difficult legal points and advising, for example, as to the strength of a client's case. More specialist practices (particularly trusts, property, tax, company, landlord and tenant, wills and conveyancing) tend to involve more paperwork, some practitioners devoting nearly all their time to advising and drafting and spending very little time in court. Barristers are not all of a type: some, as noted, specialise in certain cases (including tax, commercial, shipping, building contracts), and some have 'general' practices doing a mixture of common law work, crime and matrimonial.

Rights of advocacy (rights of audience)

Upon call to the Bar and completion of pupillage a person who is entitled to practise at the independent Bar and who has secured a tenancy in chambers has rights of advocacy in every court, from the highest to the lowest, in the English legal system. These rights of audience were confirmed by the Court and Legal Services Act 1990. Employed barristers are also permitted to exercise full rights of audience on behalf of their employer following s37 Access to Justice Act 1999: see also section 6.2 above.

An advocate (whether a barrister or solicitor) owes a duty not only to the client, but also to the court, which in fact overrides the duty to the client. The advocate must draw the court's attention to all the relevant authorities, even if harmful to that advocate's case. The advocate must not conceal the facts or set up a defence where his or her client had made a confession of guilt to that advocate. It is also the special duty of prosecuting counsel to assist the court and not to press for conviction. The nature of these obligations makes it difficult, it is said, for them to be performed by an employed advocate who may be under pressure from his or her employer to win the case. There is said to be particular danger if the employer is the state: independent prosecution barristers have frequently complained about pressure from the Crown Prosecution Service (CPS) opposing their views of the case. If CPS barristers prosecute would the case always be settled according to the CPS perspective and, if so, would it affect the quality of justice? Or is independence (and the integrity it rests on) a state of mind rather than a method of practice or payment?

Regulation and discipline

The Inns of Court are governed by the benchers, who are judges and senior members of the Bar. They exercise disciplinary powers over barristers and students through the Council of the Inns of Court, which appoints disciplinary tribunals for this purpose. Decisions of such tribunals are subject to appeal to 'visitors' to the Inns of Court, who are usually senior judges. In the most serious cases of professional misconduct a barrister can be 'disbarred' by his Inn, ie suspended from the ability to practise.

The General Council of the Bar is responsible for the professional standards of the Bar in accordance with a code laid down under the supervision of the judges. It is responsible for the receipt and investigation of complaints against barristers and for the prosecution of disciplinary charges before disciplinary tribunals.

The barristers' profession is also subject to the jurisdiction of the Legal Services Ombudsman, though the Ombudsman may not investigate, inter alia, any issue which is being or has been determined by a disciplinary tribunal of the Council of the Inns of Court.

During the 1990s the General Council of the Bar carried out a standards review and, in 1996, established the Bar Compensation Bureau to hear complaints concerning 'poor and shoddy' services. Since 1999 barristers' chambers have been 'kite-marked' (ie accredited by an approved outside organisation) for good service in such matters as management of cases, how fees are charged and how well barristers communicate with clients. The Bar Council hopes that kite-marking, the 'Bar mark', will help stamp out disreputable practices such as double-booking of cases and the problem of late-returned briefs, which cause a barrister to pull out of a trial at the last minute.

Relationships with clients

Traditionally a client cannot approach a barrister directly – the client must go through a solicitor, who chooses a barrister, negotiates a fee with the practice manager of that barrister's chamber and arranges conferences between the client and the barrister when it is necessary for the two to meet and speak directly. However, in recent years the rules prohibiting the public's access to barristers have been significantly relaxed by the Bar Council. Now under the Bar Council's 'BarDIRECT' scheme members of approved professions, companies and other approved organisations can directly contact a barrister and use his services without going through a solicitor. In most cases access is for advice only, though some organisations are permitted to instruct a barrister for court work. It may be that the Bar Council will eventually scrap all restrictions on access to barristers and if it does so one of the last restrictive practices of the legal profession will be dismantled.

Traditionally there is no contract between a barrister and the client, although s61(1) of the Courts and Legal Services Act 1990 abolished any rule of law which prevented a barrister from entering a contract for his or her services. However, the Bar Council retains the right to regulate the matter and many relationships in this field remain non-contractual; payment of fees may be a matter of professional etiquette, though the Law Society has stated that solicitors are responsible for seeing that barristers are paid for work done on their briefs.

Barristers (like solicitors) can now be sued for professional negligence for any aspect of their work, following *Arthur J S Hall* v *Simons* [2000] 3 WLR 543.

The cab-rank rule

In the past it has been said that one of the most important rules of conduct (sometimes referred to as rules of professional etiquette) is the cab-rank principle: that is, a barrister in independent practice, in any field in which he professes to practise and irrespective of whether his client is privately or publicly funded, must:

1. accept any brief to appear before a court in which he professes to practise;
2. accept any instructions; and
3. act for any person on whose behalf he is briefed or instructed.

A barrister must do this irrespective of the party on whose behalf he is briefed or instructed, the nature of the case, and any brief or opinion which he may have formed as to the character, reputation, cause, conduct, guilt or innocence of that person.

The cab-rank rule does not apply to solicitor-advocates under the rules of conduct made by the Law Society under the Courts and Legal Services Act 1990.

In practice, it seems that it is not difficult for a barrister to find a reason to avoid taking a case that he does not want. Indeed, in *Arthur J S Hall* v *Simons* (above) the House of Lords noted this reality.

6.4 The Crown Prosecution Service

Introduction

Traditionally the functions of investigating crime and prosecuting offenders belonged to the police. However, critics argued that the prosecuting function involved questions of law, evidence and public policy for which the police were not professionally trained. A high proportion of cases (approximately 40 per cent) collapsed at trial due to insufficient evidence and the cause was said to be the lack of a professional prosecutors system. Further, it was argued as a matter of principle that the investigative and prosecuting functions should be exercised by separate institutions in order that independent minds could be applied to the results of police investigations.

As a result of the pressure for reform the Crown Prosecution Service (CPS), consisting of salaried lawyers appointed and employed on civil service criteria, was established by the Prosecution of Offences Act 1985. The CPS employs about 2,000 lawyers (two-thirds solicitors and one-third barristers) as well as lay staff.

Constitution

The Director of Public Prosecutions (DPP) is head of the Crown Prosecution Service. The post of DPP had been existence for over a hundred years prior to the 1985 Act and hence the basic duties of the DPP continued in regard to prosecution, with the additional responsibilities of management of the CPS under the 1985 Act. It is the DPP's duty to commence and conduct a prosecution whenever it appears to be of importance or difficulty or which for any other reason requires the DPP's intervention. Further, the DPP always has the power to intervene in or take over any prosecution which has already been commenced. The 1985 Act established the offices of Chief Crown Prosecutor and Crown Prosecutor, who are responsible for the conduct of most prosecutions, and who work under the direction of the DPP. (For the manner in which the discretion to prosecute is exercised see Chapter 12, section 12.3.)

The DPP is accountable to Parliament through the Attorney-General, the chief law officer of the Crown, who is a member of the government and an elected MP. The DPP is required to make an annual report to the Attorney-General on the work of the CPS. The CPS is responsible for the prosecution of all criminal cases resulting from police investigations in England and Wales, with the exception of certain minor offences (such as some traffic offences).

Reorganisation

The relationship between the CPS and the police had been uneasy from the start. First, many police officers resented the transfer of their prosecuting functions to an independent agency, regarding it as a slur on their reputation for impartiality and professionalism. Second, there were severe administrative problems of co-ordination between 43 police force areas and 13 CPS area offices. This caused communication difficulties and lost paperwork which impeded the operation of the CPS. Morale among Crown Prosecutors fell as a result of overwork, staff shortages and denial of advocacy rights in jury trials in the Crown Courts, the latter remaining with the independent Bar. The loss of public confidence in the CPS led to a governmental review of its operational performance. The review was conducted by Sir Iain Glidewell, a former Court of Appeal judge. In June 1998 the Glidewell Report (Cmnd 3960; summary Cmnd 3972) recommended a decentralisation of the CPS so as to create a localised criminal justice system and to bring about closer working relationships between CPS lawyers and the police. The government accepted the Report and, as a result, since April 1999 there are 42 CPS areas, each corresponding to police force areas (there are 43 police force areas but for CPS purposes the

Metropolitan Police and City of London Police, which are two separate forces, count as one force).

The Chief Crown Prosecutors who head the 42 areas enjoy a much higher public profile, substantial autonomy and an independent budget. It was believed that the previous system concentrated too much power in a centralised bureaucracy and that the new arrangements will command greater public confidence. During the summer of 1998 Dame Barbara Mills announced her early retirement from the post of DPP. She was replaced by David Calvert-Smith QC, who was put in charge of implementing the Glidewell Report. A new post of Chief Executive has been created to relieve the DPP of much of the managerial and administrative work involved in running the CPS. The Chief Executive is in charge of a slimmed down national headquarters in the hope of ending the cumbersome bureaucracy that bedevilled the operation of the CPS since its creation.

A further development has come through the passing of the Crown Prosecution Service Inspectorate Act 2000 which came into force in October 2000. This Act establishes an independent inspectorate for the CPS with the responsibility of inspecting the operation and running of the CPS.

Rights of advocacy (rights of audience)

In magistrates' courts CPS lawyers (solicitors or barristers) conduct the daily lists of prosecutions which were previously presented by the police or local authority prosecuting solicitors. Section 53 of the Crime and Disorder Act 1998 authorises lay staff employed by the CPS to present straightforward guilty plea cases in magistrates' courts.

As employed lawyers CPS solicitors and barristers were initially denied advocacy rights in the higher courts following the setting up of the CPS. This became a source of discontent among CPS lawyers who regarded advocacy work as more attractive than much of the routine desk work which they had to handle in preparing prosecutions. They also felt that, having worked in detail on a particular prosecution, they were as able as a barrister from the independent Bar to present that prosecution in a Crown Court jury trial. The DPP, on behalf of the CPS, campaigned for such advocacy rights, arguing that granting them would boost morale among CPS lawyers and help with recruitment. The Law Society also campaigned on behalf of the employed solicitors working for the CPS: see section 6.2 above. Since 2000, s37 of the Access to Justice Act 1999 has enabled lawyers employed by the CPS to exercise rights of audience in the same way as their counterparts in private practice.

6.5 The future of the legal profession

Section 6.1 above discusses the traditional arguments put forward for and against fusion of the legal profession prior to the Courts and Legal Services Act 1990. Since the 1990 Act the legal profession has been (often despite the arguments) under pressure to change. A primary purpose of the 1990 Act is summed in s17, namely to widen legal provision to the public by means of increased competition. One of the ways provided by the Act to achieve this is to allow solicitors to extend their rights of audience to the higher courts, where the Bar traditionally has had a monopoly. However, the anticipated invasion of solicitor advocates throughout the court system failed to materialise. The Access to Justice Act 1999 is a response to this. However, there must be doubts about whether the 1999 Act will have any real impact on the Bar's dominance of advocacy, particularly in the higher courts. The reason for this is that it appears that for many solicitors it makes more financial sense to stay in the office, rather than spend time travelling to and from court. And while solicitors spend more time in the office and less time in court, they are unable to compete with the court experience of barristers.

However it is unlikely that the Bar will be able to remain complacent about all aspects of its future. Though it has reason to be optimistic about its value as a referral profession for the purposes of providing advocacy, the same is not necessarily true about its traditional position as provider of expert advice. Solicitors' firms, particularly in the cities, have adopted niche practices offering specialist advice, in many cases on par with what the Bar can offer. Here the Bar seems to have recognised that it faces real competition, and the BarDIRECT scheme (see section 6.3 earlier) can be seen as response to it. There are now over 80 different organisations approved for direct access to barristers. It is very likely that this number will grow.

In recent years there have been breaches of the traditional boundary between the professions, and there is clearly a degree of competition between them that simply did not exist 20 or 30 years ago. However, to conclude that fusion is in sight, either because of the 1999 Act, or because of the working practices of city solicitors, would be hasty. It does seem that solicitors in general will continue to value the existence of the Bar for its advocacy expertise, and that non-specialist solicitors' firms will continue to require its expert advice.

Part III: Methods of Adjudication and the Financing of Legal Services

7

Courts, Tribunals and Alternative Dispute Resolution

7.1 Divisions of the courts

7.2 The main English courts

7.3 Reform of the criminal courts: the Auld review and the Courts Act 2003

7.4 Tribunals and inquiries

7.5 Arbitration

7.6 Alternative dispute resolution (ADR)

7.7 Diagrams of the main English court structure

7.1 Divisions of the courts

The two fundamental divisions of the court are superior and inferior courts and courts of record and courts not of record.

Superior and inferior courts

Superior courts have unlimited jurisdiction, and include the House of Lords, the Privy Council, the Supreme Court and the Crown Court.

Inferior courts have jurisdiction limited either by value or geographically or both (eg county courts, magistrates' courts).

Courts of record and courts not of record

This is a historical division, based upon whether the court kept official records of its proceedings or not. This no longer applies.

Civil and criminal

English law and procedure are divided into two categories, civil and criminal, and a

137

case must be one or the other. Some courts have jurisdiction over both civil and criminal cases (eg the House of Lords, the Court of Appeal and magistrates' courts).

Courts of common law and equity

Until the Judicature Act 1873 the common law was administered solely by the courts of common law and the rules of equity by the Court of Chancery, the two being quite separate – having different procedures, being based on different principles, and offering different remedies. However, ss24–25 of the 1873 Act 'fused' the administration of law and equity. The jurisdiction of both the superior common law courts and the Court of Chancery was transferred to the High Court and judges are now required to apply both sets of rules, where relevant. Thus the modern Chancery Division of the High Court, though it is assigned some specialist matters once dealt with exclusively by the old Court of Chancery, no longer is the sole administrator of equity. Where the rules of common law and equity are in conflict, those of equity prevail.

7.2 The main English courts

The purpose of this section is to give a basic outline of each of the main English courts in the present court structure.

For the European Court of Justice see Chapter 16, section 16.2, and for the European Court of Human Rights see Chapter 18, section 18.3.

The House of Lords

Originally Parliament was a court which exercised certain judicial functions but by Tudor times this jurisdiction came to be exercised exclusively by the House of Lords. Until the Appellate Jurisdiction Act 1876 which created Lords of Appeal in Ordinary, appointed from eminent judges and lawyers, to hear appeals, any peer could hear appeals and vote on the decision, and often the only lawyer present was the Lord Chancellor. One result of this was that House of Lords' decisions before 1876 carried very little legal authority, except in cases where the judges were invited to advise the House of the law.

Appeals are heard by at least three, and usually five (and exceptionally, seven), judges who must be drawn from the Lords of Appeal in Ordinary and any other peer who has held 'high judicial office', which is defined by the 1876 Act. In practice only the Lords of Appeal ('law lords') normally sit. The law lords are usually appointed from Lord Justices of Appeal, although there are usually two who were Scottish judges because the House of Lords is also the final appeal court for Scotland. Their maximum number is 12.

Appeals are heard generally in a committee room and their lordships do not wear robes. Strictly the lords do not give 'judgments' but instead give 'opinions' stating the reasons for their vote whether to allow or dismiss the appeal. If the House is equally divided the appeal is dismissed, and while normally this situation does not arise because an uneven number sits, it can occur – such as when a law lord dies before giving judgment and the House is otherwise equally divided: see *Kennedy* v *Spratt* [1972] AC 83 (Lord Upjohn died).

The House of Lords has very little original jurisdiction. The trial of one of its members 'by his peers' was abolished in 1948 and impeachment (prosecution of political offenders) is obsolete. The only remaining matters of original jurisdiction are breaches of privilege and disputed claims to peerages.

The jurisdiction of the House is almost entirely appellate, hearing appeals from (mainly):

1. the Court of Appeal (with the leave of either the Court of Appeal or the Appeals Committee of the Lords);
2. the High Court ('leap frog' procedure, with leave of the House of Lords, on a point of law of general public importance);
3. a Divisional Court of the Queen's Bench Division in a criminal cause or matter, with the leave of that court or the House.

The Constitutional Reform Act 2005 provides for the creation of the Supreme Court of the United Kingdom which is to replace the existing system of Law Lords operating as a committee of the House of Lords.

The Court of Appeal

The Court of Appeal is composed of (1) ex officio judges who are the Lord Chief Justice (the president of the criminal division), the Master of the Rolls (the president of the civil division), the president of the Family Division, Lords of Appeal in Ordinary and former Lord Chancellors, and the Vice-Chancellor, and (2) the Lords Justices of Appeal. See also Chapter 4, section 4.3 *Circuit judges*. In practice only the Master of the Rolls and the Lord Chief Justice of the ex officio judges sit in the civil and criminal divisions respectively. High Court judges may also sit with Lords Justices, and frequently do so in the criminal division. The normal number is three, but when a difficult and important point of law is in issue, the court may consist of five. Interlocutory appeals may now be heard by a single judge sitting in chambers (in private). Further, appeals from county courts are now usually heard by two judges, though three should sit if a difficult point arises. The administrative work of the divisions is supervised by two registrars.

The Court of Appeal is a creature of statute and its powers are those conferred by the relevant Acts of Parliament. The civil appeal system is considered in Chapter 10 and the criminal appeal system in Chapter 15.

The High Court

This was established by the Judicature Acts 1873 and 1875, which abolished the old courts – Court of King's Bench, Court of Common Pleas, Court of Exchequer, Court of Chancery, the Courts of Admiralty, Probate and Divorce and Matrimonial Causes and others – and transferred their jurisdiction to the High Court. The High Court originally contained five divisions:

1. Queen's Bench Division;
2. Common Pleas Division;
3. Exchequer Division;
4. Chancery Division;
5. Probate, Divorce and Admiralty Division.

However, in 1880 the Exchequer and Common Pleas Divisions were abolished and their business transferred to the Queen's Bench Division. In the Administration of Justice Act 1970 the remaining three divisions were reorganised by the creation of a new Family Division in place of the Probate, Divorce and Admiralty Division. The admiralty work was transferred to the Queen's Bench Division, contentious probate work to the Chancery Division and the Chancery Division's jurisdiction over wards of court transferred to the new division. The great majority of puisne judges sit in the Queen's Bench Division. High Court judges are called puisne (pronounced 'puny') judges (from the law French for 'junior' or 'inferior').

Before the Courts Act 1971 the High Court sat solely in the Law Courts in the Strand, although High Court judges also tried civil cases on assize. That Act abolished the assizes and instead provided that the High Court could sit at other locations.

The High Court has both civil and criminal jurisdiction, original and appellate. Although all three divisions have equal competence, in practice they have separate jurisdiction laid down partly by the rules and partly by statutory provisions. There are no financial or geographical limitations to the High Court jurisdiction (except that its jurisdiction is confined to England and Wales, since Scotland and Northern Ireland have their own laws and legal systems).

The Queen's Bench Division of the High Court

The head of this division is the Lord Chief Justice. Its original civil jurisdiction includes tort and most contract actions; it also deals with commercial and admiralty actions. It has a lesser civil appellate jurisdiction, its Divisional Court hearing appeals by way of case stated from magistrates' courts (except in matrimonial matters) and from the Crown Court. It also hears appeals from district judges. More important is its criminal appellate function, as most of the appeals by case stated from magistrates' and the Crown Court are in criminal matters. The division exercises the supervisory jurisdiction of the old Court of King's Bench by means of the prerogative orders granted by the Divisional Court.

Judges of this division also spend part of their time trying serious criminal matters in first tier Crown Courts and hearing Queen's Bench Division actions in the same locations.

There are two specialist courts of the Queen's Bench Division with specialist judges assigned to them: the Commercial Court and the Admiralty Court. These two 'courts' have similar procedures which differ from those in general operation in the division: they deal more efficiently with the specialist nature of the subject matter.

The Chancery Division of the High Court

The effective head of this division is the Vice-Chancellor, who is now also an ex-officio judge of the Court of Appeal. Most chancery actions are heard in London, but chancery actions are also tried at certain centres in the major cities. This division tries most matters concerned with land and is given jurisdiction over contentious probate, bankruptcy, revenue matters, trusts, company matters and winding-up, and patent and trade mark actions (which are heard in the Patents Court).

The Chancery Division divisional court has appellate jurisdiction in relation to bankruptcy appeals from the county courts and land registration. Income tax appeals from the Special Commissioners of Inland Revenue are heard by a single judge.

The Family Division of the High Court

The head of this division is the President of the Family Division. Its jurisdiction includes all defended matrimonial causes, declarations of legitimacy and of validity of a marriage, proceedings for a decree of presumption of death, wardship, adoption, guardianship and certain matrimonial property matters. It deals with all proceedings under the Child Support Act 1991. The divisional court of the division hears appeals from magistrates' courts and county courts in adoption, guardianship proceedings and appeals by way of case stated in matrimonial proceedings in magistrates' courts.

The Crown Court

History

Before 1972 the courts where trials on indictment took place were the 61 Assize Courts and the 173 Quarter Sessions together with the Central Criminal Court, commonly known as 'the Old Bailey', and the Crown Courts of Liverpool and Manchester. Both Assizes and Quarter Sessions had a local jurisdiction, so that in general they could only try crimes committed within their locality and also the methods of court administration varied from area to area.

The present structure

The Courts Act 1971 abolished Assizes (both criminal and civil sides) and Quarter

Sessions. All serious crime is tried on indictment in the Crown Court (which is a single court sitting in many locations composed of many judges).

There are four types of judge in the Crown Court:

1. High Court judges;
2. circuit judges;
3. recorders;
4. assistant recorders/deputy circuit judges.

The High Court judges are usually those attached to the Queen's Bench Division. Circuit judges are full-time judges who sit in both the Crown Court and county courts, and recorders are part-time judges, appointed for a limited period. When the Crown Court is hearing an appeal from a magistrates' court, lay justices of the peace sit with a single circuit judge. Deputy circuit judges and assistant recorders are ad hoc appointments for a very short period, though used to a great extent. Assistant recorders are persons who have a ten-year Crown Court or county court qualification within s71 of the Courts and Legal Services Act 1990.

The Crown Court has exclusive jurisdiction over all criminal trials on indictment for offences wherever committed. Procedure is governed by Crown Court Rules, which are delegated legislation made by the Crown Court Rules Committee under s84 of the Supreme Court Act 1981. The Crown Court is part of the Supreme Court and is a superior court of record, but it is under the supervisory jurisdiction of the High Court as expressed by the issue of prerogative orders, and a circuit judge is not a High Court judge.

England and Wales are divided into six administrative regions called circuits, with at least two presiding judges. Crown Court cases are allocated according to the composition of the court: that is, High Court judge, circuit judge or recorder, or a court which includes justices of the peace. Allocation is made by the Lord Chief Justice with the concurrence of the Lord Chancellor (that role now being performed by the Minister for Constitutional Affairs).

County courts

Although there were county courts in earlier times, the present-day county courts were established by statute in 1846 and have only civil jurisdiction. Although they deal with many relatively minor claims they are important as they offer a comprehensive, speedy and relatively cheap procedure and deal with the bulk of civil litigation.

There are about 280 county courts in England and Wales. Some of these are specially designated divorce county courts which deal with undefended divorces and related matters and this jurisdiction is not geographically limited.

The county courts are grouped for administrative purposes into the same circuits as Crown Courts. They are staffed by circuit judges, most county courts having at least one judge virtually permanently attached to that court. The administrative business is the concern of the district judge who has a seven-year general qualification within s71 of the Courts and Legal Services Act 1990.

The district judge also deals with procedural matters and tries minor cases ('small claims'). Appeal from the district judge is to the circuit judge and from there to the Court of Appeal.

Magistrates' courts

Magistrates' courts are composed of lay Justices of the Peace or, in the big cities, a professional district judge. A district judge must have a seven-year general qualification within s71 of the Courts and Legal Services Act 1990. For trying an information summarily there must be at least two and not more than seven Justices of the Peace (in practice there are usually three) or one district judge. A single lay justice may hear committal proceedings for cases which are going for trial at the Crown Court.

Magistrates' courts have a very wide and varied jurisdiction, only part of it being criminal, but their jurisdiction is limited geographically and is confined to minor matters.

The criminal jurisdiction has two aspects, trial and committal proceedings. Certain offences can only be tried summarily (ie in a magistrates' court), and certain other offences may be tried either on indictment or summarily. Where a case is to be tried on indictment in the Crown Court then the other aspect of the jurisdiction arises. Before a case can be tried at the Crown Court it must have been sent there by a magistrates' court.

Magistrates also issue summonses and warrants which start the whole criminal process and grant bail.

There are special magistrates' courts, known as youth courts, which deal with people under the age of 17 who commit offences. A youth court is composed of at least three lay justices from a special panel, consisting of at least one man and one woman. The youth court must not sit in any place where an adult court has been sitting within the last hour and, unlike adult courts, the proceedings are not in public.

The magistrates' courts also have a very varied civil jurisdiction. Probably the most important is over family proceedings (in family proceedings courts) under which the court can grant maintenance and custody and make a non-cohabitation order, but complex cases under the Children Act 1989 should be transferred to the nearest county court. Magistrates' courts can also deal with adoption proceedings, and are responsible for the recovery of a large number of debts such as council tax, gas, electricity and water charges, income tax and national insurance contributions. They also grant and revoke several kinds of licences, especially licences to sell alcohol. Appeals on family matters go to the Divisional Court of the Family Division.

Magistrates can award compensation (maximum £5,000 for any one offence) for personal injury, loss or damage.

7.3 Reform of the criminal courts: the Auld review and the Courts Act 2003

In July 2002 the government published a White Paper outlining its plans for the criminal justice system, from crime prevention through to the punishment and rehabilitation of offenders: *Justice for All* (Cmnd 5563). This built in part on the findings of the consultation document: *Review of the Criminal Courts of England and Wales*, by Sir Robin Auld in 2001. The Courts Act 2003 is one of the products of these documents. The Act places the Lord Chancellor under the general duty of maintaining an effective and efficient court system and gives him power to make appropriate arrangements for staff and accommodation. It also abolishes Magistrates' Courts Committees and establishes local Court Administration Councils. Part 2 makes provision for Justices of the Peace and other matters relating to magistrates' courts. It replaces commission areas and petty session areas with local justice areas and also makes provision to improve fine enforcement. Part 3 deals with jurisdiction and court procedures for criminal, civil and family proceedings in magistrates' courts, providing for more effective and flexible working. Part 6 allows for alterations to the names of judicial titles and offices. This Part also allows district judges (magistrates' courts) to sit as Crown Court judges, and gives judges of the higher courts all the powers of the Justices of the Peace – allowing for greater flexibility in the use of the judiciary. It is important to note that most of the Act has not been implemented at the time of writing.

7.4 Tribunals and inquiries

Tribunals are governed by the Tribunals and Inquiries Act 1992 and by the basic characteristics of openness, fairness and impartiality. By virtue of the Franks Report 1957 (Cmnd 218) tribunals have proliferated and it is generally thought that their expertise and their expedited process makes them not only invaluable to the already overburdened courts but that they perform a useful function in themselves. Unfortunately legal aid is not often available in tribunals but there is more opportunity for representation of a party by a non-lawyer, and many individuals have the benefit of advice and assistance from, for example, trade unions.

Control of tribunals has increased over recent years. The Council on Tribunals reviews the operations of the various tribunals and the High Court can supervise their working by means of the prerogative orders even though there is often no statutory right of appeal. Such supervision takes the form of reviewing the legality of the tribunals' acts (eg for want of natural justice), not by way of rehearing on the merits.

Administrative and employment tribunals

The word 'tribunal' is defined by the Oxford Dictionary as a 'judgment seat ... A court of justice; a judicial assembly'. It is thus possible, if confusing, for an ordinary court of law to be referred to as a tribunal. The word now tends to be used in a different context from the normal court system to mean a panel to resolve disputes between, for example, the citizen and an officer of a government agency or between individuals in an area of law in which the government has legislated the conduct of their relations.

In the Social Security Appeals Tribunal the applicant is usually appealing against the decision of an adjudication officer who is an employee of the Department of Social Security. The officer may have decided that the applicant is not entitled to statutory sick pay and the applicant is informed with the adjudication officer's decision that there is a right of appeal. This is conducted by the independent tribunal, usually composed of three persons, of whom the chairman has a five-year general qualification within s71 of the Courts and Legal Services Act 1990.

Although the location and general appearance of the tribunal may make it seem as if it is an offshoot of the civil service department from which the appeal is being made, it is stressed to the appellant that the tribunal is, in fact, totally independent. Appeals from the decisions of immigration officers would be in the same category of a tribunal which deals with matters where the individual is challenging the decision of the state.

A different type of administrative tribunal is the employment tribunal where the applicant will often be appealing against his employer's decision to dismiss him and will allege that this is unfair. The tribunal in this instance will consist of a chairman having a seven-year general qualification within s71 of the 1990 Act, usually full-time, and two 'wingmen', one representing the interests of employers and the other being drawn from a trade union. Appeal lies to the Employment Appeal Tribunal.

Domestic tribunals and other forms of tribunal

The 'domestic tribunals' deal with the internal matters of professional associations. Some of these are created by statute (eg General Medical Council's disciplinary committee), others are voluntary (eg Bar Council).

Tribunals of inquiry are often set up to enquire into matters of urgent importance. This is done by Parliament.

A number of statutes empower Ministers to hold local inquiries, for example on planning schemes. These are held by an inspector who reports to the Minister who has to make the final decisions.

Reform of the tribunal system

A review of tribunals was commissioned by Lord Irvine, the Lord Chancellor, under the chairmanship of Sir Andrew Leggatt and it was reported in 2001.

The Report of Sir Anthony Leggatt, *Tribunals for Users – One System One Service* (2001) (London: Lord Chancellor's Department), is clearly an important one. The 70 different tribunals deal with over a million cases a year, more than all the civil courts put together, and are thus an important feature of the legal system, even more so since most tribunals deal with cases that involve the rights of private citizens against the state. Many deal with issues that are central to the fight against social exclusion (for example, social security, child support and mental health). The tribunals in England and Wales are administered by ten government departments and by local authorities. They range in size from the Appeals Service, which deals with over 270,000 social security appeals, to the 20 or so regulatory tribunals that rarely, if ever, sit. Tribunals are a large and important part of the justice system that have not in the past received the attention and recognition they deserve. It should be noted, however, that there has been some recent reform. This can be seen in the introduction of the unified Appeals Service, with executive agency status, to deal with social security and child support appeals, and the expanded and reformed Immigration Appellate Authorities to deal with asylum seekers.

The majority of the recommendations in the Leggatt Report are aimed at improving the services that tribunal users receive. These include recommendations concerning better access to information and advice, a customer charter setting out service standards, improved tribunal procedures, promoting better initial decision-making by departments, and better use of information technology. The Report recommends that tribunals should be administered separately from the departments whose policies and decisions they oversee, in order to enhance users' confidence in their independence. Establishing a unified Tribunal Service is also seen as being necessary. The emphasis of the Report, as the title indicates, is to concentrate on what the user needs, not the provider. In particular, the Report stresses that 'the distinctive procedures and approach of tribunals should operate so that there are few exceptions to the principle that tribunal users should be able to prepare and present their cases themselves' (recommendation 23). The Report's recommendations about service to users fall into the following main categories.

1. Users should have access to the information they need to understand their rights and the tribunal process, and to enable them wherever possible to proceed without representation. These recommendations require both decision-making departments and tribunals to provide appropriate information to users. Similarly, users should have timely access to the independent advice (and, where necessary, legal representation) they need.

2. Tribunals should publish service standards (including standards for information provision), underpinned by arrangements to spread good practice, a range of

administrative performance measures and systems for appraising judicial performance.

3. Tribunals should adopt an 'enabling approach' giving the parties confidence in both their ability to participate and in the tribunal's capacity to compensate for any lack of skills or knowledge that they may have. There should be improved training for both the judicial members of the tribunals and those who staff the tribunals. This training should focus in particular on the skills needed to implement this approach. Procedures should be fair, economic, speedy and proportionate to the issues at stake.

4. Tribunals should actively manage the progress of cases, ensuring that weak cases are weeded out at an early stage. The use of alternative dispute resolution should be encouraged.

5. Finally, it can be noted that the Report also stresses the need for tribunals, like the ordinary courts, to be independent and impartial.

7.5 Arbitration

The jurisdiction of arbitrators usually arises out of contracts, but some statutes provide for disputes to be referred to arbitration. Arbitration is used widely in shipping, commerce and the building and engineering professions.

Any provision in a contract which purports to oust the jurisdiction of the courts is void but it is usual for a contract (or sometimes a lease) to provide that a dispute be referred first to arbitration. If one party commences court proceedings without arbitration the other may, if he has taken no step in those proceedings, apply to the court to stay the proceedings until after arbitration and this order is usually granted. On the other hand, if all parties agree, the High Court may exercise the arbitrator's powers.

The governing statute must be decided according to the ordinary rules of English law (unless otherwise provided). The contract provides how the arbitrator is to be appointed, and it is common to provide that if the parties cannot agree on an arbitrator that some body or person such as the president of the Law Society shall appoint an arbitrator.

Under s69 Arbitration Act 1996 there is a right of appeal on a point of law to the High Court if the parties consent, or with the leave of the court. Appeal lies to the Court of Appeal, but only with leave on an important point of law.

There is a trend towards arbitration in the commercial world. It is usually a quicker and therefore less costly method of settling disputes. It is also possible to arrange the hearing for a time convenient to both parties. Although the parties must pay the arbitrator's fees (often quite high), arbitration may be preferred because it is a private form of dispute settlement which can be cost-effective in that the decision (known as an award) can be reached more quickly than by using the court system.

7.6 Alternative dispute resolution (ADR)

In 1990 the London Common Law and Commercial Bar Association recommended that there should be a pilot scheme in the county court and their report to this effect was adopted by the Bar Council. Alternative dispute resolution (ADR) would involve the use of lawyers to try to resolve disputes at an early stage by using conciliation and giving the parties an impartial view of the likely outcome of any trial. Decisions would not be binding, but if the procedure was successful much money would be saved and judges would be freed to deal with more difficult cases.

Subsequently, a Bar Council committee, chaired by Beldam LJ, proposed pilot schemes in county courts and the High Court to evaluate the potential of ADR in different kinds of proceedings. The legal rights of the parties would be unaffected by any mediation process and mediators would help the parties to find solutions rather then attempt to suggest or impose them. Mediators would be lawyers with at least seven years' experience and they would be given training in mediation techniques. Similar proposals have been made by the National Consumer Council.

On 8 December 1993 the then Lord Chancellor, Lord Mackay of Clashfern, urged people to resolve disputes without using the formal courts system, commending informal, accessible procedures such as those found in the small claims arbitration procedures. Ombudsman schemes had, he added, recently been gaining the confidence and imagination of the public. A characteristic that all ombudsman schemes have in common is their potential to adjudicate between disputing parties without the trappings or expense of going to court, he explained. Early settlement by informal means in most (but not all) instances was 'far more satisfactory for the parties than pursuing their disputes through the courts – however user-friendly and cost-effective court procedures might be'.

In a *Practice Statement* [1994] 1 All ER 34 Cresswell J, while emphasising the primary role of the Commercial Court as a forum for deciding commercial cases, said the judges of the court wished to encourage parties to consider the use of ADR, such as mediation and conciliation, as a possible additional means of resolving issues or disputes. The judges would not act as mediators or be involved in any ADR process but would in appropriate cases invite parties to consider whether their cases, or certain issues in their cases, could be resolved by means of ADR. By way of example only, ADR might be tried where the costs of litigation were likely to be wholly disproportionate to the amount at stake. The clerk to the Commercial Court would keep a list of individuals and bodies that offered mediation, conciliation and other ADR services. The list would also include individuals and bodies offering arbitration services.

In a *Practice Note* [1996] 3 All ER 383 the Commercial Court formally encourages the use of alternative dispute resolution (ADR) in the Commercial Court and summarises the advantages of ADR in a commercial context as follows:

1. it significantly helps to save litigants the ever-mounting cost of bringing their cases to trial;
2 it saves them the delay of litigation in reaching finality in their disputes;
3. it enables them to achieve settlement of their disputes while preserving their existing commercial relationships and market reputation;
4. it provides them with a wider range of settlement solutions than those offered by litigation; and
5. it is likely to make a substantial contribution to the more efficient use of judicial resources.

The pre-trial check list (*Practice Note* [1995] 1 All ER 385) deals specifically with ADR and asks the following.

1. Have you (the solicitor) or counsel discussed with your client(s) the possibility of attempting to resolve this dispute (or particular issues) by ADR?
2. Might some form of ADR procedure assist to resolve or narrow the issues in this case?
3. Have your or your client(s) explored with the other parties the possibility of resolving this dispute (or particular issues) by ADR?

After undertaking research on ADR, Helen Genn offered the following conclusions (*Court-based ADR Initiatives for Non-family Civil Disputes: the Commercial Court and the Court of Appeal*, (2002) London: Lord Chancellor's Department).

1. Voluntary take-up of invitations to enter ADR schemes remains at a modest level, even when the mediator's services are provided free or at a nominal cost.
2. Outside of commercial practice, the profession remains very cautious about the use of ADR. Positive experience of ADR does not appear to be producing armies of converts. Explanations may lie in the amount of work involved in preparing for mediation, the incentives and economics of mediation in low value cases, and the impact of the Woolf reforms. More pre-issue settlements and swifter post-issue settlements may diminish the perceived need for ADR in run-of-the-mill civil cases.
3. An individualised approach to the direction of cases towards ADR is likely to be more effective than general invitations at an early stage in the litigation process. This would require the development of clearly articulated selection principles.
4. The timing of invitations or directions to mediate is crucial. The early stages of proceedings may not be the best time, and should not be the only opportunity, to consider using ADR.
5. Subjective perceptions of the profession support the view that successful ADR saves the likely cost of proceeding to trial and may save expenditure by promoting earlier settlement than might otherwise have occurred. Unsuccessful ADR can increase the costs for parties.

6. ADR generally results in a high level of customer satisfaction. Mediators with excellent skills and familiarity with the subject area of the dispute produce the highest levels of satisfaction. The approach of mediators needs to be matched with the expectations of parties and their solicitors.
7. In order to maximise take-up of court-administered schemes there is a need for dedicated administrative support.

Family mediation

Tony Wells, the director of development for the Council for Family Proceedings, has said:

> 'The essential feature of mediation in family disputes is that parties are assisted to work out their own solution to their dispute. The task of the mediator is to enable the parties to do this work. The mediator sees the parties together without their legal advisers. The mediator does not offer advice or suggest solutions. He or she will clarify any proposals made and also the objections to them, as well as what might make a proposal acceptable. The work will focus on what the parties want for the future – not what has happened in the past.'

Training programmes for mediators are run by the Family Mediators' Association. Lawyers selected for training (other mediators are, for example, workers or counsellors) are expected to have had at least five years' experience as family lawyers. The National Association of Family and Conciliation Services is the biggest provider of out-of-court mediation and it has estimated that, where there was a clear outcome, in 38 per cent of cases disputed issues were completely resolved.

The Green Paper *Looking to the Future: Mediation and the Ground for Divorce*, published 6 December 1993, contained proposals for the reform of divorce, based largely on recommendations made by the Law Commission. At the heart of the proposed reform is the use of mediators to help resolve issues between the parties with minimal conflict. Trials have taken place of various mediation schemes with no clear consensus emerging as to the form that mediation should take in the family sphere.

7.7 Diagrams of the main English court structure

The civil courts

The criminal courts

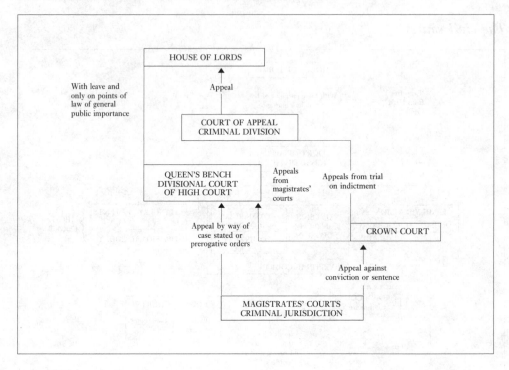

8

Funding of Legal Advice and Representation

8.1 The legal aid scheme prior to the Access to Justice Act 1999

8.2 The Access to Justice Act 1999

8.3 The Legal Services Commission

8.4 The Criminal Defence Service (CDS)

8.5 The Community Legal Service (CLS)

8.6 Alternative methods of funding: legal expenses insurance and conditional fees

8.7 Free legal services

8.1 The legal aid scheme prior to the Access to Justice Act 1999

The concept of legal aid is that the costs involved in the conduct of the defence are met by the state as opposed to by the individual. State-funded help was first introduced in 1949 and its aim was to reduce the inequality of access to justice that resulted from the inability of the poor to fund any form of legal advice or representation. This initial scheme operated in a fairly simple fashion and on the basis of solicitors in private practice being paid all, or part, of their fee for work undertaken on behalf of clients. By the mid 1980s the scheme had become cumbersome. It had divided into six different schemes and still covered most cases, civil and criminal. The cost of the scheme, however, was huge and from the mid 1980s successive governments introduced changes aimed at reducing the cost. The financial eligibility for legal advice and legal representation was changed to the extent that it eventually excluded millions of people from the scheme. In addition, the method by which lawyers were paid for legal aid work was altered so as to be a lot less favourable to them, a measure introduced to encourage firms to withdraw from the scheme, and the control over the scheme was moved from the Law Society to a Legal Aid Board set up by s3 of the Legal Aid Act 1988. Powers were then subsequently devolved to regional authorities and to particular firms through a process of franchising. The regional authorities came to be restricted to operating under 'lump-sum' amounts for each financial year that were not topped up during that year no matter how many deserving cases there might be that were without aid after the 'lump sum' had run out.

By 1996 the scheme was clearly in a state of collapse and in need of radical reform. Such reform was published in the government White Paper on *Legal Aid* (1996) but these proposals were not implemented. However, in 1996 Lord Mackay, the Lord Chancellor of the time, did use his powers under the Legal Aid Act 1988 to implement part of a plan announced in 1995 to deal with the legal aid assessments of 'apparently wealthy' applicants. This resulted from a series of cases in which defendants had obtained legal aid, both in civil and criminal cases, yet maintained a luxurious lifestyle by such tactics as setting up trusts for their children to redistribute their assets and living on subsidies obtained from wealthy family and friends. The new changes were a series of administrative changes to the way legal aid means' assessments were carried out. The operation of this was supported by a special investigations unit to assess the means of people with complex financial circumstances. The changes also included new powers for officials to scrutinise the assets of family and friends who it is thought will subsidise the claimant and a new £100,000 limit in respect of equity on the claimant's home and loans offset against its value.

By the late 1990s the effect of all these changes had brought in cuts that had reduced spending on legal aid by millions of pounds and the entire scheme had little similarity, either in concept or operation, to that originally conceived in 1949.

8.2 The Access to Justice Act 1999

In March 1998 Lord Irvine issued a consultation paper setting out ideas for reform of legal aid: *Access to Justice with Conditional Fees*. In December 1998 he published a White Paper, *Modernising Justice* (Cmnd 4155), setting out the government's finalised proposals for reform, which were to be implemented by the Access to Justice Act 1999. It stated the government's reasons for its radical reform proposals as being the need to give more people access to justice and to obtain the best value for taxpayers' money spent on legal services and the courts. The proposals were also designed to encourage more use of mediation and non-legally qualified advice workers in civil cases and increased use of conditional fees.

The Access to Justice Act came into force in July 1999. It is the present Labour government's response to the need for drastic change but is based on different criteria to those originally proposed under the former Conservative government by Lord Mackay. The former legal aid scheme (which was costing £1.6 billion per year) has effectively been dismantled and a completely new method for the state funding of civil and criminal cases has been introduced. There are now two systems of 'contracted providers' who offer services in line with the new criteria imposed by the Act. For certain cases civil legal aid is replaced purely by conditional fees, eg road accident cases where conditional fees have proved a popular and workable replacement for legal aid. In the remaining areas not covered by conditional fees (ie all criminal cases, and most family and social welfare cases) legal aid is replaced by a quality-controlled system provided by specialist lawyers working under contract.

The Lord Chancellor hailed the reforms introduced by the 1999 Act as a strategically important part of the public funding of legal information and advice. It is hoped that the changes in the legal aid scheme, combined with further development of conditional fees ('no win, no fee' arrangements), will ensure that access to justice by persons who could not otherwise afford to pay for legal representation will continue and expand.

8.3 The Legal Services Commission

The Legal Aid Board has been replaced by a new executive non-departmental public body, the Legal Services Commission. The duty of the Commission is to develop and administer in England and Wales the two new schemes introduced by the 1999 Act. The two new schemes are as follows.

1. The Criminal Defence Service (CDS): this replaces the old system of criminal legal aid and provides criminal services to all people accused of crimes. The service uses state employed 'public defenders' as well as private lawyers.
2. The Community Legal Service (CLS): this replaces the old scheme for civil legal aid, with considerable reduction of cases eligible for funding, and brings together networks of suppliers (eg solicitors) and other funders (eg local authorities) into partnerships.

The new Legal Services Commission will monitor the allocation of contracts on the basis of local needs and will be responsible for assessing the need for state-funded help in individual civil cases. It is to be guided in its work in general by the Lord Chancellor (a role now performed by the Minister for Constitutional Affairs). However, the Minister will not have any say in individual cases and the advice given to the Commission is to be made public.

Concerns were expressed about the new 'block-contracts' system that the scheme is based on. These were voiced both by MPs and peers and reflected concerns expressed by the legal profession. The Law Society warned that a system of block contracts will seriously reduce public choice; it estimates that the number of solicitors' offices offering legal aid at present could be reduced from around 10,000 to about 3,000, thereby destroying local access to justice in many areas. The Bar Council criticised the plan for block contracts as risking a 'sausage-machine mentality' to processing justice and also expressed concern over the moves towards a US-style public defender system for criminal cases on the ground that it would reduce public choice.

The contrary view in defence of the new system is that contracts under each scheme will be awarded only to those lawyers and advice centres (eg law centres and citizens' advice bureaux) who are willing to accept strictly controlled budgets and agreed standards; lawyers will no longer be paid according to the amount of work they handle, hence ending the apparent abuse of the current system under which there is no incentive to handle cases quickly or work efficiently – the scandal of unscrupulous lawyers 'milking' the legal aid fund by claiming an unreasonable number of hours per case will end.

The CDS and CLS schemes replace the six schemes that were operating under the Legal Aid Board, namely:

1. the civil legal aid scheme;
2. the criminal legal aid scheme;
3. the legal aid and assistance scheme (the 'Green Form' scheme);
4. assistance by way of legal representation (ABWOR);
5. duty solicitor schemes in police stations;
6. duty solicitor schemes for criminal cases in magistrates' courts.

8.4 The Criminal Defence Service (CDS)

There have been sweeping changes to the administration of state funding for criminal cases. In accordance with the criteria for access to justice laid down by the European Convention on Human Rights, all criminal cases are eligible for legal aid. Accordingly, the old means test has gone and state-funded assistance is now automatic for all those facing criminal charges. However, in each case the Commission has the power to investigate the financial means of the defendant to assess the true need for assistance and, upon a conviction, information on a wealthy defendant will be passed to the trial judge who will order the defendant to pay part, or all, of the costs of the defence.

In order to meet this provision, the CDS cannot be restricted by a set budget. There is, however, a set amount set aside annually for legal aid so it is to be presumed that funding for civil cases will suffer if criminal cases drain the available funds. The funding granted in an individual case can cover full legal advice and representation or any part of this, eg a duty solicitor at the police station or magistrates' court.

The services of the CDS are carried out by providers who are contracted to provide state-funded services. Any provider will give 'one-stop' provision, ie the same lawyer will deal with the client from start to finish for all services. Some criminal services will be provided by state-employed lawyers, but the Commission cannot restrict a defendant to using one of these 'public defenders'. Both sole practitioners and law firms will join 'panels' which specialise into certain forms of provision, especially for serious crime and specialist work such as serious fraud.

The upshot of this is that persons seeking legal aid for a criminal case will fall into two categories. Those whose case dictates that they must select representation from one of the 'panels', and those who may make a choice between a public defender or a private lawyer contracted by the Commission. This set-up met with considerable opposition but it does have certain advantages. In particular, the 'one-stop' provision removes the altogether unsatisfactory multiplication of schemes that were in place by the end of the old system under which lawyers sought payment from several different sources for the same case. The use of 'panels' has the advantage of allowing lawyers to specialise in certain forms of work rather than offer a wide range of state-funded criminal law provision, and, from the government's point of view, it has the advantage of allowing the Commission to maintain fairly strict control over the funding of these criminal cases. It was the employment of public defenders that provoked the most discussion. They are to be used in certain geographical areas and areas of work such as youth courts, and are intended to supplement poor legal provision in both these areas. In defence of the proposal, the government argued that it gave increased flexibility in that their own lawyers could be employed where there was insufficient provision and thereby ensure that there was proper access to justice for all.

8.5 The Community Legal Service (CLS)

This part of the Commission's brief deals with legal aid for civil cases. The old system under the Legal Aid Act 1988 has been replaced by a new set of criteria and the availability of aid is set on a wholly new footing.

The excluded categories

Some 60 per cent of civil cases previously funded under the old scheme have been excluded from the new scheme. The categories include the following.

1. All personal injury cases except medical negligence cases. Personal injury cases form the bulk of the percentage reduction of civil cases brought in by the new scheme. The exclusion forces parties to avail themselves of the conditional fee scheme. Clinical negligence cases are subject to the scrutiny of a quality assurance scheme.
2. Defamation cases and malicious falsehood cases. Defamation actions were excluded from legal aid some time ago under the old system but where it could be classed as malicious falsehood it could be eligible for legal aid. Both are now seen as being better dealt with by conditional fees.
3. Cases pursued in the course of a business. These have been removed because businesses are in a position to insure against legal costs. The message from the government by the introduction of this measure is clearly one of business responsibility: they cannot expect the taxpayer to foot the bill for legal matters

that they become engaged in and they must be prudent enough to take out sufficient insurance to cover the eventuality. There is no doubt the hope that pushing these costs back onto the businesses and their insurers will encourage out-of-court negotiation to keep insurance premiums down and thereby reduce the number of actions brought in the courts.

4. Certain types of company law claims, partnership disputes, the administration of a trust, inheritance disputes, disputes before the Lands Tribunal and neighbour boundary disputes. All of these are disputes brought by bodies or persons of sufficient means, or are otherwise considered to be matters which do not justify aid from the public purse, and can properly be dealt with by conditional fees.

It had originally been proposed that civil legal aid be replaced, apart from family and social welfare cases, with an expanded conditional fee scheme. However, following strong opposition to this plan from lawyers' groups and backbench Labour MPs, Lord Irvine, the Lord Chancellor, agreed defer the full withdrawal of civil legal aid under the new Act pending an assessment of how the system was working and modified his proposals for the current withdrawal of legal aid to the exclusions listed above.

Funding for cases in the scheme

The funding of aid for civil cases is no longer on a 'demand-led' basis, ie it is not endlessly available for all who might apply in a given year. Unlike the CDS, the CLS is to receive a fixed amount of money in each year which will be determined as part of the normal procedures for setting government spending. The money will be allocated by the Lord Chancellor (the role now being performed by the Minister for Constitutional Affairs) to two budgets, one for family cases and one for all other civil cases that fall within the new scheme. Once the fund in either budget has been exhausted, there will be no aid available until the next year. The criteria and procedures for the use of the monies in the two budgets is controlled by a Funding Code drawn up by the Legal Service Commission and approved by the Minister. The Commission is under a duty to use the money so as to combine 'price and quality'. This does not mean that they are to take the cheapest options, or even the highest quality ones, but instead there is a responsibility to balance price and quality so as to find the best value for money. The aim of promoting increased mediation underpins the criteria for the use of the funding but there is more flexibility in how funds are to be allocated than under the old system. Funding assessment is to be based on questions such as the following.

1. Would a prudent person spend his or her own money to bring or defend the action? If the answer is no, then only wider public interest reasons would justify state funding (eg for a test case that could establish liability for harm caused by a dangerous drug).
2. Is the case more suited to mediation than to adjudication? Mediation services

have proved to be very effective in reducing the number of divorce cases and also have a role to play for most other forms of action.

3. Could the action be funded in another way, eg by a conditional fee?

The services offered by the CLS vary according to the category of case, ie some will be funded only for legal advice, some will be funded only for representation by a lawyer in court, and some will be funded both for advice and representation. The Funding Code will detail the services that are offered for any area of law.

Eligibility for aid is determined on the basis of means and merits tests. Merits tests assess eligibility on the basis of whether the case is sufficiently important to justify state funding and includes consideration of whether the applicant is likely to succeed. Means tests assess eligibility on the basis of an applicant's disposable income, ie on expenditure for essential living expenses, and the test can include assessment of the applicant's disposable capital, ie money that they could draw on from their savings. The tests to be used by the CLS are more flexible than the old tests but they are also stiffer in that they are designed to identify the true wealth of a particular applicant and to determine the suitability of the case for state-funded help. The 1999 Act gives the Minister powers to pass delegated legislation to set limits which will vary according to the type of case and the type of service. However, for the start of the scheme the financial eligibility limits are remaining the same and reviews will be carried out each year.

Delegated legislation passed under powers granted by the Act details when a legally aided person who loses his/her case is to pay costs, how much these costs shall be and what proportion is to be paid by the Commission.

Funding for civil cases, under the CLS, could be restructured so that early and effective resolution outside the courts will become the favoured outcome for most cases. This is the main proposal in a consultation paper published by the Department for Constitutional Affairs and the Legal Services Commission: *The Community Legal Service* (2004). The primary objective of the consultation is to indicate possible changes that would allow the Commission to re-focus CLS funding so that early and effective dispute resolution is encouraged and litigation is seen as a last resort. The consultation paper also proposes changes designed to ensure that the limited resources of the CLS is better targeted to the areas of greatest need. Thus, legal aid funds must continue to be targeted at those who need them most and the cost of legal aid will not be allowed to increase in real terms. The historical context is that in recent years, civil legal aid has been prioritised on social exclusion, putting some legal activity into the private sector (eg 'no win, no fee' for personal injury cases). A tougher merits test was instituted, Community Legal Service Partnerships were set up to measure local needs and a greater proportion of resources was allocated to 'legal help' work to resolve cases without court intervention. As a result fewer cases in total now receive public funding, but hopefully that funding is better targeted.

In family cases, the paper proposes a significant restructuring of legal aid in order to encourage the early resolution of private family law cases outside the courts. These measures support the wider government initiative in the family justice system, which encourages people to use out of court arrangements in order to resolve sensitive issues such as child contact. Legal help and help with mediation in family cases are planned to be amalgamated into a single level of service called family help with one pay level. In addition, the paper proposes tightening up the availability of legal aid in divorce cases where there are assets in dispute which could be used to fund legal proceedings. This could create a level playing field, where legally aided clients have similar considerations to privately paying clients when reaching a decision on whether or not to go ahead with litigation. There could also be stricter controls over multiple and repeat applications in private family law cases; a reduction in legal aid costs protection; and the removal of low priority categories, such as legal advice on name changes.

New measures are also proposed to encourage claimants with claims against the National Health Service and the police to exhaust complaints channels before seeking legal aid and going to court. As a first step, a claimant should go through the improved National Health Service complaints procedure and the new Independent Police Complaints Commission. Findings obtained through these new complaints procedures should help identify the strength of the case. If the complaints channels have been exhausted, then legal aid will be available for eligible claimants for clinical negligence cases and for serious cases against the police.

In addition, the consultation paper contains a number of other proposed changes to legal aid payments, which support the routine use of mediation and other forms of ADR in many cases. Some cases should go ahead on a conditional fee agreement ('no-win, no-fee') basis, rather than using legal aid.

Contracted providers and the partnership scheme

The 'franchising' system for law firms and other advice agencies introduced in 1994 has been altered to a scheme of contracts with certain of those bodies. This has reduced the outlets which persons seeking legal aid can use, but there will nonetheless be some 6,000 providers contracted to provide legal services funded, or partly funded, by the public purse. The aim is to provide the widest possible access to information and advice, and the 1999 Act gives the Commission power to make grants to advice centres and to employ staff directly. It was feared that this latter power would be used to create a team of state-employed civil lawyers, in the same way as is being done for criminal cases (see below), but this would not appear to be in the pipeline and, for the present at least, is discrepant with the moves toward a networked system of legal services providers that is being set in motion as part of the Commission's duty to develop a network of general legal services providers through liaison with local councils and other funders of legal services. There has been such liaison with the Law Centres Federation which looks set to be a central part of the Community Legal Service and it is expected that the computerised facilities of the law centres will be used to set up an e-mail advice service.

A number of Community Legal Service partnerships have been set up, and the Commission has power to establish more, which work with the local authorities and other legal service providers and have the aim of establishing a cohesive and co-ordinated system for tailoring services to suit the needs of different areas, a valuable step towards eliminating the unequal distribution of funding that used to occur. A 'quality mark' has been introduced for all forms of service providers stating what the provider can do to assist users to make informed choices about which service they should use and reassure them that the provider meets standards set for that service. This system also applies to bodies that are less directly concerned with the funding but nonetheless play a part in assisting the user to make a choice – for example, community centres, local libraries, help groups and so on.

8.6 Alternative methods of funding: legal expenses insurance and conditional fees

Legal expenses insurance

Legal expenses insurance schemes are today generally available either free-standing or as 'add-ons' to household and motor insurance cover. About 7 per cent of the population have free-standing legal expenses insurance and that figure rises to about 27 per cent when add-on policies are included. However, this is still very low compared to insurance cover taken out by households in many European legal systems. It seems that people in this country are deterred by the costs involved or, perhaps, are unaware of the availability of such cover. It may also be that insurance companies are fixing premiums at too high a level. Insurance companies are also unwilling to offer cover for 'high-risk' areas (criminal cases, family law disputes, etc) so that only a limited amount of unmet need can be filled by legal expenses insurance. The Law Society has also stated that insurance should be seen as a supplement to the legal aid scheme and not a substitute for it. Insurance cover plays an important supplementary role to conditional fees.

Conditional fees

Conditional fees were introduced into English law by s58 of the Courts and Legal Services Act 1990 which gave the Lord Chancellor power to make orders specifying the proceedings in which agreements to charge on that basis could lawfully be made. The effect of conditional fees is that they allow lawyers and clients to share the risk of litigation by permitting the lawyer to agree to accept a case on the basis that if he loses he will not be paid a fee – hence they are also known as 'no win, no fee' arrangements. In return for the risk, the lawyer sets a 'success fee', also known as 'uplift', calculated as a percentage of normal costs, as recompense for the taking the risk of not being paid. The governing principle for this was dealt with under the 1990 Act: the higher the chance of winning, the lower the success fee that should be set, and vice versa.

Although provided for in the 1990 Act, the system came into operation in September 1995 and was part of reforms to the system of justice brought in by Lord Mackay, the then Lord Chancellor. Their introduction represented a major change since it had for centuries been accepted under the common law that any form of conditional or contingency fee was unlawful and unenforceable for being contrary to public policy. It was feared that by giving the lawyer a financial stake in the outcome of litigation it might encourage unnecessary litigation ('ambulance-chasing'!) or unethical tactics in attempting to win a case. Codes of practice for barristers and solicitors forbade such methods of payment: *Swain* v *The Law Society* [1983] 1 AC 598. The principle of conditional fee payment has, however, operated for many years in Scotland where lawyers are said to take cases 'on spec', ie on a speculative basis. American lawyers use a slightly different system of 'contingency fees', under which a lawyer may bargain for a percentage of the compensation award if he/she wins the case for the client. (In the American legal system each side pays their own costs.)

It follows that only conditional fees expressly authorised under s58 of the Courts and Legal Services Act 1990 are lawful in the English legal system: *Hughes* v *Kingston-upon-Hull City Council* (1998) The Times 9 December. Under the first regime introduced in 1995 conditional fees could only be agreed for proceedings involving personal injury, insolvency and cases before the European Commission and the European Court of Human Rights. Criminal and family proceedings were specifically excluded from the newly authorised regime. The system proved popular and successful, particularly in straightforward personal injury claims such as road accident cases where lawyers were usually confident of a win and therefore willing to take a case upon a conditional fee. In July 1998 the then Lord Chancellor, Lord Irvine, used his power under s58 of the 1990 Act to extend the conditional fee regime to all non-family civil cases. Family proceedings were not included then as it would undermine the policy of encouraging divorcing couples to settle their disputes amicably through mediation rather than hostile litigation, and for this same reason a proposal to extend conditional fees to family law disputes over property and other family assets was dropped from what would become the Access to Justice Act 1999. Criminal proceedings also remain excluded.

In 1995 the maximum amount of success fee a lawyer was entitled to charge was set at 100 per cent of the lawyer's normal fees for the work undertaken. Clients are also often expected to pay the disbursements incurred in the litigation, such as medical or other expert reports, court or enquiry agent's fees, but in some cases the lawyer may agree to fund such disbursements. Regulations were made under s58 to specify the information a conditional fee agreement had to contain, and this was followed by the Law Society producing guidance for solicitors about the use of conditional fees and a model agreement. It advised solicitors to apply a voluntary limit on the proportion of damages that could be taken by the success fee, suggesting it should not be more than 25 per cent. One of the problems with the success fee has been that it was not covered in the award of costs. Thus, even though the party had won the case, they still had to pay a success fee to their lawyer which would usually come out of the compensation award and a 100 per cent uplift can be a comparatively large deduction from that award. Following the extension of the conditional fee system in July 1998, Lord Irvine LC promised to introduce legislation so as to enable an award of costs against a losing party to cover the success element of the winning party's conditional fee and this has now been brought in by s27 of the Access to Justice Act 1999 which has changed s58 so as to permit court rules to allow the success element to be included as part of the costs order against the losing party. This is an important development; the 'no win, no fee' arrangement can now truly cost next to nothing whatever the outcome.

The biggest deterrent to the use of conditional fees is the risk of losing and having to pay costs. In the English legal system a winning litigant can usually expect to recover costs from the losing side under the rule that 'costs follow the event'. It can be argued that this serves to make litigants assess the chances of success carefully before embarking on litigation, but it can also been seen as counter-productive to the notion of access to justice if that party has a case where the law is uncertain and should be tested. Under the Access to Justice Act 1999 a case of this nature may now be able to gain legal aid as one of the 'exceptional cases' for which it is within the discretion of the Lord Chancellor (a role now performed by the Minister for Constitutional Affairs) to direct the Commission to grant state funding.

The conditional fee scheme was clearly designed as a supplement to the legal aid scheme, being aimed at middle-income groups who fell outside the financial eligibility criteria for legal aid but who were deterred from pursuing or defending claims by the very high costs of litigation. That principle has been taken up by the Access to Justice Act 1999 which excludes civil cases on the basis that they are suitable for conditional fee arrangements. The original intention had been to put all civil work onto this footing but the proposal met with such opposition that the Lord Chancellor agreed to reduce the excluded categories to those currently in the Act (see section 8.5 above) but reserved the right to move more civil cases over to conditional fees if the 1998 scheme proved successful.

The government have justified the alternative to legal aid that conditional fees represents on several grounds. It was said that it helps to ensure that the risks are managed by the lawyers who are better placed than clients to know what those risks are. It was also argued that lawyers working under conditional fee agreements are likely to be more keen to win. This may be a slight on many reputable solicitors, but there have been reports over the years of what sound like unjustifiable legally aided cases for rich and/or foreign clients who turned out to have substantial hidden assets and whose chances of success in litigation were eventually revealed with hindsight to be pretty slim. The Legal Aid Board had to share the responsibility for bad judgments on this. A counter-argument to the 'keener to win' point of view might be that some lawyers tempted to try too hard could go beyond the bounds of acceptable professional behaviour – known as 'ambulance-chasing' in the United States.

When the regime was first introduced there was speculation that lawyers would become selective about cases, preferring to take those that carried little risk of losses, for example, straightforward personal injury claims such as road accident cases where lawyers can be more confident of a win. There is little evidence of this and the scheme has, by and large, been popular and successful. Its introduction was a significant step towards removing the barrier of high costs that deterred many potential litigants from starting legal proceedings even when they had a strong case, and clients can always take out an insurance policy to mitigate the risks and expenses of losing. It can therefore be seen that the idea of conditional fees would appeal to many potential litigants and perhaps to more commercially minded members of the legal profession.

One downside of the conditional fee arrangement is that the contract can be complex and the client may not fully appreciate his obligations under it. The other downside is the cost of insurance to protect against the risk of losing. When the first scheme of conditional fees was introduced in September 1995 the Law Society negotiated with insurance companies to provide costs cover at a special low premium and by the end of 1997 some 34,000 policies had been issued with premiums ranging from about £95 for road accident cases to £150 for other cases. This cover only went some way to solving the costs of conditional fees. The insurance premium covers only ordinary legal costs and not the 'success element' charged by the winning party's lawyer and the premium itself is not recoverable as part of the costs. In addition, insurance cover is either not available or the premium is too high for cases that are regarded as highly unpredictable and potentially very costly, such as medical negligence cases. In 1998 Lord Irvine said that his Department would work on making changes to the legal insurance market so as to encourage insurers to provide cover for the success element of conditional fees, particularly in areas traditionally regarded as unpredictable/expensive.

The role of conditional fee arrangements has recently been considered by both the Court of Appeal and the House of Lords. The position that has been reached does not appear to be satisfactory. When legal aid was all but abolished for most civil litigation (family cases being the major exception) these new arrangements were to fill the void, and indeed they offered the potential to be more wide reaching than the system of legal aid had been. These arrangements, known as 'no win, no fee' arrangements, have obvious advantages for claimants. For the lawyer there can be an uplift or success fee allowing a fee greater than normal costs for the risk being taken. The claimant can also hope to recover the amount of the premiums with after the event insurance cover, which is designed to protect the claimant from the costs consequences of losing the case. The issue is: what limits should there be on such arrangements? The Conditional Fee Agreement Regulations 2000 offer obstacles in terms of the procedures to be followed. The early decisions of the courts saw their applicability as being in the area of modest road accident cases. So for claimants there is the clear dilemma that they do not know if they can rely on such arrangements. *Callery* v *Gray (No 1)* [2001] 1 WLR 2112 was such a case. The arrangements for the conditional fee and the insurance were made at an early stage of the litigation and the issue was: was this acceptable? The situation could be one in which the case was not going to be contested. The answer given by Lord Woolf for the Court of Appeal was that, in such circumstances, it was acceptable for a reasonable success fee and a reasonable insurance premium to be payable as costs by the defendant. For modest motoring personal injury cases 20 per cent would be the maximum success fee. More difficult cases could permit a higher fee. As to the insurance policy they allowed the £350 cost in the case but were unsure as to its suitability as a benchmark for other cases. When the issue of conditional fee arrangements was raised before the House of Lords (*Callery* v *Gray (Nos 1 & 2)* [2002] 1 WLR 2000) the attitude of their Lordships (by a majority verdict of three to two) was that they were not in a position to intervene in these matters. They saw the Court of Appeal as being the appropriate body to develop rules in this area.

The merits of leaving the future of conditional fee arrangements to the Court of Appeal, as espoused in *Callery*, may have to be reconsidered in the light of the decision of the Court of Appeal in *Halloran* v *Delaney* [2003] 1 WLR 28. The Court imposed a limit of 5 per cent on the success fee for run-of-the-mill personal injury cases that reach a settlement before proceedings are started. The success fee needs to be set at such a level that it will take into account the cases that lawyers lose and for which they will receive no fee at all. The danger of a figure as low as 5 per cent is that lawyers will not undertake such work and the system will be left without the provision of legal services. It should be noted that the 5 per cent figure is very different to the 20 per cent that was used in the *Callery* case.

Litigation has continued in order to refine the principles that should apply to these schemes. In *Arkin* v *Borchard Lines Limited* [2004] 1 Lloyd's Rep 88, Borchard Lines had been unsuccessfully sued by Arkin. A commercial funder had assisted Arkin by means of a conditional fee agreement. Borchard Lines now wished to recover its costs from the commercial funder: Arkin was without assets. The funder would have received a share of the damages if the action had succeeded. There was no undertaking to pay Borchard's costs if Arkin lost and after-the-event insurance had not been used. The funder argued that such an arrangement allowed impecunious claimants to bring claims in circumstances where they would otherwise be denied access to justice. Costs were refused in order to allow access to justice in cases such as this one. Whilst normally the winner could expect to recover costs, the matter fell to be determined as a question of public policy as to whether the circumstances of a case merited the making of a third party costs order. In this case the funder had not interfered in the litigation. Also, the premium for after-the-event insurance would have been so high that it was not a commercially viable option. Therefore the public interest in discouraging weak claims was subordinated to the aim of securing access to justice. To do otherwise would deter professional funders in future cases.

Legal expenses insurance and conditional fees were also considered by the government in the following report (Tackling the 'Compensation Culture' (2004), London, Department for Constitutional Affairs). This document is the Government's Response to the Better Regulation Task Force Report: 'Better Routes to Redress' (2004). It presents the law as having the role of defining people's rights and responsibilities towards each other and that the law should require people to take reasonable care towards one another and to compensate for damage they cause when they fail to do so. But the law also puts a duty on individuals to take reasonable care of their own safety and reasonable steps to reduce the cost of any damage that others cause them. People who have a genuine claim should be able to enforce their right to compensation, but the problem is the creation of a culture where people believe that if there is an injury there must inevitably be someone else to blame and someone else to pay. This creates false expectations that there is easy money just waiting to be claimed. Some personal injury advertising does just this and the problem then is that a compensation culture may emerge. Claims Management Companies offering 'no win, no fee' arrangements are perceived as being a problem in this respect. The government hopes that these companies will act to provide self regulation and discipline, otherwise the government will intervene.

The report emphasises that the Human Rights Act 1998 should not be seen as a factor in this. The Act did not create any new rights, it simply enabled people in this country to access their basic rights and liberties in their own courts instead of having to go to Strasbourg. Equally, accident claims have been reasonably static for the past four years – indeed they fell by 9.5 per cent in the year to March 2004. But there are developments that have potential to alter this situation. Advertisements that encourage people to pursue claims are becoming more and more common. The government strongly opposes advertisements in hospitals that encourage patients to claim against doctors, or doctors being paid to refer patients to a particular solicitor. It is also important that the courts award compensation for injuries caused by negligence but not otherwise. This in turn sets the standard against which claims are settled out of court. The fear is that faced with a situation of some dreadful misfortune assistance is provided on the basis of empathy rather than fault. One dimension of this is that where legal aid is sought to pursue a claim, the merits test must be applied rigorously. For example, claims against educational establishments concerning the provision of educational services, which can be made many years after education has been completed, have a low success rate and high cost.

8.7 Free legal services

To help overcome apparent unmet legal need several sources of free legal advice have grown up. Although, in general, they can be of limited assistance, the following institutions have the useful function of putting those in need of help 'on the right track', that is, providing initial basic advice and, if appropriate, informing them of the legal aid scheme and sending them to a solicitor willing to undertake such work. The following are the main sources of free legal advice.

Law centres

Law centres specialise in those areas of work which may not be well served by private practice. These include housing, welfare rights, immigration, health, family, disability rights, employment, and education. On the other hand, law centres do not undertake commercial work, conveyancing, probate, divorce, adult crime or large personal injury claims.

Law centres should employ at least one solicitor with three years' post-qualification experience, but they also employ barristers and non-lawyers. Subject to certain conditions, a solicitor employed by a member of the Law Centres Federation may give advice to, and otherwise act for, members of the public. Law centres operate mainly in poorer urban areas. At one time during the 1980s and early 1990s law centres faced acute funding problems and were often dependent on local authority grants and money from charities. Some law centres were forced to close through lack of funding. However, the future for law centres looks brighter as a result of the overhaul of the legal aid scheme, under which law centres are offered greater opportunities to participate in Community Legal Service: see further section 8.5 above.

Legal advice centres

These only provide legal advice and cannot undertake litigation. Because they are staffed by volunteers they cost very much less to run than the law centres. The majority of these centres are staffed by lawyers on a rota basis but there is no uniform pattern. Many university law faculties now run advice centres where second and third year students get practical experience of legal problems. When a client needs to start proceedings he is referred to a local solicitor.

Citizens' advice bureaux

Set up in 1939 to give emergency service during the war, the National Association of Citizens' Advice Bureaux, a registered charity, now has 594 main bureaux and 3,500 outreach centres. Most central funding comes from the Department of Trade and Industry, while local bureaux rely mainly on local authority support and the Legal Services Commission. Donations also come from the private sector and charitable trusts. Anyone may turn to a local bureau for advice and information on every subject from social security to taxation, debt counselling to consumer rights. The great majority of advisers are trained volunteers and many bureaux have honorary legal advisers solicitors or barristers who attend regular sessions in a voluntary capacity. A greater role for citizens' advice bureaux now exists under the Community Legal Service: see section 8.5 above.

Free Representation Units (FRU)

Set up by students in London in 1972, in 1993 the original unit represented over 2,000 clients, particularly in tribunals where there is usually no legal aid. Over half of these cases were in industrial tribunals (now employment tribunals) and the next largest number were before social security tribunals. The unit now has a full-time administrator and a full-time solicitor who carries out all preparatory work, but it relies on volunteers, mainly students, pupils and junior barristers, to represent the clients.

In July 1993 FRU launched, with the wholehearted support of the Bar Council, a Chambers Scheme directed at all barristers in London and the South East. The Scheme aims to meet the rapidly increasing demand for FRU's services and to enlist also the help of experienced barristers who would commit themselves to appearing in a specified number of cases every year.

Birmingham also has a Free Representation Unit and there are similar schemes in the Northern and the Wales and Chester Circuits.

In the summer of 1996 the Bar established a Pro Bono Unit, run on a charitable basis, under which a register of barristers is kept. Those on the register are prepared to offer up to three days of their time to deserving cases in any field of law where the applicant would otherwise be unable to afford legal advice or representation, provided the case does not require the assistance of a solicitor (unless the referring solicitor, or another solicitor, volunteers to assist).

Part IV:
Civil Proceedings

9

Civil Procedure

9.1   A new approach to civil litigation

Reform: the Woolf Report, *Access to Justice* (1996)

9.2   Recommendations of the Woolf Report

9.3   Reactions to the Woolf Report

Procedure from 26 April 1999

9.4   Introduction

9.5   Jurisdiction

9.6   Pre-action protocols

9.7   Judges as trial managers

9.8   Issue and service of proceedings

9.9   The defence's response

9.10 The allocation stage

9.11 Disclosure

9.12 Interlocutory applications

9.13 The listing questionnaire stage

9.14 Bringing proceedings to an end before trial

9.15 Sanctions

9.16 The trial

9.17 Judgment, interest and costs

9.18 Miscellaneous changes in terminology

9.19 Effect on precedents

9.20 Evaluation of the reforms

Small claims

9.1 A new approach to civil litigation

In 1999 a new system of civil procedure was introduced. Prior to that date civil litigation was conducted on strictly adversarial lines; the opposing parties were treated like combatants on a battlefield, with the court acting as facilitator of proceedings and the trial judge acting as neutral umpire. The burden was on the parties themselves to take the steps required of them under the rules of practice and there was much scope for delaying tactics if those suited one side. Disputes could drag on for years and the civil courts could become clogged with actions, causing further delays and hardship to parties. It was eventually accepted that radical reform was required, possibly involving an entire change of philosophy as to the conduct of civil litigation. Judges began to talk of the need for a 'cards on the table' approach to litigation and new practice directions were issued encouraging judges to be more pro-active in encouraging prompt compliance with time limits, etc.

On 24 January 1995 Lord Taylor of Gosforth CJ gave practice guidelines (*Practice Note* [1995] 1 All ER 385) applying to all lists in the Queen's Bench and Chancery Divisions, except where other directions specifically applied. His Lordship said that the paramount importance of reducing the cost and delay of civil litigation made it necessary for judges sitting at first instance to assert greater control over the preparation for and conduct of hearings than had hitherto been customary. Failure by practitioners to conduct cases economically would be visited by appropriate orders for costs, including wasted costs orders. The court would accordingly exercise its discretion to limit: discovery; the length of oral submissions; the time allowed for the examination and cross-examination of witnesses; the issues on which it wishes to be addressed; and reading aloud from documents and authorities. Other specific points included the following.

1. In cases estimated to last for more than ten days a pre-trial review should be applied for or in default could be appointed by the court. It should when practicable be conducted by the trial judge between eight and four weeks before the date of trial and should be attended by the advocates who were to represent the parties at trial.

2. Unless the court otherwise ordered, there had to be lodged with the listing officer (or equivalent) on behalf of each party (with copies to the other parties) no later than two months before the date of trial a completed pre-trial checklist in the form annexed to the practice direction. The checklist covered setting down, pleadings, evidence, documents, pre-trial review, length of trial and alternative dispute resolution.
3. No less than three clear days before the hearing of the action or application each party should lodge with the court (with copies to other parties) a skeleton argument concisely summarising that party's submissions in relation to each of the issues, and citing the main authorities relied upon.
4. The opening speech should be succinct. At its conclusion other parties could be invited briefly to amplify their skeleton arguments. In a heavy case the court could in conjunction with final speeches require written submissions, including the findings of fact for which each party contended.

This *Practice Note* paved the way for the more radical reforms that were proposed by Lord Woolf, who had been appointed to advise on the reform of civil procedure.

Reform: The Woolf Report, *Access to Justice* (1996)

9.2 Recommendations of the Woolf Report

Lord Woolf summed up his proposals as providing 'a new landscape for civil justice for the twenty-first century'. In summary the most significant of the recommendations were as follows.

1. Retention of the formal separation between the High Court and county court and retention of the separate status of High Court judge, circuit judge and district judge.
2. A framework for the High Court and county courts involving the creation of three or four new 'civil trial centres' in the regions with each centre headed by a senior civil judge to create a better working relationship between the judiciary and court administrators. There should also be specialist courts at the High Court and in the regions reserved for medical negligence cases. Housing cases should be handled by specialist judges in local county courts.
3. High Court and county court jurisdiction become a single jurisdiction with one set of procedural rules to replace those in the White and Green books. This would create 'open one-door entry' for litigants, ie litigants would be able to start a case in any court and a 'procedural judge' at that court would then take responsibility for allocating the case to the appropriate part of the system.
4. The system should consist of three tracks to which cases are allocated according to their value and complexity:

a) a 'fast track' for non-complex claims in which a hearing would be held in the county court within 30 weeks of the issue of proceedings (compared to an average of 80 weeks beforehand). The hearing should be a fixed three-hour hearing, subject to an absolute maximum of one day if extended beyond the three hours by the judge conducting the hearing. Much of the preliminary work should be done on paper rather than through oral submissions. No oral evidence from expert witnesses should be allowed. Costs would be capped at £2,500;

b) a 'small claims track' for non-complex claims;

c) a 'multi-track' with claims being allocated according to their individual complexity. Estimates of costs in each case should be either published by the court or agreed by the litigants and approved by the court. Teams of judges should be involved in making allocation decisions on the multi-track, whereas a single procedural judge (a district judge) should allocate cases on the fast track or small claims track. For the more complex cases on the multi-track there should be a case management conference before a single procedural judge (eg a High Court master if the case is in London) followed by a pre-trial review before the trial judge. The trial judge should be a High Court judge for complex cases regardless of the amount claimed. Non-complex cases should be heard by circuit or district judges under a special streamlined 'no-frills' procedure with fixed budgets.

5. Judges to be formally trained as case and trial managers so that they can become properly involved in the administration of the courts and provide 'hands on' management of cases by dictating the pace of hearings, enforcing strict time limits, taking responsibility for the calling of witnesses (especially expert witnesses) so as to ensure equality ('a level playing field') for litigants. Judges should become familiar with information technology facilities such as laptop computers and video-conference facilities. Law clerks or research assistants could be appointed from the ranks of recently qualified barristers or solicitors to assist judges working on case management.

6. It was expected that the court would appoint its own expert witness, with his or her costs being borne equally by each side, either instead of or additional to the experts to be called by each side. Meetings of experts should be ordered by the court so as to produce a single opinion if possible (or each side should agree on the use of a single expert). Agreement on expert evidence is especially relevant to fast track cases where the presentation of oral evidence from experts is not possible.

7. Oral evidence to be limited, with more emphasis on written submissions and pre-trial reading of documents by the judge. However, in his interim Report (1995) Lord Woolf emphasised that he was not proposing the abolition of the oral tradition: 'The approach ... is to preserve the best features of the present

adversary system, while giving a more interventionist management role to the court'.

8. Judges to have a greater power to strike out unworthy actions or to settle cases or parts of cases summarily (allowing only the 'core' of the dispute to go to trial). There would also be greater powers to impose sanctions (eg striking out whole or part of the claim, or ordering costs to be paid immediately, or imposing a higher rate of interest for costs) in cases where lawyers fail to meet the required deadlines. There would be a new discretionary power to allocate the burden of costs at the end of a case by reference to the conduct of the parties.

9. Greater control of pre-trial pleadings (now known as 'statements of case') and of discovery (now known as disclosure) so as to avoid verbosity and to produce precise statements of facts. There would now be 'pre-action protocols' setting out what information the parties should give one another about their cases and on what timescale.

10. Encouragement of early settlements through a 'plaintiff's offer' under which the plaintiff could suggest a sum lower than his or her actual claim at which he/she would be prepared to settle. If the defendant refuses to accept the offer and then loses the case the defendant would be penalised either in costs or in extra interest on the damages. Tough penalties are proposed in the form of interest rates of up to 25 per cent on top of the normal interest to be imposed on those unreasonably refusing settlement offers.

11. Encouragement of alternative dispute resolution (ADR) with emphasis on arbitration, mediation and ombudsmen to facilitate out-of-court settlements. For this purpose information for litigants would be improved either through advice agencies at court or electronic information kiosks.

12. There would be provision for some courts to sit in the evenings or at weekends, with mobile hearings being operated in remote rural areas.

13. The establishment of a Civil Justice Council as a general supervisory body for implementing the civil justice reforms proposed in the Final Report.

Lord Woolf summarised the advantages of the proposed reforms as follows:

1. they would end the present system of 'trial by combat' which had encouraged unreasonable behaviour by litigants;
2. they would create a simpler, more accessible, more flexible system;
3. cases would be handled in a manner proportionate to their value and complexity;
4. there would be greater certainty over the costs and duration of proceedings; and
5. the new system would ensure a 'level playing field' for litigants preventing wealthier litigants (eg insurance companies) from playing with the system to their advantage.

9.3 Reactions to the Woolf Report

The general reaction to the Woolf Report was favourable; it was welcomed by consumer groups, the legal profession, the judiciary, the government and opposition parties. Indeed the Conservative government responded quickly in 1996 to introduce legislation designed to implement the first stage of the Woolf reforms. The Civil Procedure Act 1997 established a rule-making authority to produce the single set of procedural rules for the High Court and county courts. The Act also established a Civil Justice Council to supervise the implementation of the civil procedure reforms.

The most notable criticism of the Woolf Report came from Professor Michael Zander. Writing in *The Times* (6 August 1996) Professor Zander expressed the view that most litigants want a fair hearing and will not feel that justice has been done by a short, sharp trial with restricted oral evidence and an interventionist judge chivvying the parties to a resolution of their dispute. He also argued that judges as trial managers will involve unnecessary bureaucratic costs in many cases which would normally have been settled out of court anyway, as well as resulting in longer and more complex trials for those cases that do go to court. (Zander relied on empirical evidence of the effects of judicial case management in other jurisdictions, eg the United States, for his conclusions.)

Nevertheless, the substance of the Woolf Report was implemented as from 26 April 1999. The new Civil Procedure Rules (CPR) were made in the autumn of 1998 and new Practice Directions were issued to supplement them.

Procedure from 26 April 1999

9.4 Introduction

From 26 April 1999 ('Big Bang Day') a unified code of procedural rules for the Court of Appeal (Civil Division), the High Court and the county court were introduced, save for specialist jurisdictions. The opportunity has been taken to reduce the complexity of the rules and make them more 'user-friendly' to lay persons by the use of English and simple expressions rather than traditional legal Latin. The new code is contained in the Civil Procedure Rules 1998 (CPR). Practice Directions have been and will be made to supplement the CPR. In addition, the Civil Procedure Act 1997 amended some of the law so as to prepare for the changes and also established the Civil Justice Council.

The Civil Justice Council

The Civil Procedure Act 1997 provides that the Council is an advisory body to the Lord Chancellor (whose role has been taken over by the Minister for Constitutional Affairs) and the judiciary advising on developments in the civil justice system and making proposals for research. Its objectives are to ensure that the civil justice system is accessible, fair and efficient. The Council will meet four times a year to review progress. Its members are appointed by the Lord Chancellor (whose role has been taken over by the Minister for Constitutional Affairs) and include, among others:

1. barristers;
2. solicitors;
3. persons with experience in, and knowledge of, consumer affairs;
4. persons with experience in, and knowledge of, the lay advice sector; and
5. persons able to represent the interests of particular kinds of litigant (for example, businesses or employees).

9.5 Jurisdiction

There is a three-track system based on the value and complexity of the claim.

1. Most cases worth less than £5,000 are dealt with by a district judge on the 'small claims track'.
2. Cases worth £5,000 and above up to £15,000 are dealt with under a fixed timetable on the 'fast track': cases should usually be heard within 30 weeks of allocation, with limits on procedure, disclosure, evidence and the length of the trial, and scales of fixed costs based on and in proportion to the value of the claim.
3. Cases worth £15,000 and above, or any other case which is unusually complex or raises special problems, are dealt with on the 'multi-track', closely supervised by a judge and tailored to each case. This will involve case management conferences and pre-trial hearings.

9.6 Pre-action protocols

These protocols are an essential part of the new civil justice system. Examples include those for personal injury, judicial review, professional negligence and defamation cases. The protocols require each party to complete various steps in the conduct of the case before proceedings are issued, for example sending a letter of claim in detailed form, exchanging witness statements and conducting negotiations (a process known as 'front-loading information'). The defendant has up to three months to respond to the pre-action letter of claim. If possible the parties are expected to agree on the use of a single medical expert at the trial. The protocols are designed to set standards for better communications between the parties and to facilitate earlier settlements or, failing such settlements, more efficient case management. Judges are encouraged to enforce the protocols strictly by penalising those who breach them.

9.7 Judges as trial managers

Judges have been given special training in case management techniques by the Judicial Studies Board so as to control civil litigation in accordance with the 'overriding objective' set out in Pt 1 of the CPR 1998, namely, to ensure that cases are conducted justly and with expedition and proportionality. For this purpose the judge should:

1. ensure that the parties are on an equal footing;
2. save expense;
3. deal with a case in ways which are proportionate:

   a) to the amount of money involved;
   b) to the importance of the case;
   c) to the complexity of the issues; and
   d) to each party's financial position;

4. ensure that the case is dealt with expeditiously and fairly;
5. allot to it an appropriate share of the court's resources while taking into account the need to allot resources to other cases; and
6. ensure that the parties, as well as the court, give effect to the overriding objective.

In order to achieve the overriding objective the judge should in each case:

1. identify the issues at an early stage;
2. decide promptly which issues need full investigation and trial;
3. dispose summarily of those that do not require such treatment;
4. encourage parties to use alternative dispute resolution where appropriate;
5. encourage parties to co-operate with each other in the conduct of the case;
6. help the parties to settle the whole or part of the case;
7. decide the order in which the issues are to be resolved;
8. fix timetables or otherwise control the progress of the case;
9. consider whether the likely benefits of taking a particular step will justify the cost of taking it;
10. deal with as many aspects of the case as is practicable on the same occasion;
11. deal with a case without the parties' attendance at court if this is possible;
12. make appropriate use of technology; and
13. give directions to ensure that the trial of a case proceeds quickly and efficiently.

9.8 Issue and service of proceedings

Assuming any applicable pre-action protocols have been complied with, proceedings may be commenced by the claimant issuing a claim form. Notes are provided to assist the average litigant in filling in the claim form. These notes explain the three-track system and tell the claimant to indicate in the heading of the claim form whether he/she wants the claim to be commenced in the county court or High Court. Most claims worth less than £15,000, as well as personal injury claims below £50,000, must be issued in the county court.

As before, the particulars of the claim and the remedy sought can be set out on the claim form itself or in a separate document served with the claim form or within 14 days of service of the claim form. The claimant's statement of case must be concise, of substance and specific. Points of law, as well as of fact, may be relied on. The statement of case must be verified by a statement of truth, ie sworn to be true. Hence the statement of case becomes a kind of affidavit punishable by contempt (not perjury) if the maker made a statement dishonestly and untruthfully.

Service must take place within four months of the issue of the claim form. The new rules permit modern methods of service such as e-mail and fax. The court has power to authorise 'alternative methods' of service but, if a method is unusual, the obligation will be on the claimant to prove that the method used was likely to have brought proceedings to the defendant's attention. In practice claimants will leave it to the court (either High Court or county court) to effect service by first class post. The court will then notify the claimant as to when the claim form is deemed to have been served. If a party wishes to effect service himself/herself he/she can do so but must notify the court in writing of such intention.

9.9 The defence's response

The defendant may either:

1. admit the claim and make an offer to pay; or
2. file a defence to the whole or part of the claim; or
3. file an acknowledgement of service within 14 days of service of the particulars of claim and then file a defence within 28 days of service of the particulars of claim.

A defence statement of case must be verified by a statement of truth. The right to make a counterclaim and reply are known as 'Part 20 claims' because they are regulated by Pt 20 of the CPR 1998.

Judgment in default applies and the claimant is allowed to give an estimated figure in a claim for unspecified (unliquidated) damages. Unless a defence is served judgment will be given for that estimate (or for a specified/liquidated claim) without a further assessment hearing.

9.10 The allocation stage

After the defence has been filed the court will serve an allocation questionnaire on each party so as to enable a district judge of the county court to allocate the claim to the appropriate track, unless the judge considers that the claim or defence should be struck out or summary judgment granted. Allocation will depend on the financial value of the claim, its complexity, the importance of the action and other relevant factors. Either party can also make a written request for a one month stay of proceedings so as to attempt a settlement through alternative dispute resolution.

Following the allocation decision the district judge should give the parties appropriate directions as to how to proceed (for example on disclosure of documents), together with a timetable leading to a trial date or 'window' for trial. In fast track cases there is a system of automatic directions, with a window for trial given not later than 30 weeks ahead. In multi-track cases directions similar to those for fast track cases are given unless the case is complex, in which event the judge must arrange for a case management conference and/or a pre-trial review. The trial date or trial window will still probably be fixed at the allocation stage. In small claims standard directions will apply.

9.11 Disclosure

An obligation to disclose, under Pt 1 of the CPR 1998, will arise only if ordered by the court, which has power to dispense with disclosure altogether. Unless otherwise ordered disclosure is limited in fast track and multi-track cases to 'standard disclosure', ie the only documents that will need to be disclosed will be:

1. those relied on by a party;
2. those which adversely affect a party's own case or another party's case;
3. those which support another party's case; and
4. those required to be disclosed by any relevant Practice Direction.

Disclosure must be in accordance with the overriding objective, thus interlocutory applications for general or specific disclosure which are in the nature of a 'fishing expedition' for evidence are unlikely to be successful. Staged or phased disclosure may be ordered where appropriate.

9.12 Interlocutory applications

After allocation the case will proceed through its interlocutory stages to the fixed trial date or trial window. There are opportunities to make interlocutory applications, for example for disclosure, and for 'requests for information', ie for further details of a statement of case.

9.13 The listing questionnaire stage

The listing questionnaire is sent to the parties shortly before the hearing date or trial window (probably about 20 weeks from the date of allocation). The parties are given 14 days to complete and return their copies of the questionnaire to the court. Failure to return the questionnaire may result in the claim or defence being struck out. When the court considers the listing questionnaire it will make any final directions and confirm or fix the trial date.

9.14 Bringing proceedings to an end before trial

Settlement

The opportunities to settle a case remain as before.

Summary judgment

RSC O.14 is replaced by Pt 24 of the CPR 1998.

Under the new procedure either claimant or defendant may apply for summary judgment and the test is whether the claimant has a real prospect of succeeding or the defendant has a real prospect of defending.

Payment into court and 'without prejudice offers'

'Without prejudice offers' and payments into court can be made under Pt 36 of the CPR 1998 not later than 21 days before trial, and with similar costs consequences. Without prejudice proposals (but not payments into court) can, under the new rules, be made before proceedings are issued (at least 21 days before issue of proceedings). The new rules also allow the claimant to make a settlement offer which will carry similar costs consequences for the defendant if it is refused and then not beaten by the court's award (the court has power to award the claimant interest at the rate of 10 per cent above base rate from the latest date that the offer could have been accepted). The changes are designed to put the parties on a more equal footing so far as tactics are concerned. Without prejudice offers must be kept open for 21 days and then may be withdrawn without the court's permission. Payments into court can only be withdrawn with the court's permission.

The Law Society in 2001 expressed its belief that the system whereby the defendant may pay money into court to support an offer to settle the claim should be retained. It was thought that the actual presence of the money is a strong incentive for claimants to accept a defendant's offer. The promotion of settlement was a major aim of the civil justice reforms and, therefore, this function seems to be very supportive of those reforms. The payment in satisfaction function ensures that defendants' offers are realistic and genuine. It supports the aim of the greater settlement of claims. Research shows that about 60 per cent of cases settle before trial, generally following acceptance of payments in satisfaction. The removal of this function could undermine the effectiveness of Pt 36, which is proving to be one of the most effective and popular parts of the Civil Procedure Rules 1998.

Striking out

Judges have greater powers to strike out claims or defences for 'abuse of process' or failure to comply with rules or directions.

9.15 Sanctions

Under Pt 3 of the CPR 1998 the sanctions available to a judge are made known to the parties so as to try to dissuade breach of the rules. Sanctions may be imposed for failure to comply with the CPR 1998, or Practice Directions, or pre-action protocols. Sanctions include striking out, refusals to grant extensions of time and refusals to allow documents not disclosed to be relied on.

9.16 The trial

Fast track cases will normally be limited to one day's duration, with limits on experts giving oral evidence. Jointly instructed experts should become the usual practice. The court has discretion to appoint a single expert if the parties cannot agree. In complex multi-track cases much of the groundwork will have been performed at a pre-trial case management conference conducted by the trial judge.

9.17 Judgment, interest and costs

Judgment still consists of providing the appropriate remedy, such as damages or an injunction. Penal interest rates can be set to punish misconduct during the action. In regard to costs, orders for costs and wasted costs orders can be made to punish breach of the rules of procedure, though wasted costs orders are likely to become sanctions of last resort as other penalties will usually be more appropriate and proportionate to the particular breach.

Fast track cases will eventually have fixed costs covering the costs of the trial and preparation for it. Costs will be fixed according to the amount claimed – there will be no discretion to vary the fixed costs. If counsel is used there will be a fixed fee for counsel and also a fee for the solicitor's attendance – fees will no longer be assessed according to how long a lawyer has spent on the case, hence the incentive for lawyers to deal with cases quickly. Costs of experts additional to a court appointed expert will not be recoverable from the opponent. Other miscellaneous costs will be assessed at the end of the trial by the trial judge (parties will be expected to give the judge breakdowns of such costs).

Costs in multi-track cases will be assessed at the end of the hearing and based on estimates given by the parties at the allocation and listing stages. The expression 'taxation of costs' is replaced by the description 'detailed assessment' and the taxation master becomes known as the 'costs judge'.

In general in both fast track and multi-track cases the rules will allow the court to pay closer attention to the degree of success and to the conduct of all parties.

9.18 Miscellaneous changes in terminology

The rules of procedure have been rewritten in 'plain English' and some of the more significant changes in terminology are as follows:

- 'writ' becomes 'claim form';
- 'affidavit' becomes 'statement of truth';
- 'pleading' becomes 'statement of case';
- 'plaintiff' becomes 'claimant';
- 'subpoena' becomes 'witness summons';
- 'minor/infant' becomes 'child';
- 'guardian ad litem' becomes 'litigation friend';
- 'ex parte' becomes 'without notice';
- 'inter partes' becomes 'with notice';
- 'leave' becomes 'permission';
- 'in camera' becomes 'in private';
- 'liquidated sum' becomes 'specified sum of money';
- 'unliquidated sum' becomes 'unspecified sum of money';
- 'Mareva injunction' becomes 'freezing injunction';
- 'Anton Piller order' becomes 'search order'.

9.19 Effect on precedents

Many of the precedents on the civil procedure prior to 26 April 1999 are now of historic interest only because, from 26 April 1999, the judges in exercising their powers have first recourse to the overriding objective set out in Pt 1 of the CPR 1998.

9.20 Evaluation of the reforms

The Lord Chancellor's Department issued a report in 2001 on the reforms of the civil process: *Impact of the Woolf Reforms*. From this report there is evidence that the amount of litigation is being reduced, that there is more co-operation in litigation and that litigation is less complex – all of these being positive results. On the negative side, costs may have increased. The second evaluation of the reforms was published (*Civil Justice Reform Evaluation – Further Findings* (2002) London: Lord Chancellor's Department) and the major points in this report are as follows. In general, the findings that were included in the previous report are confirmed. As to particular points, first it needs to be noted that overall there has been a drop in the number of claims issued, in particular in the types of claim most affected by the new Civil Procedure Rules 1998 introduced in April 1999. Evidence suggests that the system of pre-action protocols is working well to promote settlement and a culture of openness and co-operation. Part 36 of the Rules, which provides for payments into court and without prejudice offers, has been welcomed by all interested groups as a means of resolving claims more quickly, both in respect of claims which settle without court proceedings and those where proceedings are issued. There is evidence to show that settlements at the door of the court are now fewer and that settlements before the hearing day have increased. After a substantial rise in the first year following the introduction of the Civil Procedure Rules 1998, there has been a levelling off in the number of cases in which ADR is used. The use of single joint experts appears to have worked well. It is likely that their use has contributed to a less adversarial culture and helped achieve earlier settlements. Case management conferences are a key factor in making litigation less complex, and appear to have been a success. The time between issue and hearing for those cases that go to trial has fallen. The time between issue and hearing for small claims has risen since the introduction of the Civil Procedure Rules 1998 but may now be falling. The number of appeals in the course of proceedings appears to have fallen sharply. It is still too early to provide a definitive view on costs.

Small claims

9.21 Jurisdiction and allocation

As from 26 April 1999 the small claims jurisdiction was increased from £3,000 to £5,000. However, this small claims jurisdiction does not apply to all claims under £5,000. Personal injury claims for general damages, claims for possession of land, housing disrepair claims and harassment claims may be dealt with by the small claims procedure only if they fall below £1,000; if any such claim is above £1,000 (and below £15,000) it will usually be dealt with under the fast track system. In exceptional cases, eg where the facts or law or evidence are complex, or where there are allegations of dishonesty, the claim may be allocated to the multi-track. It is for the court to assess the true financial value of a claim, ie the claimant's assessment is not decisive.

The term 'small claim' is a misleading one as from 26 April 1999 because every claim, large or small, is now commenced by the same procedure and no claim will enter the so-called small claims track until allocated to that track by the district judge. Allocation takes place after a defence has been filed to the claimant's claim form or statement of case.

9.22 Pre-trial procedure

Standard directions apply on such matters as filing of documents: each party must supply the court and the other parties with copies of all documents (including experts' reports) to be relied on not less than 14 days before the hearing. The rules in Pt 31 of the CPR 1998 on disclosure do not apply to the small claims track. Pre-trial reviews are likely to be rare.

9.23 The trial

No more than one day will usually be allowed for the trial. There is a significant departure from the previous approach of informal arbitration. Proceedings must take place in public and be recorded. The court is no longer required to proceed in a way which will give each party an equal opportunity to have his/her case presented, or to explain legal terms or expressions to the parties. The court can adopt any procedure it considers fair, eg by an inquisitorial questioning of witnesses before the parties do so, and by imposing limits on cross-examination. Hence, there will be a dramatic shift away from the previously popular but inadequately controlled arbitration procedures to a more focused regime. The claim can be disposed of in the absence of the parties if both sides consent. The court can grant any remedy which can be granted in fast track and multi-track cases. There is no appeal available except to a circuit judge on the grounds of a serious irregularity affecting the proceedings or a mistake of law.

9.24 Costs

The so-called 'no costs' rule is applicable, although costs can be awarded to penalise a party for unreasonable conduct and to enforce an award. There is no advantage to a defendant to pay money into court since recoverable costs are in general limited to the costs stated on the summons.

10

Civil Appeals

10.1 Introduction

10.2 Appeals from orders of masters, registrars, High Court judges, circuit judges and district judges

10.3 Appeals to the Court of Appeal (Civil Division)

10.4 Appeals to the House of Lords

10.1 Introduction

In the modern civil justice system rights of appeal are statutory only and derive from the Supreme Court Act 1981 and rules and directions made under it. The directions have been somewhat piecemeal and there has now been consolidation of all principal Practice Directions relating to proceedings in the Court of Appeal (Civil Division) by *Practice Note (Court of Appeal: Procedure)* [1999] 2 All ER 490.

Radical reforms of the leave requirement were implemented in January 1999 to address the problem of delays in hearing appeals. The number of civil appeals has risen steadily over the years and in 1998 it was taking 14 months on average for an appeal to be heard. In some cases there were much longer delays with a number being subject to a wholly unacceptable delay of up to five years.

In 1998 Sir Jeffrey Bowman was appointed to review the work of the Court of Appeal (Civil Division) and this coincided with the substantial review of the whole system of justice that resulted in the 1998 White Paper *Modernising Justice* (Cmnd 4155). Both that Paper and the Bowman Report recommended that routine appeals should be settled by a single member of the Court of Appeal. The Bowman Report also went as far as suggesting that the composition of the Court of Appeal be changed, in that it recommended the appointment of specialist academic lawyers and practitioners to sit as members on appropriate occasions.

The Bowman Report made several recommendations for improving practice and procedures in the civil appeal system. One problem with changes that ease the burden of work on the Court of Appeal, and improve the efficient operation of that court, is the extent to which they in turn transfer the burden to a lower level of the judiciary and dilute the quality of judgments delivered in routine appeals. It was hoped that the whole burden on the civil courts would be lessened by the introduction of 'fast track' cases. These came in as part of the implementation of the Woolf proposals for the modernisation of the system of justice in April 1999. The new system did indeed reduce the pressure on the courts as the rate of settlements increased significantly. The Bowman Report recommended that appeals against decisions in 'fast track' cases should no longer reach the Court of Appeal (Civil Division) but be heard at a lower level. The trend has indeed been towards restricting opportunities for appeal.

10.2 Appeals from orders of masters, registrars, High Court judges, circuit judges and district judges

These appeals are from courts of first instance. Changes have been brought in by ss54–56 of the Access to Justice Act 1999 and also relevant are SI 2000/1071 and *Practice Note (Court of Appeal: Procedure)* [1999] 1 All ER 186. All of these are translated into Civil Procedure Rules Pt 52.

There has been consolidation of all principal Practice Directions relating to proceedings in the Court of Appeal (Civil Division) by *Practice Note (Court of Appeal: Procedure)* [1999] 2 All ER 490. This consolidation includes *Practice Note* [1999] 1 All ER 186 which introduced a comprehensive new leave requirement, the purpose of which was to clarify the position as to the need for leave and to reduce the number of inappropriate appeals.

Subject to any specific enactment or Practice Direction, the following applies to appeals in private civil matters, excluding family matters.

1. *An appeal lies to the next level of judge in the court hierarchy.* Where judgment is that of a district judge of a county court, appeal is made to a circuit judge. In *Tanfern Ltd* v *Cameron-McDonald and Another* [2000] 2 All ER 801 clarification was sought by the appellant on the correct destination for appeal against the decision of a district judge given in February 2000 hearing a multi-track matter. It was held, applying the procedural rule applicable in February 2000, that the correct route of appeal lay to a circuit judge in the county court. The summing-up of Brooke LJ sitting in the Court of Appeal is both interesting and useful for the review of the appeal regime he gives and which applies to the regime from May 2000 onwards.

   Where judgment is that of a master or district judge of the High Court, or is judgment of a circuit judge, appeal is made to a High Court judge. Appeal from the judgment of a High Court judge is to the Court of Appeal.

2. *Permission is generally required to appeal.* Under *Practice Note* [1999] 1 All ER 186, as consolidated by *Practice Note* [1999] 2 All ER 490, leave is now required for all appeals except appeals against: committal orders; refusals to grant habeas corpus; and secure accommodation orders made pursuant to s25 of the Children Act 1989.

3. *The criteria for permission.* The court of first instance should as a matter of routine decide whether or not to grant leave to appeal and such appeal should only be granted where the court considers that the appeal has a realistic, rather than a fanciful, prospect of success, or where there is some other compelling reason for appeal. Examples of the latter are given by Lord Woolf in *Practice Note* [1999] 1 All ER 186 and include cases which raise questions of public interest matters, questions of general policy, or reconsideration of binding precedent where the authority calls for such consideration by the Court of Appeal.

If the court of first instance is in doubt whether an appeal would have a real prospect of success or involves a point of general principle, the safe course is to refuse leave to appeal since it is always open to the Court of Appeal to grant leave.

Where there has already been one unsuccessful appeal to a court against the decision being challenged, for example from a district judge to a circuit judge or from a master to a High Court judge, and application is for leave for a further appeal to the Court of Appeal, a more restrictive approach to the test for leave to appeal should be adopted. Leave should be granted only if the case raises an important point of principle or practice or the case is one which for some other reason should be considered by the Court of Appeal.

4. *An appeal will be a review of the decision rather than a rehearing.* Appeals heard by the Court of Appeal (Civil Division) have generally been by way of a rehearing. This has, however, been on the basis of transcripts of the evidence given in the court below rather than receiving all the evidence itself, though the Court has taken into account fresh evidence which has come to light since the earlier hearing. Similarly, orders of masters or registrars of the High Court are usually heard by a High Court judge in chambers by way of a rehearing. For this it has been held that the judge is not bound by any previous exercise of discretion by the master or registrar: see *Evans v Bartlam* [1937] AC 473 (HL). In the county court appeals lie from the district judge to the circuit judge not by way of rehearing but on the basis of legal submissions only.

The position is now based on the question of serious irregularities. An appeal will only be successful where the decision of the lower court is either wrong or unjust because of such serious irregularities.

Decisions of circuit judges are challengeable in the Court of Appeal (Civil Division) and there are no 'leapfrog' appeals from the county court to the House of Lords. Decisions of High Court judges, whether in chambers or in open court, are challengeable in the Court of Appeal (Civil Division) unless expressly declared to be unappealable by statute: *Re Racal Communications Ltd* [1981] AC 374 (HL). In rare cases a 'leapfrog appeal' is available from the High Court to the House of Lords.

10.3 Appeals to the Court of Appeal (Civil Division)

Civil Appeals Office

The Civil Appeals Office is responsible for the administration of civil appeals. It is headed by the Registrar of Civil Appeals whose function is to deal expeditiously with all incidental applications which are necessary pending an appeal. The Registrar deals with these matters in chambers and an appeal lies from his decision to a single Lord Justice of Appeal and thence, with leave, to the Court of Appeal (Civil Division). Incidental applications may also be referred by the Registrar to a single judge of the Court of Appeal (Civil Division) in chambers, who in turn has power to refer such an application to the Court of Appeal (Civil Division). Appropriate applications can be made directly to a single Lord Justice or to the Court of Appeal (Civil Division).

Procedure

The appellant prepares a notice of appeal setting out the grounds of appeal and specifying the order for which he applies. The notice must be served on all parties to the action within four weeks of the judgment in the court below (this time can be extended with leave of the Registrar of Civil Appeals or the Court of Appeal) and within seven days the appellant must set down the appeal for hearing.

A respondent to an appeal may serve a notice contending that the order of the court below should be affirmed or varied on other grounds or he may cross-appeal that the decision (or part of it) is wrong. Otherwise the respondent (being the 'winner' in the court below) cannot appeal.

Skeleton arguments have become compulsory for legally represented parties in setting out the case for and against appeal. The purpose of a party's skeleton argument is to identify and summarise the principal points involved and to draw attention to the relevant legal authorities. It assists the judge to prepare for the hearing, thereby ensuring that the oral argument for the appeal can focus on the central issues in dispute between the parties. This reduces the time spent in court, and limits the costs for litigants and the legal system.

By advancing these objectives it can be said that the skeleton argument has been one of the most significant improvements in civil procedure in recent years. Under the procedural reforms introduced from 1 January 1999 (*Practice Note* [1999] 1 All ER 186) skeleton arguments are also required from represented applicants seeking leave to appeal so that the Court of Appeal can deal more efficiently with applications for leave to appeal. Two copies of the skeleton argument must accompany the bundle of documents which the applicant's solicitors lodge with the Civil Appeals Office for the application. If the application is listed for oral hearing at which both parties have the opportunity to attend, then the respondent's skeleton must be lodged and served within 14 days of receipt of the applicant's bundle.

Where leave to appeal is granted the appellant (and any respondent who has lodged a skeleton argument in response to the leave application) may use the same skeleton arguments for the purposes of the appeal or they may prepare fresh skeleton arguments for the purposes of the appeal. The appellant's solicitors must include with the appeal four copies of their skeleton argument and also include a copy of that skeleton argument with the set of bundles served on the respondent (at the same time as the appeal bundles are lodged with the Civil Appeals Office). The respondent's solicitors must lodge with the Civil Appeals Office four copies of their skeleton argument within 21 days of the date on which the appellant's bundle was served on them or, if earlier, not later than 14 days before the appeal hearing.

Since the date by which an appellant must file a bundle of documents is typically many months before the hearing, it follows that under the new procedure there is an obligation to prepare and file skeleton arguments at a much earlier stage of the appeal proceedings (previously the normal rule had been that a party could file such arguments 14 days before the fixed hearing date). It could be argued that the new procedure, by requiring the work to be done so long before the appeal hearing, will lead to a decline in the quality and focus of skeleton arguments particularly in areas of law where developments are rapid. (Revised skeleton arguments may not be lodged without the court's permission and such permission will be granted only if there is good reason for doing so.)

Appeals are heard usually by three judges or, in particularly important cases, by a 'full' court of five or more judges. Certain appeals and applications for leave to appeal can be heard by two judges. In the event of deadlock arising in the form of disagreement between the two judges, the entire case must be reargued before a reconvened Court of three judges (there cannot be an appeal to the House of Lords in such a case without a reconvened hearing).

Powers of the Court of Appeal

The Court of Appeal has full power to make any order which could have been made in the court below. However, the Court of Appeal is usually reluctant to upset the trial judge's finding of facts because he saw and heard the witnesses and was in a better position to assess their credibility. Further, the Court of Appeal is usually reluctant to interfere with a judge's exercise of his discretion where he has used it correctly, and with an award of damages unless it is out of proportion with awards in similar cases. Similarly an award of damages by a jury may be set aside only if excessive or inadequate: s8 of the Courts and Legal Services Act 1990.

A successful appellant is normally awarded the costs of both the appeal and the original trial.

In appropriate cases the Court of Appeal may order a new trial. The grounds on which this may be done include: a misdirection of the judge to the jury (in those few civil cases where it is still used); improper rejection of evidence; misconduct at the trial; and judgment obtained by fraud.

10.4 Appeals to the House of Lords

From the Court of Appeal, approximately 5 per cent of all cases are taken further to the House of Lords. A further appeal only lies with either leave of the Court of Appeal or the Appeals Committee of the House (usually three Law Lords). Such leave will only generally be granted in cases of general public importance: the House is generally influenced also by the prospects of success in an appeal and the degree of disagreement the case may have engendered in the lower courts.

In certain cases, 'leapfrog' appeals may be made directly from the High Court to the House of Lords provided all the parties consent, the trial judge certifies a point of law of general importance, and the House grants leave: ss12 and 13 of the Administration of Justice Act 1969. There is no appeal from a refusal to grant a certificate.

Argument before the House (counsel are robed, though the Law Lords are not) usually takes place in a committee room of the House of Lords, and is usually oral though the parties must provide a joint statement of facts and issues and lodge their cases after setting down. The House is usually very reluctant to interfere with a trial judge's exercise of discretion, save in those cases where the judge is demonstrably wrong either in the light of further evidence, change of circumstances, or in point of law. Such an exercise of discretion will not be interfered with 'merely on the ground that the members of the appellate court would have exercised the discretion differently': Lord Diplock in *Hadmor Productions Ltd* v *Hamilton* [1982] 1 All ER 1042 at 1046 (HL).

The House has an inherent jurisdiction to set aside a ruling, though naturally it is reluctant to reopen an appeal. It will do so in exceptional cases where a party has been subjected to an unfair procedure. Apart from such cases there is no further right of appeal from decisions of the House: *R* v *Bow Street Metropolitan Stipendiary Magistrate, ex parte Pinochet Ugarte (No 2)* [1999] 2 WLR 272; [1999] 1 All ER 577 (HL).

10.4 Appeals to the House of Lords

Part V:
Criminal Proceedings

11

Arrest, Search and Seizure and Interrogation

11.1 Introduction

In the majority of criminal cases, the defendant's first involvement in the criminal process will be his contact with the police. It is with these first stages of the criminal process that this chapter is primarily concerned.

Police powers to stop, search, detain and arrest persons were developed piecemeal across many decades. There were wide variations between rural and metropolitan areas, and many anomalies, for example inconsistencies in the scope of powers to enter, search premises and seize evidence: see *Ghani* v *Jones* [1970] 1 QB 693. Rights to stop and search were often conferred in wide and uncertain terms, such as the much-criticised and now repealed 'sus' laws, and different conditions attached to the exercise of those rights according to the particular statutes creating them. Much has now been placed upon a more consistent footing with the introduction of the Police and Criminal Evidence Act 1984 (PACE) and the Codes of Practice issued thereunder.

The Codes of Practice, issued by the Home Secretary, aim to provide guidelines as to how the discretion given to police officers under PACE 1984 should be exercised. Unlike the statute, the Codes are written in a non-technical style that should be readily comprehensible by police constables, if not the averagely educated lay person. Four Codes (A–D) were initially introduced in January 1986; now there are six. New Codes were introduced in 2004. The Codes now cover the following.

Code A: The exercise by police officers of statutory powers of stop and search.

Code B: The searching of premises by police officers and the seizure of property found by police officers on persons or premises.

Code C: The detention, treatment and questioning of persons by police officers.

Code D: The identification of persons by police officers.

Code E: The tape-recording of interviews by police officers at police stations with suspected persons.

Code F: This deals with the visual recording with sound of interviews with suspects.

Under s67(8) of PACE 1984, as originally enacted, a police officer was liable to disciplinary proceedings for a failure to comply with any provision of the Codes. This provision has, however, been repealed by s37(a) of the Criminal Justice and Public Order Act 1994, so that police forces have more discretion as to how they deal with officers who fail to follow guidelines on best practice. It is assumed that flagrant breaches of the Codes would still render an officer liable to disciplinary proceedings. Whilst a breach of the Codes may not, as such, affect the legality of an officer's action, and may not, of itself, render him liable to any criminal or civil proceedings, the Codes are admissible in evidence in civil and criminal and must be taken into account where relevant.

Although the Codes are not law in the strict sense, a trial judge can recognise non-compliance on the part of the police by excluding evidence obtained in breach of the Codes. Thus in *R* v *Saunders* [1988] Crim LR 521, where D was not shown a record of her statements made so that she could attest to their accuracy, and was not cautioned in terms that made clear her right to remain silent, the trial judge ruled the evidence inadmissible under s78. Note, however, the obiter statements of Lord Lane CJ in *R* v *Delaney* [1989] Crim LR 39, to the effect that the courts should not punish police officers for non-compliance by excluding evidence obtained in breach of the Codes. His view was that judges should only exclude evidence where it has been obtained after substantial and significant breaches that make it good sense to exclude evidence. Useful guidance is provided by the Court of Appeal in *R* v *Keenan* [1989] 3 All ER 598. D was charged with possession of an offensive weapon. Shortly before his trial defence counsel were served with copies of statements allegedly made by D to police officers in which he admitted knowledge that the weapon was in his car. D, who denied ever having made the statement, had not been invited to read and sign the statement. On appeal following conviction, the Court of Appeal held that the evidence of the statement should not have been admitted. The test to be adopted was, if the other evidence was compelling, the police would still secure a conviction, despite the exclusion of evidence obtained in breach of the Code. If the other evidence was weak, then it was right that the 'vital' evidence obtained in breach of the Code should be excluded since the safeguards designed to ensure its reliability had not been complied with.

In exercising the powers of stop, search, entry, seizure and arrest considered below, s117 of PACE 1984 makes it clear that, provided the power is not one that can only be exercised with the consent of some person, other than a police officer, the officer may use reasonable force, if necessary, in the exercise of the power.

With the enactment of the Human Rights Act 1998, the whole common law and statutory scheme of police powers will henceforth have to operate within the context of the Convention rights protected by the 1998 Act. Of particular relevance to this chapter are arts 5 and 6, dealing as they do with liberty and security of the person, and the right to a fair trial respectively.

11.2 Police powers to stop and search

Traditionally police officers have not possessed a common law power to detain suspects for questioning, short of first exercising a power of arrest. Whilst cases such as *Donnelly* v *Jackman* [1970] 1 All ER 987 confirm that a constable can commit a trivial interference with an individual's liberty, for example tapping him on the shoulder to attract his attention, without exceeding the scope of his duty, *Rice* v *Connolly* [1966] 2 QB 414 is still authority for the proposition that a citizen is not required to stop and answer police enquiries per se. In that case D refused to answer a constable's questions concerning his activities and refused to provide him with his address. D's conviction for obstructing a police officer in the execution of his duty, contrary to s51(3) of the Police Act 1964, was allowed on the ground that D had been under no legal duty to provide the police with information. (Note that to provide deliberately misleading information could give rise to liability.) Similarly in *Kenlin* v *Gardner* [1967] 2 QB 510, where the defendants, two schoolboys going from house to house to remind fellow members of their rugby team of a fixture, were stopped by a constable who produced a warrant card in order to hold the boys for questioning. The defendants struggled and assaulted the officer. The question arose as to the availability of the defence of self-defence on a charge under s51(1) of the Police Act 1964 – assaulting an officer in the execution of his duty. The court held that the defence was available, as the constable had no power short of arrest to physically detain the boys for questioning.

In theory the 1984 Act does not invalidate any of these decisions but, as indicated below, a constable can now detain a suspect in order to conduct a search under s1, and failure to provide personal details may give rise to a power to arrest without a warrant under s25.

Part I of PACE 1984 confers general powers of stop and search, not restricted to metropolitan areas, and provides for the keeping of records of searches. Section 1(2) creates a general power in constables to search a person or a vehicle or anything that is in or on a vehicle, and to detain the person or vehicle for the search. The power may only be exercised if the police constable has reasonable grounds for suspecting that he will find stolen or prohibited articles as a result of the search (s1(3)). In addition, the search may only be carried out if the person or vehicle is in any place to which at the time when the constable proposes to exercise the power the public or any section of the public has access, on payment or otherwise, as of right or by virtue of express or implied permission; or in any other place to which people have a ready access at the time when the constable proposes to exercise the power but which is not a dwelling: see s1(1).

So far as concerns searches of persons or vehicles on land adjacent to a dwelling-house, the Act provides by s1(4) and (5):

'(4) If a person is in a garden or yard occupied with and used for the purposes of a dwelling or on other land so occupied and used, a constable may not search him in the exercise of the power conferred by this section unless the constable has reasonable grounds for believing –
(a) that he does not reside in the dwelling; and
(b) that he is not in the place in question with the express or implied permission of a person who resides in the dwelling.
(5) If a vehicle is in a garden or yard occupied with and used for the purposes of a dwelling or on other land so occupied and used, a constable may not search the vehicle or anything in or on it in the exercise of the power conferred by this section unless he has reasonable grounds for believing –
(a) that the person in charge of the vehicle does not reside in the dwelling;
(b) that the vehicle is not in the place in question with the express or implied permission of a person who resides in the dwelling.'

The purpose of the search is to locate stolen goods or 'prohibited articles'. The Criminal Justice Act 2003 added the carrying of items to be used for criminal damage to this list. The definition of the former may be analogous to s24(2) of the Theft Act 1968, so that goods are 'stolen goods' if they are goods originally stolen, or which directly or indirectly represent or have at any time represented stolen goods, or are the proceeds of any disposal or realisation of stolen goods, or are goods obtained by blackmail or by deception. As regards 'prohibited articles', the Act provides by s1(7), (8) and (9) that an article is prohibited for the purposes of this part of PACE 1984 if it is an offensive weapon (defined as an article made or adapted for use for causing injury to persons, or intended by the person having it with him for such use by him or by some other person) or an article made or adapted for use in the course of or in connection with any one of a number of offences (burglary, theft, taking a conveyance, and obtaining by deception) or is intended by the person having it with him for such use by him or by some other person. Section 140 of the Criminal Justice Act 1988 extends the meaning of offensive weapon to include any article with a blade or point carried in a public place, except a folding pocket-knife.

If a search results in the discovery of what the constable has reasonable grounds to believe are stolen or prohibited articles, s1(6) confers upon him the power to seize such items.

The exercise of many of the powers granted to the police under PACE 1984 are subject to the precondition that there must be 'reasonable suspicion' or 'reasonable grounds to suspect' that a given state of affairs exists. This is particularly so in relation to the exercise of stop and search powers under s1 and also summary arrest under ss24 and 25: see further sections 11.11 and 11.12 below. Code A (as amended) gives some further guidance as to the interpretation of the phrase 'reasonable suspicion' in the context of stop and search powers. The Code provides:

'2.2 Reasonable grounds for suspicion depend on the circumstances in each case. There must be an objective basis for that suspicion based on facts, information, and/or intelligence which are relevant to the likelihood of finding an article of a certain kind or, in the case of searches under s43 of the Terrorism Act 2000, to the likelihood that the person is a terrorist. Reasonable suspicion can never be supported on the basis of personal factors alone without reliable supporting intelligence or information or some specific behaviour by the person concerned. For example, a person's race, age, appearance, or the fact that the person is known to have a previous conviction, cannot be used alone or in combination with each other as the reason for searching that person. Reasonable suspicion cannot be based on generalisations or stereotypical images of certain groups or categories of people as more likely to be involved in criminal activity.

2.3 Reasonable suspicion can sometimes exist without specific information or intelligence and on the basis of some level of generalisation stemming from the behaviour of a person. For example, if an officer encounters someone on the street at night who is obviously trying to hide something, the officer may (depending on the other surrounding circumstances) base such suspicion on the fact that this kind of behaviour is often linked to stolen or prohibited articles being carried. Similarly, for the purposes of s43 of the

Terrorism Act 2000, suspicion that a person is a terrorist may arise from the person's behaviour at or near a location which has been identified as a potential target for terrorists.

2.4 However, reasonable suspicion should normally be linked to accurate and current intelligence or information, such as information describing an article being carried, a suspected offender, or a person who has been seen carrying a type of article known to have been stolen recently from premises in the area. Searches based on accurate and current intelligence or information are more likely to be effective. Targeting searches in a particular area at specified crime problems increases their effectiveness and minimises inconvenience to law-abiding members of the public. It also helps in justifying the use of searches both to those who are searched and to the public. This does not however prevent stop and search powers being exercised in other locations where such powers may be exercised and reasonable suspicion exists.

2.5 Searches are more likely to be effective, legitimate, and secure public confidence when reasonable suspicion is based on a range of factors. The overall use of these powers is more likely to be effective when up to date and accurate intelligence or information is communicated to officers and they are well-informed about local crime patterns.

2.6 Where there is reliable information or intelligence that members of a group or gang habitually carry knives unlawfully or weapons or controlled drugs, and wear a distinctive item of clothing or other means of identification to indicate their membership of the group or gang, that distinctive item of clothing or other means of identification may provide reasonable grounds to stop and search a person.

2.7 A police officer may have reasonable grounds to suspect that a person is in innocent possession of a stolen or prohibited article or other item for which he or she is empowered to search. In that case the officer may stop and search the person even though there would be no power of arrest.

2.8 Under s43(1) of the Terrorism Act 2000 a constable may stop and search a person whom the officer reasonably suspects to be a terrorist to discover whether the person is in possession of anything which may constitute evidence that the person is a terrorist. These searches may only be carried out by an officer of the same sex as the person searched.

2.9 An officer who has reasonable grounds for suspicion may detain the person concerned in order to carry out a search. Before carrying out a search the officer may ask questions about the person's behaviour or presence in circumstances which gave rise to the suspicion. As a result of questioning the detained person, the reasonable grounds for suspicion necessary to detain that person may be confirmed or, because of a satisfactory explanation, be eliminated. Questioning may also reveal reasonable grounds to suspect the possession of a different kind of unlawful article from that originally suspected. Reasonable grounds for suspicion however cannot be provided retrospectively by such questioning during a person's detention or by refusal to answer any questions put.

2.10 If, as a result of questioning before a search, or other circumstances which come to the attention of the officer, there cease to be reasonable grounds for suspecting that an article is being carried of a kind for which there is a power to stop and search, no search may take place. In the absence of any other lawful power to detain, the person is free to leave at will and must be so informed.

2.11 There is no power to stop or detain a person in order to find grounds for a search. Police officers have many encounters with members of the public which do not involve detaining people against their will. If reasonable grounds for suspicion emerge during such an encounter, the officer may search the person, even though no grounds existed when the encounter began. If an officer is detaining someone for the purpose of a search, he or she should inform the person as soon as detention begins.'

The new version of the Code emphasises that a legal power to search must exist. Stricter provisions as to record keeping are also introduced.

11.3 Conduct of searches under s1 of the 1984 Act

Once satisfied that the conditions of s1 are met, and that there are the required 'reasonable grounds' for exercising the stop and search power, a constable must, in carrying out the search, follow the procedure laid down by s2 and must usually make a record of it in accordance with s3. If, having stopped a person or vehicle for the purpose of search, the constable thinks it unnecessary actually to make the search, he need not do so (s2(1)), but that decision does not affect the lawfulness of his initial act in detaining that person or vehicle. If the constable wishes to search a person, or a vehicle which is 'attended' (which presumably means that there is a person in it or appearing to be in charge of it nearby), s2(2) and (3) ensure that the intended object of the search is made aware of the identity of the searcher and the reasons for the search.

PACE 1984 does not state what is to be done when the constable is unable to determine which of several persons is 'in charge' of a vehicle: presumably all should be told the matters in s2(3). The requirement laid down by s2(3)(a) of PACE 1984, to the effect that a police constable about to conduct a search must provide details of his identity and of the police station to which he is attached, is mandatory. Failure to comply will render any subsequent search unlawful, even if the identity of the officer can be ascertained in broad daylight from his badge: see *Osman* v *DPP* (1999) 163 JP 725. The detainee will, presumably, be entitled to use reasonable force to resist any such search. Sedley LJ, in *Osman*, observed that a police officer could comply with the duty to inform by handing out a slip of paper detailing his name and station to a person about to be searched.

The extent of the search is governed by s2(9), which provides that neither the power conferred by s1 nor any other power to detain and search a person without first arresting him or to detain and search a vehicle without making an arrest is to be construed as authorising a constable to require a person to remove any of his clothing in public other than an outer coat, jacket or gloves; or as authorising a constable not in uniform to stop a vehicle.

The ambiguous wording of s2(9) could be taken to mean that a constable can require a person to remove other articles of clothing, provided such removal is not made 'in public'. Thus if the constable asked the subject of the search to remove his trousers, and offered to allow him to do so in the privacy of a closed police van, or inside a nearby house, it may well be that the power exists to compel the subject to comply. Code A para 3.5 clearly contemplates that such power is implied into s2(9) in that it states:

'Where on reasonable grounds it is considered necessary to conduct a more thorough search (eg by requiring someone to take off a T-shirt or headgear), this shall be done out of public view for example, in a police van or police station if there is one nearby.'

Note that such searches may only be conducted by an officer of the same sex as the person searched and may not be made in the presence of anyone of the opposite sex unless the person being searched consents to their presence.

Provided the conditions in s1 are met, vehicles that are not 'attended' may be searched even though there is no person during the search who is in charge of the vehicle or otherwise responsible for it. In such a case, s2(6) and (7) provide that the fact that a search has taken place be brought to the attention of the vehicle's owner, driver or other person responsible for it. The notice should specify the name of the constable conducting the search, and should inform the owner that an application for compensation for any damage caused by the search may be made. The notice should be left inside the vehicle unless it is not reasonably practicable to do so without damaging the vehicle.

So as to avoid excessive delay in the carrying out of a search of persons or vehicles, s2(8) imposes a statutory (if rather vague) duty upon the police where it states that: 'The time for which a person or vehicle may be detained for the purposes of such a search is such time as is reasonably required to permit a search to be carried out either at the place where the person or vehicle was first detained or nearby'.

How much time is 'reasonably required' must of course depend upon the facts of each case, but it is to be hoped that the subsection will encourage the police to make the search quickly, rather than risking a civil action for unlawful detention for a period beyond what a court could later find to have been adequate.

11.4 Other powers to stop and search

The 1984 Act significantly tidies up a confused morass of varying general and local powers. Nonetheless, several powers peculiar to particular offences, places or persons survive the Act, and some have been added since. The most notable are listed below.

1. To stop and search for prohibited drugs. The conditions for search remain those stated in s23 of the Misuse of Drugs Act 1971.
2. To search persons in public places for unlicensed firearms, or for firearms used or suspected of being intended for use in the course of crime. This power is still governed by s47 of the Firearms Act 1968.
3. To stop and search persons suspected of offences under the Terrorism Act 2000. The notion of terrorism is a wide one and can include such acts as serious violence against a person where this is designed to influence the government or intimidate the public.
4. Under s60 of the Criminal Justice and Public Order Act 1994, a police officer of

or above the rank of superintendent may, if he reasonably believes that incidents involving serious violence may take place in any locality in his area, and it is expedient to prevent their occurrence, authorise the use of stop and search powers in the area for which he is responsible for a period of up to 24 hours. The period may be extended by a further six hours where it appears to the officer who gave the initial authorisation that it is expedient to do so. The stop and search powers conferred by this section extend to stopping any pedestrian, or vehicle and searching him or the occupants of any such vehicle, or the vehicle itself, for offensive weapons or dangerous instruments (ie bladed or pointed), whether or not a constable has any grounds for suspecting that he might find such articles. If any such articles are found they may be seized by a constable.

These powers have been further extended by s25 of the Crime and Disorder Act 1998, which inserts a new subs(4A) into s60. Under this provision a police officer may require a person to remove any item that the police officer reasonably believes he is wearing wholly or mainly for the purpose of concealing his identity, such as a mask, hood or other garment. Items worn for these purposes can be seized and retained by a police officer.

Constables employed by certain statutory undertakers are also given a power of stop and search wider than that conferred on the police in general, and by s6 of the 1984 Act they may stop, detain and search any vehicle before it leaves a 'goods area' included in the premises of their employers. There is no need in such cases for the holding of 'reasonable grounds' for any suspicion of carriage by the vehicle of stolen or prohibited articles – the power is almost unlimited, though it applies only to searches of vehicles and not to searches of persons, so that any search of a person may be carried out only if the conditions mentioned in s1 of the Act are met. 'Goods area' is defined by s6(2) as 'any area used wholly or mainly for the storage or handling of goods'. The principal beneficiaries of the s6 power will be railway, dock, canal and other transport police forces, which are in theory not a part of the police force of the county in which they operate.

11.5 Road checks

Where a serious crime has been committed, it is of great assistance to the police to be able to establish roadside stations through which motor vehicles must pass and be checked to see whether they are carrying the suspect criminal or someone who may be a witness to the offence. The example of an armed raid upon an armoured security van springs first to mind; the police must act quickly if the villains are to be identified and caught before their trail becomes cold. To help in this case, and in a wide variety of others, s4 of the 1984 Act provides for short-term local powers of stop and search of vehicles. An officer may only authorise a road check under s4(3) if he has reasonable grounds for believing that a 'serious arrestable offence' has been committed; and has reasonable grounds to suspect that persons sought in connection with the offence are, or will be, in the locality in which vehicles would be stopped if the road check were authorised. Normally the authorisation to set up roadblocks must be given in writing by an officer of at least the rank of superintendent. An officer below that rank may authorise such a road check only if it appears to him that it is required as a matter of urgency.

The authorisation must specify the locality in which vehicles are to be stopped and the length of time for which the order remains in operation (normally not exceeding seven days). If a road block authorisation is granted, officers may conduct road checks for the purpose of ascertaining whether a vehicle is carrying: a person who has committed an offence other than a road traffic offence or a vehicles excise offence; a person who is a witness to such an offence; a person intending to commit such offence; or a person who is unlawfully at large. Where a vehicle is stopped in a road check, the person in charge of the vehicle at the time when it is stopped is entitled to obtain a written statement of the purpose of the road check if he applies for such a statement not later than the end of the period of 12 months from the day on which the vehicle was stopped. In practice this power will not be used to permit a full search of vehicles, but to allow for a rather a cursory inspection and interrogation to determine whether any of the persons sought is driving or being carried in the vehicle.

The phrase 'serious arrestable offence', which occurs elsewhere in PACE 1984, is defined by s116. The definition includes:

1. an offence (whether at common law or under any enactment) specified in Pt I of Sch 5 of PACE 1984 (see below);
2. any of the offences mentioned in paragraphs (a)-(dd) of the definition of 'drug trafficking offences' in s38(1) of the Drug Trafficking Offences Act 1986;
3. subject to point (4) below, any other arrestable offence is serious only if its commission has led to, or is intended or is likely to lead to: serious harm to the security of the state or to public order; serious interference with the administration of justice or with the investigation of offences or of a particular offence; the death of any person; serious injury to any person; substantial financial gain to any person; and serious financial loss to any person. Loss is serious for these purposes if, having regard to all the circumstances, it is serious for the person who suffers it. 'Injury' includes any disease and any impairment of a person's physical or mental condition.

Part I of Sch 5 lists those offences conclusively regarded as serious arrestable offences, these include: murder, rape, buggery, treason, manslaughter, kidnapping, incest with a girl under the age of 13 and so on. Part II provides details of other specific offences to be treated as serious arrestable offences, and is subject to amendment as new offences are created: see for example the offences added to Pt II by s85 of the Criminal Justice and Public Order Act 1994. Other offences will fall within the definition only if they are 'arrestable' in the meaning given by s24 of

PACE 1984, but have also caused or were intended to cause harm classified as 'serious' by s116(6). For example, theft contrary to s1 of the Theft Act 1968 is an 'arrestable' offence, but can qualify as a 'serious arrestable offence' only if it has caused or was intended to cause one of the s116(6) consequences, notably 'substantial financial gain to any person or serious financial loss to any person'. These phrases necessarily lack precision and whether or not the definitions are satisfied will be a question of fact in each case. In *R* v *Neil McIvor* [1987] Crim LR 409 (a Crown Court decision) the trial judge ruled that access to a solicitor under s58 should not have been denied as the theft alleged, 28 hunt dogs valued at £800, was not a serious arrestable offence as it did not involve a substantial loss to the victim. Similarly, in *R* v *Eric Smith* [1987] Crim LR 579, the theft of two video recorders from Woolworths plc was not regarded as involving substantial loss.

As will be seen further in this chapter the concept of 'serious arrestable offence' also has a key part to play in determining the extent of police powers to detain, isolate and interrogate arrested persons.

11.6 Powers of entry, search and seizure on premises

The powers of stop, search and seizure thus far discussed have all related to persons or vehicles in public places, whether those places be roads, pavements, or the gardens and yards provided for by s1(4) and (5). What of the police powers to enter buildings and other premises for the purpose of search or seizure? In the same way that Pt I of PACE 1984 has clarified and consolidated rights to stop and search in public places, so Pt II substantially amends the powers of entry and search of premises, and several anomalous lacunae have been closed in the process.

The police are now authorised to enter and search premises on the authority of a warrant issued by a Justice of the Peace if they suspect the commission of a 'serious arrestable offence' (see section 11.5 above) and the presence on those premises of evidence relevant to that suspected offence. For the purposes of the 1984 Act 'premises' includes any vehicle, vessel, aircraft, and any tent or movable structure: see s23.

Specifically, s8 provides:

'(1) If on an application made by a constable a Justice of the Peace is satisfied that there are reasonable grounds for believing –
(a) that a serious arrestable offence has been committed; and
(b) that there is material on premises specified in the application which is likely to be of substantial value (whether by itself or together with other material) to the investigation of the offence; and
(c) that the material is likely to be relevant evidence; and
(d) that it does not consist of or include items subject to legal privilege, excluded material or special procedure material; and
(e) that any of the conditions specified in subsection (3) below [considered below] applies, he may issue a warrant authorising a constable to enter and search the premises.'

The references to items 'subject to legal privilege', 'excluded material' and 'special procedure material' mean that no warrant may be issued by a magistrate which gives authority to enter and search for any of the following classes of evidence.

1. Documents subject to legal professional privilege according to the principles of the law of evidence and s10 of the Act. Such items are excluded from the right to search so as to preserve the defendant's right not to be compelled to incriminate himself by disclosure of anything he may have told to or been told by his legal advisers in connection with some legal matter, even though it is not the matter raised in the warrant.

2. Excluded material includes personal records of any person's physical or mental health or personal welfare acquired or created in confidence, and any human tissue or tissue fluid taken for the purposes of diagnosis or medical treatment and held in confidence, and also journalistic material held in confidence. The precise definitions of this phrase appear in s11, and a right of access to excluded material arises only on the order of a circuit judge made in an application by the police under Sch 1 of the Act. Thus, there is a safeguard against unjustified invasion of privacy.

3. Special procedure material includes certain journalistic material other than that in the definition of 'excluded material', together with certain business records held in confidence or subject to an obligation by statute not to disclose them. Such material can once again only be made the lawful object of police search and seizure on the authority of a circuit judge (s14).

Provided, therefore, that none of the evidence sought falls into the categories of 'legal privilege', 'excluded' or 'special procedure' material, a justice's warrant may issue to authorise the entry and search of premises. As s8(1)(e) provides, however, a warrant will not be issued unless one of the conditions in s8(3) applies. These conditions are designed to ensure that the draconian weapon of warrant operates only where it is impracticable or undesirable to gain access to evidence by request to the person who holds the right to grant access to it, perhaps because the evidence might be destroyed if the police are compelled to await an occupier's permission to enter, or cannot find out who has the right to allow them entry. The subsection provides:

'(3) The conditions mentioned in subsection (1)(e) above are –
(a) that it is not practicable to communicate with any person entitled to grant entry to the premises;
(b) that it is practicable to communicate with a person entitled to grant entry to the premises but it is not practicable to communicate with any person entitled to grant access to the evidence;
(c) that entry to the premises will not be granted unless a warrant is produced;
(d) that the purpose of a search may be frustrated or seriously prejudiced unless a constable arriving at the premises can secure immediate entry to them.'

The application to a Justice of the Peace for issue of the warrant must be made in the form prescribed by s15, which is intended to ensure that there is good reason for its grant, and that it clearly specifies the suspected offence and, so far as is possible, the evidence sought. The constable applying for the warrant must: state the ground on which he makes the application; state the enactment under which the warrant would be issued; specify the premises which it is desired to enter and search; and identify, so far as is practicable, the articles or persons to be sought.

Each warrant authorises entry on one occasion only (s15(5)). If granted the warrant must specify: the name of the person who applies for it; the date on which it is issued; the enactment under which it is issued; the premises to be searched; and, so far as is practicable, the articles or persons to be sought (s15(6)).

Once issued, the search warrant remains in force for only one month, and if it has not been executed within that period it lapses and must be returned to the court office from which it issued (s16(3) and (10)). It must be executed at a 'reasonable hour' unless it appears to the constable executing it that the purpose of a search may be frustrated on an entry at a reasonable hour (s16(4)). This test seems to be wholly subjective, so that the constable's honest even though unreasonable belief will be conclusive. The occupier or apparent occupier of the premises to be searched must be shown the warrant, provided with a copy of it, and given documentary evidence that the person seeking to execute it is a constable (s16(5)).

Thus far, the courts appear to be taking a hard line in requiring compliance by the police with the search warrant safeguards. In *R v South Western Magistrates' Court, ex parte Cofie* [1997] 1 WLR 885 the court granted a declaration that a search warrant was unlawful on the ground that the officer applying for it had specified the building to be searched was '78, Oxford Gardens, W10', when in fact he knew that the building was divided into flats and that only the common parts of the building, and flat 78F in particular, needed to be searched. Beldam LJ confirmed that s15(6) of PACE 1984 was to be construed strictly, and that the officer had failed to specify the premises to be searched with sufficient particularity.

In *R v Chief Constable of Lancashire, ex parte Parker* [1993] 2 WLR 428 the applicants' premises were entered by police offices purporting to act under search warrants and items were seized. The officers carrying out the searches provided the occupiers with warrants comprising photocopies of the authorisations unaccompanied by the schedules that would have detailed the articles sought. The applicants sought judicial review seeking orders of certiorari to quash the warrants and a declaration to the effect that the entries and searches had been unlawful. The Divisional Court, granting the declarations sought, held that a search warrant comprised two documents, the authorisation and the schedule of articles to be seized. Subsections 15(7) and (8) of PACE 1984 required that two certified copies should be made of any warrant, so that one might be given to the occupier, or left at the premises. The certification was required so that the occupier did not have to rely on the word of the police as to the warrant's validity. Showing the occupier a copy of the warrant would not suffice. As Nolan LJ observed:

'It seems to us clear beyond argument that when the Act refers to a warrant issued by a judge it means the whole of the original document seen and approved and put forth by him ... It would be wholly contrary to the purpose of the legislation if a judge could authorise the police to replace the whole or a part of the original warrant, for the purposes of its execution, by an uncertified photocopy which he has not seen.'

Hence the original warrant had been valid, and certiorari would not be granted to quash it, but the subsequent searches were unlawful given the failure to comply with the statutory requirements concerning authentification an completeness of copies.

Provided the documents are in order, *R* v *Longman* [1988] Crim LR 534 suggests that the police can gain entry to premises before informing the occupants as to who they are. In that case a female officer, posing as an 'Interflora' delivery woman, gained entry and then produced her warrant card. The court declared such a procedure lawful, provided the police could show that providing information prior to entry would render the subsequent search nugatory.

If the constable finds the evidence connected with the suspected offence for which the warrant issued, he may seize it (s8(2)).

11.7 Entry, search and seizure without warrant

The powers to enter and search premises thus far discussed have concerned the grant of a justices' warrant (or, if the search is for 'excluded' or 'special procedure' material, on the authority of a circuit judge), without the arrest of any suspect. It is now necessary to consider the police powers of entry and search of premises without such a warrant. These are contained in general terms in ss17 and 18. They are in addition to any other statutory powers of entry and search, and to the sole remaining such power at common law, that of entry to deal with or prevent a breach of the peace (s17(6)). Under s17 a constable may enter and search any premises for the purpose of: executing a warrant of arrest issued in connection with or arising out of criminal proceedings; arresting a person for an arrestable offence; arresting a person for an offence under s1 (prohibition of uniforms in connection with political objects) of the Public Order Act 1936, any enactment contained in ss6–8 or 10 of the Criminal Law Act 1977 (offences relating to entering and remaining on property) or s4 of the Public Order Act 1986. A constable may also enter and search any premises for the purpose of: recapturing a person who is unlawfully at large and whom he is pursuing; saving life or limb; or preventing serious damage to property.

With the exception of entry in order to save life and limb, a constable can only exercise the power of entry under s17 if he has reasonable grounds for believing that the person whom he is seeking is on the premises. In relation to premises consisting of two or more separate dwellings, the power to enter and search is limited to any parts of the premises which the occupiers of any dwelling comprised in the premises use in common with the occupiers of any other such dwelling; and any such dwelling in which the constable has reasonable grounds for believing that the person whom he is seeking may be.

The power to search provided by s17 is limited in the sense that it is a power to search to the extent that is reasonably required for the purpose for which the power of entry is exercised.

The power to enter under s17(1)(b) (to arrest a person for an arrestable offence) is only exercisable by a constable who has reasonable grounds to suspect that an arrestable offence has been committed and who believes that the suspect is in the premises to be entered. It does not permit, for example, entry in order to question a suspect (unless it could be shown that this was for a purpose closely linked to those listed in s17(1)(e)). Where the power to enter under s17(1) is exercised, the occupant must be informed of the reasons for the entry if at all possible: see further *O'Loughlin* v *Chief Constable of Essex* (1997) The Times 12 December.

The need for an arrestable offence to have been committed was considered in *Chapman* v *DPP* (1989) 89 Cr App R 190. A constable Sneller was called to assist an officer who was being assaulted by a number of youths. Sneller saw a youth he suspected of being involved in the attack run into the flat occupied by his father, the defendant. Sneller sought entry to the defendant's premises, but the defendant resisted, and was arrested for obstructing a constable in the execution of his duty. Sneller purported to be exercising his power of arrest under s24(6) PACE 1984, in relation to the defendant's son. The defendant's submission of no case to answer, in relation to the obstruction charge, was rejected by the justices, and he appealed by way of case stated, the question for the court being: 'whether the justices were right to conclude that [Sneller] at the time of the assault was exercising a statutory power of entry and so was a constable acting in the execution of his duty'. The court felt compelled to allow the appeal on the ground that the common assault on a fellow officer was not an arrestable offence, hence no power of arrest existed under s24(6), and in turn no power to enter under s17(1)(b). As Bingham LJ commented:

'What is ... inescapable and fatal to this conviction is that the justices have not found as a fact that constable Sneller reasonably suspected ... any ... arrestable offence, to have been committed, or any facts amounting to an arrestable offence to have occurred. Such a reasonable suspicion is the source from which all a police constable's powers of summary arrest flow and the justices have felt unable to make the crucial finding which the prosecutor required. This was plainly not the result of oversight or inadvertence. Had the justices found that constable Sneller reasonably suspected an arrestable offence to have been committed, it would have been incumbent on them to identify, at least in general terms, the arrestable offence which the police constable suspected and this, it is plain, the evidence adduced did not enable them to do. It is not of course to be expected that a police constable in the heat of an emergency, or while in hot pursuit of a suspected criminal, should always have in mind specific statutory provisions, or that he should mentally identify specific offences with technicality or precision. He must, in my judgment, reasonably suspect the existence of facts amounting to an arrestable offence of a kind which he has in mind. Unless he can do that he cannot comply with s28(3) of the Act by informing the suspect of grounds which justify the arrest.'

It seems clear, following the House of Lords' decision in *D'Souza* v *DPP* [1992] 1 WLR 1073, that the power to enter without a warrant under s17(1)(d) (to recapture a person unlawfully at large) is only to be used in cases of 'hot pursuit'. In that case the appellant's mother had left a hospital where she was being detained for psychiatric assessment without leave being granted as required under s17 of the Mental Health Act 1983. Several hours later, uniformed officers arrived at the house where the appellant lived with her parents in order to take her mother back to the hospital. The appellant and her father refused the police officers entry as they did not have a warrant to enter the premises, but the officers nevertheless exercised a forced entry and were attacked by the appellant and her father, who were subsequently convicted of assaulting police officers in the execution of their duty contrary to s51(1) of the Police Act 1964. Allowing their appeals against conviction, the House of Lords held that s17(1)(d) of the 1984 Act could only be used by officers seeking to enter premises where they sought to apprehend a person who was unlawfully at large, and at the time of entering the premises the police officers were in 'hot pursuit' of the said person. Whilst a person absconding from a hospital in breach of the Mental Health Act 1983 would be a person unlawfully at large, in the present case there was no evidence that the police had entered the dwelling in question whilst in hot pursuit of the appellant's mother. It would appear from this ruling that if the officers had spotted the appellant's mother entering her house and had chased after her, they would have had the power of entry without warrant provided for by s17(1)(d). As a consequence of this decision it must be the case that the subsection cannot be relied upon by a constable who, acting upon information received that a person unlawfully at large is at a particular dwelling, then proceeds to visit and enter the premises to effect the recapture of such a person. Whether a constable is in 'hot pursuit' will inevitably be a question of fact to be determined in each case.

Further powers of entry and search are also conferred by s18, which permits a search of premises following the arrest of a suspect for an 'arrestable' offence, if the suspect arrested occupies or controls the premises to be searched. Under s18(1) a constable may enter and search any premises occupied or controlled by a person who is under arrest for an arrestable offence, if he has reasonable grounds for suspecting that there is on the premises evidence, other than items subject to legal privilege, that relates to that offence or to some other arrestable offence which is connected with or similar to that offence.

As with s17 a constable exercising the power to enter and search under s18 may seize and retain anything for which he may search under s18, but his powers of search are to be exercised only to the extent that is reasonably required for the purpose of discovering such evidence.

A search under s18 must normally be authorised in advance, in writing, by an officer of the rank of inspector or above. Under s18(5) however, a constable may conduct a search under s18(1) before taking the suspect to a police station, and without obtaining the usual authorisation if the presence of the suspect at a place other than a police station is necessary for the effective investigation of the offence.

11.8 Powers of seizure

Certain powers to seize evidence have already been examined, for instance that permitting seizure of evidence specified in a search warrant under s8(2). A general power of seizure is conferred upon constables who are 'lawfully on any premises' by s19. The term 'lawfully on premises' encompasses not only lawful presence following entry to effect an arrest, or following arrest of a suspect, or on the authority of a search warrant, but also cases where the constable has been allowed into the premises by a person with the power to give him permission to enter, even though he is not there pursuant to any statutory or common law right of entry. For example, where the constable visits a suspect to question him, and the suspect invites the constable into his house. Under s19 a constable may seize anything which is on the premises if he has reasonable grounds for believing: that it has been obtained in consequence of the commission of an offence and that it is necessary to seize it in order to prevent it being concealed, lost, damaged, altered or destroyed; that it is evidence in relation to an offence which he is investigating or any other offence and that it is necessary to seize it in order to prevent the evidence being concealed, lost, altered or destroyed. Subsection 19(4) empowers a constable to require any information which is contained in a computer and is accessible from the premises to be produced in a form in which it can be taken away and in which it is visible and legible if he has reasonable grounds for believing that it is evidence in relation to an offence which he is investigating or any other offence, or it has been obtained in consequence of the commission of an offence, and that it is necessary to do so in order to prevent it being concealed, lost, tampered with or destroyed. Subsection 19(6) makes it clear that no power of seizure conferred on a constable under any enactment (including an enactment contained in an Act passed after PACE 1984) is to be taken to authorise the seizure of an item which the constable exercising the power has reasonable grounds for believing to be subject to legal privilege.

Although the powers under s18 and s19 are clearly intended to empower police officers to remove items from premises, it may be possible for police officers to seize and remove the actual premises, where they take a form that makes seizure and removal practicable: see *Cowan* v *Commissioner of Police of the Metropolis* [2000] 1 WLR 254. Hence, where the police believe that a car, boat or caravan has within it evidence of offences that can only be properly ascertained by, for example, subjecting it to examination in a forensic laboratory, it can be seized under these provisions. The only limitation seems to be whether it is physically possible for the police to remove the premises.

Where the s19 power is invoked, and articles seized, those articles may be retained 'so long as is necessary in all the circumstances', for instance for use at the trial of an accused, or to allow a forensic examination of them or to find out who is their lawful owner, but must be released to the person from whom they were seized – unless there is reason to believe that they have been obtained in consequence of the commission of an offence – if a photograph or copy of them would be sufficient for the purpose for which retention is desired. These matters are governed by s22.

11.9 Powers of arrest

Where time permits, the arrest of a suspect will often be made on the authority of a warrant issued by a justice of the peace under s1 of the Magistrates' Courts Act 1980. Such a warrant may issue in respect of any offence known to law, and is obtained by deposing to the facts of the alleged offence on oath. In addition to its use as a means of taking a suspect into custody before any charge has been made, the warrant procedure also aids in detaining those who have absconded while on bail awaiting trial, or who have failed to appear at court to answer to a summons.

In many cases, however, there is not sufficient time to apply for a warrant, and the statutory powers to arrest without it will now be considered. The 1984 Act significantly simplifies the law in this area, though several powers of arrest without warrant remain in other legislation, for example s7(3) of the Public Order Act 1936 and s28(2) of the Children and Young Persons Act 1969. These preserved additional powers of arrest are listed in Sch 2 of the 1984 Act. The Act draws a distinction between 'arrestable offences', for which a power of arrest without warrant exists in every case, subject to certain conditions, regardless of the seriousness of the harm or damage done in the actual offence, and other offences which become arrestable without warrant only if the gravity of the harm, or risk of further harm, or of the suspect's absconding without having given a true name and address, call for immediate detention.

It should be borne in mind that, notwithstanding the statutory provisions considered below, there is still a common law power to arrest for breach of the peace. As the court in *Foulkes* v *Chief Constable of Merseyside Police* [1998] 3 All ER 705 confirmed, the power can be exercised even if a breach of the peace has not yet occurred, provided the person exercising the power reasonably believes that a breach of the peace might be about to occur. There must be a sufficiently real and present threat to the peace to justify depriving a citizen of his liberty at a time when he is not actually acting unlawfully.

11.10 Arrestable offences

By virtue of s24, a power to arrest without warrant exists where an offence of the following kinds is suspected: the offence is one for which the sentence is fixed by law (eg murder); the offence is one for which a person of 21 years of age or over (not previously convicted) may be sentenced to imprisonment for a term of five years (or might be so sentenced but for the restrictions imposed by s33 of the Magistrates Courts Act 1980) – this would include serious assaults, theft, robbery and some burglaries; or the offence is one specifically stated as coming within the scope of the s24 powers. These offences include any offences: for which a person may be arrested under the Customs and Excise Acts, as defined in s1(1) of the Customs and Excise Management Act 1979; under the Official Secrets Act 1920 that are not arrestable offences by virtue of the term of imprisonment for which a person may be sentenced in respect of them; offences under any provision of the Official Secrets Act 1989 except s8(1), (4) or (5); under ss14 (indecent assault on a woman), 22 (causing prostitution of women) or 23 (procuration of girl under 21) of the Sexual Offences Act 1956; under ss12(1) (taking a motor vehicle or other conveyance without authority, etc) or 25(1) (going equipped for stealing, etc) of the Theft Act 1968; under the Football (Offences) Act 1991; under s2 of the Obscene Publications Act 1959 (publication of obscene matter); under s1 of the Protection of Children Act 1978 (indecent photographs and pseudo–photographs of children); under s166 of the Criminal Justice and Public Order Act 1994 (sale of tickets by unauthorised persons); under s19 of the Public Order Act 1986 (publishing, etc, material intended or likely to stir up racial hatred); under s167 of the Criminal Justice and Public Order Act 1994 (touting for car-hire services); or s60(8)(b) of the Criminal Justice and Public Order Act 1994 (failing to comply with requirement to remove a mask, etc). The Criminal Justice Act 2003 has introduced a power of arrest for possession of cannabis and for fraudulently obtaining a passport or a driving licence.

Without prejudice to s2 of the Criminal Attempts Act 1981, the powers of summary arrest conferred by s24 also apply to the offences of: conspiring to commit any of the offences mentioned in s24(2); attempting to commit any such offence; and inciting, aiding, abetting, counselling or procuring the commission of any such offence.

Section 26 provides that, subject to specifically provided for or preserved statutory powers of arrest without warrant (and those under s25 considered below) any power vested in a constable to arrest without a warrant shall cease to have effect. Care needs to be taken, however, in assessing the ambit of this provision. As the Court of Appeal held on *Gapper* v *Chief Constable of Avon and Somerset Constabulary* [1998] 4 All ER 248, s26 has no effect on those statutory powers of arrest vested in both police constables and private citizens not expressly repealed by PACE 1984. The plaintiff therefore failed in his action for wrongful arrest where he contended that a police constable had no power to arrest without a warrant under s6 of the Vagrancy Act 1824, on the basis that the power had not been expressly preserved by s24 and Sch 2 of PACE 1984. The Court of Appeal confirmed that s26 only abolished those statutory powers of arrest where the power was given to a police constable only (the power to arrest under s6 could be exercised by anyone); further, if the plaintiff's contention was correct it would have resulted in the manifest absurdity that a police constable's power to arrest under s6 had been abolished, whilst the citizen's power to arrest under s6 remained undiminished.

11.11 Power to arrest for arrestable offences

Given that the offence suspected falls within s24, to whom is a power of arrest allowed, and in what circumstances? There are differences between the powers of constables and those of private citizens. Section 24(4) and (5) detail the powers available to both:

'(4) Any person may arrest without a warrant –
(a) anyone who is in the act of committing an arrestable offence;
(b) anyone whom he has reasonable grounds for suspecting to be committing such an offence.
(5) Where an arrestable offence has been committed, any person may arrest without a warrant –
(a) anyone who is guilty of the offence;
(b) anyone whom he has reasonable grounds for suspecting to be guilty of it.'

It can be seen that a power to arrest arises against anyone who is in the act of committing an arrestable offence, or who is suspected on reasonable grounds to be committing such an offence, that is, someone who is still committing and has not yet completed the suspected crime, by s24(4). The power to arrest after the event given by s24(5) requires that an arrestable offence has been committed. If a private citizen arrests someone he suspected of having committed an arrestable offence, but it emerges that no arrestable offence was committed, the private citizen is liable in damages for false arrest. Such was the law prior to 1968, as enshrined in decisions such as *Walters* v *W H Smith* [1914] 1 KB 595, and it has since been confirmed in relation to s24(5) by the Court of Appeal in *R* v *Self* [1992] 1 WLR 476. Here the appellant, who was believed to have stolen a bar of chocolate, was arrested by a store detective and another member of the public. During the course of the arrest the appellant assaulted those trying to apprehend him. The appellant, who was ultimately acquitted of theft, but convicted of assault with intent to resist or prevent lawful apprehension, contrary to s38 of the Offences Against the Person Act 1861, contended that as he had been acquitted on the theft charge, neither the store detective nor any other member of the public could have been empowered to arrest him under s24(5) of the 1984 Act, since this required proof that an arrestable offence had been committed. It followed, therefore, that the detention had not been lawful, and thus he should not have been convicted under s38. Allowing the appeal, the Court confirmed that a condition precedent to the exercise of the citizen's power of arrest under s24(5) was that an arrestable offence had already been committed, and hence the contention in relation to s38 had to succeed. As Garland J observed:

'Subsection (5) makes it abundantly clear that the powers of arrest without a warrant where an arrestable offence has been committed require as a condition precedent an offence committed. If subsequently there is an acquittal of the alleged offence no offence has been committed. The power to arrest is confined to the person guilty of the offence or anyone who the person making the arrest has reasonable grounds for suspecting to be guilty of it ... If it is necessary to go further, one contrasts the words of subsection (5) with subsection (6), the very much wider powers given to a constable who has reasonable grounds for suspecting that an arrestable offence has been committed.'

Powers of arrest in wider terms are conferred on constables, in addition to those they possess in their capacity as citizens, by s24(4) and (5). These allow arrest even where no arrestable offence has in fact been committed. Under s24(6), if a constable has reasonable grounds for suspecting that an arrestable offence has been committed, he may arrest without a warrant anyone whom he has reasonable grounds for suspecting to be guilty of the offence. Under s24(7), a constable may arrest without a warrant anyone who is about to commit an arrestable offence and anyone whom he has reasonable grounds for suspecting to be about to commit an arrestable offence.

The 1984 Act does not contain a definition of what constitutes an arrest. However in *R* v *Brosch* [1988] Crim LR 743 the court held, following *Alderson* v *Booth* [1969] 2 All ER 271, that an arrest might be effected by any action or words indicating to D that he is under a compulsion and is no longer at liberty.

Reasonable suspicion

The provisions of the 1984 Act conferring powers of arrest, provided a constable has reasonable suspicion that certain preconditions exist, must be read on the basis that the officer himself must have the suspicion, ie it must be based upon matters present in the mind of the constable. The rationale for this approach is that Parliament has proceeded on the basis that police constables are independent executive officers, accountable in law for the way in which they exercise their powers. As Lawton LJ observed in *R* v *Chief Constable of Devon and Cornwall, ex parte Central Electricity Generating Board* [1982] QB 458 (at p474):

'... [chief constables] cannot give an officer under command an order to do acts which can only lawfully be done if the officer himself with reasonable cause suspects that a breach of the peace has occurred or is imminently likely to occur or an arrestable offence has been committed.'

Hence, a constable cannot be regarded as having a reasonable suspicion that a suspect has committed an offence simply because a superior officer orders him to effect an arrest of that suspect. The position was usefully summarised by Lord Steyn, in *O'Hara* v *Chief Constable of the Royal Ulster Constabulary* [1997] 2 WLR 1, as follows:

'(1) In order to have a reasonable suspicion the constable need not have evidence amounting to a prima facie case. Ex hypothesi one is considering a preliminary stage of the investigation and information from an informer or a tip-off from a member of the public may be enough: *Hussien* v *Chong Fook Kam* [1970] AC 942, 949. (2) Hearsay information may therefore afford a constable reasonable grounds to arrest. Such information may come from other officers: *Hussien*'s case, ibid. (3) The information which causes the constable to be suspicious of the individual must be in existence to the knowledge of the police officer at the time he makes the arrest. (4) The executive "discretion" to arrest or not as Lord Diplock described it in *Mohammed-Holgate* v *Duke* [1984] AC 437, 446, vests in the constable, who is engaged on the decision to arrest or not, and not in his superior officers.'

The test to be applied, therefore, is (assuming the arresting officer does suspect that circumstances justifying the exercise of the power to arrest exist) whether or not a reasonable person would have shared the officer's opinion, given the information which was in the mind of the arresting officer: see further *Castorina* v *Chief Constable of Surrey* (1988) 138 NLJ 180. In applying the test the courts appear to be willing to grant the arresting officer a margin of appreciation, given that he may have been acting in the heat of the moment: see *G* v *Superintendent of Police, Stroud* (1985) The Times 29 November.

As a police constable is a public officer (ie an officer of the executive) the legality of his actions can be tested by the application of the so-called *Wednesbury* test: see *Associated Provincial Picture Houses Ltd* v *Wednesbury Corporation* [1948] 1 KB 223. Hence he should exercise his discretion as would a reasonable police officer, not taking into account irrelevant considerations, and not failing to take into account relevant considerations. Ultimately, it will be for the court to decide whether the test has been satisfied. Hence, in *Lyons* v *Chief Constable of West Yorkshire* [1997] CLY 1359, it was held that a police officer had not acted unreasonably in exercising his power of arrest in relation to a L, notwithstanding that he had been previously informed (by a friend of L) that L had an alibi and hence could not have committed the crime under investigation. In *R* v *Chalkley* [1998] 2 All ER 155 police officers suspected the defendant of involvement in a robbery. Having obtained the necessary authorisation they decided to place a listening device in his home. In order to do so they arrested the defendant on suspicion of involvement in a number of credit card frauds so that he would be out of the house. On the basis of the evidence obtained the defendant was convicted of conspiracy to rob and appealed. One of the issues raised at the appeal was as to the legality of the arrest in relation to the credit card fraud. The Court of Appeal held that the arrest had been lawful. The Court felt that, provided the police officers had reasonable grounds to suspect that the defendant was involved in the credit card frauds, his arrest was lawful notwithstanding that his absence from his house provided the police with the opportunity to place the listening devices. Counsel for the defendant relied upon the proposition of Viscount Simon from *Christie* v *Leachinsky* [1947] 1 All ER 567 at 572, where he observed that:

'1. If a policeman arrests without warrant on reasonable suspicion of felony, or of other crime of a sort which does not require a warrant, he must in ordinary circumstances inform the person arrested of the true ground of arrest. He is not entitled to keep the

reason to himself or to give a reason which is not the true reason. In other words, a citizen is entitled to know on what charge or on suspicion of what crime he is seized.
2. If the citizen is not so informed, but is nevertheless seized, the policeman, apart from certain exceptions, is liable for false imprisonment.'

The Court, however, rejected the notion that an ulterior motive would necessarily render an arrest unlawful. As Auld LJ observed (at p176j –177g):

'In our view, the judge correctly held that the arrests were lawful. We acknowledge the importance of the liberty of the subject. It is a fundamental right of which he may only be deprived by the due process of law, which process includes an entitlement to be told why he is being deprived of it. However, a collateral motive for an arrest on otherwise good and stated grounds does not necessarily make it unlawful. It depends on the motive. That is clear from the materially different facts of *Christie* v *Leachinsky* and the qualified manner in which the members of the judicial committee expressed the important principle for which the case is famous.

First, as to the facts, there, the police informed Leachinsky of a ground of arrest which was not a valid ground for it; here the suspected credit card fraud was a valid ground for the arrests. There, there was an alternative and valid ground for arrest of which the officers had not informed him; here there was no alternative ground or reason, valid or invalid, for arrest as distinct from the object of removing [the defendant from his house] for a while to enable the installation of the device.

Second, Viscount Simon, Lord Simonds and Lord du Parcq (with whom Lord Thankerton and Lord Macmillan agreed) were all of the view that there were qualifications and possible exceptions to the general principle that the police, in making an arrest, should be motivated only by matters relevant to the suspected offence and should tell the subject the true reason for it. Viscount Simon said ([1947] 1 All ER 567 at 573, [1947] AC 573 at 588): "There may well be other exceptions to the general rule in addition to those 1 have indicated, and the above propositions are not intended to constitute a formal or complete code, but to indicate the general principles of our law on a very important matter."

Lord Simonds and Lord du Parcq ([1947] 1 All ER 567 at 575 and 581–582, [1947] AC 573 at 592 and 603–604) allowed for the legality of arrest and detention by the police of a man on one charge on which they have reasonable grounds for suspecting his guilt, but with the real or main purpose of enabling them to investigate another, possibly more serious, offence of which they have as yet no such grounds and with a view to preventing his escape from justice. As Lord Simonds observed ([1947] 1 All ER 567 at 575, [1947] AC 573 at 593): "In all such matters a wide measure of discretion must be left to those whose duty it is to preserve the peace and bring criminals to justice." The reasoning for that well-known and respectable aid to justice, "a holding charge", seems to us equally appropriate to circumstances where, as here, the police have, and have so informed the subject(s) when arresting them, reasonable grounds for doing so, but were motivated by a desire to investigate and put a stop to further, far more serious, crime. Accordingly, we agree with the judge's ruling that the arrests were lawful.'

Note that the requirement of reasonable suspicion accords with art 5(3) of the European Convention on Human Rights which requires that a person should not be deprived of his liberty except, inter alia, where he is lawfully arrested or detained for the purpose of bringing him before the competent legal authority on reasonable suspicion of having committed an offence or when it is reasonably considered necessary to prevent his committing an offence or fleeing after having done so.

11.12 Power to arrest for offences which are not arrestable

Where the suspected offence does not fall within the definition of arrestable given by s24, a power to arrest without warrant is conferred upon constables – but not upon private citizens – where it is thought undesirable to follow the normal procedure of leaving the suspected offender at large and proceeding against him by simple summons to appear at court later. The general purpose of this power is to prevent the suspect's avoiding prosecution by giving false particulars, or by refusing to give any particulars at all, or to remove the risk of further harm to the suspect himself or to the public or to property. Section 25 provides that, provided a constable has reasonable grounds for suspecting that any offence which is not an arrestable offence has been committed or attempted, or is being committed or attempted, he may arrest the 'relevant person' if it appears to him that service of a summons is impracticable or inappropriate because any of the general arrest conditions are satisfied. For these purposes 'relevant person' is defined by s25(2) as any person the constable has reasonable grounds to suspect of having committed, having attempted to commit, being in the course of committing or attempting to commit the offence.

The general arrest conditions referred to in s25(3) are: that the name of the relevant person is unknown to, and cannot be readily ascertained by, the constable; that the constable has reasonable grounds for doubting whether a name furnished by the relevant person as his name is his real name; that the relevant person has failed to furnish a satisfactory address for service, or the constable has reasonable grounds for doubting whether an address furnished by the relevant person is a satisfactory address for service; that the constable has reasonable grounds for believing that arrest is necessary to prevent the relevant person causing physical injury to himself or any other person, suffering physical injury, causing loss of or damage to property, committing an offence against public decency, or causing an unlawful obstruction of the highway; and that the constable has reasonable grounds for believing that arrest is necessary to protect a child or other vulnerable person from the relevant person.

Under s25(4) an address is a 'satisfactory address' for service if it appears to the constable that the relevant person will be at it for a sufficiently long period for it to be possible to serve him with a summons; or that some other person specified by the relevant person will accept service of a summons for the relevant person at it. A constable is not authorised to arrest under s25(3)(d)(iv) (constable has reasonable grounds for believing arrest is necessary to prevent the relevant person committing an offence against public decency) unless members of the public going about their normal business cannot reasonably be expected to avoid the person to be arrested.

In *Edwards and Others* v *DPP* (1993) 97 Cr App R 301 two men, Fox and

Sumner, were observed by police officers who believed them to be using cannabis. When challenged, the men appeared to try to dispose of certain substances. They were informed that they were being arrested for obstructing the officers in the execution of their duties under the Misuse of Drugs Act 1971. A woman named Prendergast intervened to prevent the arrest of Fox and was arrested for obstruction contrary to s51(3) Police Act 1964. Edwards intervened to prevent the arrest of Prendergast and was similarly arrested for obstruction contrary to s51(3). The defendants submitted that there was no case to answer since there was no power to arrest without warrant for obstruction under the Misuse of Drugs Act 1971. The magistrates found that in the circumstances there was a power to arrest under s25 of the 1984 Act as, on the facts now known, the arresting officer would have every reason to doubt the truth of any name he was given by the suspect, hence the arrests were lawful. On appeal by way of case stated, the Divisional Court considering the question of whether or not the arresting officer, in the circumstances of the case, had had the power to arrest Fox under s25(3)(a) and (b) and/or s25(3)(d)(i) of the 1984 Act, held that, as the power to arrest without warrant for obstruction of a police officer in the execution of his duty contrary to the Misuse of Drugs Act 1971 had been abolished by s26 PACE 1984, the only power to arrest for such obstruction would be that now arising under s25 of the 1984 Act, ie the power of summary arrest in relation to a non-arrestable offence. By simply telling Fox that he was 'nicked for obstruction', the officer had failed to give s25(1) of the 1984 Act or any of the general arrest conditions detailed in s25(3) as justification. The court confirmed that, by virtue of s28(5) of the 1984 Act, an arrest was not lawful unless the arrestee was informed of the grounds of arrest. In the instant case the court felt that there were no circumstances that precluded the giving of that information; it had obviously practicable for the officer to give reasons for the arrest, because that was precisely what he had done, although they were invalid. The arrest might have been valid if the general arrest conditions under s25 had been given as the reason for arrest, but the arrest could not be retrospectively validated. As Evans LJ observed:

> 'It may seem unrealistic that the court should be concerned after the event with the precise words that were used ... Nevertheless, it has to be borne in mind that giving correct information as to the reasons for an arrest is a matter of the utmost constitutional significance in a case where a reason can be and is given at the time.'

11.13 Information on arrest

Section 28 of the 1984 Act codifies certain established principles of common law relating to the duty of the police to inform an arrested person of the fact of and reason for his arrest. Under s28(1) where a person is arrested, otherwise than by being informed that he is under arrest, the arrest is not lawful unless the person arrested is informed that he is under arrest as soon as is practicable after his arrest. Where a person is arrested by a constable this requirement applies regardless of whether the fact of the arrest is obvious. This information does not necessarily have to be supplied by the officer who actually exercises the power of arrest: see *Dhesi* v *Chief Constable of West Midlands Police* (2000) The Times 9 May.

Some latitude is allowed to arresting officers by s28(5) which provides that there is no duty to inform a person that he is under arrest, or of the ground for the arrest, if it is not reasonably practicable at that time for him to be so informed by reason of his having escaped from arrest before the information could be given. Note that s28 accords with the requirements of art 5(2) of the European Convention on Human Rights which provides that everyone who is arrested should be informed promptly of the reasons for the arrest.

It would appear that even though reasons for an arrest are not given at the time of the arrest, the arrest can become lawful once those reasons are supplied. In *Lewis* v *Chief Constable of the South Wales Constabulary* [1991] 1 All ER 206 the plaintiffs had been arrested on suspicion of burglary and taken to a police station. One had been told the reason for the arrest ten minutes after it had occurred, the other some 23 minutes after arrest. They were detained for about five hours and then released. In an action for false arrest and wrongful imprisonment, they were awarded damages for unlawful detention of only ten and 23 minutes respectively. On appeal, Balcombe LJ rejected the contention of counsel for the plaintiffs to the effect that, if at the moment of initial apprehension the arrest was unlawful, the act was a nullity. His Lordship expressed the view that arrest was a situation; a matter of fact, citing *Spicer* v *Holt* [1976] 3 All ER 71. Whether a person has been arrested depended not on the legality of his arrest but on whether he has been deprived of his liberty to go where he pleased. There was no doubt that, on the facts of this case, the plaintiffs had been deprived of their liberty at the moment that they were arrested, and that that act was not a nullity. Arrest was a continuing act, and in his Lordship's view there was nothing inconsistent with the wording of s28(3) to say that from that moment when reasons were given the arrest became lawful, or the continued deprivation of liberty became lawful, or the continued custody became lawful. Hence the trial judge had been correct in the ruling that the period in respect of which the plaintiffs were entitled to damages was that between the arrest and the giving of reasons. The decision confirms the earlier case of *DPP* v *Hawkins* [1988] 1 WLR 1166.

Decisions such as *Abbassy* v *MPC* [1990] 1 WLR 385 confirm that a constable exercising his powers of arrest need not use technical language to indicate the offence for which D is being arrested. It is sufficient that the type of offence is identified, so that D may volunteer information that would render the arrest unnecessary. Where the arrest is made pursuant to s25, *DPP* v *Nicholas* [1987] Crim LR 474 suggests that a constable telling D that he is being arrested because of his failure to provide a name and address is enough.

The issue of information on arrest was considered in *Taylor* v *Chief Constable of Thames Valley* [2004] 3 All ER 503. The Court of Appeal considered a case in which Taylor, aged ten and a young offender, had been awarded £1,500 as damages for false imprisonment, assault and trespass to the person. This award was being appealed as was the issue of the provision of information upon arrest. Taylor had attended a demonstration, with his mother, and had been seen on videotape throwing stones. At a later demonstration he was arrested in relation to the earlier matter. The arresting officer told him that she was arresting him on suspicion of violent disorder at the earlier demonstration. The arrest was at 16.10, he arrived at the police station at 18.10; he was then processed at 19.45, interviewed at 21.21 and released at 23.00. It had been argued on behalf of Taylor, at the first hearing, that firstly he had not been given sufficient information upon arrest: that something more was required, such as a reference to throwing stones. It was also argued that there had been an unacceptable delay between 20.15 and 21.21 which amounted to false imprisonment. The decision of the court was that the arrest had been lawful but that part of the period of detention had been unlawful. The approach that a court should take in relation to arrests was to consider whether the person arrested had been told, in simple non-technical language that he could understand, the legal and factual grounds for his arrest. That satisfied the requirements of s28(3) of the 1984 Act, the Human Rights Act 1998 and obligations under art 5(2) of the European Convention on Human Rights and was in line with earlier case law.

The offence of violent disorder was such that it may not necessarily be reasonably practical for the police to give each person detailed particulars of the reason for their arrest. It was ordinarily sufficient when making an arrest in such circumstances for the officer to tell the person concerned that he was being arrested on suspicion of violent disorder at a particular time and place. Taylor had been informed of this information and therefore his arrest was lawful. On the second matter, the detention period, the judge had been entitled to find that Taylor had been unlawfully detained for a period of approximately one hour prior to his interview. This case is useful as it provides a straightforward account of the issues relating to the requirements upon arrest and the operation of the principle that detention has to have a legal justification if it is to be lawful.

11.14 Voluntary attendance at police station

At common law, the status of someone who was 'helping the police with their inquiries', but without having been formally arrested, was never very clear. It was repeatedly stated that a person was either under arrest or at liberty to leave the police station, and that the law did not recognise any form of detention as legal unless it was a lawful arrest. For the avoidance of doubt, and following the recommendations of the 1981 Royal Commission on Criminal Procedure, s29 of the 1984 Act now provides:

> 'Where for the purposes of assisting with an investigation a person attends voluntarily at a police station or at any other place where a constable is present or accompanies a constable to a police station or any such other place without having been arrested –

(a) he shall be entitled to leave at will unless he is placed under arrest;
(b) he shall be informed at once that he is under arrest if a decision is taken by a constable to prevent him from leaving at will.'

11.15 Procedure following arrest

Once a suspect has been arrested, whether with or without a warrant, he must be taken to a police station as soon as is practicable after his arrest, unless the arrest was made at such a station: s30(1). Provision is made by that section for conveying the suspect to a 'designated police station', defined by s35 as being one specified by the Chief Officer of Police for the detention of arrested persons, unless it is impracticable to do so in the short term. The suspect may be searched at the time of his arrest if there is reason to believe that he may present a danger to himself or to others, or may have upon him anything which he might use to escape from lawful custody, or which might be evidence relating to an offence: s32(1) and (2). These latter words are wide enough to allow a search for evidence of an offence other than that for which the arrest has been made. The search may also extend to premises in which the suspect was arrested, or in which he was present, immediately before his arrest, in order to discover evidence relating to the offence for which the arrest was made, if the arresting constable has reasonable grounds for believing that such evidence exists: s32(2) and (6), and see *R* v *Badham* [1987] Crim LR 202.

On arrival at a designated police station, the suspect will come under the supervision of a custody officer of at least the rank of sergeant, whose duties are prescribed by Pt IV of the 1984 Act: see also *Vince* v *Chief Constable of Dorset Police* [1993] 1 WLR 415. In brief, an arrested person should not be kept in detention, but should be released either without charge or on bail, at the earliest reasonable opportunity. The custody officer must first decide, if the arrest has been without warrant, whether there is sufficient evidence to justify a charge against the suspect (s37(1)). The Criminal Justice Act 2003 provides for the Crown Prosecution Service to be involved in charging decisions. If insufficient evidence exists, the suspect must be released, either on bail or not, unless the officer has reasonable grounds for believing that continued detention is necessary to secure or preserve evidence relating to an offence, or to obtain evidence by questioning the suspect (s37(2)). Records must be kept throughout the suspect's detention, detailing the decisions and reasons of the custody officer. If there is sufficient evidence to justify a formal charge, the suspect must be charged or released with or without bail (s37(7)). Suspects who are not in a fit state to allow the custody officer to make a charge under subs(7) or to be released under that subsection, for example, through drunkenness or the influence of drugs, may be detained until they are fit (s37(9)).

Once a charge has been made against the suspect and entered in the charge book, there is a presumption that the suspect will be released. He may be detained further only if he is an adult, his name or address cannot be ascertained or is reasonably suspected by the custody officer to be false, the custody officer has reasonable grounds for believing that the person arrested will fail to appear in court to answer to bail; in the case of a person arrested for an imprisonable offence the custody officer has reasonable grounds for believing that the detention of the arrested person is necessary to prevent him from committing an offence; in the case of case of a person arrested for a non-imprisonable offence the custody officer has reasonable grounds for believing that the detention of the arrested person is necessary to prevent him from causing physical injury to any other person or from causing loss of or damage to property; the custody officer has reasonable grounds for believing that the detention of the arrested person is necessary to prevent him interfering with the administration of justice or with the investigation of offences; or the custody officer has reasonable grounds for believing that continued detention is necessary for the protection of the suspect: see s38(1) as amended by s28 of the Criminal Justice and Public Order Act 1994.

Whether or not a charge has been made, the continued detention of every suspect depends upon a review made at intervals by the custody officer or, in the case of a suspect not yet charged, an officer of at least the rank of inspector who has not been directly involved in the investigation of the offence for which the arrest was made (s40(1)). The first review must be made not later than six hours after detention was first authorised under s37 or s38, the second review not later than nine hours after the first, and subsequent reviews at intervals of not more than nine hours (s40(3)). There is power to postpone a review if it is 'not practicable' to carry it out by the stated time, for instance if the review would interrupt a period of interrogation and the review officer is satisfied it would prejudice the investigation subject to the interrogation, or if no review officer is available at the stated time (s40(4)). In such a case, the review must take place as soon as is practicable (s40(5)).

The purpose of the review is to decide whether the reason for which detention was first authorised still holds good, for example, that the suspect was a source of harm to himself or others, or that evidence for use against him might be destroyed if he were to be released. If it does not, the suspect must be released. In deciding whether detention remains justified, s40(12) requires the officer to consider any representations made by the suspect himself or by any solicitor acting for him and available at the time of the review, though he need not consider what the suspect may have to say if the latter is asleep, or unfit to make representations by reason of his condition or behaviour (s40(14)).

Where the suspect has been arrested and is being detained without charge, s41 imposes a maximum period for which he can be detained in police custody without being brought before a court. The general maximum is 24 hours, calculated from the time of his arrival at the first police station to which he is taken after his arrest: s41(1) and (2)(d). The period is calculated from the time of arrest if he voluntarily attended at a police station and was subsequently arrested there or if he is arrested in a police area other than that in which he has been sought – for instance, the suspect who is wanted by the Metropolitan Police but who is arrested by a different police force and has not been questioned by the arresting police force with a view to discovering evidence of the offence. Other special provisions for calculating the 24-hour period are made in the cases of suspects who are removed from police detention for medical treatment in hospital, or who are arrested outside England and Wales.

Where the 24-hour period has expired and no charge has been made, the suspect must be released, with or without bail, unless detention beyond the 24 hours has been authorised by a superintendent under s42 or has been allowed by a magistrate's warrant of further detention under s43. Section 42 allows detention up to a total of 36 hours without charge on reasonable grounds for belief that it is necessary to secure or preserve evidence and that the investigation is being conducted diligently and expeditiously. A warrant under s43 is issued on very similar grounds to the superintendent's authority under s42, and permits detention in police custody and without charge beyond 36 hours and up to a maximum total of 96 hours, in periods of not more than 36 hours at a time before further application to the court is necessary: see further s42 to s44 for details of the procedure at the hearing and the grounds for warrants of further detention. The Criminal Justice Act 2003 widened the period, extending it from 24 to 36 hours for all offences: previously it was only allowed for serious arrestable offences. Review of detention over the telephone is also provided for.

The courts will construe the requirements relating to extension of detention as mandatory, unless the Act expressly provides for some discretion. Hence in *R* v *Slough Justices, ex parte Stirling* [1987] Crim LR 576, where the police arrived after 38 hours with an application to extend detention, the application was refused, on the basis that, under s43(7), it would have been reasonable for the police to apply in good time for an extension. Similarly, in *In the Matter of an Application for a Warrant of Further Detention* [1988] Crim LR 296, where detainees were not given the opportunity to make representations via a solicitor before a superintendent extended detention from 24 to 36 hours, and a brief note was placed on custody record to the effect that the superintendent considered detention necessary because the detainees might impede the course of justice if released, the justices accepted the detainees' contentions that the police had failed to comply with the mandatory requirements under s42. Detention beyond 24 hours had, therefore, been unlawful. Either the justices therefore had no jurisdiction to consider an application for further detention, or if they did they would decline to exercise it. Where a suspect is detained without the review safeguards having been observed the police may be liable in damages for the tort of unlawful imprisonment: see *Roberts* v *Chief Constable of the Cheshire Constabulary* [1999] 2 All ER 326. It makes no difference that, had the review been conducted as required, continued detention would have been authorised. Note that under s40 Terrorism Act 2000 a person suspected of involvement in terrorist activities can be detained for up to 48 hours without charge: see further *Brannigan and McBride* v *United Kingdom* (1993) 17 EHHR 539.

11.16 Appearance before magistrates following charge

An arrested person who has been charged but who, pursuant to ss38–40 of the 1984 Act, has been detained in police custody, must be brought before a magistrates' court as soon as is practicable after charge, and not later than the first sitting of the court after he has been charged with the offence (s46(2)). This will usually be on the day of the charge or the day after, but in cases where no court sitting is to be held for either of those days, detention in police custody is permitted until the next sitting, provided the clerk to the justices is informed of the fact that the suspect is in custody and awaiting appearance at the next sitting. It is then the duty of the clerk to arrange for a hearing not later than the day on which the charge was made, or, if a public holiday or weekend intervenes, the day after that holiday or weekend (s46(3)–(9)). The obligation to bring the suspect before the court does not apply if he is not well enough (s46(9)).

11.17 Interrogation of suspects and the right to legal advice

Whilst the common law recognised a general right in an accused person to communicate and consult privately with his solicitor outside the interview room (see the 'Judges' Rules'), there was no common law right entitling an accused person to have a solicitor present during police interviews: see further the speech of Lord Browne-Wilkinson in *R* v *Chief Constable of the Royal Ulster Constabulary, ex parte Begley; R* v *McWilliams* [1997] 4 All ER 833. Under PACE 1984, however, persons arrested, whether by warrant or not, and held at a police station, are given rights to have someone named by them informed of the fact and place of their detention, and are to be allowed access to legal advice from a solicitor. Although these rights are not absolute, and can be denied for a period of time in certain circumstances, the intent of PACE 1984 is clearly that they should be respected and granted in all but the clearest cases calling for their denial.

So far as concerns notification to an outside person of the fact and place of arrest, s56 provides that when a person has been arrested and is being held in custody in a police station or other premises, he shall be entitled, if he so requests, to have one friend or relative or other person who is known to him or who is likely to take an interest in his welfare told, as soon as is practicable except to the extent that delay is permitted by other provisions in s56, that he has been arrested and is being detained there.

Delay will be permitted if the detainee is being held in connection with a serious arrestable offence, and an officer of at least the rank of superintendent has authorised it in writing. The basis for delaying access must be that the authorising officer has reasonable grounds for believing that telling the named person of the arrest will lead to interference with or harm to evidence connected with a serious arrestable offence or interference with or physical injury to other persons, or will lead to the alerting of other persons suspected of having committed such an offence but not yet arrested for it, or will hinder the recovery of any property obtained as a result of such an offence. Under s56(5A) an officer may also authorise delay where the serious arrestable offence is a drug-trafficking offence. In any event access can only be delayed for 36 hours.

If a delay in granting access is authorised the detained person shall be told the reason for it and the reason for the delay must be noted on his custody record. These conditions must be complied with as soon as is practicable.

The provision governing access to legal advice by a person detained following arrest is s58. In its terms it is very similar to s56. A person arrested and held in custody in a police station or other premises is entitled, if he so requests, to consult a solicitor privately at any time. Access to a solicitor can only be delayed if the person who is in police detention is being held in connection with a serious arrestable offence and the delay is authorised by an officer of at least the rank of superintendent. The grounds for delaying access are set out in s58(8) – the officer authorising delay must have reasonable grounds for believing that the exercise of the right to consult privately with a solicitor will lead to interference with or harm to evidence connected with a serious arrestable offence, or interference with or physical injury to other persons; will lead to the alerting of other persons suspected of having committed such an offence but not yet arrested for it; or will hinder the recovery of any property obtained as a result of such an offence. Generally, access to a solicitor may only be delayed for 36 hours (s58(5)), although other provisions permit longer periods in certain specified circumstances. For example the Criminal Justice Act 1988 extends the power to delay access where serious drug trafficking offences are involved, as do various provisions relating to suspected terrorist activity (although the extent to which these provisions are in compliance with the European Convention on Human Rights may now be in question – see below).

Thus, in general terms, a person held in custody at a police station will be entitled to consult a solicitor at any time, if he so requests. The detainee may consult a solicitor of his own choice, but if he knows of none he should be informed by the police of the availability of the duty solicitor.

Simply because a detainee has a right to a solicitor, it does not follow that a solicitor has a right to enter a police station to see a detainee. The right of access to a solicitor is vested in the detainee. If it is denied the detainee can pursue an appropriate remedy in public law or raise the issue to challenge the admission of evidence at any subsequent trial. Hence no action will lie in negligence or misfeasance in public office against the police, initiated on behalf of a solicitor denied access to a client, where that solicitor has been prevented by the police from attending upon a client being held in detention at a police station: see *Rixon* v *Chief Constable of Kent* (2000) The Times 11 April.

In what circumstances, if any, will the courts permit the police to rely on evidence obtained during interrogations at a police station, where D has not been permitted to exercise his right to consult with a solicitor? In *R* v *Samuel* [1988] 2

WLR 920, the appellant was interviewed by the police on four occasions about a robbery and two burglaries. The appellant denied any involvement. During the second interview he asked for access to a solicitor, but his request was refused on the basis that there was a likelihood of other suspects involved in the robbery being inadvertently warned. At the fourth interview the appellant confessed to the two burglaries and he was charged with those offences at 4.30pm. At 4.45pm a solicitor was informed of the charges, but denied access. Shortly afterwards the appellant confessed to the robbery and the solicitor was allowed to see him one hour later. At the trial, the appellant contended that evidence of the latter confession should be excluded, but it was admitted and he was convicted of robbery. On appeal the Court of Appeal held that the conviction should be quashed as, in the circumstances, the refusal of access to a solicitor had been unjustified and the interview in question should not have taken place. The Court held that the crucial aspect of an interrogating officer's decision to exclude access to a solicitor under s58 was that, at the time of exclusion, he has reasonable grounds to believe that access will lead to or hinder one or more of the things set out in paras (a) to (c) of s58(8). As Hodson J observed:

> 'The use of the word "will" is clearly of great importance. There were available to the draftsman many words or phrases by which he could have described differing nuances as to the officer's state of mind, for example "might", "could", "there was a risk", "there was a substantial risk", etc. The choice of "will" must have been deliberately restrictive. Of course, anyone who says that be believes that something will happen, unless he is speaking of one of the immutable laws of nature, accepts the possibility that it will not happen, but the use of the word "will" in conjunction with belief implies in the believer a belief that it will very probably happen … What is it that the officer has to satisfy the court he believed? The right denied is a right "to consult a solicitor privately". The person denied that right is in police detention. In practice, the only way that the person can make any of the matters set out in paras (a) to (c) happen is by some communication from him to the solicitor. For the matters set out in paras (a) to (c) to be made to happen the solicitor must do something. If he does something knowing that it will result in anything in paras (a) to (c) happening he will, almost inevitably, commit a serious criminal offence. Therefore, inadvertent or unwitting conduct apart, the officer must believe that a solicitor will, if allowed to consult with a detained person, thereafter commit a criminal offence. Solicitors are officers of the court. We think that the number of times that a police officer could genuinely be in that state of belief will be rare. Moreover it is our view that, to sustain such a basis for refusal, the grounds put forward would have to have reference to a specific solicitor. We do not think they could ever be successfully advanced in relation to solicitors generally …'

It is submitted that to deny access to a specified solicitor may be tantamount to defamation, unless the police can produce evidence justifying the decision. As the above extract indicates, this will have to be evidence that the solicitor is likely to be duped by the suspect, or will help him pervert the course of justice. The former is perhaps possible. In *R* v *Walters* [1987] Crim LR 577, the Court accepted that access to a solicitor could be denied where there was evidence that the suspects had been using 'Delphic phrases' to communicate with each other. A solicitor could be used in such a case to convey an apparently innocent message that could alert other gang members. To suggest that a solicitor would knowingly engage in such activities would obviously be a very grave allegation indeed. *Samuel* was followed in *R* v *Alladice* (1988) 87 Cr App R 380.

Where the interrogating officers fail to inform D of his right to consult with a solicitor, or fail to act upon his request for such consultation, the trial judge will have to assess the extent to which the failure to follow the provisions of the Act and the Codes vitiates any subsequent interrogations.

In *R* v *Dunford* (1990) 91 Cr App R 150, where the Court of Appeal upheld the trial judge's decision to admit D's statement made in the absence of a solicitor on the basis that a solicitor's advice would not have added anything to the appellant's knowledge of his rights, Neill LJ expressly approved of the approach taken in *R* v *Walsh* (1990) 91 Cr App R 161, where it was stated that, whilst a breach of s58 would prima facie have an adverse effect on the fairness of proceedings:

> 'This does not mean, of course, in every case of a significant or substantial breach of s58 or the Code of Practice the evidence concerned will automatically be excluded. The task of the court is not merely to consider whether there would be an adverse effect on the fairness of the proceedings, but such an adverse effect that justice requires the evidence to be excluded ... Breaches which are in themselves significant and substantial are not rendered otherwise by the good faith of the officers concerned.'

This decision, and others, suggests that the courts are willing to adopt a causation based approach, assessing what difference access to legal advice might have had on D's conduct. Thus in *R* v *Absolam* (1989) 88 Cr App R 322, the Court of Appeal allowed D's appeal against conviction where the trial judge had allowed in evidence statements made before access to a solicitor was submitted. Bingham LJ noted that the interrogating officers should have informed D of his right to consult a solicitor when it became apparent to them that an offence had been committed, even though the series of questions and answers taking place between the officers and D was not in any formal sense a conventional interview. He continued:

> '... it seems to us that if the learned judge had been persuaded that there were here significant and substantial breaches of the Code he would, in all probability, have excluded the answers given by the appellant ... he would, we think, had he taken the same view of the Code as we have, have formed the opinion that this was a case in which, as a result of a line of questioning initiated in remarkable circumstances but with no warning to the appellant of his right, the appellant would not have given the answers that he did, and that the prosecution would not have been in receipt of these admissions if the appropriate procedures had been followed.'

Complications can arise in cases such as *R* v *Anderson* [1993] Crim LR 448, where D does not request access to a solicitor, later changes his mind, but due to a breakdown in communications, the interviewing officer is unaware that D has made such a request. In that case the Court of Appeal upheld the trial judge's decision to permit in evidence D's confession, under s78, on the basis that there was insufficient evidence that 'but for' the failure to provide legal advice D would not have made the statement, and further because there was no evidence to suggest the police had acted in any way to make the statement unreliable. See further *R* v *Parris* (1989) 89 Cr App R 68, and *R* v *Silcott* (1991) The Times 9 December.

Note that in *R* v *Chief Constable of South Wales, ex parte Merrick* [1994] 1 WLR 663, the Divisional Court ruled that whilst the statutory right to consult privately with a solicitor created by s58(1) did not extend to a prisoner held in custody at a court following a refusal of bail, such a prisoner did have a common law right to consult with a legal adviser as soon as was reasonably practicable, bearing in mind the other demands on police officers responsible for the custody of prisoners being held at the court. On this basis the policy adopted at Cardiff Magistrates' Court (of not permitting interviews between prisoners and solicitors after 10.00am, unless there were good reasons for the interview not having taken place earlier) was declared to be unlawful.

The incorporation of the European Convention on Human Rights has inevitably refocused attention on this aspect of the criminal process. Article 6(3) provides that everyone charged with a criminal offence has the right to 'defend himself ... through legal assistance'.

This does not specifically refer to access to a solicitor whilst in detention, but increasingly the European Court of Human Rights is coming to recognise what the Americans might refer to as a 'right to counsel' in so far as denial of access to a solicitor during detention might be seen as vitiating the fairness of any subsequent trial. In *Averill* v *United Kingdom* Application No 36408/97 (2000) The Times 20 June, adverse inferences where drawn from the applicant's failure to answer questions during detention. Being detained under s14(1)(b) of the Prevention of Terrorism (Temporary Measures) Act 1989, he was denied access to a lawyer for the first 24 hours of his detention. The European Court of Human Rights ruled that the concept of fairness underpinning art 6 required that the accused should have the benefit of assistance from a lawyer when faced with the dilemma of whether or not to respond to questions during police interrogations. Similarly in *Magee* v *United Kingdom* Application No 28135/95 (2000) The Times 20 June, the applicant was denied access to a solicitor for approximately the first 54 hours of detention, during which time he was subjected to intense questioning, eventually admitting his involvement in terrorist offences after approximately 48 hours of questioning. The Court held that denial of access to a solicitor would amount to a violation of arts 6(1) and 6(3) if it could be shown that the denial occurred in circumstances where the rights of the defendant were irretrievably prejudiced so that the fairness of any subsequent trial was irretrievably vitiated. The Court went on to express the view that procedural fairness required that the applicant should have been granted access to a solicitor as a counterweight to the intimidating atmosphere specifically devised to sap his will and make him confide in his interrogators.

Under Code C accurate records must be made of each interview and interrogation, and in some circumstances tape recordings of interviews will be permitted under s60. The suspect must be cautioned, and that caution must be administered as soon as the constable has grounds for believing that the suspect has committed an offence. A further caution must be given before the arrested person is interviewed, and if the interview is interrupted for more than one hour, yet another caution is to be given before it is continued. Interviews of arrested persons can be carried out only with the agreement of the custody officer responsible for them and they must be allowed at least eight hours' continuous rest in any period of 24 hours. No form of oppressive conduct is to be used in questioning, and the suspect may make a written statement if he wishes. Code C also details the records to be kept, and provides for the conduct of identification parades and interrogation of those who are physically or mentally ill or who are under the age of 17, and provides that detainees must be informed of their right to free legal advice, and must be reminded of this right before any interview takes place.

A frequently voiced criticism of PACE 1984 and the original Code on interrogation was the absence of any explicit prohibition on interviews with suspects prior to their arrival at the police station. The revised Code C goes some way to meeting these objections by providing that interviews can only be held outside a police station in certain specified circumstances. Under paragraph 11.1 exceptions can only be made where no decision to arrest the interviewee has been taken; or, the interchanges do not amount to the questioning of a person regarding his involvement or suspected involvement in criminal activity; or, delaying the interview would be likely to lead to endangering others or enabling other suspects to flee or hinder the return of any property. In *R* v *Khan* [1993] Crim LR 54, the Court of Appeal upheld the decision of the trial judge not to exclude, under s78 of PACE 1984, evidence obtained by police asking D questions whilst they were searching his dwelling. The Court confirmed that the proper venue for any interrogation was the police station, where the safeguards provided by s58 and the Codes would apply, but was satisfied that, on the facts, the main thrust of the police questioning had related to the whereabouts of property.

11.18 Searches and fingerprinting following arrest

The general power to search an arrested person at the time of arrest has already been considered. Once at the police station, a search may be conducted on the authority of the custody officer, and what is found may be seized in the circumstances provided for by s54(3) and (4). Under s54(4) clothes and personal effects may only be seized if the custody officer believes that the person from whom they are seized may use them: to cause physical injury to himself or any other person; to damage property; to interfere with evidence; or to assist him to escape; or if the custody officer has reasonable grounds for believing that the items may evidence relating to an offence.

In certain situations it will be necessary for the search carried out upon an arrested person to go beyond a simple inspection of his outer clothing and personal effects. As originally enacted, PACE 1984 provided the power to conduct an intimate search of a detainee, defining such a search as one that involved examination of the bodily orifices. This definition proved problematic in drugs cases where frequently a suspect was believed to be concealing prohibited substances in his mouth. Police officers had no right to carry out the necessary search without invoking the procedure required for intimate searches (see below). A possible loophole was identified by the court in *R* v *Hughes* [1995] Crim LR 407, where a constable conducting a search in public held D's nose and jaw causing D to expel the drugs he had been concealing in his mouth. D was subsequently convicted of possession of cannabis. The Court of Appeal, being asked to rule on whether: (1) there had been a search; (2) it had been an intimate search; (3) whether the evidence so obtained should have been excluded because the constable had failed to inform the defendant of the purpose of the search and had failed to make a formal record of it, dismissed the appeal, holding that the conduct of the police officer amounted to a search and there had, therefore, been breaches of the Codes of Practice, although they were not such as to render the evidence inadmissible on the grounds of unfairness. The search itself could not be classified as intimate as there had been no intrusion into the bodily orifices.

The problem has now been addressed by s59 of the Criminal Justice and Public Order Act 1994, which amends PACE 1984 so as to exclude searches of the mouth from the scope of intimate searches. The future relevance of *Hughes*, therefore will be as regards instances where concealed items are retrieved from a suspect's vagina or rectum without a physical examination having been carried out, although quite how this might be achieved poses an interesting anatomical question.

Section 55 of PACE 1984 provides for the carrying out of an intimate search where an officer of at least the rank of superintendent has reasonable grounds to believe that a person who has been arrested and is in police detention may have concealed on him anything which he could use to cause physical injury to himself or others, or that he might so use, while he is in police detention or in the custody of a court. Alternatively, the power can be based upon reasonable belief that such a person may have a Class A controlled drug concealed on him and was in possession of it with the appropriate criminal intent before his arrest.

An intimate search may only be carried out at a police station, hospital, doctor's surgery or other place used for medical purposes (s55(8)), and may not be made by a person of the sex opposite to the person searched. Intimate searches for evidence of drugs offences may not be made at a police station (s55(9)). Non-intimate samples, such as hair (other than pubic hair), from a nail or under a nail, from body swabs (including mouth swabs but excluding other bodily orifices), saliva and footprints or similar impressions of the body other than a part of the hand, may be taken from an arrested person without his consent under conditions very similar to those allowing intimate searches (s63).

Note that the power to take intimate and non-intimate sample extends to all recordable offences, and not merely serious arrestable offences. Following amendments introduced by the Criminal Evidence (Amendment) Act 1997, the range of persons from whom a non-intimate sample can be taken, notwithstanding that the appropriate consent has not been given has been extended to include persons convicted of an offence listed in Sch 1 to the 1997 Act (notably sexual offences and offences of violence) before 10 April 1985 who are still in custody for that offence, or detained under the Mental Health Act 1983. The 1997 Act also extends the power to take non-intimate samples without consent from those detained following an acquittal on grounds of insanity or a finding of unfitness to plead.

Intimate samples, meaning a sample of blood, semen or other body tissue, fluid, urine, pubic hair, dental impression, or a swab from a body orifice other than the mouth, may not be taken against the arrested person's will. An intimate sample, other than one of urine or a dental impression may be taken only by a registered medical practitioner, and a dental impression may only be taken by a registered dentist. A court may draw such inferences as seem justified from a person's refusal to consent to the taking of an intimate sample.

Once samples are taken, they can be used by the police to investigate offences other than that for which the suspect has been detained. Hence, in *R* v *Kelt* [1994] 2 All ER 780, the Court of Appeal held that it was permissible for the police to use a blood sample lawfully obtained from D in connection with a murder enquiry, in order to compare it with blood samples found on evidence relating to a separate incident of robbery. Express provision is now made for such cross-referencing of evidence by s65 of PACE 1984, as amended.

A significant new power, resulting from the amendment to s62 of PACE 1984 by s54 of the Criminal Justice and Public Order Act 1994, will permit the taking of intimate samples from persons not in police detention, provided such action is authorised by an officer of at least the rank of superintendent and the consent of the person is given (although adverse inferences can be drawn from a failure to grant such consent). The criteria to be satisfied are that two or more non-intimate samples must have been provided by the person in question, in the course of the investigation into an offence, which have proved insufficient (for the purposes of DNA analysis). Alternatively, non-intimate samples can be taken from a person not in detention regardless of his consent if he has been charged with a recordable offence or informed that he will be reported for such an offence and either he has not had a non-intimate sample taken from him in the course of the investigation of that offence, or if he has, it has not proved suitable for analysis.

Under a new s63B, added to PACE 1984 by s57 of the Criminal Justice and Court Services Act 2000, a sample of urine or a non-intimate sample may be taken from a person in police detention for the purpose of ascertaining whether he has any specified Class A drug in his body if a number of conditions are met. These are that the detainee has been charged with a 'trigger' offence; or has been charged with an offence and a police officer of at least the rank of inspector, who has reasonable grounds for suspecting that the misuse by that person of any specified Class A drug caused or contributed to the offence, has authorised the sample to be taken. Further conditions are that the detainee is over 18, and that a police officer has requested that the detainee give the sample. Under s57(8) it becomes a summary offence for a person to fail, without good cause, to give any sample which may be taken from him under s57. Further extensions to the powers to take non-intimate samples without consent were made by the Criminal Justice Act 2003.

Fingerprints may normally be taken from an arrested person only with his consent, but s61 provides for them to be taken without consent, on the authority of an officer of at least the rank of superintendent if he has reasonable grounds for suspecting the involvement of the person whose fingerprints are to be taken in a criminal offence; and for believing that his fingerprints will tend to confirm or disprove his involvement. Further extensions to the powers to take fingerprints without consent were made by the Criminal Justice Act 2003.

11.19 Confessions: general

Confessions are an important form of evidence in that they will presumably tend to produce a plea of guilty at trial, and hence are the best evidence that the accused has actually committed the offence with which he is charged. A defendant may, however, make a confession for a number of reasons other than guilt. For example, he may be attempting to shield the truly guilty party; he may be one of those whose psychological condition or state of mind makes him a compulsive confessor (police investigations are beset with those who invent confessions to prominent crimes which they could not possibly have committed); he may confess because he is intimidated or induced to make a statement by promises; he may feel that, if the offence is not serious a confession, a guilty plea is preferable just to 'get things over'.

In such circumstances it is clear that confessions should be treated with care and not admitted in evidence, as they are unreliable as evidence of the truth. The police can ask anyone questions despite that person's unwillingness to answer them. It is possible that those questions may lead to a confession. Leaving aside the special requirements regarding juveniles and the mentally ill or handicapped, Code C states:

'11.5 No interviewer may try to obtain answers or elicit a statement by the use of oppression. Except as in paragraph 10.9, no interviewer shall indicate, except to answer a direct question, what action will be taken by the police if the person being questioned answers questions, makes a statement or refuses to do either. If the person asks directly what action will be taken if they answer questions, make a statement or refuse to do either, the interviewer may inform them what action the police propose to take provided that action is itself proper and warranted.

11.6 The interview or further interview of a person about an offence with which that person has not been charged or for which they have not been informed they may be prosecuted, must cease when:

(a) the officer in charge of the investigation is satisfied all the questions they consider relevant to obtaining accurate and reliable information about the offence have been put to the suspect, this includes allowing the suspect an opportunity to give an innocent explanation and asking questions to test if the explanation is accurate and reliable, eg to clear up ambiguities or clarify what the suspect said;

(b) the officer in charge of the investigation has taken account of any other available evidence; and

(c) the officer in charge of the investigation, or in the case of a detained suspect, the custody officer, see paragraph 16.1, reasonably believes there is sufficient evidence to provide a realistic prospect of conviction for that offence.

This paragraph does not prevent officers in revenue cases or acting under the confiscation provisions of the Criminal Justice Act 1988 or the Drug Trafficking Act 1994 from inviting suspects to complete a formal question and answer record after the interview is concluded.'

The first part of this leads back to s76 of PACE 1984. The second shows it is not intended that, where the police have decided there is sufficient evidence to succeed in a prosecution, they should press on to secure a confession. It is perhaps unfortunate that in a number of cases a confession is the only substantial piece of evidence the police have. The confession will, after all, be a valuable constituent towards the element of the defendant's mens rea. In theory, the defendant wants to confess in order to clear his conscience and to unburden himself of guilt. Arguably, this is a very powerful compulsion. The problem in the courts is that some defendants recant and seek to withdraw their confessions. In this situation it is up to the judge to decide in the absence of the jury whether or not the confession should be admitted in evidence; this is known as a 'voir dire' or a 'trial within a trial'.

11.20 The use of the caution and the right to silence

The position at common law

Historically, the position at common law has long been that a defendant is innocent until proven guilty, and that it is the task of the prosecution to convince the court of the defendant's guilt, principles reflected in the criminal process by the existence of the so-called right to silence. The phrase 'right to silence' is something of a misnomer in that every defendant can chose to remain silent if he so wishes – there is never any possibility of a suspect being physically compelled to respond to questioning by law. What the phrase actually relates to is the proposition that the courts were not permitted to draw any adverse inferences from the defendant's failure to provide an exculpatory answer when taxed with the details of the offence he is alleged to have committed. The rationale for the common law right to silence was that the suspect and interrogator would not have been on equal terms, given that the interrogator would inevitably be a police officer. Exceptions were recognised where the defendant could be regarded as being on equal terms with his accuser, for example in *Parkes* v *R* (1976) 64 Cr App R 25, where the defendant was accused by his landlady of murdering her daughter.

The right to silence was reflected in the old form of the caution to be administered by a police officer conducting an investigation into alleged offences, ie: 'You do not have to say anything unless you wish to do so, but what you say may be given in evidence'. Minor deviations were permitted provided the sense of the caution was preserved.

The pressure for change

The view expressed in some quarters was that the right to silence was open to abuse by more sophisticated and experienced criminals and was partly responsible for some allegedly guilty defendants escaping conviction. The criticisms of the right to silence rest to a large extent on the assertion that any innocent person would seek to exculpate himself at the earliest possible moment if he had nothing to hide. Such research as has been conducted suggests that relatively few suspects choose to remain silent when interrogated by the police, although the percentage exercising this right has substantially increased since the enactment of PACE 1984.

Given the right of a detained person to consult privately with a solicitor under s58 of PACE 1984, questions have been raised as to the extent to which it remains true to say that detainee and interrogator are not on equal terms. Lawton LJ, in *R* v *Chandler* [1976] 1 WLR 585, suggested that this might be the case, but went on to observe that, once a detainee had been cautioned, no adverse inferences were to be drawn from his silence. Curiously, the effect of this view suggests that the police would be better off allowing a detainee to have access to a solicitor but not to caution him, although such a practice would undoubtedly involve a breach of the Codes. Some, such as Lord Lane CJ, commenting in *R* v *Alladice* [1988] Crim LR 608, have called for a re-assessment of the position. He stated:

> 'Paragraph 6.3 of the Code provides that a person who asks for legal advice may not be interviewed or continue to be interviewed until he has received it unless delay has been lawfully authorised ... The result is that in many cases a detainee who would otherwise have answered proper questioning by the police will be advised to remain silent. Weeks later at his trial such a person not infrequently produces an explanation of, or a defence to, the charge the truthfulness of which the police have had no chance to check. Despite the fact that the explanation or defence could, if true, have been disclosed at the outset and despite the advantage which the defendant has gained by these tactics, no comment may be made to the jury. The jury may in some cases put two and two together, but it seems to us that the effect of s58 is such that the balance of fairness between prosecution and defence cannot be maintained unless proper comment is permitted on the defendant's silence in such circumstances. It is high time that such comment should be permitted together with the necessary alteration to the words of the caution.'

In July 1993 the Royal Commission on Criminal Justice, chaired by Lord Runciman, produced its report. A majority of its members proposed no change to the common law position on the 'right to silence' at a police station, but recommended that once the prosecution case was fully disclosed, it should be possible to draw adverse inferences from the introduction of any new defence or departure from any previously disclosed defence.

As a prelude to reform of the law in England and Wales, the law in Northern Ireland was amended, by virtue of the Criminal Evidence (Northern Ireland) Order 1988, to permit the trial judge to direct the jury (or himself where the case involved a 'Diplock' court), that adverse inferences could be drawn from the defendant's failure to give evidence.

Such inferences are permitted if D is silent and offers an explanation for his conduct for the first time at his trial which he could reasonably have been expected to produce when being questioned; the prosecution satisfies the court that there is a case to answer and D declines to give evidence; he gives no explanation in relation to certain facts such as substances found, or marks on clothing; he gives no explanation for his presence in a particular place.

The changes introduced by the Criminal Justice and Public Order Act 1994

Section 34 of the 1994 Act introduces a major change in the law by providing that, if a suspect fails to mention any fact relied on in his defence (being something that he could reasonably be expected to have mentioned) either when being questioned after cautioning by a constable, or after having been charged with an offence or officially informed that he might be prosecuted, the court or jury may draw such inferences from the failure as appear proper. Section 36 provides similarly in relation to an arrested person's failure to account for any object in his possession, or any substance or mark on his person, clothing or article in his possession when required to do so by a constable investigating an offence, and s37 applies similarly to an arrested person's failure to account for his presence at a particular location.

A consequence of this change in the law is the amendment to the police caution that was used for over 30 years. In place of the previous wording (see above) para 10.4 of Code C now requires the following wording:

> 'You do not have to say anything. But it may harm your defence if you do not mention when questioned something which you later rely on in court. Anything you do say may be given in evidence.'

Under the guidelines contained in Code C a caution must be given before any questions are put to a suspect for the purpose of obtaining evidence which may be given in a court in a prosecution. The defendant, therefore, need not be cautioned if questions are put for other purposes, for example, to establish his identity, his ownership of, or responsibility for, any vehicle or the need to search him in the exercise of powers of stop and search. A person must be cautioned upon arrest for an offence unless it is impracticable to do so by reason of his condition or behaviour at the time; or he has already been cautioned immediately prior to his arrest. When there is a break in questioning under caution the interviewing officer must ensure that the person being questioned is aware that he remains under caution. If there is any doubt on this matter the caution should be given again in full when the interview resumes.

In relation to the Criminal Evidence (Northern Ireland) Order 1988, the House of Lords has confirmed, in *R* v *Murray* [1994] 1 WLR 1, that it has had the effect of changing the law and practice relating to the defendant who fails to give evidence, thus permitting the jury to infer guilt from his silence where the prosecution had established a prima facie case against him. The European Court of Human Rights has in turn considered the extent to which the Order was at odds with the requirements of art 6 of the European Convention on Human Rights and, in *Murray* v *United Kingdom* (1996) 22 EHRR 29, confirmed (by 14 votes to five) that, given the sufficiency of the procedural safeguards designed to prevent oppression, the objectives of art 6 could still be achieved, in particular the drawing of reasonable inferences from the applicant's behaviour did not have the effect of shifting the burden of proof contrary to art 6(2). It should be noted, however, that whilst this ruling clarifies the position as regards the law in the Province, some questions may still remain in respect of ss34 and 35 of the 1994 Act. The European Court of Human Rights was willing to accept the restriction imposed by the Northern Ireland Order partly because, in the Diplock courts operating in Northern Ireland, reasons will be given by the trial judge for drawing adverse inferences if any, thus there will be evidence of the weight given to the accused's decision to remain silent. In England and Wales juries will not be required to embroider their verdicts with such explanations.

11.21 Challenging the admissibility of evidence

A confession made by an accused person may be given in evidence against him at the trial provided it is relevant and has not been excluded by the court in pursuance of s76. This initial requirement is laid down because a confession is essentially an out-of-court statement and would normally be excluded by the rule against hearsay, that only testimony given under oath by a witness as to what he directly heard or otherwise experienced is to be regarded as good evidence. A confession is admitted as an exception to the hearsay rule and is tendered by the prosecution as evidence of the truth of its contents because it is thought that a person would not make a statement against himself unless it were true. According to s82 the term 'confession' includes 'any statement wholly or partly adverse to the person who made it, whether made to a person in authority or not and whether made in words or otherwise'.

A statement made by the accused that serves to exculpate him may be excluded as a self-serving statement. It may, of course, be that a statement contains material of both an inculpatory and an exculpatory nature. Both elements would then have to be put before the court.

Section 76(2) contains the vital provision with regard to the exclusion of confessions. This states that:

'If, in any proceedings where the prosecution proposes to give in evidence a confession made by an accused person, it is represented to the court that the confession was or may have been obtained –
(a) by oppression of the person who made it; or
(b) in consequence of anything said or done which was likely, in the circumstances existing at the time, to render unreliable any confession which might be made by him in consequence thereof,
the court shall not allow the confession to be given in evidence against him except in so far as the prosecution proves to the court beyond reasonable doubt that the confession (notwithstanding that it may be true) was not obtained as aforesaid.'

Thus where D alleges that the confession has been improperly obtained it is for the prosecution to prove beyond all reasonable doubt that this is not the case. Section 76(3) provides that, in any event, the court may require of its own motion that the prosecution should prove that the confession was not obtained as mentioned in s76(2). One effect of the subsection is that if there has been oppression the resulting confession so obtained can be excluded even though it is true, presumably to deter the police from using oppression. In this sense police impropriety is to be deprecated more than the obtaining of what may be a true confession. 'Oppression' is defined by s76(8) as including 'torture, inhuman or degrading treatment, and the use or threat of violence (whether or not amounting to torture)'. In *R v Fulling* [1987] 2 WLR 923 Lord Lane CJ commented:

'…"oppression" in s76(2)(a) should be given its ordinary dictionary meaning. The Oxford English Dictionary as its third definition of the word runs as follows: "Exercise of authority or power in a burdensome, harsh, or wrongful manner; unjust or cruel treatment of subjects, inferiors, etc; the imposition of unreasonable or unjust burdens." One of the quotations given under that paragraph runs as follows: "There is not a word in our language which expresses more detestable wickedness than oppression." We find it hard to envisage any circumstances in which such oppression would not entail some impropriety on the part of the interrogator.'

Fulling was applied in *R v Paris; R v Abdullahi; R v Miller* (1993) 97 Cr App R 99 (the 'Cardiff Three' case), where convictions were set aside on the basis that confessions had been obtained by means of oppression, following evidence that interrogating officers had continued to shout at one of the appellants the words they wanted him to say over 300 times, despite his denials of guilt. The court commented upon the importance of officers complying with the letter and spirit of the Codes of Practice.

Prior to the 1984 Act a confession would only be admitted if it were voluntary. This meant that it should not have been induced 'by fear of prejudice or hope of advantage exercised or held out by a person in authority'. This seems to be the general purport of s76(2)(b) although it is of wider application than the previous rule. It remains for the defendant to raise the question of the confession having been made in consequence of something said or done, and for the saying or doing to render unreliable the confession obtained in consequence. Presumably the repetition of 'in consequence' is not merely pleonastic or intended for emphasis but requires that the confession is made as a consequence as well as the unreliability being consequential.

A confession which has been excluded may not affect the admissibility in evidence of facts discovered as a result of the confession – although the facts should not be related to the confession itself – or of showing that the accused speaks, writes or expresses himself in a particular way.

At common law, following the decision in *R* v *Sang* [1980] AC 402, the judge's discretion to exclude evidence which had been improperly obtained was to be exercised on the basis that evidence should be admitted provided that its effect was not more prejudicial than probative. Pre-PACE 1984 authorities reveal a relaxed approach. Thus, in *R* v *Leatham* (1861) 8 Cox CC 489, Crompton J expressed the view that 'It matters not how you get it; if you steal it even, it would be admissible in evidence'. Similarly, in *Kuruma, Son of Kania* v *R* [1955] 1 All ER 236, Lord Goddard CJ expressed the view that if evidence was admissible the court would not be overly concerned with how it had been obtained. Lord Widgery CJ said much the same thing in *Jeffrey* v *Black* [1978] 1 All ER 555, where an unlawful search of the defendant's premises was undertaken and cannabis discovered there after he had been arrested for stealing a sandwich. He commented:

'I have not the least doubt that an irregularity in obtaining evidence does not render the evidence inadmissible. Whether or not the evidence is admissible depends on whether or not it is relevant to the issues in respect of which it is called.'

In Australia, Barwick CJ put the problem succinctly in *R* v *Ireland* (1970) 126 CLR 321:

'On the one hand there is the public need to bring to conviction those who commit criminal offences. On the other hand there is the public interest in the protection of the individual from unlawful and unfair treatment. Convictions obtained with the aid of unlawful and unfair treatment may be obtained at too high a price.'

In *R* v *Maqsud Ali*; *R* v *Ashiq Hussain* [1965] 2 All ER 464 murder suspects went voluntarily with police officers to a room where they were left alone. In their conversation incriminating remarks were made and tape-recorded by a hidden microphone. In the Court of Appeal the view was expressed that: 'The criminal does not act according to the "Queensbury rules" hence the method of the informer and of the eavesdropper is commonly used in the detection of crime'.

In *R* v *Murphy* [1965] NI 138 (Courts-Martial Appeal Court) the accused had been convicted having made disclosures of information useful to an enemy to police officers posing as subversives. Lord Macdermott CJ observed:

'Detection by deception is a form of police procedure to be directed and used sparingly and with circumspection: but as a method it is as old as the constable in plain clothes and, regrettable as the fact may be, the day has not yet come when it would be safe to say that law and order could always be enforced and the public safety protected without occasional resort to it.'

Section 78 of the 1984 Act now provides a statutory basis for the trial judge's discretion. It states:

'(1) In any proceedings the court may refuse to allow evidence on which the prosecution proposes to rely to be given if it appears to the court that, having regard to all the circumstances in which the evidence was obtained, the admission of the evidence would have such an adverse effect on the fairness of the proceedings that the court ought not to admit it.

(2) Nothing in this section shall prejudice any rule of law requiring a court to exclude evidence.'

This section curiously refers to the 'fairness of the proceedings', although it also speaks of the circumstances in which the evidence was obtained. It must be assumed that it is referring to the general fairness of the obtaining of the evidence, rather than the fairness of the proceedings as such.

In *R* v *Mason* [1988] 1 WLR 139 the Court of Appeal held that 'evidence' for the purposes of s78 included a confession notwithstanding that confessions were expressly dealt with by s76. Thus a confession that was admissible through not falling foul of s76(2) could nevertheless still be excluded on the grounds of its unfairness. Mason, who had been arrested in connection with an arson offence, was told by the police that they had glass fragments of the petrol-filled bottle used to perpetrate the offence on which they had Mason's fingerprints. In reality this was simply a trick, and the police thought it would be fair, even if deceitful, in that Mason would not have confessed if he knew that he had nothing to do with the bottle. Watkins LJ was highly critical of the tactics practised by the police, and in quashing the conviction, was clearly at pains not to be seen to be encouraging the use of such tactics.

Difficulties still exist where evidence has been obtained through the use of officers working 'under cover'. *R* v *Smurthwaite* [1994] Crim LR 53 suggests that if an officer is in the role of an agent provocateur, the courts are likely to exclude evidence thus obtained, but not where it is clearly D who initiates the criminal activity (eg soliciting a plain clothes policeman to carry out a contract killing). The problem for the court lies in making the distinction. The courts have confirmed that there is no defence in English law of entrapment, hence convictions have been upheld where police officers have used children to purchase '18' category films (see *London Borough of Ealing* v *Woolworths plc* [1995] Crim LR 58); where plain clothes officers have made test purchases of alcohol being sold in breach of liquor licence conditions (*DPP* v *Marshall* [1988] 3 All ER 683); and where police officers have posed as proprietors of a second-hand 'shop' to catch handlers selling off stolen goods: *R* v *Christou* [1992] 3 WLR 228.

What the courts will be wary of are procedures adopted by the police, eg activity that amounts to interrogation, that are not conducted in accordance with the Codes of Practice, thus undermining the reliability of evidence obtained. This problem was starkly illustrated by the decision of Ognall J to throw out the case against Colin Stagg, who had been charged with the murder of Rachel Nickell, because his 'confession' had been induced by repeated and persistent questioning by a WPC posing as Stagg's girlfriend: *R* v *Stagg* (1994) The Times 15 September.

Where there is a reliable and permanent record of the evidence, the courts may lean more in favour admitting it. In *R* v *Cadette* [1995] Crim LR 229 the appellant had been involved in a plan to unlawfully import controlled drugs. Her telephone number had been found on a courier who had been intercepted at Heathrow Airport. The courier had planned to telephone the appellant upon arrival and, following her arrest, agreed to make the telephone call as planned in order to try to persuade the appellant to come to the airport. The courier gave the appellant no indication that she had been intercepted by the authorities. The telephone conversation was taped by the police and used in evidence against the appellant at her trial. On appeal she contended, unsuccessfully, that the evidence contained in the recording should have been excluded under s78 of PACE 1984 on the ground of unfairness. The court accepted that police officers, seeking to combat those involved in the commission of drugs trafficking, might have to resort to subterfuge. The court would examine the circumstances to see if police officers were resorting to subterfuge in order to circumvent the protections provided by PACE 1984 and the relevant Codes. Unacceptable tactics would include a police officer obtaining statements by disguising his or her identity, participating in the commission of the criminal offence, or inciting the commission of the offence. In the instant case the evidence was admissible because the officers had simply given the appellant an opportunity to involve herself in the offence by allowing a pre-planned telephone conversation to take place. There was no question of the telephone conversation amounting to an 'interview'. The court was also persuaded by the reliability of the evidence (ie the fact that it was tape-recorded) and the fact that the administering of a caution at the outset of the conversation would have rendered the operation otiose.

Similarly, in *R* v *Khan (Sultan)* [1996] 3 WLR 162, the House of Lords rejected the appellant's assertions that evidence obtained by means of listening devices attached to private premises without the owner's consent should be excluded on the basis that the evidence had been obtained in breach of any right to privacy. Lord Nolan held that a trial judge had a residual discretion, under s78 of PACE 1984, to exclude evidence if its admission would render the trial unfair, and in assessing this issue art 8 of the European Convention on Human Rights was relevant, but not decisive, of the matter. As he went on to observe:

'If evidence obtained by way of entrapment is admissible, then a fortiori there can hardly be a fundamental objection to the admission of evidence obtained in breach of privacy. In *R* v *Sang* itself, Lord Diplock noted that if evidence obtained by entrapment were inadmissible, this would have the effect of establishing entrapment as a defence to a criminal charge ... By parity of reasoning, if evidence obtained by a breach of privacy were inadmissible, then privacy too would become a defence to a criminal charge where the substance of the charge consisted of acts done or words spoken in private. Such a proposition does not bear serious examination.'

Given the incorporation of Convention rights such as art 8 through the Human Rights Act 1998, it becomes positively unlawful for a public authority such as a chief constable (acting through his officers) to act in a manner that is incompatible with the Convention rights. Further, the courts will, in future, have to interpret all provisions of PACE 1984 so as to ensure consistency, so far as this is possible, with the requirements of the Convention. It remains to be seen what impact this will have on the way in which the courts exercise their powers to admit evidence. In *Khan* v *United Kingdom* Application No 35394/97 [2000] 7 CL 276 the European Court of Human Rights rejected the contention that, because evidence obtained in violation of art 8(1) had been lead at the applicant's trial, the subsequent trial was unfair, and thus in breach of art 6. The Court noted that the domestic court had had a discretion to exclude the evidence on the grounds of unfairness and had considered the issue carefully, and felt it significant that the applicant had not sought to challenge the reliability of the evidence.

Surveillance and listening devices

Prior to the enactment of the Police Act 1997 the only regulation that existed as regards the planting of listening devices by the police was in the form of the Home Office guidelines, *Covert Listening Devices and Visual Surveillance (Private Places)* 1984, under which the chief constable of the relevant force had to be satisfied that, where devices were to be used to record conversations in places where a citizen would normally be entitled to presume privacy, such surveillance was required because the investigation concerned major organised crime, particularly involving violence. The guidelines assumed that such evidence would be admissible in court. The operations of the secret intelligence services as regards the use of listening devices is governed by the Intelligence Services Act 1994, and Pt III of the 1997 Act now provides a statutory framework of regulation for such activities when carried out by police officers.

Under the 1997 Act it is envisaged that police officers, including members of NCIS or NCS, will seek permission to enter and interfere with property or wireless telegraphy equipment from 'authorising officers' – namely chief constables or the equivalent. Under s93(2) permission for interference with property can be granted where:

'... the authorising officer believes (a) that it is necessary for the action specified to be taken on the ground that it is likely to be of substantial value in the prevention or detection of serious crime, and (b) that what the action seeks to achieve cannot reasonably be achieved by other means.'

For these purposes conduct which constitutes one or more offences will be regarded as serious crime only if (under s93(4)):

'... (a) it involves the use of violence, results in substantial financial gain or is conduct by a large number of persons in pursuit of a common purpose, or (b) the offence or one of the offences is an offence for which a person who has attained the age of 21 and has no previous convictions could reasonably be expected to be sentenced to imprisonment for a term of three years or more ...'

If it is not reasonably practicable for an authorising officer to grant permission, the powers conferred on the authorising officer by s93 may, in an urgent case, be exercised by an assistant chief constable in his force (or equivalent). An authorisation must be in writing, save in an urgent case where it may be given orally. Once granted authorisations will normally remain in effect for three months (if written), or 72 hours, if oral. An oral authorisation should be renewed in the normal fashion.

As soon as is reasonably practicable an authorising officer should give notice of having granted an authorisation to a Commissioner appointed under s91(1)(b).

Appointed by the Prime Minister, the Chief Commissioner, and other Commissioners, will be persons who have held high judicial office within the meaning of the Appellate Jurisdiction Act 1876 (effectively current or former High Court judges). Each Commissioner is appointed for a term of three years (renewable) and holds office subject only to removal by a resolution passed by each House of Parliament, bankruptcy or imprisonment for an offence.

Once provided with an authorisation notice a Commissioner is under a duty to scrutinise it as soon as is reasonably practicable. Under s103(1) a Commissioner may, if satisfied that at the time an authorisation was given or renewed, there were no reasonable grounds for believing the matters specified in s93(2) existed, quash the authorisation and order the destruction of any records relating to information obtained by virtue of the authorisation. Individuals are given the right to make complaints to Commissioners concerning authorisations under s102. Authorising officers are given a statutory right of appeal against a Commissioner's refusal to grant or renew an authorisation under s104(1). Appeals are determined by the Chief Commissioner. Note that under s91(10), the decisions of the Chief Commissioner or, subject to ss104 and 106, any other Commissioner (including decisions as to his jurisdiction) shall not be subject to appeal or liable to be questioned in any court. The Chief Commissioner is under a duty to make an annual report to the Prime Minister who, in turn, is under a duty to lay the report before each House of Parliament.

In an effort to provide greater safeguards for privacy and confidentiality, certain types of authorisation will require prior approval by a Commissioner. This will be the case where the person who gives the authorisation believes the following: that any of the property specified in the authorisation is used wholly or mainly as a dwelling, or as a bedroom in a hotel; or the property constitutes office premises. This will also be the case where the action authorised by it is likely to result in any person acquiring knowledge of matters subject to legal privilege, confidential personal information, or confidential journalistic material. It should be noted, however, that s97(3) provides that: 'This section does not apply to an authorisation where the person who gives it believes that the case is one of urgency'.

The extent to which the statutory framework satisfied the requirements of the European Convention as enacted in the Human Rights Act 1998 was a problem from the outset. The fact that chief constables effectively have powers of self-authorisation, the relatively weak system of supervision, and the vague basis upon which authorisations are to be granted, suggests that the interference with the right to privacy enshrined in art 8 of the Convention may not be sufficiently 'prescribed by law'.

The protection offered by the 1997 Act reflects the law's preoccupation with property rights, in the sense that the emphasis is on trespass to property, rather than the emerging concept of the right to privacy. Hence the Act does not appear to regulate the use of long-range listening devices that can be used to pick up conversations without any trespass to property occurring. The Act also provides that the safeguards can be dispensed with where the person who can give permission in respect of a property consents to the use of listening devices. This means that devices can be placed in police cells to detect the conversations of those detained there. Surveillance not protected by the Act remains subject to the administrative guidelines mentioned above. This arrangement may also fall foul of the Human Rights Act 1998 to the extent that it permits an invasion of privacy not regulated by law. Some attempts to deal with these problems were made in the Regulation of Investigatory Powers Act 2000. This provides for a tighter system of control to that contained in the Police Act 1997. It should be noted that both systems intended to operate at the same time.

12

Criminal Procedure I: Preliminary Matters

12.1 Prosecution: introduction

If, following a period of investigation, it becomes clear that a 'suspect' should be charged with a criminal offence, the process of 'prosecution' begins. It is this prosecution which will eventually lead to the trial of a defendant, that is the person accused, either in the magistrates' court (summary trial) or in the Crown Court (trial on indictment).

12.2 The prosecutors

The police and the Crown Prosecution Service

By far the majority of prosecutions are initiated by the 43 police forces operating in England and Wales.

This is not surprising as clearly the police have many advantages over other prosecutors, including the following.

1. Wider powers of arrest than other citizens.
2. Powers, though limited, of search and seizure and detention of suspects.
3. Resources to investigate a crime and gather evidence.

Although the police remain the prime initiator of prosecutions, since the inception of the Crown Prosecution Service (CPS), the further conduct of the police's prosecutions rests with the CPS.

Private prosecutions

Any individual is entitled to prosecute any other. However, as the Queen's Bench Divisional Court explained in *R* v *Tower Bridge Metropolitan Stipendiary Magistrate, ex parte Chaudhry* [1993] 3 WLR 1154, an individual prosecutor does not have an unfettered right to pursue his prosecution to trial. A private prosecutor has two hurdles to surmount: he has to persuade a magistrate to issue a summons, and thereafter, if he wishes to retain control of the case, he may have to persuade the Director of Public Prosecutions not to take it over and, perhaps, bring it to an end. Unless there are special circumstances, eg apparent bad faith on the part of the prosecutor, magistrates should be very slow to issue a summons at the behest of a private prosecutor against a defendant who already has to answer an information laid by the Crown in respect of the same matter.

Shops and stores regularly prosecute shoplifters with the charge of theft, usually with their 'store detective' as chief witness.

Individual citizens may bring prosecutions for any offence, but most tend to be in relation to smaller incidents in which the police have taken little interest, such as a fight in relation to which a charge of assault may be brought.

Section 6 of the Prosecution of Offences Act 1985 specifically retains the right of an individual to bring a private prosecution. In *R* v *Southwark Crown Court, ex parte Tawfick* (1994) The Times 1 December the Queen's Bench Divisional Court said that, by virtue of s27(2)(c) of the Courts and Legal Services Act 1990, the courts appeared to have a discretion to grant a right of audience to any person in any proceedings. It followed that the Crown Court could allow a private prosecution to be conducted in person, although it was likely that such a discretion would be exercised only occasionally.

The police are not able to bring an action on behalf of a private individual. They must refer any case to the Crown Prosecution Service. This was seen in the case of *R* v *Ealing Magistrates, ex parte Dickson* [1989] 2 All ER 1050 in which the police charged the defendant on the behalf of the Copyright Owners Federation. The Divisional Court held that the police had no power to perform these duties on behalf of private individuals.

12.3 The decision to prosecute

Section 127 of the Magistrates' Courts Act 1980 states that a prosecution for a summary offence must, with some exceptions, be commenced within six months of the offence being committed.

At present, with some exceptions, prosecutions for indictable offences may be brought at any time.

Discretion

In 1951, Lord Shawcross, who was then Attorney-General, made the classic statement on public interest, which has been supported by Attorneys-General ever since: 'It has never been the rule in this country – I hope it never will be – that suspected criminal offences must automatically be the subject of prosecution'.

There has been a steep rise in the number of criminal suspects who are cautioned rather than prosecuted. The Home Office has admitted, however, that this may refer to a 'net-widening' process, in that previously these people would not have appeared in the statistics at all because they would have been recorded only as 'no further action'.

The intention is that children and young people should be cautioned rather than prosecuted and this represents a less interventionist approach. The critics argue that the people who are cautioned would be those against whom the police would take 'no further action'. Thus, in fact, they are brought within the criminal net when they would otherwise be left out.

A caution may have the same consequence as a conviction but without the safeguards. The recipient is more likely to be prosecuted on a subsequent occasion.

In relation to the question of discretion it is to be remembered that there is a duty of the police to enforce the law: see *R* v *Metropolitan Police Commissioner, ex parte Blackburn* [1968] 2 WLR 893. The effect of this is that each case of potential prosecution must be considered, and 'discretion' must be used in relation to the facts of the particular case. Therefore, it is not open for the police to make a general decision, for example, not to bring any prosecutions for theft unless the value of the goods stolen was over a certain sum.

It should be remembered that the Crown Prosecution Service (CPS) normally decides whether to continue or discontinue a prosecution although the police will normally be consulted before the decision is made to discontinue or to change the charges. This is the extent that the police and Crown Prosecutors will work together in decision-making. Such decisions (like refusals by the police to prosecute) are subject to judicial review, but only where it can be demonstrated that the decision was made on the basis of some unlawful policy, or because of a failure to act in accordance with established policy, or because the decision was perverse.

The Code for Crown Prosecutors is a public declaration of the principles upon which the decision to prosecute is taken. Its purpose is to promote fair and consistent decision-making.

The Code explains that there are two stages in the decision to prosecute and that the first is the evidential test. If the case does not pass this test it must not go ahead, no matter how important or serious it may be. If the case does pass the evidential test, Crown Prosecutors must decide if a prosecution also passes the public interest test, the second stage. The Crown Prosecution Service will only start or continue a prosecution when the case has passed both tests.

As to the evidential test, Crown Prosecutors must be satisfied that there is enough evidence to provide a 'realistic prospect of conviction' against each defendant on each charge. They must consider what the defence case may be and how that is likely to affect the prosecution case. A realistic prospect of conviction is an objective test. It means that a jury or bench of magistrates, properly directed in accordance with the law, is more likely than not to convict the defendant of the charge alleged. If a case fails the first test (the evidential test) there must be no prosecution even though the prosecution may be of the view that the public interest test is satisfied.

Public interest factors that can affect the decision to prosecute usually depend on the seriousness of the offence or the circumstances of the offender. Some factors may increase the need to prosecute but others may suggest that another course of action would be better. The Code lists common public interest factors, both for and against prosecution.

Factors favouring a prosecution include:

1. the likelihood of a substantial sentence being imposed on conviction;
2. use of a weapon or violence during the offence;
3. position of the victim (eg a person serving the public) and/or the position of the defendant (eg a person in position of trust or authority);
4. evidence that the offence was premeditated, carried out by a group, or that the defendant was a 'ringleader';
5. effect on the victim;
6. likelihood of the offence being repeated;
7. extent to which the offence, even though not serious, is a common occurrence in the area in which it has been committed.

Factors against a prosecution include:

1. the likelihood that only a nominal penalty will be imposed in the event of a conviction;

2. that the offence was the result of a genuine mistake or misunderstanding;
3. the lapse of time between the offence and the proceedings, except where the offence is serious, or where the delay has been caused by the defendant, or where the offence has only recently come to light, or where the complexity of the offence has necessitated a lengthy inquiry;
4. where the defendant is elderly or was suffering from a mental illness at the time of the offence, unless there is a real possibility of the offence being repeated;
5. the defendant has put right the harm or loss caused;
6. the adverse effect of certain information being made public.

Crown Prosecutors must always think very carefully about the interests of the victim, which are an important factor, when deciding, where the public interest lies. Where necessary, they should apply the Home Office guidelines as to cautioning and should look at all alternatives to prosecution when they consider the public interest. Crown Prosecutors should tell the police if they think that a caution would be more suitable than a prosecution.

Crown Prosecutors should never go ahead with more charges than are necessary just to encourage a defendant to plead guilty to a few. In the same way, they should never go ahead with a more serious charge just to encourage a defendant to plead guilty to a less serious one.

As a general rule the CPS is under no private law duty of care to those it prosecutes, unless it has assumed a special responsibility to a particular defendant: *Elguzouli-Daf* v *Commissioner of Police of the Metropolis* [1995] 1 All ER 833 (CA).

12.4 Commencing a prosecution

There are two methods of commencing a prosecution.

Laying an information

This is used in less serious offences and may be used by any type of prosecutor.

An information, which is the allegation that the person named in it has committed an offence, must be 'laid' before the magistrates' court. If an information is written, it may be laid by delivering it to the court. If the information is oral, the prosecutor must appear before the magistrate or the magistrates' clerk, and tell him what the allegation is.

On the basis of the information, a summons may be issued either by the magistrate or his clerk. Any summons is then served on the defendant by the prosecution, informing him of the allegation and requiring him to attend at the magistrates' court on a named day to answer the allegation.

Charging an accused

This is used in more serious offences and is used by the police, following either a police or citizen's arrest. The Criminal Justice Act 2003 provides for the involvement of the Crown Prosecution Service in decisions as to charge, to a much greater extent than was the case in the past.

'Charging' takes place at the police station. The procedure is simple and requires merely the writing down of the charge on a 'charge sheet' followed by the reading over of the charge to the accused by the police officer. The accused is either detained in custody or bailed (see below) to appear at a certain court on a certain date. In the meantime the charge sheet is sent to the court in question.

12.5 Bail: introduction

Once the decision to prosecute has been taken an immediate question arising is whether, pending trial of the defendant, he should be detained in custody or released on 'bail'. Bail is the release of a defendant subject to a duty to surrender to custody at an appointed place on an appointed date.

Bail may be granted either by the police (the custody officer at the police station) or by a court. Police bail is regulated by s38 of the Police and Criminal Evidence Act 1984 (as amended). Bail from the court is regulated by the Bail Act 1976 (as amended). This Chapter is mainly concerned with bail from a court, but police bail will be briefly considered. The Criminal Justice Act 2003 allows the police to grant bail in the street, thus freeing the police from the obligation of taking the suspect to the police station to be processed at that time. The Act also includes other minor amendments in relation to bail.

Bail from the police

Bail may be refused if the custody officer has good reasons for believing that the accused will not appear at court; or that he may interfere with the investigation of crime; or that it is necessary to detain the accused for his own protection; or to prevent other injury, loss or damage; or that the accused might commit an offence if granted bail: s38 Police and Criminal Evidence Act 1984, as amended by s28(2) Criminal Justice and Public Order Act 1994.

Section 27 of the 1994 Act also gives the custody officer the power to grant bail subject to conditions, though some conditions can only be imposed by a court, eg requiring residence at a bail hostel, or requiring a medical examination.

The defendant may contest a custody officer's decision by applying to a magistrates' court, either for unconditional bail or for a variation of conditional bail.

Bail from the court

The majority of applications for bail are made in the magistrates' courts. The procedure, simply, is as follows.

1. The prosecution informs the magistrates whether or not it has any objections to bail. If it has, the magistrates are likely to give weight to such objections, which usually come from the police. If the prosecution has no objections, the magistrates are unlikely to refuse bail.
2. If there are objections, the defence must indicate whether the application for bail is to be made or continued with.
3. If the application for bail is to be made, a prosecution witness, usually a police officer, must give his objections to bail under oath. The officer's objections may well be based on his own opinions and experience.
4. The defence may question the officer in order to suggest conditions of bail which might overcome his objections.
5. The defence may make a speech dealing with the objections, putting forward possible conditions of bail and emphasising factors in favour of bail.
6. The magistrates then make their decision based on all that they have heard.
7. Where the court hears full argument as to bail the clerk of the court must make a note of the argument.

12.6 A right to bail?

Section 4 of the Bail Act 1976 has the effect, in practice, of giving a 'right to bail' to a defendant. The effect of this is that the onus is put onto the prosecution to show why a defendant should not be granted bail rather than the onus being on the defendant to show why he should be granted bail.

Section 4 applies whenever a person accused of an offence appears or is brought before a magistrates' court or the Crown Court in the course of or in connection with proceedings for an offence.

There is no right to bail in the following circumstances.

1. When a station sergeant or officer not below the rank of inspector is considering bailing an arrestee from the police station.
2. The magistrates, having summarily convicted an offender, commit him to the Crown Court for sentence.
3. A defendant who has been convicted and sentenced, is appealing against conviction or sentence.

In these situations, the onus is on the defendant to show why he should be granted bail. To allay fears that murderers and rapists may be free to walk the streets, the magistrates must state their reasons for granting bail in cases of murder, manslaughter or rape or an attempt to commit the same.

Further, under s25 of the Criminal Justice and Public Order Act 1994, as amended by s56 of the Crime and Disorder Act 1998, a court (or a police custody officer) must be satisfied that there are exceptional circumstances which justify granting bail to a person charged with or convicted of murder, attempted murder, manslaughter, rape or attempted rape if that person has been previously convicted of any such offence or of culpable homicide and, in the case of a previous conviction of manslaughter or of culpable homicide, if he was then sentenced to imprisonment or (if he was then a child or young person) to long-term detention. Prior to the amendment by s56 of the 1998 Act there was a ban on bail in the specified circumstances but there was concern that such a ban might infringe the European Convention on Human Rights. In effect the amendment substitutes a strong rebuttable presumption against bail in the specified circumstances.

Even if the defendant has a right to bail, bail may be refused by the court in circumstances listed in Sch 1 to the Bail Act 1976, as amended by s26 of the 1994 Act.

Imprisonable offences

Part I of Sch 1 is applicable if the defendant is accused or convicted of at least one offence punishable with imprisonment. It states that the defendant need not be granted bail in any of the following circumstances.

1. The court is satisfied that there are substantial grounds for believing that, if released on bail, he would: fail to surrender to custody; or commit an offence while on bail; or interfere with witnesses or otherwise obstruct the course of justice, whether in relation to himself or some other person.
2. The court is satisfied that he should be kept in custody for his own protection or, if he is a child or young person, for his own welfare.
3. He is already serving a custodial sentence.
4. The court is satisfied that lack of time since the commencement of the proceedings has made it impracticable to obtain the information needed to decide properly the questions raised in (1) to (3) above.
5. He has already been bailed during the course of the proceedings, and has been arrested under s7 of the Bail Act 1976 (that is, for absconding).
6. Where a case is adjourned for inquiries or a report, it appears to the court that it would be impracticable to complete the inquiries or make the report without keeping the defendant in custody.
7. Where the offence in indictable or triable either way and the defendant was on bail in criminal proceedings at the date of the offence: s26 of the 1994 Act.

In making its decision under (1) above the court must have regard to such of the following considerations as appear to it to be relevant: that is, the nature and seriousness of the offence or default (and the probable method of dealing with the defendant for it) the character, antecedents, associations and community ties of the defendant; the defendant's record as respects the fulfilment of his obligations under previous grants of bail in criminal proceedings; and, except in the case of a defendant whose case is adjourned for inquiries or a report, the strength of the evidence of his having committed the offence or having defaulted. The court must also take into account any other considerations which appear to be relevant.

Non-imprisonable offences

Part II of Sch 1 applies to a defendant charged with or convicted of an offence or offences, none of which are punishable with imprisonment. Such a defendant need not be granted bail in any of the following circumstances.

1. It appears to the court that, having been previously granted bail in criminal proceedings, he has failed to surrender to custody in accordance with his obligations under the grant of bail, and the court believes, in view of that failure, that the defendant, if released on bail (whether subject to conditions or not) would fail to surrender to custody.
2. The court is satisfied that he should be kept in custody for his own protection or, if he is a child or young person, for his own welfare.
3. He is already serving a custodial sentence.
4. He has already been bailed during the course of the proceedings, and has been arrested under s7 of the Bail Act 1976 (that is, for absconding).

12.7 Conditions of bail

Although a defendant may be granted unconditional bail, s3 of the Bail Act 1976, as amended, provides that bail may be granted on conditions.

The possible conditions under s3 of the 1976 Act are: provision of sureties; reporting; residence; and restrictions.

Provision of one or more sureties

A surety is someone who undertakes to pay the court a certain sum of money if the defendant fails to surrender to custody as he ought to. This undertaking is known as a 'recognisance'. A surety for an adult defendant has no responsibility for seeing that he complies with any other conditions which may be imposed; the position is different in the case of a child or young person defendant when his parent or parents stand as surety for him.

Where the defendant fails to appear at the trial, it is for the trial judge, in the exercise of his wide discretion, to decide whether it would be fair or just to estreat some or all of the recognisance: *R v Crown Court at Maidstone, ex parte Lever* [1995] 2 All ER 35. If a court is satisfied that a surety was blameless throughout it might be proper to remit the whole of the amount of the recognisance: *R* v *Crown Court at Reading, ex parte Bello* [1992] 3 All ER 353.

In *R* v *Wood Green Crown Court, ex parte Howe* [1992] 1 WLR 702 the Divisional Court decided that where a bail surety had undertaken to pay a sum which he could not afford, the court should have regard to his ability to pay and to the consequences for the surety of ordering payment of an amount which would inevitably lead to a term of imprisonment in default.

Reporting

The defendant may be required to report to a certain place (usually the local police station) at a certain time each day, week or month.

Residence

The defendant may be required to live at a stated address. This will entail his sleeping at that address each evening.

Restrictions

Many different restrictions may be put upon the defendant. For example, that he should not speak to a particular witness nor go to a particular place, or a curfew restriction requiring him to be home at a certain time each evening. Section 54(2) of the Crime and Disorder Act 1998 enables a court (but not a police custody officer) to grant bail subject to obtaining legal advice prior to the time fixed for surrender to custody.

12.8 Challenges to bail decisions

Reconsideration

Section 30 of the Criminal Justice and Public Order Act 1994 inserts s5B into the Bail Act 1976. Under s5B, where a magistrates' court has granted bail in criminal proceedings in connection with an offence triable on indictment or either way, or a constable has granted bail in criminal proceedings in connection with proceedings for such an offence, that court or the appropriate court in relation to the constable may, on application by the prosecutor for the decision to be reconsidered, vary the conditions of bail, impose conditions in respect of bail which has been granted unconditionally or withhold bail. No application for reconsideration may be made unless it is based on information which was not available to the court or constable when the decision was taken.

Appeal – by the defendant

Under the Bail Act 1976, whenever bail is refused a record must be made of the decision and the reasons for it. Upon request, a copy of the record must be given to the defendant.

Part IIA of Sch 1 to the 1976 Act permits two fully argued applications for bail before the magistrates. After those the magistrates need not hear a further application unless the accused has a new argument to advance.

Appeal against the magistrates' decision to refuse bail or apply conditions may be made to the High Court or to the Crown Court.

Section 22 of the Criminal Justice Act 1967 provides that, subject to s25 of the 1994 Act (above), the High Court has jurisdiction to grant bail or vary the conditions of bail.

The Crown Court may grant bail once refused by the magistrates in the following circumstances.

1. If the magistrates remanded the defendant in custody and heard a fully argued bail application before deciding on the remand.
2. If the magistrates committed the defendant in custody to the Crown Court for trial or sentence.
3. If the magistrates convicted the defendant summarily, imposed a custodial sentence and refused to bail him pending determination of his appeal to the Crown Court.

Therefore, in almost all cases a defendant may make further application to either the High Court or the Crown Court or to both.

Appeal – by the prosecution

By virtue of s1 of the Bail (Amendment) Act 1993, where a magistrates' court grants bail to a person who is charged with or convicted of an offence punishable by a term of imprisonment of five years or more or an offence under s12 (taking a conveyance without authority) or s12A (aggravated vehicle taking) of the Theft Act 1968, the prosecution may appeal to a judge of the Crown Court against the granting of bail. This applies only where the prosecution is conducted by or on behalf of the Director of Public Prosecutions or by a person who falls within such class or description of person as may be prescribed by the Secretary of State.

Such an appeal may be made only if the prosecution made representations that bail should not be granted and the representations were made before it was granted. In the event of the prosecution wishing to exercise this right of appeal, oral notice of appeal has to be given to the magistrates' court at the conclusion of the proceedings in which bail was granted and before the release from custody of the person concerned.

Written notice of appeal must then be served on the magistrates' court and the person concerned within two hours of the conclusion of the proceedings. Upon receipt of oral notice of appeal the magistrates' must remand in custody the person concerned, until the appeal is determined or otherwise disposed of. Where the prosecution fails, within the period of two hours, to serve one or both of the written notices, the appeal is deemed to have been disposed of.

The hearing of an appeal must be commenced within 48 hours, excluding weekends and any public holiday (ie Christmas Day, Good Friday or a bank holiday), from the date on which oral notice of appeal was given.

12.9 Effect of failure to surrender

If a person who has been released on bail fails without reasonable cause to surrender to custody he is guilty of an offence: s6(1) of the Bail Act 1976. It is a single offence regardless of whether the bail was granted by the police or by a magistrates' court. In the case of failure to surrender to the Crown Court the offence will normally be dealt with as if it was a contempt. In the case of failure to surrender to a police station or a magistrates' court where bail has been granted by the police the offence must be dealt with as a summary offence. In the case of failure to surrender to a magistrates' court where bail has been granted by the magistrates' court the offence will be dealt with as if it was a contempt: see *Murphy* v *Director of Public Prosecutions* [1990] 2 All ER 390.

In *R* v *Wood Green Crown Court, ex parte Howe* [1992] 1 WLR 702 the Divisional Court considered whether a surety could 'seek to withdraw' when the defendant disappears or seems unlikely to appear for trial, or where the surety's circumstances change so that he can no longer pay the amount which he has undertaken to pay. Their Lordships believed that there is no power for a surety to withdraw unless the defendant is before the court and appropriate application is made by the prosecution or by him under s3(8) of the 1976 Act. Apart from this, s7(3) of that Act gives a constable power to arrest the defendant without warrant when a surety has made complaint in writing at a police station that the defendant is unlikely to surrender to custody. This course is, therefore, open to the surety, and it may mean that in practice the police will be able to produce the defendant in court if they can find and arrest him before the hearing. Nevertheless, the surety remains bound to produce him at the appointed time and place, and if the defendant does not appear the recognisance may be estreated.

No forfeiture of surety will be ordered if the defendant absconds after a surrender to the custody of the court, eg after arraignment: *R* v *Central Criminal Court, ex parte Guney* [1996] 2 All ER 705 (HL).

12.10 Classification of offences

In order to determine which mode of trial is suitable all criminal offences may be classified in the following three groups.

Indictable offences

An indictable offence is an offence for which an adult (aged 17 or over) must or may be tried on indictment, ie in the Crown Court before a judge and jury.

All common law offences are indictable. These include murder, manslaughter, rape and riot. Statutory offences are indictable if the statute which creates them indicates as such, for example by imposing a penalty to follow conviction on indictment.

Summary offences

Summary offences must be tried by summary trial (ie in the magistrates' court without a jury) and are all statutory offences. Examples include driving without due care and attention under the Road Traffic Act 1988, taking a pedal cycle without lawful authority under the Theft Act 1968, and all common assaults or batteries.

The statute which creates the offence will show that the offence is summary by specifying a penalty which may be imposed upon summary conviction without specifying a further penalty to be imposed upon conviction on indictment.

Offences triable either way

As has already been stated, although a summary offence must be tried summarily, an indictable offence must or may be triable on indictment. This shows that some offences may be tried either summarily or on indictment; these are said to be 'triable either way'. An offence is triable either way if it meets either of the following conditions.

1. It is to be found in Sch 1 to the Magistrates' Courts Act 1980. These include most offences under the Theft Act 1968, bigamy and indecent assault.
2. It can be seen to be triable either way from the statute which creates it, such as reckless driving under the Road Traffic Act 1988.

Offences triable either way tend to be the sort of offences which are capable of varying in seriousness, depending upon the circumstances of the particular case. Whereas murder is always a serious crime no matter what the circumstances, theft, for example, may be serious or may be trivial depending, inter alia, upon the value of the goods stolen.

12.11 Determining the mode of trial

The first question to be decided concerns the mode of trial by which the defendant is to be tried. The decision may be made by one lay magistrate, although it is usual for two or three to be present. The Criminal Justice Act 2003 provides that magistrates will be informed as to the defendant's previous convictions before they make their decision as to mode of trial.

If an offence is a summary offence or an indictable offence which must be tried on indictment, there is no choice as to the mode of trial. Therefore, the following procedure is applicable only when the offence charged is triable either way and is known as the 'plea before venue' stage of proceedings.

The procedure is contained in s17A of the Magistrates' Courts Act (MCA) 1980 (inserted by s49 of the Criminal Procedure and Investigations Act 1996), which came into force on 1 October 1997. After the charge is read to the accused the court will ask the accused to indicate his plea. Before taking that plea the court must inform the accused that if he indicates a guilty plea the court will proceed as if there has been a summary trial of the information, and that if the court then considers that it has insufficient powers to punish the accused it may send him to the Crown Court to be sentenced, using its powers under s38 MCA 1980, or may commit him if there are related offences which are to be committed for trial under s38A MCA 1980 (the latter power has been introduced by s51 Crime (Sentences) Act 1997).

The plea is then indicated by the accused. Under the law prior to 1 October 1997 magistrates had to make mode of trial decisions in the absence of any knowledge of the accused's intended plea. This led to many 'cracked trials', ie cases in which public money and administration was wasted because the accused reserved his plea for Crown Court trial but then at that trial pleaded guilty at the arraignment and was then given a sentence which the magistrates could have imposed. The new procedure is designed to ensure that cases which can properly be dealt with in the magistrates' court remain there, and to this end the taking of the plea will ensure that the magistrates are fully informed. Further, it provides an opportunity for the accused to enter a plea of guilty as soon as possible; this is a strong mitigating factor when it comes to sentencing: *R* v *Rafferty* (1998) The Times 9 April. Potentially many more cases should be retained in the magistrates' courts as a result of the new procedure, though possible problems could arise. For example, magistrates may be tempted to retain jurisdiction so as to dispose of cases swiftly in the interests of efficiency and this may result in more lenient sentences than that encouraged by official government policy. Second, there could be more adjournments in the magistrates' court in order for the defence to obtain further information in deciding what plea to indicate. For other problems: see Bavidge and Kerrigan 'Plea before Venue' [1998] NLJ 62.

If the accused indicates a plea of not guilty (or fails to plead, in which case a not guilty plea is entered on his behalf) the magistrates will proceed under ss19–23 of the Magistrates' Courts Act 1980, which are affected by the amendments brought in on 1 October 1997. The prosecution and the defence may each make submissions as to which method of trial is more suitable. The magistrates must then take account of any such submissions and the matters set out in s19(3) MCA 1980 before deciding whether the case is more suitable for summary trial than trial on indictment.

The matters set out in s19(3) should be read in conjunction with the National Mode of Trial Guidelines. These matters and guidelines may also be taken into account where there has been an indication of a guilty plea under the new procedure above because they may be relevant to the decision whether to retain jurisdiction for the purpose of sentencing the accused: *R v Warley Magistrates' Court, ex parte DPP* [1999] 1 All ER 251.

The matters set out in s19(3) are as follows:

1. the nature of the case;
2. whether the circumstances make the offence one of a serious character;
3. whether the punishment which a magistrates' court would have power to inflict for it would be adequate; and
4. any other circumstances which appear to the court to make it more suitable for the offence to be tried in one way rather than the other.

The opening general observations of the National Mode of Trial Guidelines (1995) are as follows:

1. the court should never make its decision on the grounds of convenience or expedition;
2. the court should assume that the prosecution version of the facts is correct;
3. the fact that the offences are alleged to be specimens is a relevant consideration, but the fact that the defendant will be asking for other offences to be taken into consideration, if convicted, is not a relevant consideration;
4. cases involving complex questions of fact or difficult questions of law or disclosure of sensitive material are more suitable for trial on indictment than summary trial;
5. in general, either way offences should be tried summarily unless the court considers that its sentencing powers are insufficient; and
6. the court should consider its power to commit an offender for sentence to the Crown Court if it should find that its powers of punishment are inadequate.

If the court decides that trial on indictment is the suitable mode of trial, that is a final decision, ie the accused does not have a right to insist on a summary trial. The accused will be informed of the decision and committal proceedings will follow.

If the court decides that summary trial is more suitable it will inform the accused, who is then asked whether he consents to summary trial or whether he wishes to be tried by jury at the Crown Court. Before making this choice, he should again be warned of the court's power under s38 MCA 1980 to commit him for sentence to the Crown Court if, after trying him summarily, the court convicts him and then considers that it has insufficient powers of punishment (for example because information emerges during the course of the trial which leads the court to conclude that the offence was more serious than previously thought). If the accused then chooses summary trial, the next stage will be the trial itself. If the accused elects trial by jury committal proceedings will follow.

Under s25(2) of the MCA 1980 magistrates have jurisdiction to re-open mode of trial proceedings if necessary if they have begun to try the information summarily, ie upon taking a plea of not guilty: *R v Horseferry Road Magistrates' Court, ex parte K* [1996] 3 All ER 719. It would appear in all other situations the mode of trial decision is final and cannot be re-opened.

Criminal damage offences

Offences of criminal damage contrary to s1 of the Criminal Damage Act 1971 must be tried summarily if the value of the property damaged or destroyed is £5,000 or less: s46 of the Criminal Justice and Public Order Act 1994.

12.12 Committal proceedings; sending a case for trial

Committal proceedings

These are applicable to an offence triable either way, either where the magistrates have decided the offence should be tried on indictment or where the accused has exercised his right to be tried on indictment. Committal proceedings take place in the magistrates' court and when the magistrates sit for this purpose they are known as 'examining justices'.

The examining justices are not concerned with the question of whether or not the defendant is guilty or whether or not the jury at the Crown Court will find him guilty. The question the examining justices must ask themselves is: 'Does the evidence placed before them at the committal proceedings show a "prima facie" case that the defendant has committed an indictable offence?'.

It was often said that committals were a valuable safeguard for the defence in sparing the accused the ordeal of a trial on insufficient evidence, but the need for such a safeguard became less obvious after the establishment of a professional prosecution service in 1985. Committals were abolished for serious fraud trials (Criminal Justice Act 1987) and for certain types of sexual offence, mainly involving children (Criminal Justice Act 1991), where the transfer to the Crown Court was effected through paperwork prepared by the Crown Prosecution Service. As will be seen this transfer procedure has been replaced by a new 'sending for trial' procedure, which has also replaced committal proceedings in respect of purely indictable offences (below). Where committal proceedings survive (ie for most offences triable either way) they may take one of two forms.

First, under s6(1) of the Magistrates' Courts Act 1980, as amended by s47 of and Sch 1 to the Criminal Procedure and Investigations Act (CPIA) 1996, there may be committal proceedings with consideration of the evidence (a 'long-form committal'). The procedure is as follows.

1. The prosecution outlines its case and the evidence it will call.
2. The prosecution calls its evidence. Prior to the amendment by the CPIA 1996, above, witnesses could be called to give oral evidence and could be cross-examined by the defence. However, the taking of oral evidence (including depositions) at committals was ended by the 1996 Act in an attempt to improve efficiency and protect witnesses. The prosecution evidence is therefore limited to documentary evidence (written statements) and exhibits. Any issues as to the admissibility of evidence must be determined by the justices and any error as to admissibility is subject to judicial review by the High Court: *Williams* v *Bedwellty Justices* [1996] 3 All ER 737 (HL).
3. The defence may submit that there is 'no case to answer', that is the prosecution evidence has not raised a prima facie case.
4. The examining justices must decide whether there is a case to answer, that is, a prima facie case.

    If the examining justices decide that there is a case to answer, they state in open court that they are committing the defendant to Crown Court and they state on which charge or charges he is being committed. If the examining justices decide that there is no case to answer, the defendant is discharged. A discharge, however, is not an acquittal and the prosecution is free to charge the defendant afresh for the same offence at a later date, for example if it obtains stronger evidence: *R* v *Manchester City Stipendiary Magistrate, ex parte Snelson* [1977] 1 WLR 911.

Second, under s6(2) of the Magistrates' Courts Act 1980, there may be committal proceedings without consideration of the evidence where the following three requirements are met.

1. All the evidence before the court consists of written statements tendered in evidence under s102 of the MCA 1980 (ie no party objects to their production).
2. The defendant has a legal representative acting for him.
3. There is no submission from the defence that there is no case to answer.

Compliance with these requirements ensures that a 'short-form' committal will, in practice, be used only in circumstances in which if there had been committal with consideration of the evidence, the examining justices would have found that there was a case to answer.

    The advantages of committal without consideration of the evidence are obvious, saving time and expenses for all concerned. It is not surprising, therefore, that most committals take this form. This is especially true given that a large majority of submissions of 'no case to answer' at committals, with consideration of the evidence, fail; this latter fact is understandable as the prosecution are unlikely to press ahead with a charge against a defendant if it is clear or even possible that its evidence will not satisfy even the low burden of 'prima facie case'.

Once a defendant has been committed for trial a number of final points must be considered by the examining justices.

Alibi warning

When a defendant intends to rely on an alibi at his trial (ie he intends to say that he was at a place other than the scene of the crime at the relevant time), then he must be warned of the effect of s11 of the Criminal Justice Act 1967, as amended by s5(7) of the Criminal Procedure and Investigations Act 1996 which provides that a defendant may not adduce evidence of an alibi at his trial on indictment as of right, but only with the leave of the judge, unless he has given notice of particulars of his alibi to the prosecution in advance of the trial so that the prosecution has had a reasonable opportunity to investigate the truthfulness of that alibi.

Bail

The examining justices must decide whether the defendant is to be committed on bail or in custody. It should be noted that the waiting period between committal proceedings and trial on indictment is likely to be many months and so this question is an important one, to be answered only upon full consideration of all relevant factors.

Public funding through the community legal service

The examining justices may be asked to grant public funding to the defendant to cover the costs of the defence at trial. They are unlikely to refuse, and where public funding has already been granted thus far it is generally continued automatically.

Sending a case for trial

Sections 51 and 52 of, and Sch 3 to, the Crime and Disorder Act 1998 abolish committal proceedings for all purely indictable offences. The reforms also abolish transfer for trial proceedings for such offences (eg serious fraud offences and certain sexual offences against children).

Under the new procedure (called 'sending for trial') every adult charged with an indictable only offence must first appear before a magistrates' court to determine issues concerning legal aid, bail, the taking of depositions and exhibits. The magistrate must also provide the accused with a statement of the evidence against him as well as a notice setting out the offence(s) for which he is to be sent for trial and the place where he is to be tried.

The first opportunity for a defendant to assert that there is no case to answer will be at the Crown Court, which takes over from the magistrates' court all remaining case management duties. Any submission of no case to answer must be made prior to arraignment and it will be for the judge to decide whether 'the interests of justice' require oral evidence for this purpose. If oral evidence is permitted the normal rules on reporting restrictions will apply. The normal rules on pre-trial disclosure of evidence also apply to the new sending for trial procedure.

The purpose of the new procedure is to cut delays in the criminal justice system and for this purpose new, stiffer time limits will be imposed on the prosecution to ensure efficient preparation of cases. The new time limits will be fixed after consultations and pilot trials of the new sending for trial procedures.

13

Criminal Procedure II: Summary Trial

13.1 Introduction

13.2 Attendance and representation

13.3 The information

13.4 The trial procedure

13.5 Sentencing

13.1 Introduction

Summary trial will follow automatically if the defendant is charged with a summary offence and may be chosen as the mode of trial for an offence triable either way.

Summary trial takes place in a magistrates' court before either three (exceptionally two) lay magistrates or one stipendiary magistrate. The magistrates sit as both judge and jury, that is, they decide questions of fact and law (the latter with guidance from their legally qualified clerk). Approximately 98 per cent of all criminal trials take place in the magistrates' courts.

The procedure of a summary trial is governed by the Magistrates' Courts Act (MCA) 1980.

Magistrates' courts have geographical limits to their jurisdiction – and have jurisdiction to try any summary offence committed within the county. The purpose of this is to provide a bench with 'local knowledge' (eg of a stretch of road). However, magistrates' courts have jurisdiction to try offences either way, no matter where allegedly committed.

In addition the courts have jurisdiction to try a summary offence committed outside the county in the following situations.

1. A magistrates' court which tries a person for an offence (summary or triable either way) has jurisdiction to try him in addition for any other summary offence wherever committed: s2(6) MCA 1980.
2. If one defendant is being prosecuted in a magistrates' court in Xshire and it is necessary or expedient, with a view to the better administration of justice, that he

264

be tried jointly with or in the same place as another person, Xshire magistrate may issue a summons to bring that other person before Xshire magistrates' court.

Sections 49 and 50 of the Crime and Disorder Act 1998 provide for the introduction of case management mechanisms, namely optional pre-trial reviews and early administrative hearings so as to ensure more efficient pre-trial preparations. The relevant powers to conduct such reviews and hearings are conferred on single lay justices who are also authorised to delegate certain functions (not involving significant discretionary decisions) to justices' clerks.

The Narey Report, *Review of Delays in the Criminal Justice System* (1997), has introduced further reforms to speed up the process by which persons who have been charged with criminal offences are dealt with. These came into effect on 1 November 1999. All persons charged with a criminal offence are to be brought to court the next day. Crown Prosecution staff are to be 'co-located' with the police to help to prepare 'abbreviated files' on cases, whilst at the same time carrying out their independent review of the charge. Straightforward guilty pleas will be listed exclusively for 'early first hearing' (EFH). Other cases will go to 'early administrative hearings' (EAH). Lay employees of the Crown Prosecution Service will be allowed to represent the CPS at EFHs. Legal aid will be made available to defendants who wish to be represented at EFHs or EAHs.

13.2 Attendance and representation

Attendance of the prosecution

If the prosecution fails to attend at a summary trial the magistrates have a discretion: they may either dismiss the information or adjourn the case: s15 MCA 1980. If the case is part-heard and the prosecution fails to attend, the magistrates have the further alternative of proceeding in the absence of the prosecution.

Attendance of the defendant

The defendant need not be present at his summary trial.

1. By s12 MCA 1980 the defendant (including persons aged 16 or 17) is entitled to plead guilty by post for any summary offence for which the maximum penalty does not exceed three months' imprisonment. In suitable cases, a notice explaining this option is served on the defendant with the summons. If he wishes to take advantage of this option the defendant must write to inform the clerk to the magistrates. In his letter the defendant may set out any mitigating factors he wishes the magistrates to take into account when sentencing him. The clerk will inform the prosecution of the defendant's decision so the prosecution need not attend either. On the day set for hearing, the clerk puts to the magistrates: proof

that the summons was served; the prosecution's brief statement of the facts of the offence; and the defendant's guilty plea with any mitigating circumstances.

The magistrates should then proceed to sentence. However, they may not sentence the defendant to imprisonment in his absence: s11(3) MCA 1980. If this is contemplated, the matter should be adjourned and a warrant issued for the defendant's arrest. The same course should be adopted whenever the magistrates consider the offence is in fact more serious than had been anticipated (eg if the offence is one of careless driving; this carries a fine and penalty points – the penalty points may 'tot-up' with previous ones to indicate the defendant must be disqualified from driving; this will not be done in his absence, and the matter will be adjourned, the defendant being summonsed to attend).

Section 45 of and Sch 5 to the Criminal Justice and Public Order Act 1994 substitute a new s12 of the Magistrates' Courts Act 1980, extending the procedures applicable in magistrates' courts when the accused pleads guilty. The new s12 applies when a summons has been issued requiring a person to appear before a magistrates' court, other than a youth court, to answer an information for a summary offence, not being an offence for which he is liable to be imprisoned for more than three months, and, inter alia, a concise statement of facts has been served on him. If the accused then notifies the court in writing that he wishes to plead guilty without appearing, and he does not appear, the court may (but need not) dispose of the case in his absence, taking account of any submission which he may have made with a view to mitigation of sentence. However, s11(3) and (4) (any disqualification cannot be imposed in a person's absence) of the 1980 Act still apply and any written notice may be withdrawn.

Section 12A of the 1980 Act, as inserted by the 1994 Act provisions, applies where the accused, having given written notice, nevertheless appears. If he consents, the court may proceed as if he were absent, but he must be given the opportunity to make an oral submission in mitigation.

2. Section 11 sets out the options open to the magistrates if the defendant fails to appear but has not indicated that he wishes to plead guilty under s12.

    The magistrates have a discretion to proceed in the defendant's absence – s11(1) MCA 1980 – with a plea of not guilty being entered on his behalf. The prosecution is unlikely to have difficulty in proving its case with its unchallenged evidence. For this reason, the magistrates are unlikely to adopt this course if the offence seems at all serious. This course may not be adopted without initial proof that the defendant has in fact been served with the summons.

    Where a defendant claims he is too ill to attend trial and has medical support for the claim, justices should not refuse an application for an adjournment and proceed in the defendant's absence without first satisfying themselves that the excuse was not genuine.

3. Section 13(1) gives the magistrates power to issue a warrant for the arrest of the accused so as to secure his attendance at summary trial.

    Section 48 CPIA 1996 amends s13(2) MCA 1980 relating to the conditions for issuing a warrant for the arrest of an accused who has failed to appear at his summary trial (other than an accused who has pleaded guilty by post under s12 MCA 1980).

Section 48 CPIA 1996 inserts new subss(2A) and (2B) into s13 MCA 1980. Under the new s13(2A) an arrest warrant may be issued if it is proved that the summons was served on the accused within a reasonable time before the trial or adjourned trial; and under the new s13(2B) an arrest warrant may be issued if:

a) the adjournment now being made is a second and subsequent adjournment of the trial; and
b) the accused was present at the last (or only) occasion when the trial was adjourned; and
c) on that occasion the court determined the time for the hearing at which the adjournment is now being made.

Representation

Both solicitors and barristers have a right of audience in the magistrates' courts. However, it is usual for a defendant to be represented by a solicitor or appear unrepresented (perhaps having been advised by the duty solicitor).

Where an accused is legally unrepresented, the court explains to him or her the substance of the charge in simple language. If such an accused, instead of asking a witness in support of the charge questions by way of cross-examination, makes assertions, the court puts to the witness such questions as it thinks necessary on behalf of the accused and may for this purpose question the accused in order to bring out or clear up any point arising out of such assertions.

13.3 The information

The information performs two functions.

1. It is the basis and justification for the issue of a summons ordering the defendant to appear at the magistrates' court.
2. It contains and constitutes the charge to which the defendant must plead.

It is the second function that is of relevance at the start of the summary trial.

The first stage in a summary trial is the clerk 'putting the information' to the defendant, and asking him if he pleads not guilty.

The defendant must then 'plead' to the allegations. A number of the pleas available to a defendant at a trial on indictment are not available in the magistrates' court. Put simply, the defendant must plead guilty or not guilty.

If the defendant pleads guilty, the procedure for sentencing is followed. If the defendant pleads not guilty, his trial begins.

13.4 The trial procedure

The procedure in a summary trial is as follows.

The prosecution has a right to an opening speech

Given the (usual) simplicity of most trials in the magistrates' courts, this speech is likely to be short. The purpose of an opening speech is to tell the magistrates of the charge, its background, and the nature and effect of the prosecution evidence. For instance, to open the prosecution's case in a charge of shoplifting (theft), the prosecutor may state the place and date of the offence, the nature of the goods stolen and their value, and a brief summary of what, for example, the store detective saw.

In some cases, the prosecution will not make an opening speech at all. It is clearly of less necessity in the magistrates' court, as the magistrates are experienced and do not need the preliminary explanations needed by the jury.

The prosecution calls its evidence

In all criminal trials it is for the prosecution to prove 'beyond reasonable doubt' that the defendant is guilty of the offence or offences with which he is charged. It is not for the defendant to prove his innocence. It is for this reason that it is for the prosecution to present its evidence first in order to establish at least a prima facie case against the defendant.

Generally, evidence is given orally by witnesses in court. If a witness is reluctant to attend, either side may obtain a 'subpoena' from the court which will order the witness to attend. If the witness in question then fails to attend, the magistrates, if satisfied that he has been served with the summons, that he is likely to be able to give material evidence and that he has been paid a reasonable sum of money to cover the costs of his attendance at court, may issue a warrant for his arrest.

The prosecution may call any number of witnesses who can give evidence that will work to establish any of the elements which it has to prove.

For obvious reasons, it is preferable that evidence is given orally in court; it enables the magistrates to evaluate a witness's credibility and what weight to attach to his evidence, and it enables the other side to cross-examine the witness in an attempt to challenge his evidence and cast doubt on his credibility. However, in certain circumstances, written statements may be read out and put in evidence without the attendance of the maker. In the magistrates' court these circumstances include the following.

1. Under s102 MCA 1980 a written statement is admissible in evidence if it is signed by the maker, contains a declaration that it is true to the best of the maker's knowledge and belief, has been served on all other parties, and no party

objects to its being tendered in evidence. This provision is used mainly when evidence is undisputed.

2. A deposition taken under s105 MCA 1980 from a witness who is dangerously ill and unlikely to recover may be read as evidence at the trial if it is proved that the witness is now dead or so ill that there is no reasonable probability of his ever being able to attend. The other side must have been given notice of the intention to take the deposition and given the opportunity to cross-examine the witness (eg at his bed-side).

The majority of evidence, however, is likely to be given orally. The prosecution will call its witness forward and he will stand in the witness box. Before giving evidence, the witness must promise to 'tell the truth, the whole truth and nothing but the truth'. This promise is made either by swearing to do so 'on oath', holding the Bible, Koran or whatever is the relevant book in his right hand, or by 'affirming' to do so. The latter option is to be used if the witness has no religious convictions.

The adducing of a witness's evidence is a three-stage process and is described below.

Examination-in-chief
This consists of questions asked of the witness by the side which has called him, that is, by the prosecution of a prosecution witness.

The prosecution must elicit from the witness all the evidence of that witness on which it will seek to rely. In asking questions in order to elicit such evidence, 'leading questions' must not be asked. A leading question is one which suggests the answer. For example, if the prosecution wishes to elicit from its witness evidence that at a certain time it was raining, it would be leading a witness to ask, 'it was raining, wasn't it?'. Questions should be as neutral as possible, for example, 'what were the weather conditions?'.

Cross-examination
The defence may then cross-examine the prosecution witness. In doing so, any relevant question may be asked, including leading questions. Cross-examination has two purposes. First, the defence case must be 'put' to the prosecution witness in order to give him an opportunity to reply to it. For example, if the defendant is charged with the theft of a book belonging to Mr X, Mr X may be called by the prosecution and may give evidence-in-chief that the book belongs to him and so forth. The defence 'case' may be that the defendant was given permission to take the book by Mr X. If so, this must be 'put' to Mr X: that is, he must be asked, 'Did you give the defendant permission to take your book?'. Second, questions asked in cross-examination may be used to 'discredit' the witness: that is, to show the witness up either as lying or at least as unreliable. In summary, therefore, any question is relevant if either it relates to whether the defendant committed the offence or to a

fact which increases or decreases the likelihood of his having done so, or it relates to the credibility and reliability of the witness.

Re-examination

This consists of further questions by the prosecution of its own witness. It provides the prosecution with a chance to deal with any disfavourable answers given in cross-examination; however, it is important to note that new issues and evidence may not be adduced at this stage, otherwise the other side would not have an opportunity to cross-examine the witness on that further evidence. Re-examination, therefore, is for the purpose of clarification and, possibly, amplification, of the witness evidence given in chief only, and for that reason is usually a good deal shorter than examination-in-chief or cross-examination.

All prosecution witnesses are called and, in turn, go through the above procedure. When they have all been called, that is the end of the prosecution case and, generally speaking, the prosecution will have to rely on the evidence adduced and will be unable to call any further evidence at a later stage.

Submission of 'no case to answer'

At the end of the prosecution case it is open to the defence to make a submission of 'no case to answer'. As at committal proceedings, the submission may be based on either of the following circumstances.

1. There is no evidence going to prove an essential element of the offence charged.
2. The prosecution evidence is so obviously unreliable that no reasonable tribunal could safely convict on it: *Practice Note* [1962] 1 All ER 448.

If the magistrates consider there is no case to answer they will acquit the defendant at this stage. A formal acquittal means that the defendant cannot be charged again with the offence(s) in question.

The defence case

If there is a case to answer, the defence may wish to adduce evidence, but it need not do so. It is for the prosecution to prove the defendant's guilt, and, therefore, the defendant does not have to prove his innocence. Nevertheless, if the defendant has any evidence which suggests or proves that he is not guilty the defence will wish to call that evidence. The defendant may himself give evidence, if he wishes to, but cannot be compelled to do so as other witnesses can. If the defendant chooses to give evidence he is liable to be cross-examined in the same manner as any other witness, except that he cannot normally be questioned by the prosecution on his past record, if he has one.

Defence evidence will be given orally in the same way as the prosecution evidence was given with examination-in-chief, cross-examination and re-examination.

Adjournment

In *R* v *Kingston-upon-Thames Justices, ex parte Martin* (1993) The Times 10 December, the Divisional Court said that a magistrates' court's decision as to whether to grant an adjournment to any party depended on the following factors: the importance of the proceedings, and the likely adverse consequences on the party seeking adjournment; the risk that the applicant would be prejudiced if an adjournment were refused; the risk of prejudice to his opponent if the adjournment were granted; the convenience of the court and the interests of justice in ensuring the efficient despatch of business so as not to delay other future litigants; and the extent to which the applicant had been responsible for the circumstances leading to the requirement for an adjournment.

Closing speech

The prosecution has no right to a closing speech. The defence has a choice; it may either open its case with an opening speech or finish the trial with a closing speech. It is rare for the defence not to opt for a closing speech: an opening speech adds little to the case whereas a closing speech gives the defence the opportunity to review the evidence called in its entirety and to have the last word.

The decision

On the basis of the evidence they have heard the magistrates must decide whether to find the defendant guilty or not guilty.

Lay magistrates will normally 'retire', that is, leave the court, in order to discuss the evidence and their view. They may take advice on what is the law from their legally qualified clerk. Usually three magistrates sit and they may deliver a majority verdict of two to one. However, if an even-numbered bench sits and is equally divided on its decision, the chairman has no casting vote; in that event the magistrates must adjourn the case to be reheard by a bench of three different magistrates: *R* v *Redbridge Justices, ex parte Ram* [1992] 1 All ER 652.

A stipendiary magistrate always sits alone and will usually reach his decision immediately after the defence's closing speech without retiring from the court.

If the magistrates consider that the prosecution has not proved the guilt of the defendant 'beyond reasonable doubt' they will acquit him. The defendant is then free to go and may not be charged with the offence again. If they consider that the defendant's guilt is proved they will convict him of the offence charged and proceed to sentence him.

If, after having convicted the defendant, the magistrates are unsure of the correctness of their decision, under s142 MCA 1980, they may within 28 days of their decision direct that the case be reheard by a bench of different magistrates. This direction causes their conviction and any sentence passed to be nullified.

13.5 Sentencing

The procedure prior to sentencing is dealt with in Chapter 14. This section is concerned with the magistrates' powers of sentencing only.

The magistrates have certain limits on the maximum sentences they can impose. In particular, at present the maximum fine is £5,000 for any one offence, and the maximum period of imprisonment is six months for any one offence, or one year's imprisonment for two or more offences tried together. The Criminal Justice Act 2003 provides for the maximum sentence for one offence to be increased to 12 months.

An additional option is available to the magistrates in relation to offences triable either way (but not summary offences). Although magistrates should agree to try an offence triable either way if they consider their powers of sentencing will be sufficient if there is a conviction, it may be that their powers will prove to be insufficient in the light of new material which was not available at the time of their original decision. In those events, and normally only in those events, the magistrates may commit the defendant to the Crown Court for sentencing under s38 of the MCA 1980. The Crown Court may then deal with the defendant as if he had been convicted of the offence on indictment: s42 of the Powers of Criminal Courts Act 1973.

Section 51 Crime (Sentences) Act 1997 inserts a new s38A into the Magistrates' Courts Act 1980 and enables the magistrates' court to commit the defendant to the Crown Court for sentence after a guilty plea indication to an offence triable either way if there are related offences to be committed for trial.

The magistrates may also commit the defendant to the Crown Court for sentencing in the following circumstances.

1. When they have convicted the defendant of an imprisonable offence (summary or triable either way) committed during the operational period of a suspended sentence of imprisonment passed by the Crown Court.
2. When they have convicted the defendant of any offence committed during the period of a conditional discharge order made by the Crown Court.
3. When they have convicted the defendant of an offence triable either way at a time when he is still on licence having earlier been released from prison on parole.

14

Criminal Procedure III: Trial on Indictment

14.1 Introduction

14.2 Representation

14.3 The plea; plea and directions hearings; preparatory hearings; and plea bargaining

14.4 Pre-trial disclosure

14.5 The trial procedure

14.6 Sentencing

14.1 Introduction

If the magistrates have committed a defendant to the Crown Court for trial, a 'trial on indictment' will follow several months later.

In the summary trial, the magistrates themselves decide all questions in issue, whether they are questions of fact or law. However, a trial on indictment takes place before a judge and a jury; consequently there is a division in their respective functions.

The judge in a Crown Court is always a paid professional judge. The 'adversarial' method of trial is adopted in the English legal system: this means that each side presents its own case and the judge acts as a kind of 'umpire' during the course of the trial, ensuring 'fair play'. (This is to be contrasted with the 'inquisitorial' method adopted in other legal systems in which it is the role of the judge himself to question the witnesses, although English law allows a judge to call a witness, but only to achieve the ends of justice and fairness: see *R* v *Grafton* [1992] 4 All ER 609.) At the end of the trial, it is also the function of the judge to be the sole arbiter on all questions of law and to sentence a convicted defendant.

The role of the jury is to decide all questions of fact: the jury must decide whether they believe evidence presented to them or what weight to give to each piece of evidence. The final question they must decide is whether the defendant is guilty or not guilty, that is their 'verdict'.

273

In *R* v *Crook* [1992] 2 All ER 687 the Court of Appeal stressed that the public should be excluded from a trial only when and to the extent that it is strictly necessary. While it is not sufficient that a public hearing would cause embarrassment for some or all of those concerned, each application for the exclusion of the public should be considered on its own merits.

14.2 Representation

Generally, the offences being tried in the Crown Court are more serious than those tried in the magistrates' courts. This fact is reflected in the increased formality and strictness of procedure and application of rules of evidence evident in the Crown Court. Therefore, although the defendant may represent himself, he is well advised to be legally represented (public funding is not difficult to obtain for this purpose).

Prosecuting counsel must act in the interests of justice. Although he must present prosecution evidence as persuasively as possible he should not try to win at all costs. In essence, the prosecution must act fairly towards the defence.

Defence counsel, however, need not act fairly to the prosecution; he is not in court as a 'minister of justice'. He owes a duty to the court not deliberately to mislead it, but apart from that he may use all proper means available to secure an acquittal.

The defence counsel's personal opinion is irrelevant and must not affect the way in which he presents the defence. If a defendant who insists on pleading not guilty tells his counsel he is guilty, his counsel may choose to withdraw from the case; if he continues representing the defendant he may not put forward a defence on behalf of the defendant he knows to be false but must confine himself to trying to establish that the prosecution has not proved guilt beyond reasonable doubt.

Until the Crown's case is completed, the decision whether to continue the proceedings is for the prosecution alone, and the judge cannot interfere with the prosecution's decision: *R* v *Grafton* [1992] 4 All ER 609.

14.3 The plea; plea and directions hearings; preparatory hearings; and plea bargaining

The plea

The following pleas are available.

Guilty

The effect of this is that the defendant admits the truth of all allegations made by the prosecution against him in the indictment (or in relation to the particular count in the indictment to which he is pleading guilty). A plea of guilty must be entered by the defendant himself; it may not be entered by his counsel on his behalf.

After a plea of guilty is entered, the sentencing procedure will follow. If the defendant has pleaded guilty on one count, but not guilty on another, sentencing will be postponed until after the trial of the not guilty count.

Not guilty

The effect of this plea is to deny the offence charged and thus put the whole of the prosecution case into issue. If this plea is entered the trial procedure is followed. However, it is open to the prosecution to decide not to go ahead following a not guilty plea.

Guilty to a lesser offence

Under s6(1)(b) of the Criminal Law Act (CLA) 1967 the defendant may offer a plea of not guilty as charged but guilty to a 'lesser' offence. An obvious example is in relation to a charge of murder where the defendant may offer a plea of not guilty to murder but guilty to manslaughter. However, a trial judge is only obliged to leave a lesser offence to the jury where it is necessary in the interests of justice to do so: *R v Maxwell* [1990] 1 All ER 801.

If the plea is accepted, then by s6(5) of CLA 1967, the defendant is acquitted of the offence charged but stands convicted of the lesser offence and sentencing will follow accordingly.

A plea of guilty to a lesser offence must be accepted by both the prosecution and the judge; if either is not willing to accept it it will be rejected and the defendant must choose between guilty or not guilty in relation to the offence charged.

Autrefois acquit and autrefois convict

These pleas are available to the defendant when he has been either acquitted or convicted of the offence charged in the indictment on a previous occasion. Obviously, it is rare that these pleas are suitable.

Plea and direction hearings; preparatory hearings

The charge against the defendant is contained in a formal document called an 'indictment'. An indictment may contain one or more 'counts', each of which charges one offence. A new procedure has been instituted for taking the plea: *Practice Direction (Crown Court: Plea and Directions Hearings)* [1995] 4 All ER 379 (Lord Taylor CJ).

The directions set out the detailed rules which establish plea and directions hearings (PDHs) in the Crown Court which will apply to all cases (other than serious fraud) relating to trial on indictment.

The PDH should be within six weeks of committal in cases where the defendant is on bail, and four weeks where the defendant is in custody. At the PDH arraignment will normally take place. If the defendant pleads guilty the judge should proceed to sentencing whenever possible. If the plea is not guilty, prosecution and defence will be expected to assist the judge in identifying the key issues, and to provide any additional information required for the proper listing of the case. The judge will then make such orders as appear necessary to secure the proper and efficient trial of the case.

The value of PDHs was limited by the lack of a judicial power to make binding rulings on the admissibility of evidence or on questions of law. Also the scope of a PDH did not permit a detailed examination of the issues, which might be desirable in complex or potentially lengthy cases.

The Criminal Procedure and Investigations Act (CPIA) 1996 contains provisions aimed at curing these defects.

1. Power to make binding rulings at a PDH – s40 CPIA 1996 confers jurisdiction on the judge holding a PDH to give binding rulings on the admissibility of evidence or questions of law or both. ('Binding' in this context means binding on the parties to the case, not binding in the sense of setting a judicial precedent.) A binding ruling given at a PDH will be operative until the case is disposed of either by verdict or by withdrawal of the prosecution's case. However, there is a power under s40 to discharge or vary such a ruling if it is in the interests of justice to do so, and any judge may make the order to discharge or vary the ruling, including the judge who made the original ruling.
2. A new system of preparatory hearings – s29 CPIA 1996 confers a general power on Crown Court judges to order a preparatory hearing for complex or potentially lengthy cases if substantial benefits are likely to be obtained from holding such a hearing. This follows the position in regard to serious fraud trials, where preparatory hearings can be ordered under Criminal Justice Act 1987. The purpose of a preparatory hearing is to allow a more detailed investigation of the issues than is possible at a PDH so as to assist the trial judge in the management of the trial and to assist the jury in the comprehension of the issues. The preparatory hearing is treated as the start of the trial.

The judge holding a preparatory hearing must arrange for the arraignment of the accused at the commencement of the hearing unless arraignment has already occurred at a PDH. (Many preparatory hearings will be ordered at PDHs when the new law is brought into force.) At the preparatory hearing the judge may order the prosecution to give to the court and to the accused a detailed written statement of evidence. If this is done the judge may then require the accused to give the court and prosecution a written statement of the nature of the defence, written objections which he may have to the prosecution case statement and written points of law which he wishes to take.

The judge at a preparatory hearing can only make binding rulings for the general purposes of that hearing, since the power to make binding rulings under s40 CPIA 1996 (above) is restricted to the judge holding a PDH. However, in practice rulings on questions of law and the admissibility of evidence are likely to fall within the general purpose of the preparatory hearing, so that the judge will be able to make binding rulings on these issues, unless a PDH has already been held and s40 rulings made on them.

Appeals may be taken from any ruling of a judge at a preparatory hearing to the Court of Appeal (Criminal Division) with leave of that judge or of the Court of Appeal itself. Further appeal lies to the House of Lords.

Plea bargaining

Traditionally judges pass a lighter sentence where an accused person has pleaded guilty because a guilty plea may indicate remorse, which is a mitigating factor, and because it spares prosecution witnesses the ordeal of giving evidence, as well as saving court time and costs. This practice of giving a 'sentence discount' for a guilty plea was well known and encouraged and has been described as 'implicit bargaining' between the judge and the defence, ie the earlier the plea of guilty, the greater the discount from sentence. The practice has now been given statutory recognition by s48 of the Criminal Justice and Public Order Act 1994. It should be noted that judges must not 'punish' an accused who pleads not guilty, or who enters a very late plea of guilty, by imposing upon conviction a more severe sentence than the offence demands.

Other explicit forms of plea bargaining also exist but are subject to safeguards against abuse. An example is 'charge bargaining' or 'plea arrangement' where the defence specifies to the prosecution a number of pleas relevant to the crime in question and then makes an offer of a particular plea of guilty being one of the less serious pleas. This plea of guilty is in return for the dropping of the other possible charges. Such bargaining is possible only in the presence of the trial judge, preferably in open court. The judge must also approve any arrangement reached. Whereas in other jurisdictions either side may approach the judge to obtain his view on the likely sentence in the event of a specified plea arrangement, such 'sentence canvassing' is officially discouraged in the United Kingdom jurisdictions, where there is a greater fear of improper pressure being put on an accused to plead guilty or on the judge to be unduly lenient. In England and Wales, the following safeguards have been suggested by Lord Parker CJ in *R* v *Turner* [1970] 2 WLR 1093.

1. Defence counsel may give advice, including strong advice, to his client as to his plea but must emphasise that the client should plead not guilty if he has not committed the crime in question.
2. The accused must be left with complete freedom of choice as to his plea, in full knowledge and understanding of its implications.
3. There should be freedom of access between defence counsel and the judge, but any discussions must take place in the presence of prosecuting counsel. It is always preferable for such discussions to take place in open court, although discussions in judges' chambers are allowed provided a recording device or shorthand writer is available.

4. The judge should never indicate his willingness to impose a different sentence for a plea of guilty. He should only indicate the type or range of sentence he has in mind in the event of conviction, whether after a plea of guilty or not guilty.

The guidelines were later confirmed in a *Practice Direction* [1976] Crim LR 561.

In *R* v *Pitman* [1991] 1 All ER 468 at 470–471 Lord Lane CJ gave warnings about the dangers of plea bargaining, and in particular the undesirability of secret discussions and sentence canvassing. Further warnings against sentence canvassing and plea bargaining were given in *R* v *Preston* [1993] 4 All ER 638 at 655 (per Lord Mustill) and in *R* v *Thompson* (1995) The Times 6 February (CA).

In other jurisdictions, notably the United States of America, plea bargaining is less controlled and has become a routine part of the administration of justice, with trial judges 'rubber-stamping' agreements reached between prosecution and defence (though it should be noted that in the United States, unlike the United Kingdom, the prosecution has a formal role to play in influencing the sentencing decision).

14.4 Pre-trial disclosure

The Criminal Procedure and Investigations Act 1996

Sections 3–11 CPIA 1996 set out a new three-stage procedure for the pre-trial disclosure of evidence which will apply to any type of criminal investigation except a summary trial where the accused intends to plead guilty.

Under s3 CPIA 1996 the first stage of the new procedure is known as the 'primary prosecution disclosure' stage and requires the prosecution to disclose to the accused all unused material which might in the prosecution's opinion undermine the prosecution case. This will be in the nature of a continuing duty throughout the prosecution of the case. The duty includes the obligation to provide the accused with a schedule of all other unused but possibly relevant material. The police are already obliged to make all material available to the Crown Prosecution Service, so that most decisions on pre-trial disclosure will rest with the CPS, although occasionally they will rest with others, for example customs and excise prosecutors.

The prosecution may apply to the court for permission to withhold relevant but sensitive material on the ground that it would not be in the public interest to disclose such material, for example on grounds of confidentiality or public interest immunity. It should be noted that the prosecution is under a duty not to disclose information obtained by warrants of interception issued under the Interception of Communications Act 1985.

Under s5 CPIA 1996 the second stage of pre-trial disclosure is known simply as 'defence disclosure' and requires the defence to provide the prosecution with a written statement setting out the general nature of the defence, the matters on which it takes issue with the prosecution, and the reasons why it takes such issue. The defence is not obliged to disclose the names and addresses of the witnesses intended to be called unless the defence consists of alibi evidence, in which case disclosure of alibi details is already required by s11 Criminal Justice Act 1967, which is replaced by s5(7) CPIA 1996. (The amendment simply brings the procedural requirements for the disclosure of alibi evidence into line with the new requirements for the disclosure of other evidence.)

Defence disclosure under s5 CPIA 1996 is mandatory for Crown Court trials, and appropriate inferences (including adverse inferences) may be drawn if the defence does not comply or fails adequately to comply with the disclosure requirements. Defence disclosure is voluntary for cases tried by magistrates' courts, presumably because of the more straightforward nature of summary trials.

Under s7 CPIA 1996 the third and final stage of pre-trial disclosure is known as 'secondary prosecution disclosure' and requires the prosecution to disclose any additional unused material which might reasonably assist the defence in the light of the defence disclosure under s5. Again, as under s3, the prosecution may apply to withhold sensitive material on the ground that it would not be in the public interest to disclose it.

The defence can apply at both primary and secondary prosecution disclosure stages for disclosure of specific unused prosecution material. Again the prosecution has the right to apply to withhold such material on the public interest ground.

Section 23 CPIA 1996 requires the Home Secretary to prepare a Code of Practice regulating the handling of unused material for prosecution disclosure and its preservation by the police. Such a Code also contains guidance on the handling of sensitive material, such as names of informants, and on the relevance of public interest immunity (no changes to the substantive law of public interest immunity are made by the 1996 Act).

Several notorious miscarriages of justice had been revealed during the 1980s and early 1990s and had resulted at least in part from the failure by the prosecution to disclose helpful and relevant material to the defence, a notable example being the care of Judith Ward who served 18 years in prison before her conviction was quashed on the basis of medical evidence which ought to have been disclosed by the prosecution at the time of her trial. In this case the Court of Appeal formulated common law duties of pre-trial disclosure: *R* v *Ward (Judith)* [1993] 2 All ER 577.

The effect was very favourable to defendants since it was for the defence to decide what unused material might prove helpful. The new duties were very onerous on the Crown Prosecution Service, which was faced in some cases with a huge administrative task in compiling and preserving all material connected with the case in question, whether the material appeared to be relevant or not. Dame Barbara Mills, the former head of the CPS, also voiced the fear of the police and prosecution that there were inadequate safeguards protecting sensitive material from being disclosed to the defence.

Consequently the changes made by the CPIA 1996 are designed to deal with the problems caused by the common law requirements on disclosure. It was felt appropriate for the prosecution to determine the relevancy of material to the defence because otherwise defendants would be able to make unreasonable demands for disclosure as a tactical ploy or as a 'fishing expedition' hoping to fasten upon some technical flaw in the prosecution case. The changes made by the 1996 Act should ease the heavy administrative burden shouldered by the investigating and prosecuting authorities as well as providing a procedure for the protection of sensitive information.

However, it was the proposal for defence disclosure which caused the most controversy as this change was said to undermine further the traditional rights of silence and the privilege against self-incrimination. In support of defence disclosure was the argument that defendants who were guilty should not be acquitted because of 'ambush' defences which could not be properly tested or refuted when sprung at the last minute in the court room. A miscarriage of justice occurred just as much when the guilty were acquitted as when the innocent were convicted. Defence disclosure was likely to encourage earlier resolution of cases through more pleas of guilty. Further, in some cases defence disclosure might persuade the prosecution to withdraw its case because the prosecution would realise the weakness of its hand from the details disclosed of the defence case. Hence both sides stood to benefit from the early identification of issues. Both sides would be encouraged to indulge in earlier and better preparation of their cases, thus enhancing the efficiency of the trial process.

Nevertheless some critics of the proposed new law argue that the changes simply 'turn the clock back' and raise once again the spectre of a miscarriage of justice of the kind that occurred to Judith Ward: see especially Murray 'Fair Is Foul and Foul Is Fair' [1996] NLJ 1288. The Criminal Justice Act 2003 provides for a single stage objective test to replace the above. Changes are also made so as to require more disclosure from both the defence and the prosecution.

14.5 The trial procedure

If a plea of not guilty is entered the trial must proceed. The trial procedure is as follows.

Empanelling a jury

At each Crown Court on each day a 'jury panel' is summoned, which consists of approximately 20–25 people. As soon as the defendant has pleaded not guilty the panel is brought into court. The clerk of the court has the name of each member of the panel written on a separate card; he shuffles the cards and picks out 12 at random, one at a time. Jury challenging may take place at this stage. If a juror is unchallenged, he takes his place in the jury box and takes the juror's oath:

'I swear by Almighty God that I will faithfully try the several issues joined between our Sovereign Lady the Queen and the prisoner at the bar and give a true verdict according to the evidence.'

Once 12 jurors are sworn in, the defendant is 'put in their charge'.

The prosecution case

The prosecution case begins with an opening speech by prosecution counsel. As the jury is likely to be unfamiliar with criminal procedure, the speech is likely to be explanatory of what they will see and hear and what their role is. The speech must also give the jury (and the judge) an 'overview' of the case against the defendant.

The prosecution must then call its evidence. The same procedure applies as it does in the magistrates' court. In general, witnesses must give their evidence orally in answer to questions split into examination-in-chief, cross-examination and re-examination.

The prosecution must call as witnesses all those who were called at the committal proceedings and all those who made written statements tendered under s102 of the Magistrates' Courts Act 1980. They may call further evidence provided the defence has been given notice of the same.

Evidence may be received by video link, a live television link, from two categories of witnesses, namely, those who are outside the United Kingdom and children under 14 in cases where the charge involves violence and/or sexual misconduct.

Submission of 'no case to answer'

A submission of 'no case to answer' may be made on the same basis as in the magistrates' court. There is no case to answer if the prosecution has failed to adduce evidence on which a jury, properly directed by the judge in his summing up, could properly convict.

In the Crown Court a submission of no case to answer is made in the absence of the jury and is a matter for the judge. If the judge decides there is no case to answer, the jury is called back in and directed to deliver a verdict of not guilty. If there is a case to answer – the trial continues. After the judge has ruled that there is a case to answer, the prosecution cannot be discontinued, or a plea to a lesser charge accepted, without his consent: see *R* v *Grafton* [1992] 4 All ER 609.

The defence case

The defence evidence is presented in the same way as the prosecution evidence after the defence opening speech. Where the defendant himself is being called, he should be called as the first witness for the defence.

When a decision is taken by a defendant not to go into the witness box it should be the invariable practice of counsel to have that decision recorded and to cause the defendant to sign the record giving a clear indication of (1) the fact of his having, of his own accord, decided not to give evidence and (2) that he had done that bearing in mind the advice, regardless of what it was, given to him by counsel.

Closing speeches

Both sides have a right to a closing speech. The prosecution closing speech is delivered first. He may review the evidence but may not comment on the fact that the defendant has not given evidence if that be the case. Prosecuting counsel should not comment on the potentially serious consequences to police officers of their evidence being disbelieved, even where a police officer has raised the matter in his evidence.

Finally, the defence makes its closing speech. Where part of the evidence against an accused is that he had told lies, defence counsel, in his closing speech, is entitled to suggest explanations for such lies, even beyond his client's version of the case, provided that there is other evidence in the case to support such hypotheses.

The summing up by the judge

At the end of the cases presented by the prosecution and defence the judge 'sums up' the trial to the jury. The following matters must be dealt with.

1. The functions of the judge and jury – the judge decides all questions of law and the jury all questions of fact.
2. The burden and standard of proof – the prosecution must prove that the defendant is guilty and the jury must be 'satisfied so that they are sure'.
3. An explanation of the law concerning the offence charged – the jury must accept the judge's directions on the law.
4. Any particular points concerning the evidence, for example, that the evidence of an 'accomplice' must be corroborated otherwise it is unreliable.
5. A review of the evidence actually given – the judge must give a fair summary and reminder to the jury of all material evidence given by witnesses for both sides. This will also include an appraisal of the defence put forward by the defendant.
6. In a case of any seriousness, the defendant's good character.
7. The judge must direct the jury to appoint one of their number as 'foreman' and to retire and reach a unanimous verdict.

The verdict

After the judge's summing up the jury retires to the jury room to reach their verdict. It is for the judge, not the jury, to say when they will retire: *R* v

Hawkins (1993) The Times 29 June (concern expressed by the Court of Appeal that the judge had left it to the jury to decide whether to retire in the late afternoon or following morning).

The decision of guilt or innocence is theirs alone and must be reached on the basis of the evidence they have heard and their own experience of life. Whilst doing so the jury is kept in the custody of the 'jury bailiff' (but he does not retire with them).

The jury is able to ask questions of the judge by passing him a note via the jury bailiff. The judge must show the question to counsel and if it can be answered by the judge he should do so in open court, the jury being brought back in for that purpose.

If the jury is able to reach a unanimous verdict they may return to court where their foreman will announce that verdict. The following verdicts may be returned.

1. Guilty.
2. Not guilty.
3. Not guilty as charged, but guilty of an alternative, 'lesser' offence.

However, the jury may be unable to reach a unanimous verdict. By s17 of the Juries Act 1974 the jury may acquit or convict by a majority verdict as follows:

Jury number	Majority required
12	11 to 1 or 10 to 2
11	10 to 1
10	9 to 1
9	Must be unanimous

The judge may only direct the jury that he would be willing to accept a majority verdict after the jury has been deliberating for at least two hours. The time period thereafter is within the judge's discretion.

If, despite sufficient time for deliberation, the jury is unable to reach a verdict, the judge must discharge the jury from giving one.

14.6 Sentencing

After the defendant has pleaded or been found guilty of the offence charged, the sentence procedure begins, that is, the procedure by which the punishment is fixed.

Sentencing involves a four-stage procedure: that is, the facts of the offence, the defendant's antecedents, reports on the defendant, and a plea in mitigation.

The facts of the offence

This stage is necessary only when the defendant has pleaded guilty: if he has been found guilty the judge is well aware of the facts of his offence from having listened to the evidence in the trial.

The 'facts' are given by the prosecution and, therefore, are the prosecution's version of events. However, by pleading guilty the defendant has admitted their truth.

It is necessary for the judge to know the facts of the offence in order to be able to fix the sentence. Many offences vary in their degree of seriousness; for example, a plea of guilty to theft may be a plea of guilty to stealing £10,000 from an employer's safe or to shoplifting a newspaper on the spur of the moment. The degree of seriousness of the particular offence must be reflected in the sentence given.

It is also important that the details of what happened are known generally; otherwise the justice of the sentence passed may not be checked.

The prosecution gets the facts of the case from the statements and proofs of evidence of the witnesses who would have been called by them had there been a trial.

The prosecution must not ask for any particular sentence to be passed nor should they comment on how severe or lenient the judge should be.

The defendant's antecedents

These involve previous convictions, recorded cautions, and other personal or relevant details pertaining to the convicted person.

It should be noted that any previous convictions which are 'spent' must be marked as such on the antecedents. Under the Rehabilitation of Offenders Act 1974, as amended, it is possible for a conviction to be 'spent' after a specified period of time – the rehabilitation period. The Act provided that a person need not declare a spent conviction for certain purposes (eg when applying for certain jobs). However, although a spent previous conviction must be marked as such on the defendant's antecedents, a judge is entitled to take account of it in fixing sentence for a subsequent offence.

Reports on the defendant

Reports on the defendant are often prepared for the judge in the Crown Court (magistrates rarely see any when sentencing in the magistrates' court).

The types of reports which may be prepared are as follows.

Pre-sentence reports
Prepared by a court welfare officer (or local authority social worker), after interviewing the defendant. It deals with the defendant's circumstances and income and any social problems he may have. The conclusion is a recommendation as to how the defendant could be dealt with. The officer who prepared the report may be required to give evidence and may be cross-examined by the defence.

Medical and psychiatric reports
There must be consideration of medical reports before a defendant may be ordered to be detained in a mental hospital.

Plea in mitigation

Finally, a plea in mitigation may be delivered by the defence. The purpose of the plea is to persuade the judge to pass as lenient a sentence as can be justified in all the circumstances. In order to so persuade the judge, the defence will usually deal with the following aspects of the defendant and the offence.

The offence itself
The defence should put forward any factor which shows the offence up in a less serious light. For example, its commission was unplanned.

Explanation of the offence
There may be factors which explain why the offence was committed. For example, the defendant is young and inexperienced and was led astray by older people, or the defendant stole when he was in great financial difficulty.

The defendant's future
Factors such as a new job, becoming engaged to be married or other indications of a stable domestic background may be put forward as indicating that it is unlikely that the defendant will offend again.

Finally, if the defendant has no previous convictions, co-operated with the police after arrest pleaded guilty and shown remorse, all these factors may be put forward in favour of the defendant.

Sentences

A wide range of sentencing options, including fines and imprisonment, are available to the Crown Court judge.

15

Criminal Appeals

15.1 Appeals following a summary trial

15.2 Appeals following a trial on indictment

15.3 Miscarriages of justice: the historical position

15.4 The Criminal Cases Review Commission (CCRC)

15.1 Appeals following a summary trial

Appeal to the Crown Court

A defendant may appeal from the magistrates' court to the Crown Court: on conviction and sentence if he pleaded not guilty; and on sentence only if he pleaded guilty. No leave to appeal is required. The prosecution has no right of appeal against an acquittal or an unduly lenient sentence.

There is no right of appeal against a committal to the Crown Court for sentencing. The procedure for appeal is as follows.

1. Defendant gives notice of appeal within 21 days after the day on which the decision of the magistrates was given, to the magistrates' clerk and to the prosecution.
2. The hearing before the Crown Court is a complete rehearing of the case. Therefore, the prosecution must prove its case afresh by calling its witnesses. New evidence may be tendered without leave of the court.
3. On appeals against conviction, the Crown Court may confirm, reverse or vary the decision of the magistrates' court. This includes the power to increase the sentence to whatever the magistrates had the jurisdiction to impose.
4. On appeals against sentence, the Crown Court may impose any sentence which the magistrates' court could have passed.
5. By s48(2) of the Supreme Court Act 1981 the Crown Court may 'make such other order in the matter as the court thinks just, and by such order exercise any power which the said authority might have exercised'.
6. It may remit the matter with its opinion to the magistrates' court.

Appeals against conviction are allowed on one broad ground, namely that the conviction was against the weight of the evidence.

A Crown Court sitting in an appellate capacity has to give reasons for its decision, ie enough to show that it had identified the main contentious issues and how it had resolved each of them. A refusal to give such reasons could amount to a denial of natural justice and lead to the quashing of the decision: *R* v *Harrow Crown Court, ex parte Dave* [1994] 1 WLR 98.

Appeal to the Queen's Bench Division of the High Court by way of case stated

By s111(1) of the Magistrates' Courts Act 1980, any person who was a party to proceedings before or aggrieved by the decision of the magistrates, may appeal against the proceeding on the ground that it is wrong in law or in excess of jurisdiction by applying to the magistrates' court to state a case for the opinion of a Divisional Court of the Queen's Bench Division.

Application must be in writing, made within 21 days after the date of the decision of the magistrates and indicating the point of law on which the opinion of the High Court is sought.

The 'case' to be stated by the magistrates must include the arguments which they heard, the facts found by them and their decision. In settling a statement of the case the parties should also be consulted.

At the hearing before the High Court the parties will (usually) be represented by counsel and the court will determine the questions of law raised. The magistrates themselves are not usually represented, although they may file an affidavit dealing with any matters they consider to be of importance and relevance.

The High Court may:

1. reverse, affirm or amend the magistrates' decision;
2. remit the matter to the magistrates with its opinion;
3. make such other order as it sees fit, eg, order a re-hearing by the same or a different bench: *Griffith* v *Jenkins* [1992] 2 WLR 28.

In *Tucker* v *Director of Public Prosecutions* [1992] 4 All ER 901 the Divisional Court stressed that a severe sentence imposed at the discretion of justices would be varied on an appeal to the Divisional Court only if it appeared to be astonishing by any acceptable standards. In all but the most exceptional circumstances the appropriate course for those dissatisfied by the sentence imposed by magistrates was to go to the Crown Court for a re-hearing.

Any order, judgment or other decision of the Crown Court may be questioned by any party to the proceedings, on the ground that it is wrong in law or is in excess of jurisdiction, by applying to the Crown Court to have a case stated by that court for the opinion of the High Court: s28(1) of the Supreme Court Act 1981. The power of the High Court to review decisions of the Crown Court is limited to the provisions of ss28 and 29 of the Supreme Court Act 1981. The general power of judicial review in s31 is subject to those sections: *R* v *Chelmsford Crown Court, ex parte Chief Constable of Essex Police* [1994] 1 WLR 359.

Appeal to the House of Lords

An appeal to the House of Lords may be made from the Divisional Court of the Queen's Bench Division. In order to do so there must be a certificate from the Divisional Court that a point of law of general public importance is involved. Further, there must be leave to appeal either from the Divisional Court or from the House of Lords itself.

15.2 Appeals following a trial on indictment

Introduction

The position is governed by the Criminal Appeal Act (CAA) 1968, as amended by the Criminal Appeal Act 1995. Appeal is to the Court of Appeal (Criminal Division). The changes made by the 1995 Act give effect to many of the recommendations of the Royal Commission on Criminal Justice (1993) Cmnd 2263, and are designed to deal with some of the problems which caused notorious miscarriages of justice, such as the cases of the Birmingham Six, the Guildford Four, Judith Ward and the 'Bridgewater Three' (three men released after serving 18 years in prison, convictions being quashed because of forged confessions concocted by a corrupt police unit. The three men, together with a fourth man who died in prison in 1981, had been wrongly convicted of the murder of a newspaper delivery boy, Carl Bridgewater, in 1979). A further attempt to address such problems culminated in the creation of the Criminal Cases Review Commission.

Appeal against conviction: the ground of appeal

There may be an appeal against conviction based on:

1. a question of law alone; or
2. a question of fact alone; or
3. a mixed question of law and fact.

Leave to appeal is required from the Court of Appeal, unless the trial judge certifies that the case is fit for appeal: s1(1) of the 1995 Act.

Even if the defendant pleaded guilty, there may be an appeal against conviction if the court is satisfied that a ground of appeal is established: *R* v *Lee* [1984] 1 WLR 578. However, for this purpose the plea of guilty must have been tendered mistakenly or without intention to admit the truth of the offence charged.

Sometimes such a plea may be tendered as a result of an erroneous ruling by the trial judge which appeared to make an acquittal legally impossible; in such circumstances an appeal against the conviction is available. However, it is not available if the plea of guilty was not founded upon such a ruling, eg where the ruling may have made the case against the defendant appear factually overwhelming but not legally conclusive. There is no appeal available against a plea of guilty tendered in those circumstances: *R* v *Chalkley; R* v *Jeffries* [1998] 2 All ER 155 (CA). Under the 1968 Act there were three grounds of appeal:

1. that the conviction was unsafe or unsatisfactory;
2. that there had been a wrong decision by the trial judge on any question of law; and
3. that there had been a material irregularity in the course of the trial: s2(1) of the 1968 Act.

Even if grounds (2) and (3) were established, the Court of Appeal had discretion to dismiss the appeal if it considered that no miscarriage of justice had actually occurred: the 'proviso' to s2(1) of the 1968 Act. The use of the proviso was controversial since it required the appeal judges to ask themselves whether a reasonable jury, properly directed, would still have reached the same verdict: *R* v *McIlkenny* [1992] 2 All ER 417; *R* v *Maguire* [1992] 2 All ER 433. Yet this was logically impossible since, whereas a jury sees and hears all the witnesses, the appeal judges rely mainly on the transcript of the trial and submissions from appeal counsel, and only rarely receive new oral evidence from witnesses. It was feared that the appeal judges, perceived to be part of the 'Establishment', would be reluctant to set aside convictions and, in order to reassure public opinion, it was made clear that the appeal should be allowed if the appeal judges had a 'lurking doubt' about the safety of the conviction: *Stafford* v *DPP* [1974] AC 878; [1973] 3 All ER 762 (HL).

Nevertheless, criticism continued of the narrow grounds of appeal, which were said to be a 'strait jacket' fettering the exercise of discretion by appeal judges. The Royal Commission on Criminal Justice (1993) Cmnd 2263 recommended the substitution of one broad ground of appeal, namely that the conviction is 'unsafe or may be unsafe'. The reform enacted by s2(1) of the 1995 Act substitutes a single ground of appeal, namely that the conviction 'is unsafe'. Whilst the reform has been welcomed by some as creating a broader ground of appeal than under the 1968 Act, it has also been criticised for not following the wording recommended by the Royal Commission. Is the omission of the words 'or may be unsafe' an indication that the appeal judges need no longer apply the 'lurking doubt' principle? This possibility was suggested by Professor J C Smith ([1995] NLJ 533 and 572) and his view has been confirmed by the Court of Appeal: *R* v *Farrow* (1998) The Times 20 October. In this case it was said that the new test of 'unsafeness' under the amended s2(1) of the 1968 Act has the advantages of brevity and simplicity and that it would not be appropriate to place a gloss on that test in the form of the 'lurking doubt' concept.

The basis of an appeal contending an unsafe conviction will usually be a misdirection of law by the trial judge, either during the course of the trial or in the summing-up to the jury. In a notorious miscarriage of justice case the conviction of a man executed for murder in 1953 was quashed 45 years later because the Court of Appeal was at long last persuaded that the trial judge's summing-up was so defective and biased that the accused had been denied a fair trial: *R* v *Bentley* (1998) The Times 31 July (CA).

Apart from misdirection it is possible that other matters that would have been classified as 'material irregularities' under the unamended 1968 Act will today form the basis of an appeal based simply on the unsafeness of the conviction under s2(1) of the amended 1968 Act, eg constant interruptions by the trial judge which prevent the fair presentation of a witness's testimony or of the defence case as a whole.

In *R* v *Clinton* [1993] 2 All ER 998 it was argued that the negligence of defence counsel in the presentation of the defence could constitute a material irregularity but it was held that only 'flagrantly incompetent' advice or advocacy could constitute a ground of appeal. The Royal Commission had recommended that a mistaken decision of defence counsel, eg in not calling a particular witness, should be a basis for appeal, but this view was rejected in *R* v *Satpal Ram* (1995) The Times 7 December, where it was held that a 'reasonable' decision of defence counsel, even though mistaken or unwise in hindsight, could not form a basis for appeal since otherwise the adversary system of justice, which depended heavily on the honest and independent judgment of counsel, would be undermined.

It is perhaps not surprising that in view of the notorious reluctance of appeal judges to set aside convictions some critics still contend that, even after the reforms introduced by the 1995 Act, the appeal judges will continue to be difficult to persuade of the need to allow an appeal. This view appears to be confirmed by the approach adopted in *R* v *Chalkley; R* v *Jeffries* [1998] 2 All ER 155, where the appellants had contended, inter alia, that the Court of Appeal should consider not only the safeness of the conviction but also whether it was a 'satisfactory' conviction (the language used in the unamended 1968 Act). The contention was rejected – under the amended s2(1) of the 1968 Act the sole ground for appeal is the safety of the conviction and it is not open to the Court of Appeal to consider whether a 'safe' conviction might in some other respect be 'unsatisfactory'. The former tests of 'unsatisfactoriness' and 'material irregularity' are no longer available as grounds of appeal, although they can be used as aids to determining the safety of a conviction.

Appeal against conviction: fresh evidence

Section 23 of the 1968 Act empowered the Court of Appeal to receive fresh evidence which was 'likely to be credible': see further *R* v *Gilfoyle* [1996] 3 All ER 883. Critics argued that the Court of Appeal interpreted this power too narrowly by displaying a sceptical attitude toward such evidence, in line with its general reluctance to overturn convictions. Section 23 is amended by s4(1) of the 1995 Act, ostensibly to try to deal with this problem. The new power to receive fresh evidence is made subject to a duty to consider the same factors as under s23 of the 1968 Act, namely:

1. credibility;
2. relevance to the safety of the conviction;
3. admissibility at trial; and
4. reasonableness of the explanation for any failure to adduce evidence at trial.

The change brought in by s4(1) of the 1995 Act is in the wording of the test on credibility: the appeal judges are encouraged to receive fresh evidence which is 'capable of belief' rather than 'likely to be credible'. The change was apparently designed to encourage the appeal judges to take a broader, more sympathetic approach to the issue of fresh evidence, but some critics have argued that it is a semantic change which will make no difference. Only time will tell, but in view of the need to restore public confidence in the appeal system after several notorious miscarriages of justice it would be surprising and disappointing if in future the Court of Appeal does not display a more sympathetic treatment of fresh evidence. It appears that the Court of Appeal will be reluctant to receive fresh expert evidence, either because the appellant should have been aware of its availability at the time of the trial or because the new test of credibility is more appropriately applied to factual evidence: *R* v *Jones (Steven Martin)* (1996) The Times 23 July.

The House of Lords suggested, in the case of *R* v *Pendleton (Donald)* [2002] 1 All ER 524 that the question for the Court of Appeal on an appeal against conviction was whether the conviction was safe, and not whether the accused was guilty. When assessing fresh evidence in a case of any difficulty it would usually be wise for the Court of Appeal to test its own provisional view by asking whether the evidence, if given at trial, might reasonably have affected the decision of the trial jury to convict. If so, the conviction would be unsafe. However, trial by jury did not mean trial by jury in the first instance and trial by judges of the Court of Appeal in the second.

Appeal against conviction: powers of the Court of Appeal in disposing of an appeal

The Court of Appeal may either:

1. allow the appeal and quash the conviction: or
2. allow the appeal, quash the conviction but substitute a conviction of some other offence and sentence the defendant accordingly. This power is contained in s3(1) of the 1968 Act and should be exercised only where the appeal judges are satisfied that the jury could have found the defendant guilty of the other offence on the facts presented at the trial: *R* v *Graham (HK) and Others* [1997] 1 Cr App R 302. The power is not available if the defendant pleaded guilty to offences prior to being put in charge of the jury because s3(1) of the 1968 Act expressly contemplates a verdict from a jury: *R* v *Horsman* [1997] 3 All ER 385

(appellant had pleaded guilty to obtaining property by deception but successfully appealed on the basis of the reinterpretation of law that occurred in *R* v *Preddy* [1996] 3 All ER 481; his conviction had to be quashed, the s3(1) power being unavailable); or

3. allow the appeal, quash the conviction but order a retrial if it is in the interests of justice to do so, bearing in mind the lapse of time since the trial, the continuing availability of witnesses, etc: s53 Criminal Justice Act 1988 and *R* v *Grafton* [1992] 4 All ER 609; or

4. dismiss the appeal. If the Court of Appeal takes the view that the appeal was frivolous it can order that any time spent by the defendant in custody pending the appeal, which normally would count as part of the sentence, shall not count as part of the sentence. Apart from this, the Court of Appeal has no power to increase a sentence when dismissing an appeal against conviction.

It should also be noted that, although the prosecution has no right of appeal against an acquittal, there is a right of appeal on a point of law to enable the Court of Appeal to deal with a misdirection without affecting the jury's verdict of not guilty: s36 Criminal Justice Act 1972. There is also a power to set aside an acquittal obtained by intimidation: see s51 Criminal Justice and Public Order Act 1994. The Criminal Justice Act 2003 provides for a right of appeal for the prosecution against judicial decisions to direct or order an acquittal before the jury has been asked to consider the evidence. This would be introduced to balance the defendant's right of appeal against both conviction and sentence. The Act also makes it possible in certain very serious cases for a retrial to take place despite an earlier acquittal if there is new and compelling evidence of guilt.

Appeal against sentence

The defendant may appeal against the sentence passed by the Crown Court, but only with the leave of the Court of Appeal or the Crown Court judge: s9 and s11, as amended, CAA 1968. There is no appeal against a sentence fixed by law.

The Court of Appeal will not interfere with the discretion of the judge below and will only interfere if the sentence is wrong in principle or manifestly excessive. It has power to reduce the sentence or substitute one form of detention for another.

On the recommendation of the Attorney-General the prosecution may appeal against an unduly lenient sentence to the Court of Appeal: ss35, as amended, and 36 of the Criminal Justice Act 1988. This measure was introduced following an outcry in the media at the sentences imposed in certain cases. It has been applied, for example, to substitute detention for two years, pursuant to s53(2) of the Children and Young Persons Act 1933, for a non-custodial sentence passed on a 15-year-old boy convicted of rape (*R* v *W* (1993) The Times 16 March) and to increase a sentence for careless driving causing death having consumed alcohol above the prescribed limit: *Attorney-General's Reference (No 14 of 1993)* [1994] RTR 49.

Until 1 March 1994 s36 of the 1988 Act applied only to cases where the offence was triable on indictment only. Since that date it has applied also to three triable either way offences, ie indecent assault, cruelty to or neglect of children and making threats to kill. However, these extended rights of appeal apply only where the case was heard, or sentence was passed, in the Crown Court.

Appeals to the House of Lords

Either the prosecution or the defence may appeal from the Court of Appeal to the House of Lords if both the following requirements are satisfied.

1. The Court of Appeal certifies that a point of law of general public importance is involved in the decisions.
2. Either the Court of Appeal or the House of Lords gives leave on the ground that the point in issue is one which ought to be considered by the House of Lords.

The House of Lords may exercise the same powers as those exercised by the Court of Appeal: *R* v *Mandair* [1994] 2 All ER 715.

Once a criminal appeal has been decided by the House of Lords, either dismissing the defendant's appeal or directing that his conviction be restored, it is not open to him to apply to the Court of Appeal to have his appeal relisted for the hearing of grounds of appeal not considered by the House of Lords: *R* v *Berry (No 2)* [1991] 1 WLR 125. However, the House of Lords may remit a case to the Court of Appeal where a ground of appeal had not been disposed of by the Court of Appeal: see *R* v *Mandair*, above.

Further, in exceptional cases the House of Lords has inherent jurisdiction to set aside an earlier ruling of the House if it has caused injustice. Whilst the House is naturally reluctant to re-open an appeal it will do so if a party has been subject to an unfair procedure. Apart from such exceptional cases there is no right of appeal from decisions of the House: *Pinochet Ugarte (No 2)* [1999] 2 WLR 272.

15.3 Miscarriages of justice: the historical position

Section 17 of the 1968 Act enabled the Home Secretary to refer to the Court of Appeal any conviction which the Home Secretary had reason to believe might be unsafe. This referral power was an important device for ensuring reconsideration of cases since, once an appeal had been dismissed, no further appeals could be brought under s2 of the 1968 Act: *R* v *Pinfold* [1988] 2 All ER 217. However, the Home Office only had limited resources to investigate petitions alleging miscarriages of justice, and even where a case was referred the Court of Appeal demonstrated its traditional reluctance to interfere with convictions, notably on such cases as the Birmingham Six, who were the subject of several referrals before the Court of Appeal was persuaded to quash the convictions.

The Royal Commission on Criminal Justice recommended the abolition of the Home Secretary's role in appeals and the establishment of an independent Criminal Cases Review authority to take its place. The implementation of this proposal by the 1995 Act forms the centrepiece of the new appeal system.

15.4 The Criminal Cases Review Commission (CCRC)

The Commission was established by ss 8–14 and Sch 1 to the Criminal Appeal Act 1995 and began its work on 1 April 1997. It has the power to review and investigate cases of suspected wrongful conviction and/or sentence in England, Wales and Northern Ireland, and to refer cases to the appropriate court for an appeal whenever it considers that there is a real possibility that the conviction, verdict, finding or sentence would not be upheld.

Section 4(2) of the Act states that the CCRC 'shall not be regarded as the servant or agent of the Crown'. The impartiality of the Commission was seen as important to public perception of the way in which miscarriage of justice cases are dealt with and, therefore, to the success of the Commission. The Home Secretary had been too open to the conflicting accusations of making a reference out of political motivation and failing to make a reference out of reluctance to interfere with the judicial process. Whilst the Commission can refer cases to the Secretary of State with a view to his recommending to the Queen the exercise of the Royal Prerogative of Mercy, the main import of the Act was the fostering of an independent but close relationship between the Commission and the court with the Commission referring matters to the court for advice and the court requiring the Commission to undertake investigations and report back.

The constitutional independence of the CCRC from both from the executive and the judiciary was welcomed by the Bar, the Law Society, by civil liberties groups and by senior members of the judiciary, such as the Lord Chief Justice. It was seen as being a good means by which to remove the quasi-judicial involvement that the Home Secretary had in the appeal process which was constitutionally unsound and was suggested by some to be a reason for the traditional reluctance of the courts to interfere with convictions referred to them.

The Act requires that the Commission have a composition which includes a two-thirds lay majority made up of people who have some experience of the criminal justice and complaints system. It may consider on broad grounds any allegation of a miscarriage of justice resulting from either a conviction or a sentence in either the Crown Court or the magistrates' courts, either upon referral with leave of the Court of Appeal (which may wish to have the matter investigated in an inquisitorial manner) or after dismissal of an appeal. Complaints may also be received direct from members of the public and, for the first time, it has become possible to make referrals in summary cases. By s13 it may reinvestigate cases where there is a 'real possibility' that a miscarriage of justice has occurred. This is a wide power and the

Commission has the power to interview all applicants, including prisoners. The lawfulness of the Commission to refuse to refer a case to the Court of Appeal was tested for the first time in *R* v *Criminal Cases Review Commission, ex parte Pearson* [1999] 3 All ER 498. The applicant had been convicted of murder and some years later obtained fresh evidence in the form of a psychiatric report which indicated that she may have been suffering from what is now recognised as 'battered women syndrome'. The Commission refused to refer the case on the ground that there was not a 'real possibility' of the conviction being quashed since, in its view, there was no likelihood of the Court of Appeal receiving the fresh evidence. The applicant sought judicial review of the Commission's decision. The application was dismissed. It was held that the Commission had correctly applied the s13 test which was equally applicable to the question of the reception of fresh evidence as to the question of upholding a conviction. In applying the test the Commission had correctly made its own assessment of the merits of the applicant's case without unlawfully usurping the functions of the Court of Appeal. For the purposes of s13 a 'real possibility' was something more than an outside chance or bare possibility, but might be less than a probability, or a likelihood or a racing certainty: per Lord Bingham CJ.

At the time the Commission was set up three main areas of doubt about the likely effectiveness of their work sat with: the procedure for investigation of cases; the lack of provision of legal aid to applicants in prison; and the lack of representation on its membership of persons experienced in criminal defence work. The lack of ability for the Commission to rely on its own investigators to carry out an investigation was probably the most controversial of the issues. For cases originally investigated by the police the basic duty of investigation lies with the chief constable who may appoint an investigating officer either from his own force or from another. The Runciman Report concluded that there was no suitable alternative to this method of investigation and the Commission was set up with the intention that it be analogous to the Police Complaints Authority which instructs the police to carry out investigations. Since some of the most notorious of the miscarriages of justice have been caused and covered up by police misconduct, this continuing reliance on police investigations is seen as undermining the apparent independence of the Commission from the police. The Labour Party in opposition and lawyers' groups such as the Legal Action Group argued that the police become judges and jury in their own cause. Chris Mullin, the Labour MP who campaigned successfully on behalf of the Birmingham Six, described it as 'an absolutely fatal flaw' in the new system, but others might regard this as an overreaction: it is insulting and false to suggest that no policeman can be trusted to carry out such work. Indeed, the wrongdoings of the West Midlands police force in the Birmingham Six case were uncovered and exposed by the officers of the Devon and Cornwall police force.

The failure to provide public funding to convicted persons who have lost their appeal for the costs of advice and assistance in making representations to the

Commission was contrary to the proposals of the Runciman Report, which had envisaged that it would be available but would end once the Commission decided to investigate unless the Commission required further information or assistance from the applicant's solicitor. It was feared that this would prove to seriously restrict the work of the Commission who would have to be mindful of costs during their investigations and may find it difficult to instigate the investigation they require for some cases. In the event, these fears proved unfounded and, conversely, the problem has instead been the workload that the Commission have. As a result, the main complaint about the Commission has been the long delays in dealing with cases.

It was expected that the Commission would deal with an average of 800 cases each year. By the end of their first year they had received 1,000 applications. It had also inherited some 280 Home Office and Northern Ireland cases when it took office in 1997. That figure doubled over the second year, and its third Annual Report for the period up to March 2000 records receipt of 3,193 cases over the three-year period of its existence. The figures for February 2005 revealed that the total applications received to date was 7,493, and 6,744 cases have been completed. By the end of its first year the Commission had referred 12 cases to the relevant courts of appeal and two appeals had been heard and had been successful. The Commission reported in its first Annual Report: 'These are creditable statistics for the Commission's first year of caseworking, with potential for improvement as casework experience grows'. By February 2005 there had been 268 referrals, with the Court of Appeal having made a decision in 215 of them of which 149 saw the sentence being quashed. By a strange irony, the first high profile success of the Commission was its success with the referral of the case of Derek Bentley to the Court of Appeal. Bentley was convicted of the murder of a policeman and was executed in January 1953. The circumstances of his conviction gave rise to one of the longest campaigns for justice in the history of the English legal system and even became the subject of a major feature film, 'Let Him Have It', in 1993. A Royal Pardon was eventually granted but only in respect of the sentence. The family continued its campaign for the conviction itself to be quashed and when the Commission took office they persuaded it to refer the case to the Court of Appeal which quashed the conviction on the ground of a defective summing-up by the trial judge: *R* v *Bentley* (1998) The Times 31 July.

Any evaluation of the success of the Commission has to be made in the context of the other reforms introduced by the 1995 Act. Two changes are of particular importance: the substitution of a conviction that 'is unsafe' as the single ground for appeal to replace the three overlapping grounds under the 1968 Act; and the lowering of the threshold for the admission of fresh evidence. These changes were intended to keep cases of merit within the appeal system and so reduce the number of applications for post-appeal referral. The conditions placed on the power of the Commission to make a referral clearly intends to limit referrals to cases with strong fresh evidence which have exhausted their appeal remedies: there must be 'a real possibility' that the conviction will be quashed, an appeal must have been heard or leave to appeal refused, and the reference must be because of an argument or evidence not raised at trial or on appeal. Provision for post-appeal referral is thus seen as being confined to exceptional cases of particular merit. A government discussion paper published in 1994, reflected this sentiment: 'A "last resort" procedure should be precisely that: a vehicle for remedying miscarriages of justice not an extra stage in the ordinary criminal justice process to be used routinely'.

Part VI: European
Legal Systems

16

The European Community and the European Union I

16.1 Introduction

16.2 The institutions of the European Union

16.3 The sources of European Community law

16.1 Introduction

The European Union, as it is has been called since 1992, can trace its origins back to the immediate post-war era of the late 1940s and early 1950s. Europe had been ravaged by two World Wars, and there was a political will to ensure that such a catastrophic breakdown in diplomatic relations, with consequent loss of life and systematic abuse of human rights, should not be allowed to recur. The belief was that the more the individual states of Europe became integrated and interdependent, the less likely it would be that any one state would resort to armed force against another. In May 1950 the French Foreign Minister, Robert Schuman (working closely with Jean Monnet) outlined the aims and methods of the so-called 'Schuman' plan, which sought to integrate the coal and steel industries of those Western European countries wishing participate in the scheme. It will be noted that the coal and steel industries were central to any country having militaristic ambitions, hence the impetus to achieve integration in these areas. The result was the European Coal and Steel Community (ECSC), formally established in 1951 when six countries – Belgium, France, the Federal Republic of Germany, Italy, Luxembourg and The Netherlands – signed the Treaty of Paris 1951. Common institutions were established to govern the operation and development of the coal and steel industries in the Member States. The establishment of the ECSC was seen by many as the first step towards greater unity in Europe, the intention being that, following the integration in areas of coal and steel production, economies as a whole of the member countries would be integrated. Once economic integration was completed it was thought that the way might be open to the formation of a United States of Europe. In 1957, the process of integration was taken a step further with the signing of the Treaty of Rome establishing what was, until 1992, known as the European

301

Economic Community (EEC). This period also saw the formation of the European Atomic Energy Community (Euratom), to encourage co-operation in the peaceful use and development of nuclear energy.

Terminology

Following the signing of the Treaty on European Union (TEU) 1992 or 'Maastricht Treaty', the term 'European Economic Community' (EEC) was dropped in favour of 'European Community' (EC). The TEU 1992 also made it clear that the original Treaty of Rome, as amended by the Single European Act (SEA) 1986 and the TEU 1992, was henceforth to be known as the EC Treaty. Other terminological changes flowing from TEU 1992 were as follows: the Council of Ministers became the 'Council of the European Union'; the Commission became the 'European Commission'. The Treaty on European Union (TEU) 1997 or 'Amsterdam Treaty' provides that the EC is itself now part of a wider entity, the European Union (EU). The EU is based on three 'pillars': (1) the EC, including the European Coal and Steel Community and Euratom; (2) the common foreign and security policy; and (3) co-operation in the fields of justice and home affairs. EC institutions have no jurisdiction in relation to (2) and (3) unless the Council of the EC decides otherwise. Matters in (2) and (3) are governed by inter-governmental co-operation at a national level.

Although there is a tendency to use the terms 'EU law' and 'EC law' interchangeably, it is technically incorrect to use the former expression as the EU does not actually enact legislation. In the technical sense the expression 'Community law' should now only be used in respect of law arising under the EC Treaty.

The objectives of the European Union

The EC has as its aim the welding of Europe into a single prosperous area by abolishing restrictions affecting the movement of people, goods and capital; in effect an internal market without internal frontiers in which the free movement of goods, persons, services and capital can be achieved. Article 2 of the EC Treaty provides:

> 'The Community shall have as its task, by establishing a common market and progressively approximating the economic policies of Member States, to promote throughout the Community a harmonious development of economic activities, a continuous and balanced expansion, an increase in stability, an accelerated raising of the standard of living and closer relations between the states belonging to it.'

Article 3 of the Treaty details the means by which these aims are to be achieved. This includes, for example, the elimination of customs duties and quantitative restrictions on the import and export of goods between Member States. With the abolition of all customs duties between Member States there will be a single European market of approximately 270 million customers available to producers in

Europe, and European manufacturers will be able to produce goods more cheaply on the scale that is practised for example in the United States. Article 3 also envisages the establishment of a common commercial policy, an internal market characterised by the abolition, as between Member States, of obstacles to free movement of goods, persons, services and capital. Under the common agricultural policy, designed to keep the price of foodstuffs at a sufficiently high level to ensure an adequate return for farmers without the need for subsidies, foodstuffs entering Member States from outside the European Union have levies placed upon them to make them as expensive as those offered for sale by producers in the EC. Prices are not allowed to fall to their natural level because producers can insist on designated national authorities intervening to buy foodstuffs at a certain price – the 'intervention' price fixed each year by the Council. Provision is also made in art 3 for the approximation of laws of Member States to the extent required for the proper functioning of internal market; development of a policy on environmental matters; and a common policy on transport. In all the above the EC aims to eliminate inequalities and to promote equality between men and women.

In 1973 the original six Member countries were joined by Denmark, Ireland and the United Kingdom. In January 1981 Greece joined the Community and Spain and Portugal also became Members on 1 January 1986. With effect from 1 January 1995 membership increased to 15, with the addition of Austria, Finland and Sweden. Following the Amsterdam Summit in 1997 negotiations are in train to admit Poland, Hungary, the Czech Republic, Slovenia, Estonia and Cyprus to an enlarged EU. The preconditions for membership are: stable democratic political institutions; observance of the rule of law; respect for human rights; and a viable market economy able to withstand competition from other Member States.

Towards a federal Europe: the Maastricht and Amsterdam Treaties

Following a meeting of heads of government of Members States in Maastricht in December 1991, the TEU 1992 (the 'Maastricht Treaty') was signed by all Member States, with certain exceptions being made by the United Kingdom, on 7 February 1992. The Treaty accelerated the move towards a federal, unified, Europe, providing, for example, that every national of each Member State was to be granted the status of citizen of the EU, in addition to national citizenship. The TEU 1992 laid down a timetable for monetary union, with the aim that a single currency (the ECU) should be in circulation by 1999.

As with previous EC treaties, and in accordance with constitutional requirements, the TEU 1992 had to be incorporated into United Kingdom law by means of domestic legislation, hence the enactment of the European Communities (Amendment) Act 1993. The Conservative government of the day sought an opt-out for the United Kingdom as regards certain aspects of the TEU 1992 'package' (eg limitation upon working hours, etc), but the Labour government elected in May 1997 has agreed that the United Kingdom should be bound by them.

The ratification of the TEU 1992 prompted an application for judicial review in *R v Secretary of State for Foreign and Commonwealth Affairs, ex parte Rees Mogg* [1994] 2 WLR 115. The applicant sought a declaration that any such ratification would be unlawful on the ground (inter alia) that the establishment of a common foreign policy (under Title V of TEU 1992) would involve a loss of prerogative power, which could only be achieved by way of statutory enactment. Dismissing the application, the court held that, on the facts, the ratification of Title V of the Maastricht Treaty did not involve a diminution of prerogative power as it would be open to the United Kingdom to renege on its obligations under the Treaty, and re-assert the prerogative power to formulate and execute foreign policy in the areas affected.

The 'Amsterdam Treaty' (ie TEU 1997) seeks to consolidate each of the three 'pillars' of the EU put in place by TEU 1992. The Treaty was incorporated into domestic law by virtue of the European Communities (Amendment) Act 1998. In addition to addressing issues related to strengthening the operation of the EU institutions (as to which see below), specific matters addressed by TEU 1997 are as follows.

Rights of EU citizens

The EU will co-ordinate policies aimed at reducing unemployment, via the European Investment Bank. With the signing of the Treaty the United Kingdom has accepted the agreement on social policy providing for a maximum working week and a minimum wage. Under the Treaty the EU will monitor the extent to which Member States adhere to their obligations under the European Convention on Human Rights. The TEU 1997 contains a non-discrimination clause that allows the EU to take action against all forms of discrimination.

Removing remaining obstacles to freedom of movement and strengthening security

In accordance with the 1990 Schengen Agreement, identity checks will be abolished at internal frontiers with the exception of the borders of Ireland and the United Kingdom. Controls at external frontiers and ports will remain in place. The TEU 1997 also envisages a harmonisation of rules on the issuing of visas and the granting of asylum to those arriving from outside the EU. Minimum European norms will be established regarding facilities provided for asylum seekers. The role of Europol will be expanded and developed in respect of its data-gathering activities and investigative roles. There is no proposal that it should take over any of the policing functions of the forces of Member States. Note that the TEU 1997 moves some aspects of justice and home affairs, such as asylum and immigration, from the third pillar of the EU to the first, thus bringing them within the jurisdiction of the EC institutions, notably the European Court of Justice.

16.2 The institutions of the European Union

The Council of the European Union

The Council is the EC's principal decision-making body. The government of each of the 25 nations in the European Union has a seat on the Council. The foreign minister is usually a country's main representative, but a government is free to send any of its ministers to Council meetings. The Council's membership thus varies with the subject scheduled for discussion. Finance ministers will attend for discussion of economic issues, transport ministers for discussion of transport policy, agriculture ministers for discussion of the common agricultural policy, and so on. Unlike the European Commission, the Council's members represent their national interests first and foremost. The presidency of the Council rotates between the Member governments at six-monthly intervals.

Under art 202 EC Treaty the functions of the Council are stated as being to ensure that the objectives of the EC Treaty are attained, and to ensure the co-ordination of economic policies of Member States. The Council carries out these functions by making policy decisions, issuing regulations and directives, and acting upon proposals from the Commission.

The Council can determine issues by a simple majority vote, by qualified majority voting, or by means of a unanimous decision, depending on the procedure required by the EC Treaty, as amended. The provisions regulating the voting procedures of the Council attempt to fulfil two aims: first, to ensure that the Council cannot easily take a high-handed approach to Commission proposals; and, second, to ensure that important proposals aimed at promoting greater integration of Member States should not be held back by the veto of one Member State. Hence the Council may be able to accept Commission proposals by a qualified majority, but unanimity is required if it seeks to amend a Commission proposal against the wishes of the Commission. For some particularly important decisions, such as acceptance of a new Member State or changes in the number of commissioners, unanimity is required.

As art 205 EC Treaty explains, under the system of qualified majority voting the votes of Members are 'weighted' according to population, although there are anomalies in respect of the smaller nations so as to ensure that their views are not totally marginalised. The Treaty of Nice increased the total number of votes to 321, and the number of votes needed to form a 'blocking minority' has increased proportionately to 90. The use of qualified majority voting gradually increased through measures introduced in the SEA 1986, and later in the TEU 1997, the latter extending its use to areas such as social exclusion, public health, equal opportunities and employment incentives.

Although in theory it should become more difficult for any one Member State to exercise a power of veto by opposing a measure in Council, in reality the Council has recognised that there may be a heavy political price to pay for enforcing on a

Member State a measure that it bitterly opposes, and which is likely to cause widespread anti-EC sentiment within that Member State. Hence, under what is known as the Luxembourg Accord (the Luxembourg Agreement of 1966) the Council will not normally impose a decision on a Member State by way of qualified majority voting if a Member State can show that the decision would be detrimental to its vital national interests. The Luxembourg Accord has no legal status but has proved an important factor in negotiations between Member States. The Council is not bound to accept an assertion by a Member State that a matter ought not to be decided by qualified majority voting on the grounds that a vital national interest is affected. The ultimate decision rests with the Council.

Although the Council has a shifting membership, some stability and consistency is ensured by the work of the Committee of Permanent Representatives of Member States (COREPER), which not only undertakes the preparatory work for Council meetings but also co-ordinates meetings of senior civil servants from Member States. COREPER is organised on a committee basis, with work being split between the first committee dealing with social affairs and transport, and the second dealing with economic and foreign affairs. Agricultural issues fall under the responsibility of a separate agriculture committee.

The European Commission

The treaties assign the European Commission a wide range of duties. It is the guardian of the treaties setting up the EC and is responsible for seeing that they are implemented. It is the initiator of Community policy and oversees the execution of policy initiatives. The Commission can investigate instances of Member States failing to fulfil treaty obligations, and if necessary deliver a reasoned opinion. Non-compliance with such an opinion will result in the Commission referring the matter to the European Court of Justice: see art 226 EC Treaty.

The European Commission, an independent body with executive powers and responsibility, comprises 25 commissioners chosen for their all-round capability by agreement between the governments of the Member States. At present Germany, United Kingdom, France, Italy and Ireland have two commissioners each. A commissioner is obliged to act in the Community's interests as opposed to the interests of the country of which he or she is a national. Throughout their four-year term of office commissioners remain independent of their respective governments and of the Council.

The Council cannot remove any commissioner from office; only the European Parliament can compel the European Commission to resign as a body by passing a motion of censure. In January 1999 such a censure motion was only narrowly defeated following mounting concern regarding the failure of the Commission to deal properly with fraud, corruption and allegations of poor accountability. The Commission agreed to the appointment of a team of independent investigators who could look into the allegations. The resulting report, published in March 1999, was very critical of the way in which the Commission had conducted itself, and of the behaviour of certain individual commissioners. As a result all 20 serving commissioners resigned. Some were subsequently invited to take up different posts within the Commission; others, pointedly, were not.

The Commission as a whole is headed by a President, appointed by the Commission in consultation with Member States. Each commissioner heads a department with special responsibilities for one area of Community policy, such as economic affairs, agriculture, the environment and transport. Regular discussions are held between a commissioner's department and interested parties. As a result of these discussions the relevant commissioner formulates draft proposals which he believes will help to improve the quality of life of Community citizens. The draft proposals are discussed by all the commissioners who then decide on the nature of the final proposal. Decisions are taken on a collegiate basis.

Economic and Social Committee

In addition, there is also a body known as the Economic and Social Committee that plays a consultative role in the decision-making processes of the Council and Commission. The Committee represents a wide spectrum of European Community interests, such as those of workers, consumers and farmers.

The European Parliament

The EC Parliament is not to be equated with the Westminster model. It cannot legislate in its own right and does not possess any form of parliamentary sovereignty. It does, however, exercise a limited, but growing, supervisory power in relation to legislative measures. In particular the Parliament:

1. advises the Council of the European Union on Commission proposals;
2. with the Council of the European Union, determines the budget for the EC;
3. exerts some political control over the Council and Commission; and
4. by debate can attract publicity to issues that then have to be considered by the Commission or the Council.

The European Parliament now has 732 members who represent the citizens of the European Union. Members are directly elected and serve for a period of five years. The composition of Parliament makes it a fully integrated Community institution, as the members do not sit in national groups but in political party groups. The six main political party groups at present are the Communists, Socialists, European People's Party, European Progressive Democrats, European Democrats and the Liberal and Democratic Group. The United Kingdom has 87 MEPs.

The European Parliament meets on average once a month, for sessions which last up to a week. It has 18 standing committees that discuss proposals put forward by the Commission under the consultation procedure. The committees present reports on these proposals for debate by the full Parliament. The Commission is not obliged to act upon the recommendations of these committees. Similarly, the Parliament can put forward its own policy initiatives, but the Commission is under no obligation to act upon them.

Despite worryingly low turnouts, particularly in the United Kingdom, direct elections have given the Parliament greater political authority and new prestige both inside and outside the European Union. The Parliament has the right to question members of the Commission and Council and is therefore able, to a limited extent, to monitor the work of these institutions. It has the power to dismiss the European Commission by a two-thirds majority vote, and can similarly reject the Council's proposals for the Community budget. As noted above, the inquiry into fraud and corruption within the Commission, instigated by the EC Parliament in January 1999, led to the resignation of all of the commissioners in March 1999.

The role of the Parliament has been strengthened by the provisions of the SEA 1986, TEU 1992 and TEU 1997. As a result the Parliament has a power of co-decision in relation to a wide range of matters such as freedom of movement, non-discrimination, transport policy, social security, rights of establishment of foreign nationals and rules governing professions. The Parliament considers the Council of Ministers' proposals, within a strict time limit, and can adopt, amend or reject them. Rejection or amendment requires an absolute majority of members. In the event of rejection or amendment, the conciliation procedures come into play whereby a Conciliation Committee, comprised equally of Parliament and Council members, seeks to achieve agreement. If agreement cannot be reached the measure in question is dropped.

The European Parliament now has an effective power of veto over applications for EU membership, can veto nominations for the appointment of commissioners, and the appointment of the EU President will require the endorsement of the Parliament.

The EC Ombudsman

In the wake of the 1994 European Parliament elections an Ombudsman for the EC was appointed by the European Parliament, pursuant to art 195 of the EC Treaty, to investigate allegations of maladministration made by any EU citizen or resident against any EC institution other than the European Court of Justice. Complaints considered by the EC Ombudsman do not have to pass through an MEP filter (he can act on his own initiative), and are not subject to any specific time limit. Given that serious violations of EC law can be pursued by individuals taking cases to the European Court of Justice, it seems likely that the EC Ombudsman will be concerned with less serious cases, perhaps where there may be no obvious judicial remedy, and where political pressure to achieve a settlement or redress is more appropriate. The only sanction available to the EC Ombudsman in the event that he finds an institution guilty of maladministration is the making of an adverse report to the European Parliament.

The Court of Justice of the European Communities

The Court is the European Union's supreme judicial authority; there is no appeal against its rulings. Each of the treaties establishing the European Communities uses the same broad terms to define the specific responsibilities of the Court of Justice, which are to ensure that in the interpretation and application of these treaties the law is observed. The Court therefore interprets and applies the whole corpus of EC law from the basic treaties to the various implementing regulations, directives and decisions issued by the Council and the European Commission.

Although its jurisdiction is principally concerned with EC law, the Court is not cut off from national law, since it draws its inspiration from the legal traditions that are common to the Member States. This ensures respect both for the general principles of law and for fundamental human rights in so far as they have been incorporated into the European Community legal order.

The 15 judges of the Court are appointed by common accord of the governments of the Member States. The treaties require them to be chosen 'from persons whose independence is beyond doubt and who possess the qualifications required for appointment to the highest judicial offices in their respective countries or who are jurisconsults of recognised competence'. There is no specific nationality requirement, but at the present time the Court has one judge from each Member State. The judges select one of their number to be President for a renewable term of three years. Members of the Court hold office for a renewable term of six years. Every three years there is a partial replacement of the Court's membership: five or six judges and two or three advocates-general are replaced alternately. This ensures continuity of the Court's decisions, especially as most of the judges have had their term of office renewed at least once and sometimes twice. The independence of the judges is guaranteed by their status and is based on three fundamental rules of procedure: their deliberations are secret; judgments are reached by majority vote; and judgments are signed by all the judges who have taken part in the proceedings. Dissenting opinions are never published.

The Court is assisted in its work by the advocates-general who are appointed on the same terms as the judges, although nationality is immaterial. According to art 222 EC Treaty the functions of the advocates-general are to act with complete impartiality and independence, and to make, in open court, reasoned submissions on cases brought before the Court, in order to assist the Court in the performance of the tasks assigned to it. The advocates-general do not represent the Communities and cannot initiate proceedings themselves. At a separate hearing, some weeks after the lawyers have addressed the Court, the advocate-general comments on the various aspects of the case, weighs up the provisions of EC law involved, compares the case in point with previous rulings, and proposes a legal solution to the dispute. The advocate-general does not participate in the Court's deliberations. Once the advocate-general has delivered his opinion it is not open to the parties to submit any further written submissions unless requested to do so: see further *Emesa Sugar (Free Zone) NV* v *Aruba* (2000) The Times 29 February.

Since 1988 the European Court has been assisted in its work by the Court of First Instance, comprising 12 judges, created under the SEA 1986. Advocates-general may assist the Court of First Instance but there are none specifically assigned to it. The role of the Court of First Instance is to deal with cases that turn primarily on issues of fact, rather than law, brought by natural or legal persons, rather than Member States. Initially its caseload was limited to disputes related to production quotas, competition law and staff cases, but since 1993 its jurisdiction has been extended to all matters, other than cases involving anti-dumping proceedings. Appeal on a point of law lies to the European Court of Justice.

There are a variety of ways in which legal disputes can be brought before the European Court of Justice. A distinction is made between direct actions, which involve disputes between parties, and requests for preliminary rulings, which take the form of questions put by national judges. Direct actions may be divided into four categories:

1. proceedings against a Member State for failure to fulfil an obligation;
2. proceedings for annulment;
3. proceedings for failure to act; and
4. proceedings to establish liability.

As indicated above, if the Commission considers that any part of the administration of a Member State has not honoured an EC obligation, it asks that Member State to make its comments and then issues a reasoned opinion. If the Member State does not act on the opinion within the time allowed, the Commission may refer the matter to the Court on the basis that the Member State has failed to act as required: see art 226 EC Treaty. If the Court agrees that the case is well founded, it declares that an obligation has not been fulfilled: see for example *EC Commission* v *Italy* Case 39/72 [1973] ECR 101. All the authorities of the Member State concerned are required to take the necessary measures to comply with the Court's judgment in their respective areas of competence. If a state does not comply with the initial ruling, new proceedings may be brought for a declaration by the Court that the obligations arising from its first decision have not been complied with. *EC Commission* v *Italy* [1989] 3 CMLR 25 makes it clear that the Member State's duty in such cases is to make the necessary amendments to its domestic law. The TEU 1992 provided a framework for the introduction of a system of fines imposed upon Member States for non-compliance with EC obligations: see art 68 EC Treaty. The European Commission has agreed that fines are to be imposed on a sliding scale, related to the 'wealth' of Member States.

Proceedings for annulment under art 230 EC Treaty are a way of reviewing the legality, under the treaties, of Community acts, Commission decisions and regulations, and of settling conflicts between the institutions over their respective powers under the treaties. The proceedings, which can be instigated by a Member State, the Council or the Commission, are directed against binding Community acts, be they general regulations and directives or decisions addressed to individuals, taken by the Council and the European Commission. The basis of such a challenge is that the impugned acts are unlawful because of lack of legal competence, infringement of an essential procedural requirement, infringement of the EC Treaty or any rule of law relating to its application, or misuse of powers. A notable example was the unsuccessful attempt by the United Kingdom to challenge the validity of the adoption of the 'working time directive' which sought to limit the average working week to 48 hours' duration: see further *United Kingdom* v *Council of Ministers of the European Communities* [1996] All ER (EC) 877. Because opinions and recommendations do not have binding force, proceedings may not be brought in respect of them.

Private citizens, companies and non-EC Member States may also initiate proceedings for annulment, but only against decisions which are specifically addressed to them or which, despite being in the form of regulations or decisions addressed to another person, concern them directly and individually. If the Court regards the action as well founded, it declares the act in question void and of no effect and the act then ceases to have any legal force as from the date when it originally took effect.

Proceedings for failure to act (under art 232 EC Treaty) provide a means of penalising inactivity on the part of the Council or the European Commission. Should the Council or the European Commission infringe the EC Treaty by failing to act, the Member States and the other institutions of the Community may bring an action before the Court of Justice to have the infringement established. Such actions are admissible only if the institution in question has previously been called upon to act. If it has not acted within two months of being invited to do so, an action may be brought within a further two months. Proceedings for failure to act can also be brought under identical conditions by private individuals or firms, who can accuse a Community institution of having failed to take a binding decision (ie one other than a recommendation or opinion) concerning them. Admissibility is subject to the same conditions as those that apply to actions for annulment – the act not taken must have been of direct and personal concern to the party initiating the proceedings.

Finally, the civil liability can be imposed by the Court for damage caused by EU institutions or servants in the performance of their duties in accordance with the general principles common to the laws of the Member States. The treaties confer on the Court of Justice the exclusive jurisdiction to order the EC to pay damages because of its actions or its legislative acts, on the principle of non-contractual liability. In exercising its unlimited jurisdiction, the Court decides the basis on which liability is to be determined, whether the damage is due to Community action, the amount of damage caused and the sum to be paid in compensation. By contrast, the EC's contractual liability is subject to the general law of the Member States and to the jurisdiction of their courts.

The European Court of Justice is, by its very nature, the supreme guardian of Community law. But it is not the only court that has the power to apply and interpret this body of law that is common to all the Member States. Unlike most classical forms of international treaty, there is a mass of provisions set out in the treaties themselves and in the secondary legislation of the Council and the European Commission, and in agreements entered into by the Community that are directly and immediately applicable in the legal systems of all the Member States. These acts have a direct effect in that they can confer individual rights on nationals of Member States (see below for an explanation of direct effect). Private individuals may invoke them in their national courts in relation to the national authorities and, in some circumstances, in relation to other private individuals and companies. The courts in each Member State have thus become, in a sense, 'Community courts'. To avoid differing and even conflicting interpretations, art 234 EC Treaty introduced a system of preliminary rulings that can be requested in order to test the validity of acts adopted by the institutions, and to provide clarification regarding the extent to which the domestic law of a Member State is at variance with the dictates of EC law.

Under the EC Treaty, where a national court from which appeals be made finds there is a problem regarding the interpretation of the treaties or of measures taken by the institutions, or some question arises as to the validity of these measures, it may apply, under art 234, to the European Court for a preliminary ruling if it considers that it needs to do so in order to come to its judgment. When a problem or question of this type arises in a national court against whose decisions there is no judicial remedy under national law (eg the House of Lords), that court must refer the matter to the Court of Justice. This system has resulted in valuable collaboration between the Court of Justice and national courts in ensuring the uniform application and interpretation of Community law.

In *Srl CILFIT* v *Ministry of Health* [1982] ECR 3415 the Court defined the extent and limits of the obligation on courts of final instance to request preliminary rulings. The Court stated that national courts did not need to refer questions if: the question raised was irrelevant, as, for instance, if it could have no possible influence on the outcome of the dispute; the Community rule in question had already been interpreted by the Court (whatever the circumstances and without the matters in dispute necessarily being absolutely identical); and there was no reasonable doubt about how the question should be answered.

Opinions vary on the authority enjoyed by preliminary rulings and particularly on whether they have general effect or are binding only on the parties concerned. However, three points seem to have been accepted regarding references for interpretation: the interpretation given by the Court is binding on the judge who requested it – he can refer the matter back to the Court if he considers that there is still a question to be answered; the interpretation serves as a basis for applying the relevant law in any subsequent case and other courts may invoke it without further reference to the Court of Justice; and a judge may always ask the Court of Justice for a new interpretation. A preliminary ruling may only be applied for by a national court or tribunal and not by the parties to the case. Once a ruling has been given the matter is taken back to the domestic court that made the reference for that court to give its ruling in the light of the European Court's decision.

As a consequence of the fact that any domestic court can, in theory, refer a case for consideration under art 234, concern is increasing at the extent to which the process is becoming overburdened by the number of cases so referred. At present the average length of time taken in dealing with a reference is 18 months. One possible reform that may be considered is to only permit the exercise of the right to make references once all domestic appeal procedures have been exhausted.

Given that the EC Treaty reflects its continental legal origins in the way in which it is drafted, as does the output of the Council in terms of other sources of EC law, it is not surprising to find that the approach of the European Court to the interpretation of the EC Treaty and other measures is markedly different from the approach adopted by UK courts when interpreting domestic legislation. As Lord Diplock observed in *Henn and Darby* v *DPP* [1981] AC 850 (at p852):

'The European Court, in contrast to English courts, applies teleological rather than historical methods to the interpretation of the treaties and other Community legislation. It seeks to give effect to what it conceives to be the spirit rather than the letter of the treaties; sometimes, indeed, to an English judge, it may seem to the exclusion of the letter. It views the Community as living and expanding organisms and the interpretation of the provisions of the treaties as changing to match their growth.'

The Council of Europe and the European Council

The Council of Europe exists quite independently of the EU, being the creation of the Treaty of Westminster in 1949. It has a much larger membership than the EU, comprising many states that, for political or economic reasons, find the concept of EU membership unacceptable or unattainable. The Council of Europe operates essentially as an inter-governmental organisation, that from time to time generates conventions on key aspects of international law. Its most notable achievement is the European Convention on Human Rights. A possible consequence of failing to comply with the Convention's requirements is expulsion from the Council of Europe. In 1967 Greece had its membership suspended following the military take-over and attendant human rights abuses. Similarly, in April 1995, the Council of Europe approved a resolution ordering Turkey's suspension unless it showed progress in withdrawing from Northern Iraq where it had intervened in relation to the Kurds.

The European Council has existed since the early 1970s and is comprised of the heads of EC Member States and the President of the European Commission. Although it originally existed as an ad hoc organisation, its existence has now been formerly recognised by the SEA 1986, and has had its status increased by virtue of the TEU 1997. The European Council provides a forum for discussion of strategic issues related to EU policy, such as economic and social matters, constitutional issues, and for reviewing the operation of the EU. Meetings, normally held three times a year, are chaired by the head of the Member State currently holding the Presidency of EC.

The Treaty of Nice

A number of factors underpinned the agreement reached by EU Member States at the Nice summit in December 2000. The first was the desire to enlarge membership from 15 to 27 Member States. The Treaty of Nice therefore paves the way for the admission of 12 new Member States: Bulgaria; Cyprus; the Czech Republic; Estonia; Hungary; Latvia; Lithuania; Malta; Poland; Romania; Slovakia; and Slovenia.

The second factor was the recognition that enlargement would necessitate a streamlining of decision making processes, especially with regard to qualified majority voting (QMV). Under the Treaty QMV is extended to 23 new areas including external border controls; freedom of movement for non-EU nationals; aspects of asylum and immigration rules; intra EU judicial co-operation on civil matters; social security provisions; state aid for industry; regional subsidies; and various procedural and administrative matters. Areas that remain outside the scope of QMV are taxation, core social security policy, trade issues concerning cultural and audio/visual sectors and core immigration policy.

The third factor was the desire on the part of the larger Member States to ensure that their influence was not diluted by an influx of many smaller Member States following enlargement. Although large Member States such as the United Kingdom, France, Germany and Italy have each lost one of their commissioners now that we are in 2005 (the total number of commissioners being capped at 27), between them Germany, France and the United Kingdom will form a dominant power block able to control the future direction of EU policy. The United Kingdom's influence within the EU is, arguably, strengthened under the Treaty by virtue of the fact that it has a larger share of votes in the Council of Ministers (29 out of 237 – ie 12.24 per cent, instead of 10 out of 87 – ie 11.49 per cent); there is a higher threshold for a qualified majority vote (74 per cent of 239 votes, instead of 71.4 per cent).

The European Communities (Amendment) Act 2002, which received Royal Assent on 26 February 2002, provides for the implementation of the provisions in the Treaty of Nice. That Treaty provided for reform of the European Union so as to enable the European Union to operate effectively after the accession of the new applicant Member States. The key institutional changes include:

1. changes to the size and organisation of the College of Commissioners;
2. revision of the current system of weighted votes in the Council;

3. extension of qualified majority voting in the Council and co-decision with the European Parliament;
4. changes to the procedures set out in the Amsterdam Treaty for authorising a group of Member States to use the European Union's institutions to move ahead with activity in certain areas, even though not all Member States want to take part (enhanced co-operation);
5. changes to the distribution of seats in the European Parliament after enlargement;
6. a package of reforms to alleviate the growing burden on the European Court of Justice and the Court of First Instance.

The European Union (Accessions) Act 2003 provides for the accession to the European Union of an additional ten Member States.

16.3 The sources of European Community law

There are three main sources of EC law: the Community treaties; the Acts of the Community institutions; and the decisions of the Court of Justice of the European Communities. Essential to the effective operation of the EC is the principle that its primary law, the treaties, applies to the same extent in the legal system of each Member State, and that it takes precedence over the domestic law of any Member State, to the extent that there is any conflict between the two.

Article 10 of the EC Treaty provides:

> 'Member States shall take all appropriate measures, whether general or particular, to ensure fulfilment of the obligations arising out of this Treaty or resulting from action taken by the institutions of the Community. They shall facilitate the achievement of the Community's tasks. They shall abstain from any measure which could jeopardise the attainment of the objectives of this Treaty.'

The 'appropriate measures' for the implementation of the Treaty depend upon the nature of the Member State's legal system. Where it is monist, the Treaty will automatically become part of domestic law that can be relied upon in the courts of that Member State (to the extent that it creates rights for individual litigants, as to which see below). Where the Member State has a dualist system, as is the case with the United Kingdom, the Treaty has to be incorporated into domestic law in order to be effective: see the European Communities Act 1972, the impact of which (as regards UK parliamentary sovereignty) is considered further in Chapter 17.

As regards the secondary legislation of the European Union, namely regulations, directives and decisions, art 249 of the EC Treaty provides:

> 'A regulation shall have general application. It shall be binding in its entirety and directly applicable in all Member States. A directive shall be binding, as to the result to be achieved, upon each Member State to whom it is addressed, but shall leave to the national authorities the choice of form and methods. A decision shall be binding in its entirety

upon those to whom it is addressed. Recommendations and opinions shall have no binding force.'

Decisions of the Court of Justice may be treated as a secondary source of EC. The Court is not bound to follow its previous decisions and they may therefore be treated as persuasive rather than binding authority.

Any doubt as to the primacy of EC law over national law was resolved by the European Court of Justice in *Costa* v *ENEL* [1964] ECR 585 where the Court stated:

'By creating a Community of unlimited duration, having its own institutions, its own personality, its own legal capacity of representation on the international plane and, more particularly, real powers stemming from a limitation of sovereignty or a transfer of powers from the States to the Community, the Member States have limited their sovereign rights, albeit within limited fields, and have thus created a body of law which binds both their nationals and themselves. The integration into the laws of each Member State of provisions which derive from the Community, and more generally the terms and spirit of the Treaty, make it impossible for the States, as a corollary, to afford precedence to a unilateral and subsequent measure over a legal system accepted by them on a basis of reciprocity ... The executive force of Community law cannot vary from one State to another in deference to subsequent domestic laws, without jeopardising the attainment of the objectives of the Treaty ... and giving rise to the discrimination prohibited by art [6]. The obligations undertaken under the Treaty establishing the Community would not be unconditional, but merely contingent, if they could be called in question by subsequent legislative acts of the signatories ...'

The primacy of EC law prevails even where the domestic law is penal in nature, thus creating a defence of reliance on European Community law: see *Pubblico Ministero* v *Ratti* Case 148/78 [1979] ECR 1629.

Direct applicability

It will be seen, therefore, that provisions contained in the treaties and regulations enacted by the Council are of 'direct applicability', by which is meant that they become part of the law of a Member State without further intervention by the Member State: see further *Van Duyn* v *Home Office* Case 41/74 [1974] ECR 1337 and *Re Export Tax on Art Treasures (No 2)* [1972] CMLR 699. As indicated above, proceedings can be brought in the European Court by any Member State against another Member State failing to fulfil its obligations under the treaties. Directives, by contrast, are not directly applicable in that they require further enactment by a Member State before they can take effect within its domestic law. Member States have no discretion as regards the object to be achieved by the implementation of the directive, but do have discretion as to how that objective is to be achieved. In the United Kingdom, for example, the implementation of a directive may take the form of primary or delegated legislation as appropriate. As to the consequences of an EC directive creating a conflict with existing UK primary legislation: see Chapter 17.

Direct effect

The extent to which the primacy of EC law is made effective depends largely upon the degree to which compliance is policed. Clearly, large-scale failure by a Member State to comply with the requirements of EC law would be raised by the European Commission, or other Member States. It is through the empowerment of individual EU citizens, however, that the monitoring process is made most effective, and this has been achieved by the European Court's development of the concept of 'direct effect'. In basic terms, if a given provision of EC law is held to have the characteristic of direct effect it can be invoked by a individual against a Member State in the courts of the relevant Member State.

This form of direct effect is sometime referred to as 'vertical' direct effect to distinguish it from 'horizontal' direct effect (considered below) where an individual seeks to invoke a provision of EC law against another private party.

Broadly, the criteria to be satisfied before a provision can be regarded as having direct effect are that it is sufficiently precise in its terms to be said to be creating individual rights, and does not require any further implementation in order to become effective in law.

That treaty provisions can have direct effect, where they are found to be sufficiently precise and unconditional in their effect, was established in *Van Gend en Loos* v *Nederlandse Administratie der Belastingen* [1963] ECR 1, where the Court observed that:

'The objective of the [EC Treaty], which is to establish a Common Market, the functioning of which is of direct concern to interested parties in the Community, implies that this Treaty is more than an agreement which merely creates mutual obligations between the contracting states. This view is confirmed by the preamble to the Treaty, which refers not only to governments but also to peoples. It is also confirmed more specifically by the establishment of institutions endowed with sovereign rights, the exercise of which affects Member States and also their citizens. Furthermore, it must be noted that the nationals of the states brought together in the Community are called upon to co-operate in the functioning of this Community through the intermediary of the European Parliament and the Economic and Social Committee ... the task assigned to the Court of Justice under art [234], the object of which is to secure uniform interpretation of the Treaty by national courts and tribunals, confirms that the states have acknowledged that Community law has an authority which can be invoked by their nationals before those courts and tribunals. The conclusion to be drawn from this is that the Community constitutes a new legal order of international law for the benefit of which the States have limited their sovereign rights, albeit within limited fields, and the subjects of which comprise not only Member States but also their nationals. Independently of the legislation of Member States, Community law therefore not only imposes obligations on individuals but is also intended to confer upon them rights which become part of their legal heritage. These rights arise not only where they are expressly granted by the Treaty, but also by reason of obligations which the Treaty imposes in a clearly defined way upon individuals as well as upon the Member States and upon the institutions of the Community ...'

The same reasoning can be applied to regulations, provided the preconditions for direct effect are met: see *Politi* v *Ministry of Finance* [1971] ECR 1039.

Subject to certain conditions, directives can also have direct effect. The issue was considered by the European Court of Justice in *Van Duyn* v *Home Office* Case 41/74 [1974] ECR 1337. The United Kingdom government allowed the Church of Scientology to operate in England, but sought to limit its activities by not granting work permits to foreign nationals seeking to take up employment with the Church in England. Ms Van Duyn, a Dutch national offered employment by the Church in England, was refused a work permit by the Home Office. She sought a declaration that the minister's prohibition was in contravention of what is now art 39 of the EC Treaty, and was not permitted under Council Directive 64/221/EEC. Amongst the question referred under what is now the art 234 procedure, the court asked whether the directive in issue was directly applicable so as to confer rights on individuals enforceable by them in the courts of a Member State. The European Court of Justice, holding that the directive could have direct effect, observed:

'If ... by virtue of the provisions of art [249] regulations are directly applicable and, consequently, may by their very nature have direct effect, it does not follow from this that other categories of acts mentioned in that article can never have similar effects. It would be incompatible with the binding effect attributed to a directive by art [249] to exclude, in principle, the possibility that the obligation which it imposes may be invoked by those concerned. In particular, where the Community authorities have, by directive, imposed on Member States the obligation to pursue a particular course of conduct, the useful effect of such an act would be weakened if individuals were prevented from relying on it before their national courts and if the latter were prevented from taking it into consideration as an element of Community law. Article [234], which empowers national courts to refer to the Court questions concerning the validity and interpretation of all acts of the Community institutions, without distinction, implies furthermore that these acts may be invoked by individuals in the national courts. It is necessary to examine, in every case, whether the nature, general scheme and wording of the provisions in question are capable of having direct effects on the relations between Member States and individuals.'

Becker v *Finanzamt Munster-Innenstadt* [1982] ECR 1-53 makes clear that the conditions for the direct effect of directives are that the Member State against whom the action is brought must have failed to transpose the directive into domestic law, or failed to do so correctly, and the directive must be sufficiently unconditional and precise in its terms. As was noted in *Marks & Spencer plc* v *Commissioner of Customs and Excise* [2000] STC 16, direct effect cannot be invoked where the directive has been correctly transposed but wrongly implemented. A further factor to be taken into account was highlighted by the Court in *Francovich (and Others)* v *Italian Republic* (see below), where the Court noted [at paras 11 and 26] that:

'Wherever the provisions of a directive appear, as far as their subject matter is concerned, to be unconditional and sufficiently precise, those provisions may ... be relied upon as against any national provision which is incompatible with the directive or insofar as the provisions of the directive define rights which individuals are able to assert against the

State ... [but] ... even though the provisions ... [are] sufficiently precise and unconditional as regard[s] the determination of the persons entitled to the guarantee and as regards the content of that guarantee, those elements [may not be] sufficient to enable individuals to rely on those provisions before the national courts. [If] those provisions do not identify the person liable to provide the guarantee ... the State cannot be considered liable on the sole ground that it has failed to take transposition measures within the prescribed period.'

On this basis the Court of Appeal, in *Evans* v *Motor Insurers Bureau; Mighell* v *Reading and Another; White* v *White and Another* (1998) The Times 12 October held that the Second Council Directive 84/5/EEC (OJ 1984 L8/17), which dealt with the approximation of the laws of EU Member States regarding civil liability arising from the use of motor vehicles, was not of direct effect as it left it to the United Kingdom government to determine who should provide the scheme of compensation for those suffering losses caused by uninsured drivers.

What is a public body for the purposes of 'vertical' direct effect?

As has been noted above, the term vertical direct effect has been used to describe the position where a directive can be invoked by an individual against a Member State. The scope of vertical direct effect depends, therefore, on the extent to which defendant bodies are perceived to be emanations of the state, eg the armed forces, the police, regulatory bodies, colleges and universities, etc. The extent to which an employer could be regarded as falling within the sphere of public law (and hence amenable to the doctrine) was considered in *Marshall* v *Southampton and South West Hampshire Area Health Authority* (below) and *Johnstone* v *Chief Constable of the Royal Ulster Constabulary* [1987] QB 129, where the European Court of Justice ruled respectively that employees of the National Health Service, and those of constitutionally independent authorities responsible for maintaining law and order, could invoke provisions contained in directives against their employers on the basis that they were agents of the national authority. In *Foster* v *British Gas* [1991] QB 405 the European Court of Justice suggested that:

'... a body, whatever its legal form, which has been made responsible pursuant to a measure adopted by the State, for providing a public service under the control of the State and which has for that purpose special powers beyond those which result from the normal rules applicable in relations between individuals is included in any event among the bodies against which the provisions of a directive capable of having direct effect may be relied upon.'

Following this ruling the House of Lords proceeded on the basis that British Gas was a state body for the purposes of vertical effect. Similarly, in *National Union of Teachers and Others* v *Governing Body of St Mary's Church of England (Aided) Junior School and Others* [1997] ICR 334, the Court of Appeal held that the governing body of a voluntary aided school was an emanation of the state, for the purposes of the direct enforceability of a European Community directive. Citing *Foster*, Schiemann

LJ noted that voluntary schools, once they chose to come within the state system, were subject to a considerable degree of control and influence by the Secretary of State, such that they could be regarded as coming within the 'control' of the state. In contrast see *Doughty* v *Rolls Royce* [1992] CMLR 1045 (ownership by the Crown not the sole determining factor).

Horizontal direct effect

Given the development of the doctrine of vertical direct effect, the question has arisen as to the extent to which treaty provisions, regulations and directives can have 'horizontal' direct effect, in the sense that they can be invoked by one individual against another natural or private legal person in the courts of Member States.

The horizontal direct effect of treaty provisions has been recognised by the European Court of Justice in decisions such as *Walrave and Koch* v *Union Cycliste Internationale* [1974] ECR 1405 and *Defrenne* v *Sabena* [1976] ECR 455, where it has been seen as a necessary step towards ensuring that the objectives of the Union are not thwarted by private law bodies exercising their rights to legal autonomy. A distinction has been drawn, however, between treaty provisions and regulations on the one hand, that are directly applicable and hence become part of domestic law without further enactment, and directives on the other, that require the State to which they are addressed to carry out the necessary procedures for implementation. Whilst it might be justifiable to permit proceedings against a private party for non-compliance with a treaty provision or regulation, should that private party be at risk of litigation because of the Member State's failure to implement a directive? In a number of cases, most notably *Marshall* v *Southampton and South West Hampshire Area Health Authority* [1986] QB 401 and *Faccini Dori* v *Recreb Srl* Case C–91/92 [1995] CMLR 833, the European Court of Justice has ruled that directives cannot have horizontal direct effect so as to impose liabilities and duties on individuals and private companies. As the Court observed, recognising the limits of the scope of Community law in *Faccini Dori* v *Recreb Srl*:

> 'The effect of extending ... to the sphere of relations between individuals [the case law on horizontal direct effect to directives] would be to recognise a power in the Community to enact obligations for individuals with immediate effect, whereas it has competence to do so only where it is empowered to adopt regulations.'

The unwillingness of the European Court of Justice to recognise the horizontal direct effect of directives has, however, to be seen in the light of two other factors: the doctrine of indirect horizontal effect and the availability of damages against Member States for failure to implement directives.

Indirect effect

Although the European Court of Justice has balked at the prospect of openly recognising horizontal direct effect in respect of directives, not least because they are addressed to Member States and not individuals, it has developed a doctrine, sometimes referred to as indirect effect, whereby the responsibility of the Member State for the application by its courts of EC law is regarded as being the means by which they can be compelled to ensure that the objective of a given directive is achieved in the resolution of disputes in domestic courts.

In two cases, *Von Colson* v *Land Nordrhein-Westfalen* [1984] ECR 1891 and *Harz* v *Deutsche Tradex GmbH* [1984] ECR 1921, the plaintiffs sought compensation having had their job applications turned down on grounds of gender. Under German law the rejection of their applications was lawful, and their only entitlement was to reimbursement of their travelling expenses. The plaintiffs claimed that there had been a breach of art 6 of the Equal Treatment Directive. The European Court held that, notwithstanding whether the Directive gave rise to direct effect, the German State was obliged, under art 10 of the EC Treaty, to ensure that its domestic courts interpreted domestic law in such a way as to secure compliance with the objectives of the Directive. Hence, even if the Directive was not one having direct effect, by this means it could be given indirect effect. Note that although Von Colson was pursuing her action against a public body (the German prison service), the claim in *Harz* v *Deutsche Tradex GmbH* was against a private company. This is significant because it means that the doctrine of indirect effect can operate vertically and horizontally.

Indirect effect places UK courts in a particular dilemma as the traditional approach is to give domestic legislation its ordinary and everyday meaning. How far should UK courts now go in attempting to interpret domestic law so as to ensure conformity with directives? In *Lister* v *Forth Dry Dock & Engineering Co Ltd* [1990] 1 AC 546 the House of Lords was willing to disregard the prima facie meaning of a statutory instrument in order to ensure compliance with a directive, notably because it was felt that the statutory instrument had been introduced specifically to ensure compliance with the directive (note also that this was litigation against a private party). Even where domestic legislation has not been enacted to secure compliance with a directive, the courts are still likely to strive for a meaning that ensures compatibility provided this can be done without doing undue violence to the terms of the domestic law: see *Webb* v *EMO Air Cargo Ltd (UK) (No 2)* [1995] 1 WLR 1454. Where no such accommodation is possible, the plaintiff would be advised to pursue a claim in damages against the Member State for non-compliance.

In *Marleasing SA* v *La Comercial Internacional de Alimentacion SA* [1992] 1 CMLR 305 the doctrine of indirect effect was developed further to cover the situation where a directive had not been implemented. The plaintiff company had sought the nullification, in the Spanish courts, of the creation of the defendant company, on the basis that it had been formed with the sole purpose of defrauding creditors. The plaintiff's legal challenge was based on the provisions of Spanish law (sections 1261 and 1275 of the Civil Code) which rendered invalid contracts which were without legal purpose or caused unlawful consequences. The defendants called in aid art 11 of Council Directive 68/151 claiming that it listed exhaustively the circumstances in which the nullity of a company could be declared, and that the ground relied upon by the plaintiff was not listed therein. The Directive had not, at the time this issue came before the Spanish courts, been incorporated into the domestic law of Spain. The question referred to the European Court of Justice was as to whether the article in question was directly applicable so as to preclude a declaration of nullity of a public limited company on a ground other than those set out in the article. The European Court of Justice ruled that, whilst directives were not of themselves capable of having direct effect between individuals, the national courts of Member States were obliged to interpret domestic law so as to ensure conformity with EC directives, whether the domestic law originated before or after the incorporation of the directive. The effect of the decision was to prevent the Spanish court from declaring the defendant company to be a nullity on any ground other than one listed in the relevant directive: see further *Faccini Dori* v *Recreb Srl* (above). Note again that the decision gives rise to a measure having horizontal indirect effect. If it is simply impossible for the domestic court to interpret existing domestic law so as to achieve conformity with the objectives of the directive, the Member State may be liable in damages: see further *Wagner Miret* v *Fondo de Garantia Salaria* [1993] ECR 1–6911.

Remedies for non-compliance with Community law

The failure of a Member State to ensure compliance with the provisions of the EC Treaty or other Community legislation, or indeed to implement directives accurately and within given time limits, may give rise to a right in damages on the part of an individual adversely affected by the failure. The development of this form of State liability is of particular significance where there is no relevant domestic law upon which a plaintiff can base a legal claim. The possibility of such liability being imposed was recognised by the European Court of Justice in *Francovich (and Others)* v *Italian Republic* [1992] IRLR 84. A number of Italian workers who had been made redundant found that, following their employer's insolvency, there were insufficient funds to pay their salaries. The workers complained that the Italian government had failed to implement legislation, required by a directive, to guarantee that such salary arrears should be paid by the State. The European Court of Justice held that, even in situations such as presented by the case under consideration where (because of uncertainties relating to implementation) the directive in question could not be regarded as one having direct effect, Member States were obliged to provide protection for clearly defined individual rights granted by EC law to specific groups, and a failure to provide such protection, if resulting in economic loss to individuals within those groups, rendered the Member State in question liable in damages.

The Court based its reasoning on the ground that the full effectiveness of EC law might be called into question, and the protection of the rights which they conferred would be weakened, if individuals could not obtain compensation where their rights were infringed by a breach of EC law for which a Member State was responsible. In other words, a Member State should not be able to hide behind its own failure to implement a directive when defending such proceedings. The Court identified three precondition to liability: the directive had to be one conferring individual rights; the rights had to be identifiable on the basis of the provisions of the directive; and there had to be a causal link between the Member State's failure and the damage suffered. For these purposes a directive will generally be regarded as conferring individual rights if it is intended to provide protection for economic welfare (eg as regards consumer contracts), health (eg drinking water standards) or safety (eg product liability). In many ways this development is a logical extension of the doctrine that compliance with Community law will be most effectively policed by individuals within Member States. It simply provides them with a financial incentive to bring instances of non-implementation before the courts.

The European Court of Justice has since gone on to extend this right to damages to other instances of non-compliance by Member States, notably in *Brasserie du Pêcheur SA* v *Federal Republic of Germany* Case C–46/93; *R* v *Secretary of State for Transport, ex parte Factortame Ltd and Others (No 4)* Case C–48/93 [1996] 2 WLR 506. The first case concerned an action brought by a French beer producer in respect of losses caused through not being able to export its beer to Germany, following a ruling by the German authorities that its products did not comply with the German beer purity laws. The restriction imposed by the German authorities had, in previous proceedings, been found to be in contravention of EC Treaty articles seeking to eliminate quantitative restrictions on imports. The second case was brought by Spanish trawlermen seeking damages for losses caused by the enactment of Pt II of the Merchant Shipping Act 1988 that had prevented them from operating fishing vessels that could be registered in the United Kingdom and thus permitted to fish against the British quota under the Common Fisheries policy. The 1988 Act had, in previous proceedings, been found to be in breach of Community law, in particular of the EC Treaty provisions ensuring freedom of establishment. The European Court ruled that the principle established in *Francovich* applied equally where the non-compliance was caused by any organ of government of the State, including the State's legislature, provided three conditions were met:

1. the rule of law infringed must be intended to confer rights on individuals;
2. the breach must be sufficiently serious; and
3. there must be a direct causal link between the breach of the obligation resting on the State and the damage sustained by the injured party.

On the facts the Court was satisfied that condition (1) was clearly satisfied in both cases. As regards condition (2), the test was whether or not a Member State had manifestly and gravely disregarded the limits on its discretion regarding the measures to be taken in ensuring compliance, due regard being had to factors such as whether the breach was intentional or voluntary, whether an excusable error of law had been made, whether the action of any Community institution might have contributed to the breach, and whether or not there were previous decisions of the European Court making clear the incompatibility of the domestic law in question. The issue of causation was to be determined by the domestic courts of Member States. See further *R* v *Secretary of State for Social Security, ex parte Sutton* [1997] 3 All ER (EC) 497.

Exemplary damages could be awarded in respect of such claims, provided they could be awarded on a similar basis under the domestic law of a Member State, subject always to the proviso that domestic law should not operate so as to make the obtaining of such reparation excessively difficult or impossible. In this regard, the requirement of English domestic law, to the effect that damages would only be recoverable in cases of misfeasance, was a measure that made the recovery of damages excessively difficult, if not impossible, given that the action that was the subject matter of the claim for damages was that of the legislature. Under EC law, the only permissible fault requirement for the award of damages was that there had been non-compliance with EC law. The measure of damages awarded had to be commensurate with the nature of the loss and damage suffered by the plaintiff, due regard being had to the extent to which the plaintiff had shown due diligence in mitigating the extent of any loss. In this respect, the proper protection of EC rights militated against the exclusion of a right to recover damages for loss of profit. Note that the Court rejected the contention that the right to damages should be limited to losses occurring only after the ruling by a competent court that there had been a violation of EC law.

The matter returned to the domestic courts of the UK in *R* v *Secretary of State for Transport, ex parte Factortame Ltd and Others (No 5)* [1999] 3 WLR 1062, where the House of Lords held that breaches of EC law by the United Kingdom in implementing the Merchant Shipping Act 1988 were sufficiently serious to give rise to liability in damages. The Secretary of State had contended that there should be no liability in damages as the legislation had been introduced to deal with a serious economic problem, the UK had enjoyed a wide margin of appreciation as regards the appropriate measure to introduce, and because there should be no liability in damages where the breach of EC law was 'excusable'. Rejecting these contentions Lord Slynn observed that the prohibition of discrimination on grounds of nationality was not to be found in an ambiguous directive but was clearly stated in (what had been) art 7. The action adopted by the UK government, albeit in good faith, had been deliberate, not accidental, and had (as its inevitable consequence) the harming of the interests of Spanish fishermen. The transitional period for compliance had been very short, as UK law stood at the time there was no effective means of securing interim relief, and the UK government had pressed ahead with the legislation despite the strong opposition expressed by the European Commission. His Lordship concluded that, taking all these factors into account, there had been the deliberate adoption of legislation that was clearly discriminatory amounting to a manifest breach of treaty obligations. The breach was grave both intrinsically and in terms of the consequences for those affected. The 'domicile' requirement fell to be regarded in the same way as the nationality requirement and was thus also a serious breach of EC law.

Lord Hoffmann expressed the view that what was fatal to the UK government's case was the divergence between the rhetoric and the solution adopted to deal with the problem of 'quota-hopping'. The rhetoric presented the problem as one of UK fishermen being robbed of the opportunity to fish in their own waters by Spanish fishermen effectively poaching the catch. The legislative solution adopted actually concerned itself with the residence of those who owned shares in the companies operating the fishing vessels. Lord Hope, concurring, added the view that if damages were not recoverable in a case such as this it would be hard to envisage when they would ever be available.

It is doubtful whether any one of these matters is, taken by itself, decisive as regards the availability of damages. Much will depend on the facts of a particular case. Where, for example, there is a lack of clarity as regards the relevant EC law, particularly where the meaning attributed to a provision of EC law by the UK legislature is one shared by other Member States acting in good faith, it seems that damages would not be forthcoming; see further *R v HM Treasury ex parte British Telecommunications plc* [1996] 3 WLR 203. The view of the European Commission as to how a provision of EC law should operate will be highly persuasive, but not decisive of the matter. In cases of doubt a Member State ought to be guided by the Commission; see further *R v Ministry of Agriculture ex parte Headley Lomas (Ireland) Ltd* [1996] 3 WLR 787, where the United Kingdom ban on the export of live sheep to Spain, on the basis that methods used in Spanish slaughterhouses were not consistent with those required by Council Directive 74/577/EEC, was held to give rise to a right to damages because art 34 (quantitative restriction on imports) created individual rights, and the breach of that article had been serious (there was no evidence that the slaughterhouses used by applicants were breaching the Directive).

As to the availability of punitive or exemplary damages see *Bourgoin SA and Others v MAAF* [1986] QB 716. It is submitted that, unless a statute provides for punitive damages, only compensatory damages will be available. A breach of EC law by a Crown servant is not necessarily to be equated with misfeasance. As to what would be required to establish an action based upon the tort of misfeasance (and hence open up the possibility of punitive damages): see further *Three Rivers District Council v Bank of England (No 3)* [2000] 3 All ER 1.

Where a causal link cannot be established between the failure to implement Community law and financial loss on the part of the applicant, declaratory relief will be more appropriate: see *R v Secretary of State for Employment, ex parte Equal Opportunities Commission and Another* [1994] 2 WLR 409.

17

The European Community and the European Union II

17.1 EC law in the United Kingdom

17.2 EC law and United Kingdom sovereignty

17.3 Conclusion

17.1 EC law in the United Kingdom

The United Kingdom became a member of the European Communities with effect from 1 January 1973, by virtue of the Treaty of Accession 1972. Given the dualist nature of the United Kingdom's legal system it was necessary for the Treaty of Accession and the Community treaties to be incorporated into domestic law in order for them to have effect in the domestic courts. This was achieved by the European Communities Act 1972, as amended.

With the benefit of hindsight it might be said that what the politicians of the day, and most voters, thought that they were agreeing to was membership of an enlarged free trade area. It is clear that the true legal implications of membership were not grasped at the time, in particular the consequences for parliamentary sovereignty. The level playing field required for fair competition between manufacturers and suppliers in Member States brings with it many restraints that go beyond the prohibition of anti-competitive tariffs. The institutions of the European Union have turned their attentions to related matters such as conditions of working, equal opportunities, sex discrimination, pollution, etc. As will have been seen from Chapter 16, a central tenet of the European Union's philosophy is that EC law should apply to the same extent within each Member State. Inevitably, therefore, situations have arisen where the United Kingdom's domestic law has been found to be in conflict with the provision of EC law. Given the provisions of the European Communities Act 1972 (considered below), the courts have had to try and resolve these conflicts, constrained by the doctrine of parliamentary sovereignty on the one hand and the realities of EU membership on the other.

What the European Communities Act 1972 provides

Section 1 of the 1972 Act defines the Community treaties to which the Act relates and includes the treaties entered into by the Communities prior to 22 January 1972. Any subsequent treaties entered into by the Communities may be incorporated into United Kingdom law by Order in Council. Section 2(1) is arguably the most important provision of the Act in that it provides that:

> 'All such rights, powers, liabilities, obligations and restrictions from time to time created or arising by or under the treaties, and all such remedies and procedures from time to time provided for by or under the treaties, as in accordance with the treaties are without further enactment to be given legal effect or used in the United Kingdom shall be recognised and available in law, and be enforced, allowed and followed accordingly; and the expression enforceable Community right and similar expressions shall be read as referring to one to which this subsection applies.'

The effect of this subsection is that all the provisions of EC law which are, in accordance with EC law, intended to take direct effect in the United Kingdom, are given the force of law. This applies to EC law made both before and after the coming into force of the Act. Section 2(2) provides that where EC law requires legislative implementation in the United Kingdom, for example, directives, this may be achieved by means of delegated legislation.

Section 2(4) addresses the issue of conflict between domestic legislation and EC law by providing that:

> 'The provision that may be made under subsection (2) … includes, subject to Sch 2 to this Act, any such provision (of any such extent) as might be made by Act of Parliament, and any enactment passed or to be passed, other than one contained in this Part of this Act, shall be construed and have effect subject to the foregoing provisions of this section; but, except as may be provided by an Act passed after this Act, Sch 2 shall have effect in connection with the powers conferred by this and the following sections of this Act to make Orders in Council and regulations.'

The 'foregoing provisions' for these purposes include s2(1), which states that directly applicable EC law shall have effect in the United Kingdom. Therefore, s2(4) seems to amount to a statement that United Kingdom Acts of Parliament shall be construed and have effect subject to directly applicable EC law.

Section 3(1) provides that, for the purposes of all legal proceedings, any question as to the meaning or effect of any of the treaties or as to the validity, meaning or effect of any Community instrument, shall be treated as a question of law (and if not referred to the European Court of Justice) be for determination as such in accordance with the principles laid down by the European Court of Justice.

17.2 EC law and United Kingdom sovereignty

Despite Lord Denning's words in *Bulmer* v *Bollinger* [1974] Ch 401, to the effect that:

> '... when we come to matters with a European element the [T]reaty is like an incoming tide. It flows into the estuaries and up the rivers. It cannot be held back ...'

there are several possible interpretations of s2(4) European Communities Act 1972.

It could be seen as amounting to a statement that all United Kingdom legislation shall only take effect to the extent that it is consistent with EC law, however clearly it may appear from the United Kingdom legislation that it is intended to have effect notwithstanding any EC law to the contrary. It is clear both from the Treaty and from statements made by the European Court of Justice, that the Community view is that EC law should prevail over national law in all circumstances. The European Court of Justice, in *Costa* v *ENEL* [1964] CMLR 425, stated that accession to the European Communities has as a corollary the impossibility, for the Member State, to give preference to an unilateral and subsequent measure against a legal order accepted by them on a basis of reciprocity. In *Re Export Tax on Art Treasures (No 2)* [1972] CMLR 699 the European Court of Justice stated:

> 'The grant to the Community by the Member States of the rights and powers envisaged by the provisions of the Treaty implies in fact a definitive limitation of their sovereign powers over which no appeal to provisions of international law of any kind whatever can prevail.'

This makes it clear that, as far as the European Court of Justice is concerned, any United Kingdom constitutional law doctrine of the legislative sovereignty of Parliament is irrelevant.

The approach of the European Court of Justice runs contrary to the traditional doctrine of the sovereignty of Parliament as enunciated in *Vauxhall Estates Ltd* v *Liverpool Corporation* [1932] 1 KB 733 and *Ellen Street Estates* v *Minister of Health* [1934] 1 KB 590. The strict traditionalist, who insists on the retention of the doctrine of implied repeal as set out in *Ellen Street Estates*, would refuse to give full effect to s2(4), insisting that later United Kingdom legislation always, by implication, repeals earlier legislative provision with which it is inconsistent.

A third approach to s2(4) is to treat it as amounting to a rule of interpretation that there shall be a presumption that the United Kingdom Parliament, in passing legislation, intends to legislate consistently with EC law. This approach differs from the first since it allows that if the United Kingdom Parliament were to make it clear in an Act that it intended to legislate contrary to EC law, or that it intended the legislation to take effect notwithstanding any provision of EC law to the contrary, then the United Kingdom legislation would prevail to the extent that it was in conflict with EC law. This is the approach that was favoured by the Court of Appeal in *Macarthys Ltd* v *Wendy Smith* [1979] 3 All ER 325. A man had been employed as a stockroom keeper at £60 per week. Subsequently a woman was employed in this position at £50 per week. She took the matter to an industrial tribunal on the grounds that this was contrary to law. Three main questions arose: first, was this arrangement contrary to the Equal Pay Act 1970 as amended by the Sex Discrimination Act 1975; second, if it was not, was it contrary to art 119 of the Treaty of Rome (now art 141 EC Treaty) which provides: 'Each Member State shall ... ensure and ... maintain the application of the principle that men and women should receive equal pay for equal work'; third, in the event of a conflict between the United Kingdom legislation and art 119 (now art 141) EC Treaty, which should prevail in the United Kingdom courts? The employment appeal tribunal held that the 1970 Act provided Ms Smith with the right to equal pay where she had performed identical duties in succession to a male employee. The employers appealed to the Court of Appeal. It was held (per Lawton and Cumming Bruce LJJ) that the Equal Pay Act 1970, as amended by the Sex Discrimination Act 1975, only required equal pay for men and women employed in like work contemporaneously, and thus afforded no protection for the female plaintiff in the present case. There was uncertainty, however, as to whether or not art 119 covered the situation where a woman was employed on certain work that had previously been performed by a man. Since the proper interpretation of art 119 was uncertain, the matter was referred to the European Court of Justice under art 177 (now art 234 EC Treaty) for a preliminary ruling.

It is interesting to note the views that were expressed by Lord Denning MR regarding the primacy of EC law:

'It is unnecessary, however, for these courts to wait until all that procedure has been gone through. Under s2(1) and (4) of the European Communities Act 1972 the principles laid down in the Treaty are without further enactment to be given legal effect in the United Kingdom; and have priority over any enactment passed or to be passed by our Parliament. So we are entitled and I think bound to look at art 119 [now art 141 EC Treaty] ... because it is directly applicable here; and also any directive which is directly applicable here: see *Van Duyn* v *Home Office (No 2)*. We should, I think, look to see what those provisions require about equal pay for men and women. Then we should look at our own legislation on the point, giving it, of course, full faith and credit, assuming that it does fully comply with the obligation under the Treaty. In construing our statute, we are entitled to look to the Treaty as an aid to its construction, but not only as an aid but as an overriding force. If on close investigation it should appear that our legislation is deficient or is inconsistent with [EC law] by some oversight of our draftsmen then it is our bounden duty to give priority to [EC law]. Such is the result of s2(1) and (4) of the European Communities Act 1972 ... I pause here, however, to make one observation on a constitutional point. Thus far I have assumed that our Parliament, whenever it passes legislation, intends to fulfil its obligations under the Treaty. If the time should come when our Parliament deliberately passes an Act with the intention of repudiating the Treaty or any provision in it or intentionally of acting inconsistently with it and says so in express terms then I should have thought that it would be the duty of our courts to follow the statute of our Parliament. I do not however envisage any such situation.'

Thus Lord Denning put forward the view that if Parliament in an Act stated an express intention to legislate contrary to EC law or notwithstanding EC law, then in that one situation the United Kingdom court would give preference to the United Kingdom legislation over the EC law. The other members of the Court expressed the same view, Lawton LJ saying:

'... I can see nothing in this case which infringes the sovereignty of Parliament ... Parliament by its own act in the exercise of its sovereign powers has enacted and followed in the United Kingdom (s1(1) European Communities Act 1972) and that any enactment passed or to be passed ... shall be construed and have effect subject to (s2 in accordance with s2(4) of the Act). Parliament's recognition of [EC law] and the jurisdiction of the European Court of Justice by one enactment can be withdrawn by another. There is nothing in the Equal Pay Act 1970 as amended by the Sex Discrimination Act 1975, to indicate that Parliament intended to amend the European Communities Act 1972, or to limit its application ...'

On the reference under art 177 (now art 234), the European Court of Justice ruled that art 119 (now art 141) did not require contemporaneous employment (*Macarthys Ltd* v *Smith* [1980] ECR 1275), and the case was referred back to the Court of Appeal for the implementation of this interpretation: *Macarthys Ltd* v *Smith* [1981] QB 180. Although his comments were obiter Lord Denning took the opportunity afforded by the second hearing to state the following view:

'Art 119 [now art 141 EC Treaty] now takes priority over our English statute ... [EC law] is now part of our law; and, whenever there is any inconsistency, [EC law] has priority. It is not supplanting English law. It is part of our law which overrides any other part which is inconsistent with it.'

This 'rule of construction' approach, whereby domestic law is always interpreted in a manner that ensures its compliance with EC law, amounts to a retention of the doctrine of express repeal of earlier law by later legislation, but involves the abandonment of the doctrine of implied repeal as far as EC law is concerned. In this approach it is neither consistent with the traditional United Kingdom doctrine of the sovereignty of Parliament, nor with the Community doctrine of the supremacy of EC law over national law.

The matter was considered further by the House of Lords in *Garland* v *British Rail Engineering Ltd* [1983] 2 AC 751. The appellant was a female employee of the respondent company. Employees enjoyed (ex gratia) free travel on British Rail. Upon retirement male employees continued to enjoy this benefit for themselves and their families. In the case of retiring female employees, the benefit did not extend to their families. The appellant contended that this discrimination was not permitted by s6(4) of the Sex Discrimination Act 1964, and was in breach of art 119 (now art 141) EC Treaty. The complaint was dismissed by an industrial tribunal, allowed on appeal to the employment appeal tribunal, and the respondent employers appealed successfully to the Court of Appeal. On appeal to the House of Lords, the issue was referred to the European Court of Justice, which held that the discrimination was in breach of art 119 (now art 141) EC Treaty, which was directly applicable where a domestic court found such discrimination to exist. On reference back to the House of Lords the decision of the employment appeal tribunal was restored. Lord Diplock observed that:

'... it is a principle of construction of United Kingdom statutes, now too well established to call for citation of authority, that the words of a statute passed after the Treaty has been signed and dealing with the subject matter of the international obligation of the United Kingdom, are to be construed, if they are reasonably capable of bearing such a meaning, as intended to carry out the obligation, and not to be inconsistent with it. A fortiori is this the case where the Treaty obligation arises under one of the Community treaties to which s2 of the European Communities Act 1972 applies ...'

To some extent Lord Diplock side-stepped the key question of when, if ever, domestic law would be allowed to prevail where it was in conflict with EC law. He expressed the view that:

'The instant appeal does not present an appropriate occasion to consider whether, having regard to the express direction as to the construction of enactments to be passed which is contained in s2(4), anything short of an express positive statement in an Act of Parliament passed after 1 January 1973, that a particular provision is intended to be made in breach of an obligation assumed by the United Kingdom under a Community treaty, would justify a [domestic] court in construing that provision in a manner inconsistent with a Community treaty obligation of the United Kingdom, however wide a departure from the prima facie meaning of the language of the provision might be needed in order to achieve consistency.'

As will have been seen in Chapter 16, the growing influence of the doctrine of indirect effect means that domestic courts are now expected to interpret domestic law to achieve conformity with EC law, regardless of whether the measure in question is directly applicable or of direct effect: see again *Von Colson* v *Land Nordrhein-Westfalen* [1984] ECR 1891; *Harz* v *Deutsche Tradex GmbH* [1984] ECR 1921; and *Marleasing SA* v *La Comercial Internacional de Alimentacion SA* [1992] 1 CMLR 305. These decisions have had some influence on the courts of the United Kingdom, as evidenced by their willingness to interpret domestic legislation to ensure compliance with directives, even if this means straining the natural language of the domestic law: see further *Pickstone* v *Freemans plc* [1989] 1 AC 66; *Lister* v *Forth Dry Dock & Engineering Co Ltd* [1990] 1 AC 546; and *Webb* v *EMO Air Cargo Ltd (UK) (No 2)* [1995] 1 WLR 1454. Where the United Kingdom courts have drawn the line is in refusing to give retrospective effect to domestic law enacted to give effect to a directive, in the absence of clear evidence that Parliament intended the domestic law to operate retrospectively: see *Duke* v *GEC Reliance Ltd* [1988] 1 All ER 626.

A situation where there is an irreconcilable conflict between domestic law and EC law, in the sense that there has been a deliberate attempt by the United Kingdom legislature to repudiate its international obligations under EC law, may seem a remote possibility, but where a conflict arises that cannot be resolved by means of an 'elastic' approach to the interpretation of domestic law to ensure compliance, the United Kingdom courts will have little option but to refer the matter to the European Court of Justice under art 234 EC Treaty. Pending the consideration of the reference by the European Court of Justice, questions arise as to the legal position of those litigants who claim that their rights under EC law are being infringed by the courts giving effect to domestic law. If domestic law is applied until the European Court of Justice rules that it is in conflict with the proper application of EC law, the litigant may have suffered financial loss. If such loss is to be prevented, the operation of the domestic law will have to be suspended by the domestic court pending the European Court of Justice's ruling.

Such a situation arose in *R* v *Secretary of State for Transport, ex parte Factortame (No 2)* [1990] 3 WLR 818. Fishing quotas were introduced by the EC to prevent overfishing. The United Kingdom Parliament enacted the Merchant Shipping Act 1988 (Pt II) to protect British fishing interests by restricting the number of vessels whose catch could be counted against the British quota. The Secretary of State issued regulations under the Act that required any vessel wishing to fish as part of the British fleet to be registered under the 1988 Act. Registration was contingent upon a vessel's owner being a British citizen or domiciled in Britain. In the case of companies, the shareholders would have to meet these requirements. The applicants were British-registered companies operating fishing vessels in British waters. These companies now found it impossible to obtain registration because their shareholders and directors were Spanish. The applicants contended that the regulations effectively prevented them from exercising their rights under EC law to fish as part of the British fleet. The Secretary of State contended that EC law did not prevent the United Kingdom from introducing domestic legislation determining which companies where 'British nationals' and which were not.

The applicants sought judicial review of the minister's decision that their registration should cease; the minister's determination that they were no longer 'British' ships; and the relevant parts of the Act and regulations which would have the effect of preventing them from fishing. In terms of remedies the applicants sought a declaration that the minister's decision should not take effect because of its inconsistency with EC law; an order of prohibition to prevent the minister from regarding the ships as de-registered; damages under s35 of the Supreme Court Act 1981; and an interim injunction suspending the operation of the legislation pending the ruling of the European Court of Justice.

As regards the interpretation of EC law, the Divisional Court requested a preliminary ruling under art 234 (formerly art 177) so that the questions relating to the applicant's rights could be resolved. Pending that ruling, the Court granted the applicants interim relief in the form of an injunction to suspend the operation of the legislation by restraining the minister from enforcing it, thus enabling the applicants to continue fishing. The Secretary of State sought to challenge the order for interim relief, which was set aside by the Court of Appeal. On appeal the House of Lords held that domestic courts had no power to grant interim relief to prevent the operation of a statute passed by Parliament, unless it could be shown that there was some overriding principle of EC law which provided that Member States must provide such relief. The question of whether such a principle existed was referred to the European Court of Justice under art 234 EC Treaty.

In responding to the House of Lords' reference, the European Court of Justice held that EC law required the courts of Member States to give effect to the directly enforceable provision of EC law, such EC laws rendering any conflicting national law inapplicable. A court that would grant interim relief, but for a rule of domestic law, should set aside that rule of domestic law in favour of observing EC law. On the reference back, the House of Lords held that, in determining whether interim relief by way of an injunction should be granted, the determining factor should not be the availability of damages as a remedy, but the balance of convenience, taking into account the importance of upholding duly enacted laws. Damages are not available against a public body exercising its powers in good faith. The court should not restrain a public authority from enforcing an apparently valid law unless it is satisfied, having regard to all the circumstances, that the challenge to the validity of the law is prima facie so firmly based as to justify so exceptional a course being taken. On the significance of this litigation, Lord Bridge observed (at p857):

> 'Some public comments on the decision of the European Court of Justice, affirming the jurisdiction of the courts of Member States to override national legislation if necessary to enable interim relief to be granted in protection of rights under [EC law], have suggested that this was a novel and dangerous invasion by a Community institution of the sovereignty of the United Kingdom Parliament. But such comments are based on a misconception. If the supremacy within the European Community of [EC law] over the national law of Member States was not always inherent in the EEC Treaty (Cmnd 5179–11) it was certainly well established in the jurisprudence of the European Court of Justice long before the United Kingdom joined the Community. Thus, whatever limitation of its sovereignty Parliament accepted when it enacted the European Communities Act 1972 was entirely voluntary. Under the terms of the Act of 1972 it has always been clear that it was the duty of a United Kingdom court, when delivering final judgment, to override any rule of national law found to be in conflict with any directly enforceable rule of [EC law]. Similarly, when decisions of the European Court of Justice have exposed areas of United Kingdom statute law which failed to implement Council directives, Parliament has always loyally accepted the obligation to make appropriate and prompt amendments. Thus there is nothing in any way novel in according supremacy to rules of [EC law] in those areas to which they apply and to insist that, in the protection of rights under [EC law], national courts must not be inhibited by rules of national law from granting interim relief in appropriate cases is no more than a logical recognition of that supremacy.'

The limits of applicability

It should be obvious from the foregoing that domestic courts will only have to apply EC law in the form of treaty provisions, regulations or directives where it is relevant to the issue that is the subject of the litigation. The more subtle question of whether the fundamental principles of EC law, such a proportionality, equal treatment and non-discrimination are of general application in domestic law was considered by the Divisional Court in *R* v *MAFF, ex parte First City Trading Ltd and Others* [1997] 1 CMLR 250. Following the ban placed on the export of British beef by the European Commission, the Ministry of Agriculture, Fisheries and Food (MAFF) had introduced a scheme of financial aid – the Slaughtering Industry (Emergency Aid) Scheme 1996 – to assist exporters who had been adversely affected. The applicants sought, unsuccessfully, to challenge the legality of the scheme on the basis that it discriminated against those exporters who lacked their own slaughtering and cutting up facilities, and was thus in breach of fundamental principles of EC law, namely the principles of equal treatment and non-discrimination. In dismissing the application, Laws J observed that the fundamental principles of EC law referred to had been developed by the European Court of Justice in the course of deciding cases raising issues regarding the interpretation of the key Community treaties. Hence they were only relevant where an issue of EC law was under consideration. EC law might be under consideration where a Member State took action required by EC law, or acted under domestic law in an area that fell within the scope of the EC law. The scheme in question, however, had not been implemented at the behest of the European Community and the United Kingdom government had not had to seek the permission of the European Community prior to its implementation. The fact that the scheme had been introduced in response to action taken by the European Commission was irrelevant. Hence the principles evolved through the case law of the European Court of Justice were not binding upon a domestic court assessing the legality of the scheme.

17.3 Conclusion

The United Kingdom Parliament appears to have forfeited its sovereignty by enacting the European Communities Act 1972, which provides for the direct applicability of EC law in the United Kingdom, and the enforceability of rights arising under EC law before United Kingdom courts. It may be, however, that this apparent forfeiture of sovereignty is, in reality, limited and partial. The European Communities Act 1972 is not entrenched. Parliament can, in theory, repeal the Act at any time and thus regain its full supremacy as a sovereign legislature. With the passage of time, however, this regaining of sovereignty becomes more theoretical and less practical. The political realities of the situation will dictate that the greater the degree of integration in terms of economic, monetary and commercial union, the more difficult it will be for any United Kingdom government to extricate itself from the European Union. As successive generations grow up not having known anything of life prior to membership, it may be unlikely that any prospective United

Kingdom government would receive a mandate for withdrawal. A further move towards integration is seen in the proposals for a European Constitution.

The view expressed by Hoffmann J in *Stoke-on-Trent City Council* v *B & Q plc* [1991] 2 WLR 42 displays increasing realism on the part of the judiciary. His Lordship stated (at p45):

'The EEC Treaty is the supreme law of this country, taking precedence over Acts of Parliament. Our entry into the European Economic Community meant that (subject to our undoubted but probably theoretical right to withdraw from the Community altogether) Parliament surrendered its sovereign right to legislate contrary to the provisions of the Treaty on matters of social and economic policy which it regulated.'

18

The European Convention on Human Rights

18.1 Introduction: the political background

18.2 The place of the ECHR in English law

18.3 The Human Rights Act 1998: the rights protected

18.4 Pursuing a Human Rights Act claim before the domestic courts

18.5 Taking a case to Strasbourg

18.6 The European Convention on Human Rights and EC law

18.1 Introduction: the political background

Although the Bill of Rights 1689 has been a feature of the British constitutional landscape for over 300 years, it would be quite inappropriate to contend that it provides anything like the comprehensive protection for basic individual rights and freedoms that one normally associates with a modern Bill of Rights. The British constitution has traditionally looked to the common law to ensure that individual rights are recognised and upheld, but this has operated in an essentially negative fashion. Hence citizens have been entitled to do as they please, subject to the restrictions imposed by common law and statute, rather than being able to point to positive legal rights to things such as freedom of expression, association or privacy.

While the protection of fundamental rights and freedoms on the international plane has proved a slow and difficult process (witness the implementation of the Universal Declaration of Human Rights since 1948), the protection of human rights on the regional level among groups of states sharing common ideals and standards has been more effective. One of the most highly regarded of the regional conventions for the protection of human rights is the European Convention on Human Rights (hereinafter the ECHR). The ECHR is very much a product of the determination amongst the Allies in the immediate post-war years to ensure that the wide spread atrocities, witnessed during the Second World War, and the concomitant violations of human rights should not be repeated in mainland Europe. There was a realisation that the way in which individual States treated their citizens

336

was no longer a purely domestic matter. The evidence was all too clear that any State that started out by denying the basic rights of its own citizens would, in all likelihood, be only too willing to treat inhabitants of neighbouring States in a like fashion if the opportunity arose. The essential concept underpinning the ECHR is that signatory States should police each other and, where applicable, the nationals of signatory States should be able to draw attention to violations.

The United Kingdom was one of the original signatories of the ECHR, on 4 November 1950, and of its First Protocol on 8 March 1952. The instruments of ratification of the ECHR and its First Protocol were deposited with the Secretary-General of the Council of Europe on 8 March 1951 and 3 November 1952, respectively. The ECHR entered into force on 3 September 1953. On 23 October 1953 a declaration was made under art 63(1) extending the ECHR's force to certain territories for whose international relations the United Kingdom was responsible. On 14 January 1966, the United Kingdom recognised the competence of the European Commission on Human Rights (hereinafter 'the Commission') to receive individual applications, and recognised the compulsory jurisdiction of the European Court of Human Rights. With the enactment of the Human Rights Act 1998 those rights have now been 'brought home' with the effect that, since 2 October 2000, certain Convention provisions have direct effect as part of the domestic law of the United Kingdom (see section 18.4 below).

18.2 The place of the ECHR in English law

Historically the approach of United Kingdom governments and courts has, to a large extent, been that the incorporation of the ECHR was unnecessary, given the track record of the United Kingdom in respecting human rights, and the ability of the common law to respond to changing circumstances. As indicated above, the Human Rights Act 1998 marks a significant departure from this approach by placing positively expressed rights firmly in the context of domestic law of the United Kingdom. The enactment of the 1998 Act was necessary because the United Kingdom legal system is dualist in nature. Whilst the Crown has power to enter into treaty obligations on the international plane, such treaties can only resound in domestic law if incorporated by an Act of Parliament. Hence, although the ECHR and its First Protocol have (subject to derogations and reservations) been signed and ratified by United Kingdom governments, they could not become part of domestic law without first being enacted in an Act of Parliament. This mirrors the position regarding the Treaty of Rome (as it was then known) and the European Communities Act 1972, which incorporated that Treaty into domestic law. By contrast, many other signatory states have monist legal systems, whereby the ECHR became part of their domestic law once ratified.

Whilst the incorporation of the ECHR is doubtless of huge totemic significance, one should not lose sight of the basic fact that the Human Rights Act 1998 does not create any new substantive rights. The real change effected by the 1998 Act is procedural – litigants are now allowed to take ECHR points in argument before domestic courts, rather than having to opt for the rather daunting prospect of taking a case to Strasbourg: see further section 18.5.

The pre-incorporation era

To understand the impact of the Human Rights Act 1998 on the United Kingdom constitution it is instructive to review the position as it was in the pre-incorporation era, not least because it may prove to be the case that the courts are not as willing to accede to arguments based on the ECHR as might be assumed. The courts have always been willing to use the ECHR to resolve ambiguities in domestic legislation, on the basis that it was presumed that Parliament would not have legislated in contravention of those obligations without clearly flagging that fact. What the United Kingdom courts refused to do was to recognise rights created by the ECHR where no such corresponding right existed in domestic law.

For example, in *Uppal* v *Home Office* (1980) 3 EHRR 391, the applicants, illegal immigrants, applied for declarations that they should not be deported from the United Kingdom until the European Commission on Human Rights had determined whether deportation would contravene their right to respect for family life under art 8 of the ECHR, and argued that deportation would hinder the effective exercise of the right of individual petition. In his judgment, Sir Robert Megarry doubted the validity of this argument; but in any event held that obligations in international law which were not enforceable as part of English law could not be the subject of declaratory judgments or orders. Subsequently, when considering the legality of telephone tapping in *Malone* v *Metropolitan Police Commissioner* [1979] Ch 344, he reaffirmed his decision in *Uppal* after full argument on the point.

Whilst Lord Denning MR in *R* v *Home Secretary, ex parte Bhajan Singh* [1976] QB 198, observed that the executive should have regard to the ECHR in exercising its discretion because it was, in his view, only a statement of the principles of fair dealing, the House of Lords made it clear in *R* v *Secretary of State for the Home Department, ex parte Brind* [1991] 2 WLR 588, that public bodies exercising discretion were not bound to take into account the terms of the ECHR as a precondition of acting intra vires. The House of Lords recognised that to have accepted such a contention would have amounted to the incorporation of the ECHR via the 'back door'. This was true whether the power in question was one derived from statute, or the prerogative: see *R* v *Secretary of State for the Home Department, ex parte Ahmed and Others* [1998] INLR 570.

Elsewhere the courts tended to adopt the view that the common law and the ECHR provided, in any event, the same rights and freedoms. For example, in holding that a local authority could not use the law of defamation against a newspaper that had been critical of its conduct in certain financial matters, the House of Lords appeared to regard any argument based on art 10 of the ECHR as redundant. Whilst Balcombe LJ, in the Court of Appeal, felt that domestic law was uncertain on the point and observed that 'where the law is uncertain, it must be right for the court to approach the issue before it with a predilection to ensure that our law should not involve a breach of art 10', Lord Keith expressed the view that he had reached his conclusion based on the common law of England, adding only that it was 'consistent with obligations assumed by the Crown under the Treaty in this particular field': see *Derbyshire County Council* v *Times Newspapers Ltd and Others* [1993] 2 WLR 449.

A more positive approach to reliance on the ECHR was expressed in *Rantzen* v *Mirror Group Newspapers (1986) Ltd* [1993] 3 WLR 953, where the Court of Appeal held that to allow juries to award unlimited amounts of damages to successful plaintiffs in defamation actions could amount to a breach of art 10, in the sense that as a restriction on free speech the threatened sanction of a large award of damages had to be shown to be necessary in a democratic society, and 'prescribed by law'. Like the House of Lords in the *Derbyshire County Council* case the Court expressed the view that art 10 reflected the rules of the common law in relation to freedom of expression.

The Human Rights Act 1998: the debate over incorporation

The 20-year period prior to the enactment of the Human Rights Act 1998 saw growing support for the notion that the United Kingdom should 'bring human rights home' by incorporating the ECHR into domestic law. Significantly, the Labour Party, which won the May 1997 general election with a huge majority, included a commitment to incorporating the ECHR at the earliest opportunity as part of its manifesto.

In observance of this promise, the Human Rights Bill was duly introduced into the House of Lords in November 1997, at the same time as the publication of the White Paper *Rights Brought Home: The Human Rights Bill* (Cmnd 3782).

Various arguments were advanced in favour of incorporation. Essentially they stressed the following; that it was better for the United Kingdom's reputation (as a nation that was taking human rights seriously) for human rights issues to be determined by domestic courts; that the provision of domestic remedies would provide litigants with cheaper and speedier legal redress; and that was illogical for the United Kingdom to agree to protect various rights in an international treaty but not extend that protection via incorporation of those rights into its domestic law.

As the White Paper stated:

> 'It is plainly unsatisfactory that someone should be the victim of a breach of the Convention standards by the State yet be unable to bring any case at all in the British courts, simply because British law does not recognise the right in the same terms as one contained in the Convention.' (at para 1.16)

Further, there was the view, expressed by Lord Irvine LC (introducing the Human

Rights Bill in the House of Lords) that an unwritten constitution could not provide the citizen with adequate protection from abuses of state power that infringe human rights.

The proposals for incorporation were, at least superficially, seductive, particularly to those who equated the provision of rights with some form of political empowerment. They marked a shift from rights being associated with freedoms, towards rights being seen as entitlements given by the state. On the other hand, traditionalists, such as Lord Donaldson, argued that incorporation was 'constitutionally unacceptable' and that Parliament's right to govern should not be curtailed by Strasbourg. Other objections raised were that: the ECHR was out of keeping with the traditional style of domestic legislation; it represented an imported written constitution, whereas it would be preferable for the United Kingdom to be devising its own; it was undemocratic, because it sought to transfer power from the elected legislature to the courts; and that if enacted as domestic law, it could cause an unnecessary increase in litigation. Lord Mackay, speaking during a two-day debate on the constitution in the House of Lords in July 1996, expressed the view that the common law offered sufficient protection, and warned of judges being dragged into political controversy. The point has been made by many commentators that judges declaring domestic legislation to be incompatible with the ECHR (see further section 18.4) would effectively be ordering the legislature to act, a complete reversal of the doctrines of the separation of powers and parliamentary sovereignty.

The statistics concerning cases brought against the United Kingdom were frequently relied upon to support the contention that the human rights of United Kingdom citizens were not sufficiently safeguarded by United Kingdom law, and that justice could only be obtained by resort to Strasbourg, or by incorporation of the ECHR into domestic law. It is true that, in the period from 1990–1995, the United Kingdom was the subject of over 3,000 claims lodged by individuals with the Commission, of which approximately 600 were declared admissible, and that the United Kingdom has lost over 50 cases at Strasbourg. Few signatory States, other than Turkey and Italy, have suffered a higher rate of successful challenge. Against this some argued that many of the cases involved what some might regard as peripheral human rights issues, as opposed to dealing with matters of life and death, and many cases turned upon issues in relation to which perfectly reasonable persons could agree to differ without either forfeiting the right to be described as reasonable. Furthermore, the frequency with which a signatory state was cited as a respondent before the Court at Strasbourg did not necessarily have any correlation with its having incorporated the ECHR, as the track records of Turkey and Italy indicated.

18.3 The Human Rights Act 1998: the rights protected

The Human Rights Act 1998 received Royal Assent in early November 1998. Sections 18, 20 and 21(5) came into effect on enactment, with the remaining sections coming into effect on 2 October 2000. The Act seeks to give effect to the European Convention on Human Rights in the domestic law of the United Kingdom, but the actual Convention rights to be incorporated are stated in s1 as being arts 2–12 and 14 of the Convention, arts 1–3 of the First Protocol, and arts 1 and 2 of the Sixth Protocol, as read with arts 16–18 of the Convention. This restricted definition of Convention rights must also be read in the light of the derogations and reservations claimed by the United Kingdom in respect of art 5(3) and art 2 of the First Protocol.

The rights protected under the ECHR

A detailed examination of the working of the ECHR and its jurisprudence is beyond the scope of a text of this nature, but what follows is a summary of the main provisions of the ECHR with illustrative case law reflecting the impact of the ECHR on domestic law.

Article 2: right to life

Article 2 provides as follows:

> '(1) Everyone's right to life shall be protected by law. No one shall be deprived of his life intentionally save in the execution of a sentence of a court following his conviction of a crime for which this penalty is provided by law.
> (2) Deprivation of life shall not be regarded as inflicted in contravention of this article when it results from the use of force which is no more than absolutely necessary:
> (a) in defence of any person from unlawful violence;
> (b) in order to effect a lawful arrest or to prevent the escape of a person lawfully detained;
> (c) in action lawfully taken for the purpose of quelling a riot or insurrection.'

The scope of this article was considered in *McCann and Others* v *United Kingdom* Case No 17/1994/464/545 (1995) 21 EHRR 97. The applicants were parents of IRA terrorists who had been killed by members of the SAS in Gibraltar in March 1988. The soldiers carrying out the killings did so in the belief that such action was necessary to prevent the suspects from remotely detonating a car bomb, with subsequent loss of life on a large scale. The applicants alleged that the killings amounted to a violation of art 2. The Commission ruled, by 11 votes to six, that the United Kingdom had not breached the ECHR but the European Court of Human Rights viewed the matter differently. Whilst holding, by ten votes to nine, that the actions of the SAS soldiers, given the information on which they acted, did not in themselves amount to a violation of art 2, the Court held that the lack of care on the part of the authorities regarding the execution of the control operation, led to the conclusion that the force used had been in excess of what was absolutely necessary in order to defend others from unlawful violence. In particular, the majority of the Court took the view that the suspects could have been detained upon entering Gibraltar, and that the authorities unjustifiably assumed that the intelligence available was correct. Hence the conditions set forth in art 2(2) were not met. Despite its finding against the United Kingdom, the Court declined to award any monetary compensation.

One area where art 2 may become significant is in relation to the NHS's treatment of patients with life-threatening conditions, especially where health authorities make questionable decisions regarding the allocation of resources, such as the rationing of health care by reference to age, life-style or even postcode. The applicant may be able to contend that the denial of treatment is inconsistent with the right to life: see further *D* v *United Kingdom* (1997) 24 EHRR 423.

Article 3: prohibition of torture

Article 3 provides that 'No one shall be subjected to torture or to inhuman or degrading treatment or punishment'.

The landmark decision involving the United Kingdom regarding art 3 was *Ireland* v *United Kingdom* (1978) 2 EHRR 25, concerning the interrogation techniques employed by security forces operating in Northern Ireland, where the European Court of Human Rights found that individuals had been subjected to inhuman treatment by members of the armed forces. It was also successfully invoked against the United Kingdom so as to prevent deportation, following refusal of a request for political asylum, in *Chahal* v *United Kingdom* (1996) 23 EHRR 413. The European Court of Human Rights emphasised that the prohibition of torture under art 3 of the Convention was absolute. Given that there was compelling evidence that, if deported, the applicant would be mistreated by certain elements in the Indian security forces, the refusal of asylum would amount to a breach of art 3, notwithstanding the national security issues put forward by the United Kingdom.

In *D* v *United Kingdom* (1997) 24 EHRR 423, the applicant, a native of St Kitts, was a drugs courier who had been detained whilst trying to enter the United Kingdom in possession of £120,000 worth of cocaine. He was subsequently convicted of drugs offences and imprisoned for six years. One year into his sentence the applicant was diagnosed as being HIV positive and began a course of treatment on the NHS. His condition continued to deteriorate and a few days before he was due to be released on licence the immigration authorities ordered his removal to St Kitts. The applicant unsuccessfully sought judicial review of this decision. The Court of Appeal noted that, as the applicant's case was, technically, one of seeking leave to enter, rather than remain in, the United Kingdom, the immigration authorities were not bound to take into account the government guidelines on the treatment of an applicant suffering from AIDS. The Commission found that his removal to St Kitts would amount to inhuman and degrading treatment contrary to art 3 of the ECHR, a decision upheld on referral to the Court. The protection offered by art 3 applied notwithstanding that the applicant had been convicted of a serious criminal offence which itself created grave social dangers. Whether or not a violation of art 3 would occur was not to be decided merely by reference to the actions of a third party (ie the actions of those who might provide some help and support in St Kitts). The Court looked at the effect of the applicant's removal from the United Kingdom. There was no way in which the care available in St Kitts could match that being provided to the applicant in the United Kingdom. The applicant had reached a stage in his illness where the removal of care would have catastrophic personal consequences for him, and the real possibility of his dying in the most distressing circumstances created the risk of inhuman and degrading treatment that art 3 was designed to prohibit.

Physical chastisement of children by parents and guardians was also declared to be a violation of art 3 in *A* v *United Kingdom* Case No 100/1997/884/1096 (1998) The Times 1 October. The applicant's stepfather, who regularly beat him with a stick, had been acquitted on charges of causing actual bodily harm after raising the common law defence of lawful chastisement.

The European Court of Human Rights in (unanimously) holding that there had been a violation of art 3 concluded that the ill treatment attained the minimum level of severity required for it to fall within art 3. In reaching its decision, the Court had regard to the circumstances of the case, including the nature of the punishment, its duration, the age and health of the victim and its effect on the mental health of the victim. Although the ECHR created obligations for Member States, not private individuals, the court reiterated its view that the State was required to ensure that all those within its jurisdiction enjoyed the rights protected by the ECHR. In particular the State was required to ensure that these rights were secured for vulnerable groups such as children. The existing state of English criminal law, which permitted a defence in law of reasonable chastisement, did not provide adequate protection for children.

Article 4: prohibition of slavery and forced labour

Article 4 provides that 'No one shall be held in slavery or servitude' and that 'No one shall be required to perform forced or compulsory labour'. For these purposes the term 'forced or compulsory labour' does not include:

'(a) any work required to be done in the ordinary course of detention imposed according to the provisions of art 5 of this Convention or during conditional release from such detention;
(b) any service of a military character or, in the case of conscientious objectors in countries where they are recognised, service exacted instead of compulsory military service;
(c) any service exacted in case of an emergency or calamity threatening the life or well-being of the community;
(d) any work or service which forms part of normal civic obligations.'

Article 5: right to liberty and security

Article 5 seeks to ensure that the deprivation of liberty should only occur where sanctioned by law and following the correct procedure. It provides thus:

'(1) Everyone has the right to liberty and security of person. No one shall be deprived of his liberty save in the following cases and in accordance with a procedure prescribed by law:

(a) the lawful detention of a person after conviction by a competent court;

(b) the lawful arrest or detention of a person for non-compliance with the lawful order of a court or in order to secure the fulfilment of any obligation prescribed by law;

(c) the lawful arrest or detention of a person effected for the purpose of bringing him before the competent legal authority on reasonable suspicion of having committed an offence or when it is reasonably considered necessary to prevent his committing an offence or fleeing after having done so;

(d) the detention of a minor by lawful order for the purpose of educational supervision or his lawful detention for the purpose of bringing him before the competent legal authority;

(e) the lawful detention of persons for the prevention of the spreading of infectious diseases, of persons of unsound mind, alcoholics or drug addicts or vagrants;

(f) the lawful arrest or detention of a person to prevent his effecting an unauthorised entry into the country or of a person against whom action is being taken with a view to deportation or extradition.'

Hence in *Johnson* v *United Kingdom* Case No 19/1996/738/937 (1997) The Times 4 December the absence of safeguards, to ensure that the continued detention of a patient at a mental hospital was still required, was held to be a violation of art 5(1) where it resulted in the applicant's release being unnecessarily delayed. Further, in *Benham* v *United Kingdom* (1995) The Independent 8 February, the applicant, who had been summonsed in respect of his failure to pay his community charge, was found guilty and ordered to serve 30 days in prison, even though he had no means to pay, had no assets, and was not entitled to receive income support. The European Court of Human Rights held that the failure by the justices to conduct an adequate inquiry as to why the applicant had not paid his community charge prior to ordering his detention amounted to a denial of the right to liberty contrary to art 5.

The wording of art 5 suggests that obscurely or vaguely worded criminal provisions will be in breach of the ECHR because they do not satisfy the requirement that the deprivation of liberty should be 'prescribed by law'. This contention was tested in *Steel and Others* v *United Kingdom* (1998) 5 BHRC 339 in respect of the common law power of a police constable to arrest and detain in respect of alleged breaches of the peace (breach of the peace being treated as an offence for these purposes). The European Court of Human Rights held that where a defendant's actions clearly gave rise to a breach of the peace, or created an obvious possibility that a breach of the peace might occur, the common law was sufficiently clear so as not to amount to a breach of art 5. Where, however, powers to arrest for breach of the peace were used against peaceful demonstrators, a violation of art 5 would occur, there being no grounds to justify the use of the power.

Further safeguards provided under art 5 are that: 'Everyone who is arrested shall be informed promptly, in a language which he understands, of the reasons for his arrest and of any charge against him' (5(2)); and 'Everyone arrested or detained in accordance with the provisions of paragraph [5(1)(c)] of this article shall be brought promptly before a judge or other officer authorised by law to exercise judicial power and shall be entitled to trial within a reasonable time or to release pending trial'. Release may be conditioned by guarantees to appear for trial (5(3)). In *Brogan* v *United Kingdom* (1989) 11 EHRR 117, it was held that the detention of terrorist suspects without charge for more than four days was in breach of art 5(3), but see the discussion of derogations, below.

Predictably, the provisions of s25 of the Criminal Justice and Public Order Act 1994, which sought to automatically prohibit the granting of bail to certain categories of accused persons, such as those charged with rape or murder, were found to be in breach of art 5(3) by the European Court of Human Rights in *Caballero* v *United Kingdom* (2000) The Times 29 February.

The right of anyone who is deprived of his liberty by arrest or detention to 'take proceedings by which the lawfulness of his detention shall be decided speedily by a court and his release ordered if the detention is not lawful' (5(4)), was found to have been violated by the United Kingdom in *T* v *United Kingdom; V* v *United Kingdom* (1999) The Times 17 December. The Home Secretary had determined the original tariff period (ie the length of time the applicants would have to be imprisoned to satisfy the requirements of punishment and retribution) and, when the period imposed by him was declared unlawful by the House of Lords, he had failed to impose a substitute tariff. The Parole Board would only be able to review the continued detention of the applicants after the expiry of a tariff period. Hence not only had a member of the executive performed a judicial function (thus violating the requirement of an independent tribunal for sentencing), the Parole Board had been prevented from supervising the continued detention (thus violating the requirement that there should be an independent judicial supervision of detention): see further *Hussain* v *United Kingdom* (1996) 22 EHRR 1. Similarly, in *Chahal* v *United Kingdom* (above), the determination of appeals against deportation orders by an advisory panel, where issues of national security were involved, was deemed to be a violation of art 5(4), because the panel did not provide sufficient procedural safeguards to amount to a 'court' as that term was used in the Convention.

Under art 5(5), everyone who has been the victim of arrest or detention in contravention of art 5 should have an enforceable right to compensation.

Article 6: right to a fair trial

Article 6 is effectively a 'due process' clause designed to ensure that both civil and criminal proceedings provide adequate protection for the parties involved. Article 6(1) provides:

'In the determination of his civil rights and obligations or of any criminal charge against him, everyone is entitled to a fair and public hearing within a reasonable time by an independent and impartial tribunal established by law. Judgment shall be pronounced publicly but the press and public may be excluded from all or part of the trial in the interest of morals, public order or national security in a democratic society, where the interests of juveniles or the protection of the private life of the parties so require, or to the extent strictly necessary in the opinion of the court in special circumstances where publicity would prejudice the interests of justice.'

In *T* v *United Kingdom; V* v *United Kingdom* (above), the applicants had been convicted of murder in November 1993. At the time they were aged ten and 11. The trial took place in public in the Crown Court. The European Court of Human Rights, holding that the applicants had been denied a fair trial, expressed the view that proceedings involving children that were likely to invoke a high level of media interest should be conducted in private with only those strictly required in attendance. Whilst the Court noted that special measures were taken in respect of the applicants, such as providing them with explanations of the procedure, allowing them to see the courtroom in advance and reducing the length of hearings so as to avoid tiredness, some other measures had actually been counter-productive, such as raising the dock so as to provide the applicants with a better view of the proceedings. The Court felt that this simply emphasised the level of scrutiny felt by the applicants. Although the applicants had been represented by skilled and experienced lawyers seated in court within 'whispering distance' of the applicants, the Court felt that they had been so intimidated and traumatised by the proceedings that they were not able to communicate effectively with their lawyers or give information for the purposes of the defence.

In *Findlay* v *United Kingdom* Case No 110/1995/616/706 (1997) 24 EHRR 221, the European Court of Human Rights ruled unanimously that the procedures for court martials, laid down by the Army Act 1955, whereby the convening officer was responsible for appointing the prosecutor and members of the court, amounted to a violation of art 6: see also *Coyne* v *United Kingdom* Case No 124/1996/743/942 (1997) The Times 24 October; *Hood* v *United Kingdom* (2000) 29 EHRR 365; *Cable and Others* v *United Kingdom* (1999) The Times 11 March; and *Jordan* v *United Kingdom* (2000) The Times 17 March.

As regards the right to a hearing before a court or tribunal for the determination of civil rights, the European Court of Human Rights has held, in *Stubbings* v *United Kingdom* (1996) 23 EHRR 213, that the limitation periods for actions in tort, laid down by the Limitation Act 1980, did not amount to a denial of access contrary to art 6(1). The Court expressed the view that limitation periods served legitimate aims of ensuring that stale claims were not pursued to the prejudice of third parties, and prevented injustice from occurring, as might be the case where a court proceeded on the basis of evidence that had become unreliable with the passing of time. The failure to determine liability to costs within a reasonable time (due to the incompetence of public officials) was found to be a breach of art 6(1) in *Robins* v

United Kingdom Case No 118/1996/737/936 (1997) The Times 24 October. Other measures that restrict or effectively deny access to a court or tribunal for the determination of rights may fall foul of art 6 if they go further than is necessary to secure some other legitimate aim. Hence in *Tinnelly and Sons Ltd and Others* v *United Kingdom*; *McElduff and Others* v *United Kingdom* (1998) 4 BHRC 393, the European Court of Human Rights held that certificates issued by the Secretary of State for Northern Ireland, under s42 of the Fair Employment Act (Northern Ireland) 1976, to the effect that the decision not to award the applicants a contract for work on electricity stations was an act done 'for the purpose of safeguarding national security or the protection of public safety or order' amounted to a violation of art 6(1). Section 42(2) of the 1976 Act provided that such a certificate was conclusive proof that the act in question was carried out for the purposes stated, and in judicial review proceedings challenging the legality of the certificate the Court had upheld ministerial claims that relevant documents were protected from disclosure by public interest immunity. The European Court of Human Rights accepted the need for vigilance as regards ensuring the security of essentials such as electricity, and the threat posed by terrorist organisations having access to sensitive information. It was felt, however, that the total ban imposed by the s42 certificates had a disproportionate effect on the applicants' rights of access to the courts. The Court was also concerned that rights guaranteed by art 6 could be overridden by the ipse dixit of a member of the executive. Overall the United Kingdom government had failed to demonstrate why some compromise arrangement could not have been arrived at that would have provided the applicants with more information whilst at the same time ensuring security matters were adequately safeguarded.

Under art 6(2) everyone charged with a criminal offence shall be presumed innocent until proved guilty according to law. The extent which the removal of the right to silence pursuant to the introduction of the Criminal Evidence (Northern Ireland) Order 1988 (SI 1988/1987 (NI 20)) amounted to a violation of art 6 was contested in *Murray* v *United Kingdom* (1996) 22 EHRR 29, the Court holding (by 14 votes to five) that although the right to remain silent under questioning and the privilege against self-incrimination were generally recognised international standards which lay at the heart of the notion of a fair procedure under art 6, they were not absolute rights. The matter had to be viewed in the light of the sufficiency of the procedural safeguards designed to prevent oppression, such as regular cautioning and access to legal advice, and the amount of evidence against the accused that was regarded as justifying the drawing of adverse inference in the event of his failing to refute it. The Court was satisfied that sufficient safeguards were in place to ensure that the objectives of art 6 could still be achieved, and that the drawing of reasonable inferences from the applicant's behaviour did not have the effect of shifting the burden of proof contrary to art 6(2).

Note, however, that the tribunal of fact in *Murray* was an experienced judge (sitting in a 'Diplock' court). Much more care may be needed when directing a jury as to the drawing of adverse inferences from silence, and a failure to do so adequately will amount to a violation of art 6, not withstanding provisions of domestic law that appear to permit such inferences: see further *Condron* v *United Kingdom* (2000) The Times 9 May.

Article 6 has also raised questions as to the legality of provisions of domestic law that place an individual under some compulsion to provide information to the authorities, under threat of prosecution if the information is withheld. In *Saunders* v *United Kingdom* (1996) 23 EHRR 313, the use by the prosecution, during the applicant's trial for fraud, of statements made by him during investigations conducted by the Department of Trade and Industry, was found to be a violation of art 6(1) because the applicant had faced the possibility of imprisonment for contempt of court if he refused to answer. By contrast in *Brown (Margaret)* v *Stott; Stott (Procurator Fiscal)* v *Brown* [2001] 1 CL 639, the Privy Council held that a reply given to a police office by a motorist, confirming that she had been the driver of a car, could be lead in evidence by the prosecutor in a drink-driving case, notwithstanding the fact that the motorist had faced the prospect of a conviction under s172 of the Road Traffic Act 1988 if she had refused to provide the information to the police officer. Lord Bingham explained that the ECHR did not expressly provide any guarantee of the privilege against self-incrimination. In determining whether any given statutory provision compromised the overall fairness of a trial, there were a number of factors the court had to take into account, in particular the need to strike the right balance between the interests of the individual and the general interest of the community as a whole. Given the high incidence of death and injury caused by the misuse of motor vehicles there was a clear public interest in the effective enforcement of road traffic legislation. Whilst the operation of s172 could result in a suspect being coerced (under pain of prosecution for not providing evidence) into making a statement that could result in his or her being convicted of a criminal offence, it did not represent a disproportionate response to the problem created by the need to identify vehicles and their drivers. Further, reliance on the evidence so obtained had not undermined the defendant's right to a fair trial. His Lordship distinguished the instant case from that of *Saunders* v *United Kingdom* on the basis that under s172 the questioning was limited to a simple query, there was no prolonged interrogation, and the penalties for refusing to supply information were moderate and non-custodial. The court accepted the prosecutor's argument that it was illogical to allow the use in evidence of body samples taken by force, but to prohibit reliance on the use of statements provided under threat of prosecution. More generally the court thought it significant that those who chose to drive cars knowingly subjected themselves to a regulatory regime which did not apply to the public as a whole. That regime was imposed because of the potential for serious harm that could be caused by the misuse of motor vehicles.

Article 6(3) lists the minimum rights of an individual charged with a criminal offence as being:

'(a) to be informed promptly, in a language which he understands and in detail, of the nature and cause of the accusation against him;

(b) to have adequate time and facilities for the preparation of his defence;

(c) to defend himself in person or through legal assistance of his own choosing or, if he has not sufficient means to pay for legal assistance, to be given it free when the interests of justice so require;

(d) to examine or have examined witnesses against him and to obtain the attendance and examination of witnesses on his behalf under the same conditions as witnesses against him;

(e) to have the free assistance of an interpreter if he cannot understand or speak the language used in court.'

In a series of cases the European Court of Human Rights has confirmed that compliance with art 6 requires the provision of legal representation in any proceedings that could be regarded as punitive, for example proceedings for tax enforcement or proceedings that could result in the loss of liberty: see further *Benham* v *United Kingdom* (1995) The Independent 8 February, and *Wynne* v *United Kingdom* (1994) 19 EHRR 333. In *Bonner* v *United Kingdom; Maxwell* v *United Kingdom* (1994) The Times 1 November, the Court held that the rights guaranteed by art 6 extended to the provision of legal aid to everyone charged with a criminal offence where the interests of justice so required, in light of the importance of the hearing (as regards the sentences imposed on the applicants), the limited scope for the unrepresented applicant to present his case competently, the nature of the proceedings, and clear evidence that the applicants lacked the financial resources to pay for their own lawyers. Similarly the denial of access to a solicitor during the first 48 hours of police questioning has been held to be a violation of art 6(3)(c): see *Murray* v *United Kingdom* (1996) 22 EHRR 29.

The concept of 'equality of arms' underpins much of art 6(3), hence any action, or failure to act, on the part of the prosecution that has the result of undermining the ability of the defendant to represent his case adequately may amount to a violation of the provision. Hence, in *Rowe and Others* v *United Kingdom* [2000] 4 CL 358 the ECHR ruled that the prosecution's failure to provide a trial judge with the opportunity of ruling upon whether evidence, to be relied on by the prosecution in the course of the trial, should be disclosed to the defence or withheld on the grounds of public interest immunity, resulted in the applicants being denied a fair trial. (Note that the domestic law relating to pre-trial disclosure was changed after the domestic trials giving rise to the application but before the applications were considered by the ECHR.)

The 'equality of arms' principle was also invoked in *R* v *Secretary of State for the Home Department, ex parte Quaquah* (2000) The Times 21 January, where the Divisional Court quashed a direction ordering the removal of the applicant, an unsuccessful asylum seeker, from the jurisdiction. Prior to the direction being given the applicant had commenced an action against the Secretary of State for malicious prosecution arising out of an alleged involvement in disturbances whilst the applicant was being held at a detention centre. The court could find no compelling argument to justify the interference with the applicant's right to a fair trial of his action, and also found no evidence that his need to remain in the jurisdiction to properly conduct the litigation had been taken into account.

The Dowsett case is a good reminder that equality of arms is a fundamental principle that the courts will be prepared to protect: *Dowsett* v *United Kingdom* (2004) 38 EHRR 41. Dowsett complained that the United Kingdom had violated his right to a fair trial under art 6(1) European Convention on Human Rights. Dowsett had been convicted of murdering his business partner. This was done by paying two persons to carry out a contract killing. One of these people gave evidence against Dowsett at the trial. Dowsett's defence included the submission that he had only requested an assault to be carried out. This was rejected by the jury and he was convicted. Shortly before his appeal, previously undisclosed material was made available to Dowsett, but the Crown indicated that other documents would still be withheld on the ground of public interest immunity. Dowsett's appeal was dismissed. A letter then came into his possession which seemed to suggest that one of the hired killers had been offered inducements to give evidence against Dowsett. In his current application, Dowsett contended that the principle of equality of arms had been damaged by the Crown's withholding of evidence which could have been of benefit to Dowsett, and that there had been no adequate scrutiny of the Crown's reasons for withholding the material. The application was allowed; there had been a violation of art 6(1). Although there would be instances where genuine reasons required the withholding of evidence, in this case, evidence was withheld which could have assisted Dowsett's defence. That evidence should have been put to the trial judge to assess whether public interest immunity applied. The Court of Appeal would not have been adequately able to assess its relevance, and therefore Dowsett could not be criticised for failing to request that it do so.

Article 7: no punishment without law

Article 7 provides for a prohibition on retrospective legislation creating any criminal offence or increasing the penalty for an offence, by providing that: 'No one shall be held guilty of any criminal offence on account of any act or omission which did not constitute a criminal offence under national or international law at the time when it was committed. Nor shall a heavier penalty be imposed than the one that was applicable at the time the criminal offence was committed.'

This prohibition is modified by art 7(2) to the extent that it should apply without prejudice to the possibility of a person being tried and punished for any act or omission which, at the time when it was committed, was criminal according to the general principles of law recognised by civilised nations.

This provision was successfully invoked by the applicant in *Welch* v *United Kingdom* (1995) 20 EHRR 247, who had been convicted of drug related offences and sentenced to a long term of imprisonment. An order was made under the Drug Trafficking Offences Act 1986 (now the 1994 Act) which resulted in the confiscation of certain of the applicant's assets that could be regarded as the proceeds of drug dealing, even though the offences in question had been committed prior to the commencement of the Act.

The applicant complained that the operation of the 1986 Act was a violation of art 7(1) of the ECHR as it involved the imposition of a heavier penalty than could lawfully have been imposed at the time the offence was committed. Granting the application, the Court held that the measure was clearly penal in nature, and did violate art 7(1) by providing for a more severe penalty than could have been imposed when the drug dealing offences were carried out.

More generally, the way in which judges develop the principles of the common law within the English legal system has lead to questions as to whether defendants are victims of retrospective law-making. In *SW* v *United Kingdom* Case No 47/1994/576; *CR* v *United Kingdom* Case No 48/1994/577 (1995) The Times 5 December, both applicants, who had been convicted of the rape and attempted rape of their wives, claimed that there had been a violation of art 7 of the ECHR since, at the time the incidents giving rise to the convictions had occurred, there was, at common law, a rule that a husband could not be guilty of raping his wife. In rejecting the applicants' contention that the decision of the English court (see *R* v *R* [1991] 3 WLR 767) to disregard the common law rule and uphold the convictions amounted to the imposition of retrospective criminal liability, as their actions had not been contrary to the common law at the time they were committed, the Court held that art 7 did not prohibit the gradual clarification of the principles of criminal liability on a case-by-case basis provided the development could be reasonably foreseen. The gradual evolution of restrictions upon the husband's immunity from liability for marital rape, and the mounting criticism of the immunity, made the judicial development in the instant case reasonably foreseeable.

Article 8: right to respect for private and family life

Article 8 provides that: 'Everyone has the right to respect for his private and family life, his home and his correspondence' (8(1)); and that 'There shall be no interference by a public authority with the exercise of this right except such as is in accordance with the law and is necessary in a democratic society in the interests of national security, public safety or the economic well-being of the country, for the prevention of disorder or crime, for the protection of health or morals, or for the protection of the rights and freedoms of others' (8(2)).

This provision was successfully invoked against the United Kingdom in *Malone* v *United Kingdom* (1985) 7 EHRR 14, the European Court of Human Rights ruling unanimously that the (then) current law relating to the interception of communications was insufficiently precise. The Court accepted that such interception might be necessary in order to investigate crime, but again stressed that this should be in accordance with the law and, in the absence of any clear law, the United Kingdom was unable to satisfy this condition. The consequence of this ruling was the introduction of the Interception of Communications Act 1985. Note also that in *Halford* v *United Kingdom* (1997) 24 EHRR 523, the European Court of Human Rights ruled that the right to privacy extended to telephone calls made from the workplace if no warning was given by an employer that calls would be monitored. If such calls were intercepted on an internal communications system, there would be a breach of art 8. The interception could not be justified as being in accordance with the law because, given that the 1985 Act did not apply to private telephone systems, there was no relevant law covering such interceptions.

In *Khan* v *United Kingdom* Application No 35394/97 [2000] 7 CL 276, art 8 was successfully invoked before the European Court of Human Rights in relation to the use by police officers of a surveillance device attached (without permission) to the exterior of the premises in order to record the conversations of suspected drugs dealers. The respondents accepted that the applicant's privacy had been invaded by the eavesdropping, but contended that it was permissible as being 'in accordance with law and justified in a democratic society'. Rejecting this contention the Court noted that, at the time the surveillance had taken place, the only regulation of the eavesdropping took the form of Home Office guidelines: *Covert Listening Devices and Visual Surveillance (Private Places)* 1984. Under these guidelines the chief constable of the relevant force had to be satisfied that, where devices were to be used to record conversations in places where a citizen would normally be entitled to presume privacy, such surveillance was required because the investigation concerned major organised crime, particularly violence. Given the absence of statutory controls, and the fact that the guidelines were not readily available to the public, the Court concluded that it could not be said that the violation of the applicant's privacy had been in 'accordance with the law'.

Note that the use of such devices by the police is now regulated by the provisions of the Police Act 1997, and the Regulation of Investigatory Powers Act 2000.

Article 8 could, in theory, be invoked by those who feel that their right to adopt an 'alternative' lifestyle is being hampered by the state, but note that in *Buckley* v *United Kingdom* (1996) 23 EHRR 191, the applicant, a gypsy, unsuccessfully argued that the planning laws that led to her being forbidden to site caravans on land that she had purchased for her own occupation amounted to a violation of art 8. The planning legislation was regarded by the European Court of Human Rights as having 'legitimate aims', and as having been applied in a non-discriminatory fashion. Note that the applicant had also sought to argue that both the Caravan Sites Act 1968 and the Criminal Justice and Public Order Act 1994 were discriminatory in seeking to penalise or incriminate those who led a gypsy lifestyle, but the Court declined to consider these questions given that no specific action had been taken against the applicant under the auspices of either piece of legislation.

Many of the cases brought against the United Kingdom under art 8 have involved questions concerning status arising from sexuality or sexual disposition.

In *Dudgeon* v *United Kingdom* (1981) 4 EHRR 149, the European Court of Human Rights upheld (by a majority) a claim that the Northern Ireland laws prohibiting buggery between consenting adult males amounted to a violation of the right to privacy under art 8, as the police had relied upon the law to justify questioning the applicant about his sex life. The Homosexual Offences (Northern Ireland) Order 1982 was introduced to meet the requirements of the Court's ruling.

Similarly in *ADT* v *UK* (2000) The Times 8 August, the European Court of Human Rights held that s13 of the Sexual Offences Act 1956, as amended by s1(2)(a) of the Sexual Offences Act 1967 (relating to male homosexual acts committed in private not being unlawful provided that no more than two persons are present) did amount to a violation of art 8, where the applicant had been convicted of gross indecency between men, after the police had seized his video tapes of sexual acts he had performed at his house with up to four other consenting adult males. Whilst the Court was satisfied that the interference with the applicant's private life was in accordance with the law, in that s13 of the 1956 Act and s1(2)(a) of the 1967 Act provided for a clear scheme of prohibitions and sanctions, it could not accept that the domestic law was, on the facts, necessary in a democratic society. The applicant's activities were non-violent, raised no general public health concerns and were restricted to a small number of consenting adults. They were, therefore, 'genuinely private' leading the Court to adopt a narrow margin of appreciation in reviewing the domestic law. On this basis the interference caused by the domestic law could not be justified.

Neither has the Ministry of Defence policy prohibiting individuals with homosexual proclivities from serving in the armed forces survived the scrutiny of the European Court of Human Rights when viewed in the light of art 8. In *Lustig-Prean and Becket* v *United Kingdom; Smith and Grady* v *United Kingdom* (1999) The Times 11 October, the Court held that the policy violated art 8, noting that the investigations into the homosexuality of the applicants had been intrusive and constituted grave interferences with their private lives. The Court was unwilling to accept alleged homophobia amongst members of the armed forces as a justification for the policy. To the extent that such prejudice existed, the Court felt that it was incumbent upon the United Kingdom government to take steps to eradicate it, as was the case with racial or gender-based discrimination. The Court was also influenced by the fact that other contracting States appeared to be adopting more liberal policies on the admission of homosexuals to their armed forces.

Applicants claiming that their right to privacy has been violated because their changed sexual status has not been recorded by variations to their birth certificates have met with less success. In *Rees* v *United Kingdom* (1986) 9 EHRR 56 (woman having sex change operation to become a man), and *Cossey* v *United Kingdom* [1991] 2 FLR 492 (man having sex change operation to become a woman) the Court recognised that the margin of appreciation allowed to signatory States permitted them to insist on a system of recording births that identified the sex of a child when born. In *Rees* the Court noted the importance of the fact that the register of births recorded facts of legal significance and the establishment of family ties in connection with succession, legitimate descent and the distribution of property. The European

Court of Human Rights rejected the argument advanced in *X, Y, and Z* v *United Kingdom* (1997) 24 EHRR 143 to the effect that it was a breach of art 8 to refuse to register as the father of a child a person who had undergone female to male gender reassignment surgery, and whose partner had conceived by artificial insemination. Given the margin of appreciation granted to signatory States, they were entitled to adopt the view that only someone who was a 'biological male' could be registered as a child's father.

In *Sheffield and Horsham* v *United Kingdom* [1998] 2 FLR 928, the European Court of Human Rights saw no reason to depart from the above decisions regarding the refusal of signatory States to alter birth certificates, but the Court did stress the need for States to keep the matter under review in the light of emerging medical evidence. Pending such evidence the Court was not persuaded that the frequency of incidents when the applicants would have to produce documents showing their sex at birth was such as to amount to a disproportionate interference with the right to respect for their private lives. The Court also observed that, as regards the right to marry enshrined in art 12, the marriage there referred to meant a traditional marriage between persons who were of the opposite biological sex, and that the right was concerned to protect marriage as the basis of family life. To allow the applicants to succeed under art 12 would result in an impairment of the very basis on which art 12 had been included in the Convention. See further on other aspects of art 8: *Laskey, Jaggard and Brown* v *United Kingdom* Case No 109/1995/615/703–5 (1997) 24 EHRR 39.

In *R* v *Secretary of State for the Home Department, ex parte Mellor* [2000] 3 FCR 148, the applicant was a prisoner serving a life sentence for murder. He requested that a sample of his semen be taken so that his wife, who he had married whilst he was in prison, could be artificially inseminated. The applicant feared that, by the time the tariff period of his sentence had been served and he became eligible for release, his wife would be too old to have children. The Secretary of State refused the request stating that it was his department's policy to accede to such requests only in the most exceptional circumstances. It was also contended that there was no need for the procedure and that there were doubts as to the stability of the applicant's relationship with his wife. The applicant sought judicial review of the refusal, stressing that prisoners retained all civil rights not expressly or impliedly removed as a result of incarceration. In particular he contended that his right to found a family had not been given sufficient weight by the Secretary of State.

Dismissing the application, the Court accepted that, whilst art 8 of the ECHR did require respect for family life where it existed, it did not necessarily give rise to any right to start a family. Article 12 (considered below) could not be relied on to create any such right either. Prisoners did not have any right as such of access to facilities for artificial insemination. The Secretary of State therefore had a discretion as to whether or not to allow access to such facilities, and the adoption of a policy to govern the exercise of that discretion was lawful provided, as in the present case, the policy was rational. Further, it was legitimate for the Secretary of State to take into account factors such as the interests of the unborn child, and public concern over the provision of artificial insemination facilities to prisoners serving custodial sentences. Note that although the decision was made prior to the Human Rights Act 1998 coming into effect, it serves as a good example of the Court carrying out the balancing act required when considering arguments relating to alleged the violation of those rights where the interest of both the individual and society at large have to be considered.

Article 9: freedom of thought, conscience and religion

Article 9 provides that: 'Everyone has the right to freedom of thought, conscience and religion; this right includes freedom to change his religion or belief and freedom, either alone or in community with others and in public or private, to manifest his religion or belief, in worship, teaching, practice and observance' (9(1)); 'Freedom to manifest one's religion or beliefs shall be subject only to such limitations as are prescribed by law and are necessary in a democratic society in the interests of public safety, for the protection of public order, health or morals, or for the protection of the rights and freedoms of others' (9(2)).

Article 10: freedom of expression

Article 10(1) provides that:

> 'Everyone has the right to freedom of expression. This right shall include freedom to hold opinions and to receive and impart information and ideas without interference by public authority and regardless of frontiers. This article shall not prevent States from requiring the licensing of broadcasting, television or cinema enterprises.'

Limitations upon this right are envisaged by art 10(2), which goes on to provide that:

> 'The exercise of these freedoms, since it carries with it duties and responsibilities, may be subject to such formalities, conditions, restrictions or penalties as are prescribed by law and are necessary in a democratic society, in the interests of national security, territorial integrity or public safety, for the prevention of disorder or crime, for the protection of health or morals, for the protection of the reputation or rights of others, for preventing the disclosure of information received in confidence, or for maintaining the authority and impartiality of the judiciary.'

Note that it allows for what is referred to as a margin of appreciation to contracting States regarding restrictions upon the right to free expression. Hence in *Handyside* v *United Kingdom* (1976) 1 EHRR 737, where the Court held that obscene publications laws in the United Kingdom did not, on the facts, amount to a violation of art 10, it was noted that:

> 'By reason of their direct and continuous contact with the vital forces of their countries, State authorities are in principle in a better position than the international judge to give

an opinion on the exact content of those requirements ... as well as on the "necessity" of a "restriction" or "penalty" intended to meet them.'

In *Bowman* v *United Kingdom* (1998) 26 EHRR 1 the European Court of Human Rights held, by a majority, that the limitation imposed on unauthorised election expenditure under s75 of the Representation of the People Act 1983 amounted to a violation of art 10 on the basis that it could not be justified as necessary in a democratic society. Note that the application was considered admissible even though the criminal prosecution brought against the applicant had been unsuccessful. The European Court of Human Rights was mindful of the deterrent that the threat of future prosecutions might have.

In *Ahmed and Others* v *United Kingdom* (1998) 5 BHRC 111 the European Court of Human Rights rejected claims that restrictions imposed on senior local authority officers in 'politically restricted posts' from standing for elections as MPs or serving as councillors amounted to a violation of rights under art 10. The Court accepted that the regulations did interfere with the applicants' rights under art 10, but found, contrary to the applicants' submissions, that the restrictions were sufficiently precise to meet the requirement that they should be 'prescribed by law'. The Court noted that the regulations could not be expected to define political activity with absolute precision, bearing in mind also that they applied to a substantial number of officers. Secondly, the Court concluded that the restrictions imposed by the regulations were in pursuit of a legitimate aim, namely ensuring the effectiveness of local political democracy and preventing the diminution of the neutrality of certain categories of officers. The regulations were also seen as protecting the rights of council members and the electorate to effective political democracy at the local level. In particular, the Court attached great importance to what it saw as the long tradition of political neutrality which local government officers owed to elected council members. Thirdly, the Court held that the regulations were 'necessary in a democratic society'. In reaching this conclusion the Court took notice of the work done by the Widdicombe Committee in 1985 and the evidence of abuse that it had uncovered. The response, in the form of the regulations, was within the respondent State's margin of appreciation.

By restricting the operation of the regulations to certain specified categories of officer, and restricting only partisan comment, the government had tried to ensure that the interference with rights under the ECHR had been minimised insofar as this was possible given the purpose of the regulations. Rights such as freedom to join political parties remained unaffected by the regulations. Note that the Court regarded it as significant that the Labour government elected in May 1997 had reviewed the operation of the regulations and determined that they should remain in effect.

In the case of *Roddy (A Child) (Identification: Restriction on Publication), Re; Torbay Borough Council* v *News Group Newspapers* [2003] EWHC 2927; [2004] EMLR 8, a newspaper publisher wanted to publish details of the story of two 12 year olds before and after the birth of their child (Y). In 1999 and 2000 various actions to obtain and challenge injunctions were undertaken and care proceedings were instituted in relation to all three children. The upshot was that the identity of the parents was to be protected and all were placed in care. Later the mother returned to her parents and her care order was ended. She then wished to be able to offer her story to the newspaper. The local authority was opposed to this in relation to Y (the identification of the child was the issue) but not the mother. The newspaper wished to challenge such a restriction. The newspaper's application was allowed. The right to communicate one's story was protected not only by the Human Rights Act 1998 (in Sch 1, Pt 1, art 10) but also by art 8, which protected an individual's physical and social identity. Whilst both the father and the baby deserved protection it should not prevent the story being told anonymously. As to the mother's position, she had sufficient understanding and maturity to decide for herself what should remain private, and the court had a duty to protect her right to make a choice: *Gillick* v *West Norfolk and Wisbech Area Health Authority* [1986] AC 112 applied. By allowing one party to publicise their life, perhaps for no better reason in some cases than to make a financial gain, the position of the other parties is likely to be jeopardised. Of course the court has to take into account competing claims to rights, but you do wonder if the infant was given sufficient protection here.

Article 11: freedom of assembly and association

Article 11 provides that:

'(1) Everyone has the right to freedom of peaceful assembly and to freedom of association with others, including the right to form and to join trade unions for the protection of his interests.

(2) No restrictions shall be placed on the exercise of these rights other than such as are prescribed by law and are necessary in a democratic society in the interests of national security or public safety, for the prevention of disorder or crime, for the protection of health or morals or for the protection of the rights and freedoms of others. This article shall not prevent the imposition of lawful restrictions on the exercise of these rights by members of the armed forces, of the police or of the administration of the State.'

Article 12: right to marry

Men and women of marriageable age have the right to marry and to found a family, according to the national laws governing the exercise of this right: see *Sheffield and Horsham* v *United Kingdom* (above), where the Court held that as regards the right to marry enshrined in art 12 it meant a traditional marriage between persons who were of the opposite biological sex.

Article 14: prohibition of discrimination

The enjoyment of the rights and freedoms set forth in the Convention are to be secured by the contracting States without discrimination on any ground such as sex, race, colour, language, religion, political or other opinion, national or social origin, association with a national minority, property, birth or other status.

Article 16: restrictions on political activity of aliens

Nothing in arts 10, 11 and 14 should be regarded as preventing the contracting States from imposing restrictions on the political activity of aliens.

Article 17: prohibition of abuse of rights

Nothing in the Convention may be interpreted as implying for any State, group or person any right to engage in any activity or perform any act aimed at the destruction of any of the rights and freedoms set forth in the Convention or at their limitation to a greater extent than is provided for in the Convention.

The First Protocol

There are a number of protocols to the ECHR that States can sign up to as they see fit. In effect they are 'optional extras' on the human rights menu. The First Protocol, to which the United Kingdom is a signatory, provides (under art 1) that:

> 'Every natural or legal person is entitled to the peaceful enjoyment of his possessions. No one shall be deprived of his possessions except in the public interest and subject to the conditions provided for by law and by the general principles of international law.
>
> The preceding provisions shall not, however, in any way impair the right of a State to enforce such laws as it deems necessary to control the use of property in accordance with the general interest or to secure the payment of taxes or other contributions or penalties.'

See further *National and Provincial Building Society and Others* v *United Kingdom* (1997) 25 EHRR 127.

Article 2 details a right to education:

> 'No person shall be denied the right to education. In the exercise of any functions which it assumes in relation to education and to teaching, the State shall respect the right of parents to ensure such education and teaching in conformity with their own religious and philosophical convictions.'

Note that the United Kingdom has filed a reservation in respect of art 2 to the First Protocol to the effect that the principle affirmed in the second sentence of art 2 is accepted 'only so far as it is compatible with the provision of efficient instruction and training, and the avoidance of unreasonable public expenditure' (reservation dated 20 March 1952).

As the White Paper *Rights Brought Home: The Human Rights Bill* (Cmnd 3782) indicates:

> 'The reservation reflects the fundamental principle originally enacted in the Education Act 1944, and now contained in s9 of the Education Act 1996, "that pupils are to be educated in accordance with the wishes of their parents so far as that is compatible with the provision of efficient instruction and training and the avoidance of unreasonable public expenditure". There is similar provision in Scottish legislation. The reservation does not affect the right to education in art 2. Nor does it deny parents the right to have account taken of their religious or philosophical convictions. Its purpose is to recognise that in the provision of State-funded education a balance must be struck in some cases between the convictions of parents and what is educationally sound and affordable.' (at para 4.5)

Article 3 provides for a right to free elections:

> 'The High Contracting Parties undertake to hold free elections at reasonable intervals by secret ballot, under conditions which will ensure the free expression of the opinion of the people in the choice of the legislature.'

See further *Matthews* v *United Kingdom* (1999) 28 EHRR 361.

Other Protocols

Protocol Four prohibits deprivation of liberty on grounds of inability to fulfil contractual obligations; provides a right to liberty of movement; a right to non-expulsion from the home State; a right of entry to the State of which a person is a national; and a prohibition on the collective expulsion of aliens. The United Kingdom signed Protocol Four in 1963 but has not subsequently ratified it because of concerns regarding the compatibility of domestic law. Protocol Six prohibits the death penalty. Again this has not been ratified on the basis that the issue of whether or not to retain the death penalty has always been regarded as one best determined by individual MPs as a matter of conscience. Protocol Seven prohibits the expulsion of aliens without a decision in accordance with the law or opportunities for review; a right to a review of conviction or sentence after criminal conviction; a right to compensation following a miscarriage of justice; a prohibition on double jeopardy in criminal cases; and a right to equality between spouses. The present government intends to ratify Protocol Seven once certain aspects of domestic law have been rationalised.

Limitations, restrictions and derogations

A number of articles contain express exemption provisions; for example, arts 11(2), 8(2), 9(2) and 10(2). As regards derogation in time of war or public emergency, art 15 provides:

> '(1) In time of war or other public emergency threatening the life of the nation any High Contracting Party may take measures derogating from its obligations under this

Convention to the extent strictly required by the exigencies of the situation, provided that such measures are not inconsistent with its other obligations under international law. But: (2) No derogation from art 2, except in respect of deaths resulting from lawful acts of war, or from arts 3, 4(1) and 7 shall be made under this provision.'

Following the *Brogan* case (above) the United Kingdom applied for a derogation in respect of art 5(3) in the light of that fact that:

'There have been in the United Kingdom in recent years campaigns of organised terrorism connected with the affairs of Northern Ireland which have manifested themselves in activities which have included repeated murder, attempted murder, maiming, intimidation and violent civil disturbance and in bombing and fire raising which have resulted in death, injury and widespread destruction of property. As a result, a public emergency within the meaning of art 15(1) of the Convention exists in the United Kingdom.' (Derogation notification of 23 December 1988.)

In *Brannigan and McBride* v *United Kingdom* (1993) 17 EHRR 539, the European Court of Human Rights accepted the contention of the United Kingdom that the situation in Northern Ireland justified a derogation under art 15 in respect of the provisions of the ECHR relating to detention without charge. Hence the detention of the applicants under the Prevention of Terrorism (Temporary Provisions) Act 1984 (see now s14 and para 6 of Sch 5 to the Prevention of Terrorism (Temporary Provisions) Act 1989, which make comparable provision) did not amount to a violation of the ECHR, vindicating, to some extent, the refusal of the United Kingdom government to alter the law relating to the detention of suspected terrorists following the ruling in *Brogan* v *United Kingdom* (above). It should be noted that the relevant statute, for the detention of suspected terrorists, is now the Terrorism Act 2000, s40 of which allows detention without charge for up to 48 hours.

18.4 Pursuing a Human Rights Act claim before the domestic courts

Procedure for enforcement

The Human Rights Act 1998 does not expressly create a new procedure for raising alleged violations of Convention rights. Section 7(1) envisages that individuals will be able to bring proceedings (or a counterclaim) against a public body in the appropriate court or tribunal 'as may be determined in accordance with rules' (s7(2)). Section 7(9) provides that these rules are to be made by the Lord Chancellor. Alternatively litigants will be allowed to 'rely on the Convention right or rights concerned in any legal proceedings' (s7(1)(b)), legal proceedings including, for these purposes 'proceedings brought by or at the instigation of a public authority; and ... an appeal against the decision of a court or tribunal' (s7(6)(a) and (b)). Section 22(4) provides that proceedings can only be brought against a public body by an individual under s7(1)(b) in respect of acts taking place after the Act came into force; however, an individual seeking to rely on Convention rights in proceedings brought by or at the instigation of a public body is able to do so after October 2000 regardless of when the impugned action of the public body took place: see *R v Director of Public Prosecutions, ex parte Kebilene; R v Director of Public Prosecutions, ex parte Rechachi* [1999] 3 WLR 175.

Only the 'victim' of the alleged unlawful act is permitted to bring proceedings or rely on the Convention in legal proceedings (s7(1)). The 'victim' in this context can be a limited company: see *County Properties Ltd v The Scottish Ministers* 2000 SLT 965.

It is clear that many of the cases involving reliance on Convention rights will take the form of applications for judicial review – given that the Act is of direct application to public bodies (see below). The result is that a narrower test for locus standi will be applied in applications alleging a breach of Convention rights, as compared to applications for review generally. As s7(3) makes clear: 'If the proceedings are brought on an application for judicial review, the applicant is to be taken to have a sufficient interest in relation to the unlawful act only if he is, or would be, a victim of that act'. 'Victim' for the purposes of s7 is defined as 'a victim for the purposes of art 34 of the Convention if proceedings were brought in the European Court of Human Rights' (s7(7)). In particular, whereas pressure groups are increasingly seen as having 'sufficient interest' for the purposes of applying for judicial review, it will be difficult for them to satisfy the 'victim' test adopted by the Act. Section 7(5) provides for a time limit of 12 months for the bringing of proceedings where it is claimed that a public authority has acted in breach of Convention rights, time running from the date on which the act complained of took place. Beyond this a court or tribunal will have a discretion to allow proceedings outside this time limit if it considers it equitable to do so having regard to all the circumstances. This time limit would apply subject to any rule imposing a stricter time limit, hence, the three-month rule in relation to applications for judicial review would still apply.

Significantly the Act makes no provision for a Human Rights Commission to oversee compliance with the Act and bring proceedings in respect of non-compliance. This omission has drawn criticism from some quarters, particularly where comparisons have been drawn with the work of the Equal Opportunities Commission and the Commission for Racial Equality in overseeing legislation dealing with discrimination on the grounds of gender and ethnicity. Northern Ireland does have a Human Rights Commission, but not one instituted as a result of the Human Rights Act 1998.

Who can be the subject of these proceedings?

By virtue of s6(1) it becomes unlawful for a public authority to act (or fail to act: see s6(6)) in a way which is incompatible with a Convention right. A public body for these purposes includes a court or tribunal, and 'any person certain of whose functions are functions of a public nature, but does not include either House of the

[United Kingdom] Parliament or a person exercising functions in connection with proceedings in the [United Kingdom] Parliament' (s6(3)). The term 'Parliament' as used in s6(3) does not include the House of Lords in its judicial capacity. By contrast the Scottish Parliament and the Welsh Assembly, as subordinate legislatures, are bound by the 1998 Act. Section 29(2)(d) of the Scotland Act 1998 provides that the Scottish Parliament does not have legislative competence to enact legislation that is incompatible with Convention rights, and Sch 4 to the 1998 Act further provides that no Act of the Scottish Parliament can modify the Human Rights Act 1998. Section 107 of the Government of Wales Act 1998 imposes similar restraints on the Welsh Assembly, subject to the fact that the Assembly is not, in any event, empowered to enact primary legislation.

Under s6(1) a public body such as a tribunal or local authority will be bound to observe the ECHR whether it is engaged in a public law or private law activity. Other bodies may be regarded as public bodies if certain of their functions are of a public nature (see s6(3)(b)), but the 1998 Act will only apply to acts of such bodies that are of a public nature. In determining whether or not a body has public law functions it seems likely that the courts will be influenced by the jurisprudence built up in relation to applications for judicial review where the issue has been whether a non-statutory body can be regarded as a public authority: see for example *R v Panel on Take-overs and Mergers, ex parte Datafin plc* [1987] 2 WLR 699; *R v Disciplinary Committee of the Jockey Club, ex parte The Aga Khan* [1993] 1 WLR 909; and *R v Insurance Ombudsman Bureau and the Insurance Ombudsman, ex parte Aegon Life* [1994] COD 426. It is possible that bodies such as the BBC, the Church of England and other religious bodies, universities, the governing bodies of various sports, self-regulatory bodies, and any organisation that has taken over what was previously a public law function, such as running prisons, could come within the scope of 'public authority' for the purposes of the Act as regards their public law functions. The Press will presumably not come within the scope of the Act, raising the possibility of different approaches being taken to the right to privacy under art 8 depending on whether it is a television broadcast or newspaper article that is complained of. The Press Complaints Commission (PCC) will, it is submitted, be regarded as a public body. If the PCC fails to safeguard the right to privacy, or indeed the right to freedom of expression as defined in the ECHR, it could find itself involved in lengthy litigation.

Where the claim of unlawfulness under s6 is based upon a judicial act, proceedings under s7(1)(a) may only be brought by exercising a right of appeal, making an application for judicial review, or by following such procedure as may be laid down in rules made from time to time (s9(1)). So-called 'ouster' clauses that seek to remove rights of appeal or exclude judicial review would not be affected by this requirement; see s9(2).

Section 6(1) effectively creates a new 'head' of ultra vires as regards applications for judicial review of public bodies. If a public body fails to pay due regard to the terms of the Convention, or indeed the jurisprudence of the European Court of

Justice, in exercising its discretion, prima facie grounds for review will exist. The situation is similar where a public body exercises a statutory power and the interpretation of the relevant statutory provision in the light of the ECHR shows the power to have been exercised in an ultra vires manner. In particular the notion of proportionality as developed by the European Court of Human Rights (ie comparing what was needed to deal with a situation with the extent of the power actually used) becomes a facet of domestic law to which reviewing courts will now be obliged to have regard.

Section 6(2) restricts the scope of s6(1) by providing that the latter does not apply if, as the result of one or more provisions of primary legislation, or because of the way in which subordinate legislation has to be applied in the light of primary legislation, the public body alleged to have acted unlawfully could not have acted differently. If such a situation arises the court may still be willing to make a declaration of incompatibility, as to which, see below.

It remains to be seen to what extent the courts are willing to allow the concept of a 'constitutional tort' to develop under s6 whereby claimants seek damages for the failure on the part of a public body to observe its duty under s6 not to act in a manner incompatible with the rights set forth in the ECHR.

Further, no action will lie against a minister for not laying a proposal for legislation before Parliament or for not making any primary legislation or remedial order: see s6(6)(a) and (b), and below.

Given that it includes the courts and tribunals, the definition of public authority in s6 creates the possibility of the Convention having indirect 'horizontal' effect. Although the 1998 Act does not expressly create any obligation on the part of private individuals to abide by the terms of the Convention, proceedings could be brought against a court that failed to uphold a Convention right in proceedings between private individuals. An example might be an allegation that a newspaper had invaded the privacy of an individual. There is no common law right to privacy as such. Article 8 of the Convention is now part of domestic law, but appears only to apply to public authorities, not newspapers. If a court were to strike out proceedings brought by a private individual against a newspaper alleging invasion of privacy as disclosing no cause of action, the court might itself then become the focus of an action for not upholding Convention rights. It might be further argued that whether or not there has been a violation of an individual's human rights should be judged by looking at the effect of the actions on the victim, rather than concentrating on the legal niceties of the status of the perpetrator. Suppose a group of anti-abortionists terrorised doctors willing to carry out abortions to the point where the doctors were too frightened to express their views publicly. Could the doctors claim that their right to free speech had been violated on the basis that the State had not provided adequate protection in respect of the actions of other private individuals?

What is required of a court considering a case involving an allegation that a Convention right has been violated?

A court or tribunal called upon to do so must interpret primary legislation and subordinate legislation 'in a way which is compatible with the Convention rights' (s3(1)). This duty applies whether the legislation was enacted before or after the coming into force of the Human Rights Act 1998.

In effect it means that a court will try to ensure it arrives at an interpretation of domestic law that is consistent with the ECHR even if this means resorting to creative or dynamic methods of statutory interpretation. Bear in mind that this applies to legislation enacted both before and after the Human Rights Act 1998. This means that the doctrine of implied repeal does not operate fully in respect of the 1998 Act. Normally the 1998 Act would prevail over any inconsistent provision in earlier legislation. The effect of s3, however, is that earlier inconsistent legislation might still prevail over the 1998 Act if the courts cannot arrive at an interpretation of the earlier legislation that is consistent with the terms of the ECHR (see judicial remedies, below).

Section 2(1) of the 1998 Act makes it clear that any court or tribunal determining a question arising in connection with a Convention right must take into account: any judgment, decision, declaration or advisory opinion of the European Court of Human Rights; any opinion of the Commission given in a report adopted under art 31 of the Convention; any decision of the Commission in connection with art 26 or 27(2) of the Convention, or any decision of the Committee of Ministers taken under art 46 of the Convention, 'whenever made or given, so far as, in the opinion of the court or tribunal, it is relevant to the proceedings in which that question has arisen'.

This is a much weaker obligation than that created by s3(1) as a court may take into account the jurisprudence of the ECHR, such as the doctrine of the 'margin of appreciation' and the role of proportionality in justifying interference with rights, but then decide not to give effect to it when considering the compatibility of domestic law.

It may also be the case that the courts take into account rulings of the Privy Council in appeals concerning constitutional rights for those countries having written constitutions incorporating terms similar to those found in the ECHR: see for example *DPP* v *Tokai* [1996] AC 856; and *Robinson* v *The Queen* [1985] AC 956. In *R* v *Director of Public Prosecutions, ex parte Kebilene; R* v *Director of Public Prosecutions, ex parte Rechachi* (see above), Lord Hope, referring to the likely impact of the 1998 Act once in force, observed:

'... the vigorous public debate which [has accompanied the passage through Parliament of the Human Rights Act 1998] has already had a profound influence on thinking about issues of human rights. It is now plain that the incorporation of the European Convention on Human Rights into our domestic law will subject the entire legal system to a fundamental process of review and, where necessary, reform by the judiciary ... Lord Wilberforce ... in *Minister of Home Affairs* v *Fisher* [1980] AC 319, 328 [observed] that instruments of this nature call for a generous interpretation suitable to give to individuals the full measure of the fundamental rights and freedoms referred to, and Lord Diplock's comment in *Attorney-General of The Gambia* v *Momodou Jobe* [1984] AC 689, 700 that a generous and purposive construction is to be given to that part of a constitution which protects and entrenches fundamental rights and freedoms to which all persons in the State are to be entitled. The same approach will now have to be applied in this country when issues are raised under the 1998 Act about the compatibility of domestic legislation and of acts of public authorities with the fundamental rights and freedoms which are enshrined in the Convention.'

See also comments of Lord Woolf in *AG of Hong Kong* v *Lee Kwong-Kut* [1993] AC 951 at 975, where he referred to the need [as regards the Hong Kong Bill of Rights] to ensure that disputes did not get out of hand, to ensure that the Bill was approached with realism and a sense of proportion so that it did not become a 'source of injustice' and thereby 'debased in the eyes of the public'. If the Scottish experience is any guidance the courts will be robust in their treatment of vexatious or outlandish claims: see observations of Lord President, Lord Rodger of Earlsferry *Anderson* v *The Scottish Ministers and Another* (2000) The Times 21 June.

It seems inevitable that the courts are going to have to adopt a new approach to statutory interpretation where Convention rights are concerned, rather than stick rigidly to the traditional rules of interpretation. The tradition of the European Court of Human Rights is to be more flexible and evaluative in its exercise of its interpretative functions. Thus domestic judges will have a more explicit role in assessing the merits of executive decision-making (ie its legitimacy within the context of the ECHR), whereas their role to date, at least in theory, has been limited to scrutinising the legality of executive action by means of judicial review.

As Lord Irvine LC observed:

'[Once the ECHR is incorporated in domestic law] The courts' decisions will be based on a more overtly principled, indeed moral, basis. The court will look at the positive right. It will only accept an interference with that right where a justification, allowed under the Convention, is made out. The scrutiny will not be limited to seeing if the words of an exception can be satisfied. The court will need to be satisfied that the spirit of this exception is made out. It will need to be satisfied that the interference with the protected right is justified in the public interests in a free democratic society. Moreover, the courts will in this area have to apply the Convention principle of proportionality. This means the court will be looking substantively at that question. It will not be limited to a secondary review of the decision making process but at the primary question of the merits of the decision itself.

In reaching its judgment, therefore, the court will need to expand and explain its own view of whether the conduct is legitimate. It will produce in short a decision on the morality of the conduct and not simply its compliance with the bare letter of the law.' (Tom Sargant Memorial Lecture, December 1997.)

During the passage of the Human Rights Bill great concern was expressed by religious organisations as to the effect of incorporation on their rights to act in accordance with their religious beliefs, and by sections of the media concerned at the impact of a right to privacy on the common law notion of free speech. Section 11 provides that the incorporation of the Convention should not be regarded by a court as necessarily restricting any other rights and freedoms conferred on an individual by common law or statute. Section 12 goes on to deal more specifically with the issue of free speech by providing (in s12(4)) that the courts must have:

> '... particular regard to the importance of the Convention right to freedom of expression and, where the proceedings relate to material which the respondent [ie person against whom the application for relief is made] claims, or which appears to the court, to be journalistic, literary or artistic material (or to conduct connected with such material), to – (a) the extent to which – (i) the material has, or is about to, become available to the public; or (ii) it is, or would be, in the public interest for the material to be published; (b) any relevant privacy code.'

Where a court is considering whether to grant any relief which, if granted, might affect the exercise of the Convention right to freedom of expression, and the respondent is neither present nor represented, no such relief should be granted unless the court is satisfied: '(a) that the applicant has taken all practicable steps to notify the respondent; or (b) that there are compelling reasons why the respondent should not be notified' (s12(2)(a) and (b)). Further, 'no such relief is to be granted so as to restrain publication before trial unless the court is satisfied that the applicant is likely to establish that publication should not be allowed': see s12(3).

Section 13 provides that a court determining a question arising under the 1998 Act that 'might affect the exercise by a religious organisation (itself or its members collectively) of the Convention right to freedom of thought, conscience and religion' must 'have particular regard to the importance of that right'.

The usefulness of both ss12 and 13 must be questioned. They seek to assist the courts in the interpretation of domestic legislation and Convention rights, but ultimately the United Kingdom courts will be bound by the jurisprudence of the European Court of Human Rights as regards the 'hierarchy' of rights (ie whether freedom of expression outweighs the right to privacy). If domestic courts restrict the scope of Convention rights in a manner that is contrary to the rulings of the European Court of Human Rights, the way lies open to have the matter determined at Strasbourg with the prospect of the United Kingdom being found in breach of its Convention rights, notwithstanding incorporation.

Judicial remedies

A court dealing with an application for judicial review of subordinate legislation would be able to declare it to be ultra vires if it was found to be incompatible with the Convention rights. The courts have no such power in relation to primary legislation, however. Indeed s3(2)(b) expressly provides that the section 'does not affect the validity, continuing operation or enforcement of any incompatible primary legislation'. Further, the section cannot be relied upon to invalidate incompatible subordinate legislation if '(disregarding any possibility of revocation) primary legislation prevents removal of the incompatibility' (s3(2)(c)). Where an irreconcilable issue of compatibility arises before the House of Lords, the Judicial Committee of the Privy Council, the Courts-Martial Appeal Court, the High Court or the Court of Appeal, that court will be empowered to grant a declaration of incompatibility. In relation to subordinate legislation the power to make such declarations will arise provided (disregarding any possibility of revocation) the primary legislation concerned prevents removal of the incompatibility. Where such a declaration is made it does not 'affect the validity, continuing operation or enforcement of the provision in respect of which it is given; and ... is not binding on the parties to the proceedings in which it is made' (s4(6)). The Crown can be joined as a party to the proceedings if a court is considering whether to make a declaration of incompatibility (s5(1)). Where legislation of the Scottish Parliament is concerned the court does have the power to declare it to be ultra vires on the basis of non-compliance with the ECHR as the legislation is the product of a body of limited jurisdiction, unlike the United Kingdom Parliament at Westminster.

It could be argued that the 1998 Act is further evidence of the steady erosion of parliamentary sovereignty. Although a declaration of incompatibility does not place a minister under a duty to take remedial action (see below), the political pressure to do so will be intense. It suggests more clearly than ever before that it is the judiciary that are to be the protectors of minority groups, not a legislature that represents, by definition, the interests of majority groups.

Whilst the 1998 Act does not provide for any new judicial remedies (other than the declaration of incompatibility), a court finding that a public authority as acted unlawfully within the terms of s6 'may grant such relief or remedy, or make such order, within its powers as it considers just and appropriate' (s8(1)). In particular there is no new power to award damages simply because Convention rights have been violated: see s8(2). Even if a power to award damages exists an award should only be made if, having taken into account all the circumstances of the case, including 'any other relief or remedy granted, or order made, in relation to the act in question (by that or any other court), and ... the consequences of any decision (of that or any other court) in respect of that act, the court is satisfied that the award is necessary to afford just satisfaction to the person in whose favour it is made' (s8(3)). A court should also have regard to 'the principles applied by the European Court of Human Rights in relation to the award of compensation under art 41 of the Convention' in determining whether to make an award and in determining quantum.

Remedial action by ministers

Where a declaration of incompatibility has been made and rights of appeal have been exhausted, abandoned or become time barred, or it appears to a minister that (in the light of a finding of the European Court of Human Rights) a provision of legislation is incompatible with obligations under the Convention, a minister may, if he considers that there are compelling reasons for so doing, make orders to amend the relevant legislation to the extent that he considers necessary to remove the incompatibility: see s10(1) and (2).

Note the far-reaching effect of these provisions. A minister will be able to amend primary legislation by means of a statutory instrument (s20(1)). Amendments can be retrospective in effect (but not so as to create criminal liability): see Sch 2 paras 1(1)(b) and 1(4). Schedule 2 provides for two types of procedure for the making of remedial orders, depending upon the urgency of the situation. In most cases a minister will prepare a 'document' comprising the draft order and other details required by Sch 2 para 1(5) (ie details of the incompatibility to be removed and the reasons for proceeding under s10). There then follows a 60-day consultation period during which representations can be made both inside and outside Parliament. Following this period of consultation the minister lays before Parliament the draft remedial order together with a summary of the representations made and details of any revisions made to the order in the light of those representations. To come into effect the draft order must have been laid before Parliament for 60 days and must then be approved by Parliament. In urgent cases a minister will be able to bring an order into effect without parliamentary approval. The safeguards take the form of requirements that the minister should then lay the 'made' order before Parliament with the details required by Sch 2, para 1(5). Once 60 days have passed the minister must lay before Parliament a summary of the representations made and details (if any) of revisions made to the order in the light of those representations. At the end of a period of 120 days from the date when the order was first laid before Parliament it will cease to have effect unless approved by both Houses of Parliament. The failure by Parliament to affirm such an order does not affect the validity of actions taken pursuant to that order within the 120-day period.

Pre-enactment procedures

Section 19 places the relevant minister in charge of a Bill under a duty to 'make a statement to the effect that in his view the provisions of the Bill are compatible with the Convention rights' or to make a statement to the effect that 'although he is unable to make a statement of compatibility the government nevertheless wishes the House to proceed with the Bill'. Such statements must be made before the Second Reading of a Bill, must be in writing and should be published in such manner as the minister considers appropriate. Presumably a statement of non-compliance would only ever be made where the government had already secured derogations or reservations in respect of certain Convention provisions, or had at least indicated that it intended to do so. Otherwise Parliament would be being invited to enact legislation acknowledged to be in breach of the Convention. Were such legislation to be enacted the courts would then be in a position to grant declarations of incompatibility to litigants alleging that action taken on the basis of the non-compliant legislation was unlawful. If no remedial order was forthcoming, the litigant would presumably take his case to the European Court of Human Rights and have the United Kingdom found to be in breach of its obligations.

The Human Rights Act 1998 in action

Like the ill-fated 'Poll Tax' the Human Rights Act 1998 was 'road tested' in Scotland prior to its coming into effect in England and Wales. In a number of highly publicised cases the effect of the Act quickly became apparent. The use of temporary sheriffs (judges) to determine criminal cases was successfully challenged on the basis that they were not sufficiently independent to satisfy the requirements of art 6 – dependent as they were on the gift of appointment from the Lord Advocate. New rules for part-time judicial appointments were introduced. The practice of requiring motorists to provide evidence (under threat of conviction if refusing) of whether or not they had been driving a car at a particular time was also successfully challenged. Not surprisingly these instances lead to suggestions that the Act would cause chaos when introduced in England and Wales, but it should be noted that during the first year of the Act's operation in Scotland 98 per cent of the 980 claims under the Act were rejected by the courts.

The approach of the courts should vary according to the type or right in question. Where 'absolute rights' are involved, such as art 3 (freedom from torture) or art 7 (non-retrospective criminal law) there is little scope from allowing a public body any 'margin of appreciation'. Where rights subject to specified narrow limitations are involved, such as art 2 (the right to life) or art 5 (liberty of the person) the court must investigate whether or not the conditions for satisfying the exception have been made out. Finally there are those rights that are provided subject to general exceptions, typically the rights to privacy, freedom of expression, freedom of religion and freedom of assembly. Where these rights are concerned the court, in addition to considering whether the preconditions for any exception are met, will also have to apply a broad test of proportionality, for example questioning whether the restrictions imposed on the enjoyment of a particular right are necessary in a democratic society, or are necessary to maintain public order. This inquiry also involves consideration of whether or not the restrictions went further than was required. It is in relation to this last group of rights that the doctrine of 'margin of appreciation' is likely to become most significant. Under the Strasbourg jurisprudence it is accepted that national judges are best placed to conduct the sort of 'balancing of rights' that arises under arts 8 to 11: see *Handyside* v *United Kingdom* (1976) 1 EHRR 737. The less uniformity there is between Member States in their approach to a particular issue (for example the age of criminal responsibility), the greater the margin of appreciation allowed. Compare this to very narrow margin of appreciation allowed where commonly agreed standards are involved, such as the desirability of democracy.

The early decisions under the 1998 Act in England and Wales indicated that this was indeed the approach being taken by the courts. In *R* v *Secretary of State for*

Health, ex parte Lally (2000) The Times 26 October, the Divisional Court upheld the validity of a Health Service circular prohibiting visits by children to certain categories of patients in prison hospitals. The applicant (a patient at a secure hospital) had argued that the circular, in its operation, amounted to a violation to his right to a family life under art 8. Scott Baker J confirmed that where there were conflicting rights under art 8, a Member State, and hence the Secretary of State for Health, was entitled to a wider margin of appreciation. He went on to confirm that the directions contained in the circular were not disproportionate to the aim they sought to achieve, ie the protection of children.

The courts have had quite a number of opportunities in recent years to comment on the impact of the Human Rights Act 1998 and no doubt this will continue for the foreseeable future. The following are two examples of the approach of the House of Lords. In *Attorney-General* v *Punch and Steen* [2003] 2 WLR 49 the House had to apply art 10 of the Convention, which deals with freedom of expression. It decided in the particular circumstances that other considerations should prevail over the needs of a claim to freedom of expression. The House ruled that former *Punch* editor James Steen was in contempt by publishing an article by former MI5 officer David Shayler – which was done in breach of a gagging order on Shayler. *Punch* had published an article by Mr Shayler in July 2000 claiming MI5 had not taken sufficient security precautions in the run-up to the 1993 IRA Bishopsgate bombing. The issue was whether or not they (*Punch*) should have obtained clearance from the Attorney-General before publication. The injunction had contained a proviso that the order did not apply to any information in respect of which the Attorney-General had stated in writing that the information was not information whose publication the Crown sought to restrain. Whilst the Court of Appeal viewed this as an imposition of a restriction on freedom of the press that was disproportionate to any public interest, and thus in breach of art 10 of the European Convention on Human Rights, the approach that the House of Lords took was quite different. It thought that the purpose of the court in granting an interlocutory injunction (the gagging order) was that, pending a decision by the court on the claims in the proceedings, the restrained acts should not be done. Third parties were in contempt of court if they wilfully interfered with the administration of justice. This was despite the fact that they were not parties to the original litigation in which the gagging order was issued. Third parties were in contempt of court if they wilfully interfered with the administration of justice by thwarting the achievement of the purpose of the injunction, ie retaining the confidentiality of the material. It is interesting to note that whilst the Attorney-General was prepared to give guidance in this case, he felt unable to undertake a similar endeavour in the next case.

In *R (On the Application of Pretty)* v *Director of Public Prosecutions* [2001] 3 WLR 1598, the House of Lords had the opportunity to comment on the issues surrounding the application of the European Convention on Human Rights to the crime of assisted suicide in the case of the terminally ill. A conservative approach was taken in relation to both this issue and in relation to the possibilities of judicial control of the law officers of the Crown. Diane Pretty attempted in the litigation to ensure that her husband would be able to assist her to end her own life, before she entered the terminal stage of motor neurone disease, without risking prosecution for the offence of aiding and abetting her suicide. The principal obstacle was s2(1) Suicide Act 1961 which makes it a criminal offence to aid, abet, counsel, or procure the suicide of another. The first problem in mounting a challenge to s2 was to bring the matter to court. Mrs Pretty's solicitor, the legal officer of Liberty, adopted the ingenious device of requesting the Director of Public Prosecutions (DPP) to undertake that he would not consent to such a prosecution under s2(4) of the 1961 Act. He then sought judicial review of the Director of Public Prosecution's refusal to give such an undertaking. The claim was based on the Director of Public Prosecution's duty as a 'public authority', under s6 Human Rights Act 1998, to act compatibly with Mrs Pretty's rights under the European Convention on Human Rights, and the House's jurisdiction under s3, to grant a declaration of incompatibility in the event that they considered any provisions of the Suicide Act 1961 to contravene those rights. Mrs Pretty relied on her rights under arts 2, 3, 8, 9 and 14 of the Convention. She claimed that art 2 protected a right to self-determination, entitling her to commit suicide with assistance, that failure to alleviate her suffering by refusing the undertaking amounted to inhuman and degrading treatment proscribed by art 3, that without justifications her rights to privacy and freedoms of conscience under arts 8 and 9 were infringed and that in breach of art 14 she had suffered discrimination, since an able-bodied person might exercise the right to suicide, whereas her incapacities prevented her from doing so without assistance. She further claimed that if s2 of the 1961 Act prevented her assisted suicide, or the DPP giving the undertaking, it was incompatible with the Convention. In terms of the approach of the House of Lords the simple answer is that they felt that none of these claims should succeed, and rather, as with the first case, one might wonder as to the degree of protection that is in reality being given to human rights.

What was heralded as the most important constitutional case ever was decided in December 2004: *A v Secretary of State for the Home Department; X v Secretary of State for the Home Department* [2005] 2 WLR 87; [2004] UKHL 56. It concerned the detention of foreign terrorist suspects without trial. The legislation under which they were being held was the Anti-Terrorism, Crime and Security Act 2001. The government had opted out of part of the European Convention on Human Rights concerning the right to a fair trial, in order to bring in the legislation in response to the 11 September attacks in the United States. The House of Lords ruled by an eight to one majority in favour of appeals by nine detainees. The Law Lords said the measures were incompatible with European human rights laws. The judgment did not impact upon the legality of the provisions: they have remained in force. Despite the initial publicity there was no immediate action taken. In 2005 the government faced the prospect of having to release the detainees as the powers under the 2001 Act were due to expire. The government sought to obtain new legislative powers under the Prevention of Terrorism Act 2005. This 2005 Act provided for a system of control orders in the community and they were used for the detainees who were released from custody.

18.5 Taking a case to Strasbourg

Article 1 of the ECHR provides that the High Contracting Parties shall secure to everyone within their jurisdiction the rights and freedoms defined in the ECHR. To help achieve compliance with this objective the ECHR established a procedure for enforcement (arts 19–56). As originally enacted this enforcement process comprised a Commission on Human Rights, a Committee of Ministers and a Court of Human Rights. The Commission itself comprised a number of members equal to that of the High Contracting Parties, with members elected by the Committee of Ministers of the Council of Europe for a period of six years. Inter-State applications could be received by the Commission, and individual applications were accepted where a signatory State accepted the right of individual petition. Approximately 90 per cent of the petitions submitted by individuals under art 25 were declared inadmissible by the Commission at this stage, which suggests that there was still widespread misunderstanding of the scope and purpose of the ECHR.

The Commission, on accepting a petition referred to it, would then ascertain the facts and try to secure a friendly settlement of the matter on the basis of respect for human rights as defined in the ECHR. If a solution was not reached the Commission would draw up a report on the facts and state its opinion as to whether the facts found disclosed a breach by the State concerned of its obligations under the ECHR. The report would then be forwarded to the Committee of Ministers together with such proposals as the Commission thinks fit. Absenting any settlement, the case would then have to be referred, in due course, to the European Court of Human Rights.

With an increasing number of States accepting the right of individual petition it became evident that the effective protection offered by the Commission and the Court was in danger of being undermined by its inability to deal with the ever-growing caseload. Between 5,000–6,000 applications were received each year, of which approximately 1,600 were registered, and approximately 200 declared admissible. Between 1959 and 1973 only 11 cases where referred to the European Court of Human Rights. In 1991 alone 93 cases were referred. The backlog of unconsidered cases as a whole reached over 1,500. The average time taken for an application to reach the European Court of Human Rights had stretched to five years. With Eastern European countries applying to join the Council of Europe the prospect emerged of some 800 million citizens having the right to have recourse to the European Court of Human Rights.

The procedure under Protocol Eleven

In response to the pressures outlined above the text of what is now known as Protocol Eleven was opened for signature in April 1994. The purpose of the Protocol was to completely overhaul the procedure for dealing with applications under the Convention. Because the Protocol altered the provisions of the Convention itself it could not come into force until all States had signed – a process that was completed in time for it to come into effect in November 1998.

The changes introduced by Protocol Eleven had been trailed by limited reforms introduced in 1990, with Committees being used to rule on admissibility, and Chambers determining routine cases. There was a resultant improvement in processing rates, but concerns about the system being overwhelmed continued.

As a result of Protocol Eleven there is now a permanent European Court of Human Rights, replacing the previous structure of Commission and Court. The new Court comprises 40 judges (one from each Member State) allocated to Committees (three judges to each Committee), Chambers (comprising seven judges) and a Grand Chamber of 17 judges. The Court is assisted by a single registry comprising the Commission secretariat and the Court secretariat (around 100 lawyers in total). The Court of Human Rights heard its first case under the new procedure in November 1998 and delivered its first judgment in January 1999.

The right of individual petition to the new Court becomes mandatory upon Member States. The ECHR is itself restructured so that Section I deals with the rights protected; Section II with the machinery for enforcement; and Section III with miscellaneous matters.

The revised procedure involves an applicant filing his application with the Court's registry, which assigns it to a Chamber and a judge rapporteur who has responsibility for overseeing the progress of the application. A Committee, or tribunal, of judges considers the admissibility of the application, and provided at least one of the three considers it to be admissible, the ruling is communicated to the Member State against whom the application has been made. If a friendly settlement cannot be reached the Chamber (seven judges) will give its judgment. The procedure also applies to applications between States. The authors of these reforms envisage that an application will only need to be referred to the Grand Chamber in exceptional cases, and a panel of five Grand Chamber judges will decide whether there are grounds for re-examination, unless the case is one where the Chamber itself has relinquished jurisdiction. Early indications are that there are still major problems in terms of a backlog of applications. A year after the new system came into operation there were 12,500 applications waiting to be considered. By 2004 there was a five-year backlog of cases. Attempts to address such issues under Protocol 14, which requires ratification by Member States, in terms of the streamlining and simplification of decision-making offers the alternative worry of lower quality decision-making.

The Committee of Ministers becomes responsible for overseeing the enforcement of the Court's rulings and can check on the steps taken by signatory States to comply with rulings of the Court. The Committee can also request Member States to address specific issues of general concern, such as the treatment of asylum seekers.

Alternative mechanisms for entrenching rights

The Human Rights Act 1998 is a cleverly worded compromise between the demands of those who wished to see the courts being given the power to invalidate primary legislation found to be incompatible with Convention rights, and those who feared that the Act would, almost by default, mark a serious erosion of parliamentary sovereignty. It is nevertheless instructive to examine briefly the alternative strategies that could have been adopted to ensure that the courts accord special status given to human rights provisions. First, the Act could have avoided any reference to incompatibility altogether, and simply allowed existing constitutional principles to apply. This would clearly have been unsatisfactory for a government wanting to be seen to take the incorporation of the Convention seriously. The resulting Act would have taken precedence over previous incompatible legislation by virtue of implied repeal, but would have been at the mercy of any subsequent legislation; see further the Hong Kong Bill of Rights Ordinance 1991. Second, at the other extreme, the model provided by the Canadian Charter of Rights and Freedoms could have been adopted, whereby the Canadian courts have been given the power to disapply incompatible legislation, unless the legislation in question expressly states that it is to apply notwithstanding any such incompatibility. In practice this means that the Canadian courts 'read in' the missing rights, or make it clear that, for certain purposes, a statute no longer applies. The Canadian Parliament remains at liberty to amend legislation as it sees fit following such a ruling. Third, the government could have copied the approach taken following the incorporation of the Treaty of Rome (as it then was), whereby the European Communities Act 1972 operates to make certain aspects of EU directly part of domestic law. This latter proposal was rejected, however, on the basis that it is a prerequisite of EU membership that Member States give priority to EC law, whilst becoming a signatory to the Convention creates no such obligation.

The approach adopted for the incorporation of the ECHR in the United Kingdom bears close similarity to the New Zealand Bill of Rights Act 1990, which adopts what is known as an 'interpretative' approach, requiring courts to strive for an interpretation which gives effect to the human rights legislation, but leaving intact legislation that cannot be complied with in a manner consistent with those rights. Defending the adoption of this method the White Paper states:

'The Government has reached the conclusion that courts should not have the power to set aside primary legislation, past or future, on the ground of incompatibility with the Convention. This conclusion arises from the importance that the Government attaches to parliamentary sovereignty. In this context, Parliamentary sovereignty means that

Parliament is competent to make any law on any matter of its choosing and no court may question the validity of any Act that it passes. In enacting legislation, Parliament is making decisions about important matters of public policy. The authority to make those decisions derives from a democratic mandate. Members of Parliament in the House of Commons possess such a mandate because they are elected, accountable and representative. To make provision in the Bill for the courts to set aside Acts of Parliament would confer on the judiciary a general power over the decisions of Parliament which under our present constitutional arrangements they do not possess, and would be likely on occasions to draw the judiciary into serious conflict with Parliament. There is no evidence to suggest that they desire this power, nor that the public wishes them to have it. Certainly, this Government has no mandate for any such change.' (at para 2.13)

18.6 The European Convention on Human Rights and EC law

The ECHR does not form part of EC law in the strict sense, but it is accepted that respect for fundamental human rights is a precondition for the lawfulness of Community acts: see comments in *Opinion No 2/94* [1996] ECR I–1759. The preamble to SEA 1986 also makes express reference to the need to respect such fundamental rights, and similar commitments to respect fundamental human rights are to be found in TEU 1992 art 6 (formerly art F of TEU 1992) and art 6(3) (formerly art F.1 of TEU 1997). In *Opinion No 2/94*, the opinion of the European Court of Justice was sought on the question of whether the accession of the European Community to the ECHR would be compatible with the EC Treaty. Whilst the Court declined to answer the question as posed, it held that, as EC law presently stood, the Community had no competence to accede to the ECHR. Notwithstanding the provisions of art 308 of the EC Treaty empowering the Council to take appropriate measures to ensure that the Community was empowered to achieve its objectives, there was no specific Treaty power that enabled the Community institutions to enact rules relating to human rights or to become a party to international conventions on human rights. In the Court's view, accession to the ECHR would effectively make its provisions part of Community law, with profound consequences for the institutions of the Community and for Member States, and would hence involve changes of such constitutional significance that it could only be brought about by amendment of the EC Treaty.

An individual asserting that the domestic legislation of a Member State is in breach of the ECHR, and thus EC law, will not succeed before the ECJ where the domestic legislation does not deal with a matter falling within the field of application of Community law, and has not been enacted by a Member State so as to ensure compliance with Community law: see further *Kremzow* v *Republik Osterreich* [1997] ECR I–2629. There remains the possibility of the ECHR being indirectly invoked where the application of EC law having direct effect is held, by the European Court of Justice, to require reference to, and conformity with, provisions of the ECHR: see for example *R* v *Kirk* [1984] CMLR 522.

Index

Internet Law

Dr Charles Wild, BSc (London), LLM, PhD (Sheffield), Pg Cert HE, CPE, LPC,
Head of the University of Hertfordshire School of Law,
Head of the Centre for International Law,
Mr Stuart Weinstein, BA (Williams), JD (Columbia), Attorney-at-Law
(California, District of Columbia and New York), Solicitor
and Mr Neil MacEwan, LLB, LLM, LPC

This new text offers, for the first time, a complete review of the area of Internet law. The discussion commences with an analysis of e-contracts, ranging from details of their formation, on-line terms and conditions through to a consideration of associated jurisdictional and choice of law issues. In addition, e-finance is considered, focusing on the use and regulation of credit cards on the Internet together with an evaluation of other methods of payment, including Smart Cards and electronic money. The text also covers intellectual property and data protection issues which specifically arise from the transfer and subsequent utilisation of data on the Internet, including responses in the form of cryptography, privacy enhanced technology and regional legislative responses. Finally, more specific topics such as domain names and spam will be included so as to provide the student with comprehensive coverage of this dynamic and challenging area of law. Whilst the legal content is UK based, the combination of UK, US and EU authors ensures that every aspect of this global subject is dealt with from a cross-jurisdictional perspective. An essential text for any student studying this subject or anyone interested in issues surrounding the Internet.

For further information on contents or to place an order, please contact:

Customer Services
Old Bailey Press
at Holborn College
Woolwich Road
Charlton
London
SE7 8LN

Telephone: 020 8317 6039
Fax: 020 8317 6004
Website: www.oldbaileypress.co.uk
E-Mail: customerservices@oldbaileypress.co.uk

ISBN 1 85836 573 2
Soft cover 246 x 175 mm
400 pages approx
£15.95
Due September 2005

Revision Aids

Designed for the undergraduate, the 101 Questions & Answers series and the Suggested Solutions series are for all those who have a positive commitment to passing their law examinations. Each series covers a different examinable topic and comprises a selection of answers to examination questions and, in the case of the 101 Questions and Answers, interrograms. The majority of questions represent examination 'bankers' and are supported by full-length essay solutions. These titles will undoubtedly assist you with your research and further your understanding of the subject in question.

101 Questions & Answers Series

Only £7.95 Published December 2003

Constitutional Law
ISBN: 1 85836 522 8

Criminal Law
ISBN: 1 85836 432 9

Land Law
ISBN: 1 85836 515 5

Law of Contract
ISBN: 1 85836 517 1

Law of Tort
ISBN: 1 85836 516 3

Suggested Solutions to Past Examination Questions 2001–2002 Series

Only £6.95 Published December 2003

Company Law
ISBN: 1 85836 519 8

Employment Law
ISBN: 1 85836 520 1

European Union Law
ISBN: 1 85836 524 4

Evidence
ISBN: 1 85836 521 X

Family Law
ISBN: 1 85836 525 2

For further information or to place an order, please contact:

Mail Order
Old Bailey Press at Holborn College
Woolwich Road
Charlton
London
SE7 8LN

Telephone: 020 8317 6039
Fax: 020 8317 6004
Website: www.oldbaileypress.co.uk
E-Mail: mailorder@oldbaileypress.co.uk

Unannotated Cracknell's Statutes for Use in Examinations

New Editions of Cracknell's Statutes

Only £11.95   Due 2005

Cracknell's Statutes provide a comprehensive series of essential statutory provisions for each subject. Amendments are consolidated, avoiding the need to cross-refer to amending legislation. Unannotated, they are suitable for use in examinations, and provide the precise wording of vital Acts of Parliament for the diligent student.

Company Law
ISBN: 1 85836 563 5

Equity and Trusts
ISBN: 1 85836 589 9

Constitutional & Administrative Law
ISBN: 1 85836 584 8

European Union Legislation
ISBN: 1 85836 590 2

Contract, Tort and Remedies
ISBN: 1 85836 583 X

Family Law
ISBN: 1 85836 566 X

Criminal Law
ISBN: 1 85836 586 4

Land: The Law of Real Property
ISBN: 1 85836 585 6

Employment Law
ISBN: 1 85836 587 2

Law of International Trade
ISBN: 1 85836 582 1

English Legal System
ISBN: 1 85836 588 0

Medical Law
ISBN: 1 85836 567 8

Revenue Law
ISBN: 1 85836 569 4

For further information or to place an order, please contact:

Customer Services
Old Bailey Press at Holborn College
Woolwich Road, Charlton
London, SE7 8LN
Telephone: 020 8317 6039
Fax: 020 8317 6004
Website: www.oldbaileypress.co.uk
E-Mail: customerservices@oldbaileypress.co.uk

Old Bailey Press

The Old Bailey Press Integrated Student Law Library is tailor-made to help you at every stage of your studies, from the preliminaries of each subject through to the final examination. The series of Textbooks, Revision WorkBooks, 150 Leading Cases and Cracknell's Statutes are interrelated to provide you with a comprehensive set of study materials.

You can buy Old Bailey Press books from your University Bookshop, your local Bookshop, directly using this form, or you can order a free catalogue of our titles from the address shown overleaf.

The following subjects each have a Textbook, 150 Leading Cases, Revision WorkBook and Cracknell's Statutes unless otherwise stated.

Administrative Law
Commercial Law
Company Law
Conflict of Laws
Constitutional Law
Conveyancing (Textbook and 150 Leading Cases)
Criminal Law
Criminology (Textbook and Sourcebook)
Employment Law (Textbook and Cracknell's Statutes)
English and European Legal Systems
Equity and Trusts
Evidence
Family Law
Jurisprudence: The Philosophy of Law (Textbook, Sourcebook and
    Revision WorkBook)
Land: The Law of Real Property
Law of International Trade
Law of the European Union
Legal Skills and System
    (Textbook)
Obligations: Contract Law
Obligations: The Law of Tort
Public International Law
Revenue Law (Textbook,
    Revision WorkBook and
    Cracknell's Statutes)
Succession (Textbook, Revision
    WorkBook and Cracknell's
    Statutes)

Mail order prices:	
Textbook	£15.95
150 Leading Cases	£12.95
Revision WorkBook	£10.95
Cracknell's Statutes	£11.95
Suggested Solutions 1999–2000	£6.95
Suggested Solutions 2000–2001	£6.95
Suggested Solutions 2001–2002	£6.95
101 Questions and Answers	£7.95
Law Update 2004	£10.95
Law Update 2005	£10.95

Please note details and prices are subject to alteration.

To complete your order, please fill in the form below:

Module	Books required	Quantity	Price	Cost
		Postage		
		TOTAL		

For the UK and Europe, add £4.95 for the first book ordered, then add £1.00 for each subsequent book ordered for postage and packing.

For the rest of the world, add 50% for airmail.

ORDERING

By telephone to Customer Services at 020 8317 6039, with your credit card to hand.

By fax to 020 8317 6004 (giving your credit card details).

Website: www.oldbaileypress.co.uk

E-Mail: customerservices@oldbaileypress.co.uk

By post to: Customer Services, Old Bailey Press at Holborn College, Woolwich Road, Charlton, London, SE7 8LN.

When ordering by post, please enclose full payment by cheque or banker's draft, or complete the credit card details below. You may also order a free catalogue of our complete range of titles from this address.

We aim to despatch your books within 3 working days of receiving your order. All parts of the form must be completed.

Name

Address

E-Mail

Postcode   Telephone

Total value of order, including postage: £

I enclose a cheque/banker's draft for the above sum, or

charge my   ☐ Access/Mastercard   ☐ Visa   ☐ American Express

Cardholder: ....

Card number

☐☐☐☐ ☐☐☐☐ ☐☐☐☐ ☐☐☐☐

Expiry date   ☐☐☐☐

Signature: ....Date: ....